'Aidan McGlynn has constructed an admirably clear and well-balanced Introduction to issues of epistemic injustice. While partly designed to be the valuable teaching resource it will surely prove to be, I suspect his book will also make its mark as a welcome addition to the scholarly literature.'

Miranda Fricker, New York University, USA

'In a time when "epistemic injustice" is often a mere buzzword, Aidan McGlynn's well-rounded introduction offers readers the opportunity to understand the profound value of the nuanced philosophical debate about "epistemic injustice" and reasserts the concept's practical relevance.'

Melanie Altanian, University of Freiburg, Germany

'Razor sharp and incisive, this book scrutinises a new philosophical field: epistemic injustice. A much-needed analysis carried out with acuity and sensitivity.'

Havi Carel, University of Bristol, UK

'A wonderful resource for anyone interested in the topic. Full of examples, it is accessible without thereby losing the complexity of the debate and the topic itself. It is also remarkable in its sensitivity to the history that the contemporary debate on epistemic injustice has and the relevance of debates of epistemic oppression, epistemic violence, and contributory injustice. A great contribution to philosophy!'

Hilkje Hänel, University of Potsdam, Germany

'I have learned a great deal from reading this, due in large part to how easy it is to pick up where I left off, and that is due to McGlynn's expertise and skill as a writer...it is an excellent teaching resource.'

Nate Sheff, Visiting Assistant Professor, Fairfield University, USA

Epistemic Injustice: An Introduction

Epistemic injustice is one of the most important yet complex subjects to have emerged in philosophy in recent years. It refers to the idea that a person can be wronged when they are not properly believed or understood due to factors like prejudice and ignorance. In this clear and much-needed introduction, Aidan McGlynn explains what epistemic injustice is and examines it from a philosophical standpoint. He covers the following key topics and questions:

- What is epistemic injustice and why is it significant?
- What is epistemic oppression, and how does it differ from epistemic injustice?
- The relationship between different theories of epistemic injustice
- Testimonial injustice
- Hermeneutical injustice
- Primary harms of epistemic injustice
- How to make progress towards epistemic justice

Throughout this book McGlynn connects the conceptual aspects of epistemic injustice to pressing real-life examples of prejudice and ignorance, including those relating to gender, race, and disability.

With the inclusion of chapter summaries, suggestions for further reading, and a glossary of key terms, *Epistemic Injustice: An Introduction* is an ideal starting point for anyone coming to the topic for the first time. In addition to philosophy, it is essential reading for those in related disciplines such as gender studies, sociology, ethnic and racial studies, law, education, politics, and health and disability studies.

Aidan McGlynn is a Senior Lecturer in the Philosophy Department at the University of Edinburgh, Scotland, and a Senior Research Associate at the African Centre for Epistemology and Philosophy of Science, University of Johannesburg, South Africa. He is author of *Knowledge First?* (2014), a co-editor-in-chief of *Hypatia: A Journal of Feminist Philosophy*, and co-editor with Jennifer Lackey of *The Oxford Handbook of Social Epistemology* (2025).

Epistemic Injustice

An Introduction

Aidan McGlynn

Taylor & Francis Group

LONDON AND NEW YORK

Cover image: courtesy of Getty images.

First published 2026
by Routledge
4 Park Square, Milton Park, Abingdon, Oxon OX14 4RN

and by Routledge
605 Third Avenue, New York, NY 10158

Routledge is an imprint of the Taylor & Francis Group, an informa business

© 2026 Aidan McGlynn

The right of Aidan McGlynn to be identified as author of this work has been asserted by them in accordance with sections 77 and 78 of the Copyright, Designs and Patents Act 1988.

All rights reserved. No part of this book may be reprinted or reproduced or utilised in any form or by any electronic, mechanical, or other means, now known or hereafter invented, including photocopying and recording, or in any information storage or retrieval system, without permission in writing from the publishers.

For Product Safety Concerns and Information please contact our EU representative GPSR@taylorandfrancis.com. Taylor & Francis Verlag GmbH, Kaufingerstraße 24, 80331 München, Germany.

Trademark notice: Product or corporate names may be trademarks or registered trademarks, and are used only for identification and explanation without intent to infringe.

British Library Cataloguing-in-Publication Data
A catalogue record for this book is available from the British Library

ISBN: 978-1-032-25161-5 (hbk)
ISBN: 978-1-032-25160-8 (pbk)
ISBN: 978-1-003-28186-3 (ebk)

DOI: 10.4324/9781003281863

Typeset in Joanna
by codeMantra

In memory of my mother, and dedicated with love to Malcolm

Contents

ACKNOWLEDGEMENTS   XI
PREFACE   XVII

Part 1
What Is Epistemic Injustice?   1
1. Introduction: Epistemic Matters   3
2. Crying for the Moon: Examples of Epistemic Injustice   23
3. The Nature and Scope of Epistemic Injustice   49
4. Situating Epistemic Oppression   66

Part 2
Being Believed   91
5. The Central Case of Testimonial Injustice   93
6. Testimonial Injustice, Prejudices, and Credibility Deficits and Excesses   117
7. Epistemic Violence and Silencing   141

Part 3
Being Understood — 165
8. The Central Case of Hermeneutical Injustice — 167
9. Incidental Hermeneutical Injustice and Hermeneutical Marginalisation — 185
10. Contributory Injustice and Epistemic Oppression — 205

Part 4
Primary Harms of Epistemic Injustice — 235
11. Identifying Primary Harms of Testimonial and Hermeneutical Injustice — 237

Part 5
Epistemic Justice — 263
12. Towards Epistemic Justice — 265

GLOSSARY OF KEY TERMS — 287
INDEX — 293

Acknowledgements

This book grew out of my attempt to write a short (8,000-word maximum) chapter on epistemic injustice for a handbook which I edited with Jennifer Lackey and which was finally published in 2025. Having planned out what I wanted to cover in my chapter, I quickly found that I had written close to 30,000 words without coming close to completing my plan. It started to seem like I had outlined a book rather than a chapter, and so I approached Routledge. In the meantime, I had another shot at writing my 8,000-word chapter (and failed a second time, with the published chapter being around 17,000 words—one of the perils of being one's own editor). This chapter appeared as 'Epistemic Injustice: Phenomena and Theories' in *The Oxford Handbook of Social Epistemology*, edited by Jennifer Lackey and Aidan McGlynn, and published by Oxford University Press in 2025. I haven't reused much text from the chapter here, but they share a lot of D.N.A., and for permission to use the strands of text that have made it into the present work, I thank Oxford University Press.

This book inherits all of the intellectual debts of that chapter, and adds a great deal more. Perhaps most significantly, I'd like to thank the members of the Scottish Feminist Philosophy Network, who read drafts of various chapters as part of our regular work-in-progress sessions: thanks to Matthew Cull, Jade Fletcher, Katharine Jenkins, Fed Luzzi, Filipa Melo Lopes, Aness Webster, and others who participated in those discussions.

My gratitude is also due to the Cogito group at Glasgow, in particular Adam Carter, Chris Kelp, and Mona Simion. I presented a version of Chapter 11 to one of the fantastic online work-in-progress groups they ran during the years that the Covid-19 pandemic prevented in-person gatherings, and a version of the material that became Chapter 9 at an event jointly organised by myself, Adam, and Mona in Edinburgh. These events proved crucial opportunities to get feedback on the ideas in those chapters, not least of all feedback from Adam, Chris, and Mona themselves.

The EPIC—Epistemic Injustice in Healthcare—project held an online seminar on my handbook chapter which I was able to join, and they subsequently invited me to their launch event in Bristol in 2024, where they held a discussion of two draft chapters, and I was able to give a talk to the Bristol department colloquium about a third chapter. This was a terrific opportunity, and I'm really thankful to all of the members of the project and the department that contributed to these discussions. As I suggest in the final chapter of this book, I think that the EPIC project offers a model of how to go about a serious effort to address epistemic injustice. A workshop on epistemic injustice in Global Health at Queen Margaret University organised by Paul Kadetz in September 2024 offered another valuable chance to discuss ideas about how theories of epistemic injustice might contribute to conversations about healthcare (as well as the limitations of these theories).

I had several chances to present material to the Arche research centre in St Andrews. The direction taken in Chapter 11 was very influenced by feedback at an online epistemology seminar in 2021: particularly from Sandy Goldberg and Alessandra Tanesini, who have both been sources of support and insight more generally. The material in Chapter 8 began life as a talk for the Epistemology of #BelieveWomen workshop in St Andrews in 2023, organised by Jade Fletcher, and Chapters 4, 7, and 10 were the subject of a very enjoyable seminar of the Feminist Philosophy and Social Theory group organised by Emma Holmes in July 2025, and again I'm very grateful for the feedback I received on those occasions.

Three of my teachers during my undergraduate degree at St Andrews died within a few months of each other in 2021: Sarah Broadie, Peter Clark, and Katherine Hawley. I'm grateful for all that I learned about how to be excellent philosophers and excellent people from all three of them (though I have misapplied or forgotten much of it in the intervening years). Katherine's work in particular shaped the approach to epistemic injustice I have taken in this book much more deeply than will be apparent from the text. It was thinking about the picture of epistemic injustice that was hinted at in Chapter 5 of her wonderful final book *How to be Trustworthy* that helped me begin to see how much myself and others were conflating Fricker's theoretical views with the phenomena we were theorising about, and how badly this had distorted our conception of Fricker's contribution, not to mention the alternatives to Fricker's view produced by Kristie Dotson and others. I presented on this at the memorial symposium for Katherine organised by Jade Fletcher at St Andrews in July 2022, and that became the basis for a paper in a special issue of *Philosophical Psychology* dedicated to Katherine's memory, but the observation about the need to carefully distinguish theories of epistemic injustice from the phenomena mostly dropped out and instead became the starting point of my handbook chapter, as well as the present book.

Two of the PhD students working with me recently, Rory Wilson and Yinmei Wu, have been writing on epistemic injustice, and I have learned a lot from having the chance to talk regularly with each of them. I have also had the considerable benefit of teaching hundreds of students, across all levels of undergraduate and postgraduate study about epistemic injustice, and this has greatly shaped how this book has developed. Thanks to all of my students in 'Knowledge and Reality,' 'Social Philosophy,' 'Advanced Epistemology,' and especially 'Knowledge, Ignorance, and Power' over the past ten years. It would be impossible for me to credit each of the particular students that have improved my understanding of the topic of this book over the years, though I will mention Lochlan Atak and Rachel Ram in this connection. I presented a version of Chapter 9 at an 'epistemology paper jam' organised by Stacie Friend at Edinburgh in March 2025, and offer my gratitude to all of the participants in that event. I also thank the University of Edinburgh for a period of sabbatical in Fall 2022, which enabled me to make progress on this book, and the PPLS student support team for all that they do for our students and for being such a pleasure to work with this past year.

I have benefitted enormously from discussing the issues in Chapters 9 and 12 with Nick Clanchy, and they kindly offered feedback on a version of Chapter 12 that was largely eaten in editing. I still got a lot from their comments, and I hope to return to those issues in other work, so I don't think their efforts were in vain, and I appreciated them greatly.

I have been very glad of my team of fellow editors at *Hypatia*, as we have together figured out what it takes to keep a journal (and in particular a feminist philosophy journal) running: Victoria Browne, Katharine Jenkins, Charlotte Knowles, Aness Webster, and for the first year, Simona Capisani. I have learned a lot from them over the past two years, and it's been a privilege to work with them all. Likewise, my co-editor for *The Oxford Handbook of Social Epistemology*, Jennifer Lackey, has offered a model of what an engaged epistemologist, philosopher, and academic looks like, although she has set a standard for what can be accomplished in these roles that few can even come close to matching.

For other support, feedback, encouragement, and discussion relating to the topics covered in this book, I'd like to say thanks to Melanie Altanian, Solmu Anttila, Natalie Ashton, Zara Bain, Derek Ball, Cristina Borgoni, Alice Bosna, Jessica Brown, Rebecca Buxton, Havi Carel, Amandine Catala, Annalisa Coliva, Francis Darling, Emmalon Davis, Gerry Dunne, Catarina Dutilh Novaes, Paul Giladi, Emma Gordon, Josh Habgood-Coote, Hilkje Hänel, Jules Holroyd, Matt Jope, Jordan Karausky, Alkis Kotsonis, Thirza Lagewaard, Karl Landström, Jon Matheson, Michela Massami, Ellie Mason, Robin McKenna, Emily Colleen McWilliams, Veli Mitova, Kris Moody, Kathleen Murphy-Hollies, Hadeel Naeem, Susan Notess, Nick Ollivere, Richard Pettigrew, Lukas Schwengerer, Kegan Shaw, Martin Smith, Jason Stanley, Bryan Pickel, Jer Steeger, Lani Watson, and Emilia Wilson. I have almost certainly left someone important off this list, and so my apologies for that. Of course, responsibility for any errors or other deficiencies rests entirely with me.

When I arrived in Austin, Texas in August 2005 to start my PhD, I had never even visited the city before, and it became very quickly apparent that I was entirely underprepared—coming from Scotland, it hadn't even occurred to me that I was moving into an unfurnished flat without the electricity turned on. Tristan (who was also starting the programme) and Sharmane picked me up from the airport, and let me stay with them for the first period I was in Austin, until I (sort of) had my act together. It's not clear how I would have made it through even my first week there without their help, and that was far from the last time I relied on them during my time in Texas. Tristan died suddenly and unexpectedly at the end of 2023, as I was finishing up the first draft manuscript of this book. He and Sharmane have been very much on my mind the past year and a half. One aspect of how difficult it is to lose someone is that the rest of the world keeps relentless churning on, which is understandable and natural, but it can leave one with the impression that everyone and everything else is acting like it doesn't matter that this person ever existed. But nothing could be further from the truth, and when I think about the various forms of good fortune and kindness that I've undoubtedly benefitted from over the years, those I associate with Tristan and Sharmane stand out.

I have completed this book under unusual and difficult circumstances. I finished the first full draft early in 2024 and received three very helpful referee reports as well as editorial guidance on how to revise the manuscript a couple of months later. I was confident the finish line was close at hand, but in July, a back injury flared very badly during a trip to the Joint Session of the Aristotelian Society and the Mind Association in Birmingham, and has stubbornly refused to settle down since then. This injury has completely turned my professional and personal life upside down for the past year. My situation worsened and worsened across the second half of 2024, but I turned a corner around the new year, and as I've slowly recovered throughout 2025, I have been able to return to this book and finally finish the revisions it needed. I'm grateful to the referees for giving my earlier manuscript their attention and for their encouragement and constructive comments, to Adam Johnson at Routledge, and to my editor, Tony Bruce, who has offered sometimes challenging, but always helpful advice and feedback throughout, and who has been patient with me during this horrible past year. On a more personal note, I'd like to thank all of the medical professionals who have been involved in my care, as well as Robin McKenna, who helped me during that initial awful trip to the Joint Session; I found myself navigating a city I didn't know while struggling with a completely unexpected and unexplained onslaught of pain and loss of mobility, and Robin went out of his way to make that much more manageable than it would otherwise have been.

Last, but of course not least, I'd like to thank my family: Lauren and Arthur; my father and Linda, Frankie, Ronnie, Ciaran, and Katy; Finn, Nora, Calum, Lewis, Rowan, and Maeve; and all the other relatives who have helped support me in this and in everything else. Lauren and Arthur have not only had to endure me writing (and complaining about writing) another book, having suffered through the first, but have also had to deal with the tremendous additional strain caused by my injury this past year. Finally, this book is dedicated to my mother, Moyna McGlynn, and to my younger son, Malcolm. In a life-changing couple of weeks in the middle of 2016, Malcolm was born and my mother died, and everything I have done (or tried to do) since then has happened in the shockwaves of those twin events, one as devastating as the other was joyful. These don't ever cancel each other out, of course; you just eventually learn to live, and very occasionally write books, within the contradiction.

Preface

This book is a highly opinionated introduction to the main philosophical issues that have gone under the banner of 'epistemic injustice' in the past 20 years. The term comes from Miranda Fricker's work, and in particular from her 2007 book *Epistemic Injustice: Power and the Ethics of Knowing*, which is responsible for the huge explosion of interest in this topic from academic philosophers, as well as other academics and a number of people working outside academia (such as lawyers, teachers, and healthcare professionals). It's unusual for a topic with its roots in feminist philosophy to have such a big impact on philosophy in general, let alone to attract so much attention from non-philosophers.

One reason for such widespread interest in this topic surely stems from Fricker's book, which was relatively easy and pleasurable to read for a work of philosophy, and which was also packed with rich and seemingly compelling examples, as well as ready-made labels and definitions that seemed to immediately enable us to make sense of the examples and organise them into a helpful taxonomy. However, another reason for the attention the topic has received is that epistemic injustice and the various subtypes identified by Fricker and others have seemed explanatorily powerful, illuminating problematic dynamics across all domains of human interaction. Subsequent work on the topic has explored a great many of these avenues, applying, refining, stretching, and replacing Fricker's terminology and framework.

However, there has also been increasing recognition that epistemic injustice as a topic has a much longer history, both within philosophy and in other disciplines, and Fricker has been criticised for not locating her work against this background. (I'll consider this criticism in more detail in Chapter 4.) While I can't pretend to be able to offer anything close to a comprehensive overview of all of the contributions to my topic predating the contemporary debate, I do cover some of the most significant; moreover, I will try to illustrate some of the ways that these older contributions still have enormous relevance for contemporary attempts to understand the nature and scope of epistemic injustice.

I have tried to keep the discussion in this book very example-focused, laying out a large number of examples in Chapter 2 as a kind of ostensive definition of what it is that this book is concerned with, and returning to many of those examples for more detailed discussion in later chapters. Still, I suspect some readers will be disappointed by how theoretical the book is, and by the fact that I don't attempt to survey the various applications of the theories discussed on different areas of our lives. One reason for the lack of any such survey is that I think we're already at the point where that would be impossible, at least if one wanted to avoid offering something dated and superficial; there are several papers each week making applications of ideas from the literature on epistemic injustice to various aspects of our interactions with each other, and any attempt to keep up would inevitably fail. I also don't have sufficient knowledge of each of these different domains—healthcare, the criminal justice system, genocide denial, systematic data gaps in research into the safety of products and medicine, the reception of people's avowals concerning their racial and gender identities, to name just a few—to be able to do justice to almost any of them. Perhaps I'm being too pessimistic, and someone could write a survey that covered enough of these developments in enough detail to be worthwhile; I am certain, at least, that I couldn't write such a survey (though I'd be very interested to read one!). Where I do think I have a contribution to make is in offering an introduction to the theoretical ideas and terminology which these broader discussions usually appeal to, and to try to put these underlying theoretical notions on a more secure footing by clarifying what makes the different frameworks that have been developed distinct from one another and offering a sense of some of their main strengths and weaknesses. My hope is that this makes it easier for those working to understand and counter particular forms of epistemic injustice that arise within different domains to select the right theoretical tools to help them in those tasks.

Within academic philosophy, epistemic injustice is a topic that sits in the intersection of a wide range of different areas: epistemology (and in particular social epistemology), philosophy of language, political philosophy, feminist philosophy, philosophy of race, philosophy of disability, moral philosophy and moral psychology, and so on. My own philosophical background is in epistemology and feminist philosophy, and this has undoubtedly shaped the particular way I have approached the topic of epistemic injustice in this book. To give a concrete example, Miranda Fricker begins her book with a lengthy discussion of power, but that's not a notion I give much explicit attention here, even though it's certainly relevant to my discussion. It's hard to imagine a political philosopher having so little to say on this or being content to leave it unanalysed, and it's correspondingly easy to imagine a very different book to this one that took it as one of the central theoretical topics that discussions of epistemic injustice must address. Such an author might well entirely skip over the topic of Chapter 11, primary harms of epistemic injustice, which has been the focus of my own research on epistemic injustice prior to this book. There would be nothing wrong or misguided with such an approach; it would just require a very different author. Because epistemic injustice covers such a broad range of areas, understanding it will require many philosophers with complimentary areas of expertise working together. In this book, I contribute what I have to offer.

A similar point can be made regarding traditions within philosophy. To the extent that the customary division of philosophy into analytic and continental camps still makes sense (assuming it ever did), my background and training has been in the analytic tradition associated with figures like Gottlob Frege, Bertrand Russell, G. E. Moore, Ludwig Wittgenstein, the Logical Positivists, the Post-War Oxford Ordinary Language philosophers, and so on. To a large extent, the way I approach this book is still very analytic in character (though I do engage with figures who are not a part of the analytic tradition at various points). This is another place where someone else could write a quite different book, and again I would have no quarrel with a contrasting approach; I'm sceptical that any one tradition has a monopoly on fruitful philosophical discussion of this topic, and some of the best contemporary work on epistemic injustice takes inspiration from figures outside of the tradition I mostly associate myself with.

Let me say a few words about who this book is for, and how to get the most out of it. I have intentionally tried to make this book as accessible as I can, and so I have tried to write it without presupposing that the reader is already familiar with the jargon, theories, and methodologies of academic philosophy and epistemology. Each chapter includes an annotated list of further readings where I make suggestions about where an interested reader might follow up on various issues covered in that chapter, and there is a glossary at the end of the book which gives the reader struggling to keep track of the various labels a place to quickly check their understanding (though precisely what is meant by many of the terms listed is part of what's under contention in the chapters).

Despite these steps, I don't think I have wholly succeeded in making all of the topics and chapters accessible to all readers; some of the discussions remain unavoidably complex, and I have kept them in only because I judged them too central and significant for the topic of this book to leave out. What I have done is try to restrict the most difficult material to later chapters in each part of this book. This means that the text builds up to the more difficult chapters, in a way that hopefully keeps as many readers as possible on board, but it also means that readers can choose how deeply they want to engage with a particular topic. Chapters 10 and 11 are probably the most difficult in the whole book.

Much the same point holds for using this book in teaching. Suppose you want to use this book to teach students about the first variety of epistemic injustice identified by Fricker, which she calls testimonial injustice. This is the subject of Part 2 of this book. Within Part 2, Chapter 5 gives an overview of the main features of Fricker's account of testimonial injustice and discusses the principal examples she uses to motivate that account. Chapter 6 builds on this, getting more under the hood of Fricker's account, and discussing some of the challenges it faces, while Chapter 7 lays out an alternative account of more or less the same phenomena due to Kristie Dotson. This structure gives a lecturer who wants to assign a reading on this topic several options, depending on how much they can ask students to read and how deeply they want them to understand the various issues. Part 3 of this book features almost exactly the same structure, and so gives people teaching on what Fricker calls hermeneutical injustice and related topics a precisely similar range of options.

I have used the text in my own recent teaching in this fashion. My second-year undergraduate class is an introduction to epistemology that's compulsory for anyone who wants to do a Philosophy degree, and I ask them to read Chapter 5 and perhaps also 6, as well as Chapter 8 (but not 9 or 10) so that they also have a basic grasp of what hermeneutical injustice is and the primary examples Fricker uses to try to illustrate it. In contrast, my fourth-year students have opted to take an entire course focused on epistemic injustice, and so I ask them to read all three chapters of Parts 2 and 3. Other lecturers might make different choices for these groups, or be teaching this material to students at different levels and different degrees of knowledge and experience, and they'll find that the organisation of the book should give them the flexibility to do that.

The literature I'll be discussing has often been guilty of using disability metaphors to make points about ignorance, silencing, and so on, and it has been important to me not to replicate this practice. The reader will occasionally find such metaphors in the text in direct quotations from other philosophers, but I have tried to avoid using them myself. Throughout, I discuss both fictional and real-life examples of racism, misogyny, sexual harassment, sexual violence, ableism, and other forms of violence and oppression, with Chapter 2 being a particularly difficult read in this regard.

Part 1

WHAT IS EPISTEMIC INJUSTICE?

1

INTRODUCTION

Epistemic Matters

1.1 EPISTEMIC EVERYTHING EVERYWHERE ALL AT ONCE

A recent pattern in academic philosophy over the past 20 or so years has involved relentlessly adding the word 'epistemic' in front of almost every other word. Examples include epistemic infringement; epistemic apprenticeships; epistemic oppression; epistemic failure; epistemic vices; epistemic atonement; epistemic weaponry; epistemic injustice; epistemic phariseeism; epistemic slurs; the epistemic apocalypse; epistemic health; epistemic inoculation; epistemic complicity; epistemic dehumanisation; epistemic appropriation; epistemic trespassing; epistemic violence; epistemic rights; epistemic death; epistemic exploitation; epistemic redlining; epistemic reparations; epistemic sanity; the epistemic IKEA effect; epistemic apathy; epistemic shamelessness; epistemic utopia; and epistemic exhaustion.[1] This trend shows no sign of slowing down; on the contrary, it can seem like we're only a short distance along an exponential curve, with new additions to the list almost every week.

Epistemology is the branch of philosophy that studies things like knowledge, evidence, understanding, justification, wisdom, warrant, and so on. Traditionally, it examines how we learn about the world and ourselves, the nature of knowledge and understanding and other states of this kind, the scope and limits of what we can know, how to respond to the 'sceptic' who argues that our beliefs are rarely if ever justified or warranted, and other issues like these. 'Epistemic' is an adjective that picks out things as falling under epistemology's remit; the epistemic is what epistemology studies. Knowledge is an epistemic state; indeed, it's the *paradigm* of an epistemic state. Knowledge is a relationship between thinkers (or perhaps groups of thinkers) and the world, involving those thinkers recognising how things are in the world. That might sound rather abstract, but examples couldn't be more familiar; I know where my keys are right now, and I know the last four digits of my phone number (at least when I have had sufficient caffeine), and this is a matter of me recognising certain things about the world—the location of my keys in it, and the digits of my phone number. To describe something as epistemic is a way of somehow relating it to knowledge and other epistemic states, such as those I've already mentioned.

So why has there been such an explosion of interest in epistemic…stuff? In particular, why has there been such a focus on prefixing 'epistemic' to stuff that doesn't seem all that closely related to epistemology's traditional concerns (for example, weaponry, slurs, violence)? Is there anything philosophically interesting behind the 'epistemic X' pattern? Is it just herd-mentality combined with the influence of a few philosophical trend-setters (dynamics which philosophers are not always as immune to as we like to think, or like others to think)? Or is it a slightly odd marketing-gimmick: a way to try to make research that might pass by relatively unnoticed seem like it's part of a hot new trend?

I don't want to wholly dismiss these kinds of unflattering explanations, but perhaps unsurprisingly this book takes the line that there is something philosophically important going on here, at least for many of the examples I started with. To start to see why, it's worth thinking about the broader context in which the 'epistemic X' pattern occurs. The tradition within philosophy that it has primarily emerged in, analytic philosophy, is usually associated with giants of the 19th and 20th centuries such as Gottlob Frege, G. E. Moore, Bertrand Russell, and Ludwig Wittgenstein. In the century or so since these 'fathers of analytic philosophy' produced their pivotal works, analytic philosophy has gained a reputation for dry, technical analyses and 'logic-chopping,' blithely (and sometimes proudly) unconcerned with any of the pressing social and political issues of our times, and published in books and academic articles that read like dishwasher instruction manuals. That's something of a caricature, but it's one that has stuck because it contains some elements of truth.

The past two or three decades have seen a significant shift, with analytic philosophers increasingly open to the idea that the kind of skills, training, concepts, and theories that they have developed might be useful for attempts to understand and address socially pressing issues.[2] Relatedly, areas of philosophy that were once pushed to the margins, such as feminist philosophy, philosophy of race, philosophy of disability, and trans philosophy have increasingly come to find more mainstream acceptance; it's more and more common to find these topics taught as part of introductory courses in philosophy, included in overviews of the subject, taken seriously as areas of active research, published in 'general' philosophy journals rather than 'specialist' ones, and so on (though there still remains considerable room for improvement).[3]

It's this larger 'applied' turn in philosophy that forms the context for the recent tendency to prefix 'epistemic' to things, particularly to things that don't have any obvious or inherent link to what epistemologists tend to study. If we look again at the list I started with, several items on it may now pop out: epistemic injustice; epistemic oppression; epistemic violence; and perhaps some others. These express the idea that there are kinds of injustice or oppression or violence that are somehow epistemic in nature, and so fall at least in part within the purview of epistemology, broadly construed. The enthusiasm we're now witnessing for the 'epistemic X' formula is in large part a result of those who work on issues in epistemology—epistemologists—embracing a much broader and more exciting and pressing set of concerns than previously seemed possible, or of those who haven't thought of themselves as epistemologists coming to see the epistemic as more central to their concerns than they had realised.

Looking at our list of supposedly epistemic things one last time, at least a couple of the items seem clearly hyperbolic or metaphorical. The 'epistemic apocalypse' isn't really an apocalypse, but the hyperbole serves to bring out how catastrophic our epistemic position is meant to be in a world in which deepfakes—realistic, AI-generated images, videos, and audio-clips of things that never happened, and people doing and saying things they never did or said—are ubiquitous. Someone who suffers an 'epistemic death' isn't really dead; rather, it's a metaphor designed to capture the severe harms inflicted on someone who is persistently excluded from contributing to our collective epistemic lives (in ways I'll make much more precise in the chapters to follow). This metaphor draws a parallel to the more familiar notion of 'social death,' influentially used by the sociologist Orlando Patterson (1982) to convey the degree of dehumanisation and neglect inflicted on those treated as slaves. What this suggests is that we can take the talk of an epistemic apocalypse or epistemic death relatively seriously—we can treat it as picking out real phenomena which deserve our attention and concern—without taking it all that literally.

This naturally prompts the question of whether we should understand other items on the list in the same spirit. Is talk of epistemic injustice, epistemic oppression, and epistemic violence similarly hyperbolic or metaphorical? For example, someone might suggest that what philosophers call 'epistemic injustice' isn't *really* a form of injustice, but is at most an illuminating way of speaking due to parallels that we can draw to genuine cases of injustice. Is this what's going on? Well, perhaps—I don't think that's a view we should simply rule out from the start. However, it's not the approach that philosophers tend to advocate for, nor is it the approach I will recommend in this book. Instead, I want to take more literally and seriously the idea that there can be epistemic forms of injustice and oppression (and perhaps even violence), and to see how best to make sense of this idea and to think about what we stand to gain, theoretically and practically, from accepting it.

At the root of the 'epistemic X' pattern in recent analytic philosophy is the explosion of interest in the notion of *epistemic injustice*, which is why I've taken that as the central focus of this book (as reflected in its title). We'll see that our topic has a longer history, as I indicated already in the preface, but the main impetus for this explosion is Miranda Fricker's (2007) book *Epistemic Injustice: Power and the Ethics of Knowing*, which quickly popularised the term 'epistemic injustice' and has generated an enormous and rapidly growing literature within philosophy and beyond, largely conducted in Fricker's terminology and with many of her views taken explicitly or implicitly as starting assumptions. The other 'epistemic X's have largely followed in the wake of the remarkable uptake of the notion of epistemic injustice; as I hinted above, there *is* a little bit of trend-following in the story of how we got to epistemic everything everywhere all at once.[4]

The term 'epistemic oppression' is less prevalent in philosophical discussions, though Fricker has also used it in her writing (Fricker 1999), and more recently, it has been given new significance in the work of the philosopher Kristie Dotson (2012, 2014). 'Epistemic oppression' is sometimes treated as if it's just another name for what Fricker calls 'epistemic injustice,' but that's not how I'll present things in this book. Rather, I take these to be alternative—and perhaps rival—theoretical frameworks for trying to make sense of certain phenomena (illustrated by examples which we will meet in Chapter 2).

This brings us to the leading questions of this book:

- Are there, literally speaking, cases of epistemic injustice and/or epistemic oppression?
- What are they like? If they are not all alike, what different forms do they take?
- What is their significance?

I've left that last question deliberately vague. Is it asking about the significance of cases of epistemic injustice and the like for the study of epistemology, or for philosophy more generally? Or for our social and political lives? Or all of the above? Or for something else? I don't think we should pin ourselves down on this too much in advance; instead, let's keep an open mind for now, and see what emerges from the discussion in the chapters to follow.

You might protest, quite fairly, that *all* of my questions are vague, since I haven't said all that much about what it is for something to be epistemic, and less still about what injustice and oppression are. Admittedly in these last two cases, the reader will be approaching this book with at least an intuitive understanding; these are everyday terms, and I intend to use them here in ways that don't distort their usual, familiar meanings. Still, I do need to say something about how I'm going to understand them. In what's left of this chapter, I want to sketch out how I'm understanding the notions of injustice (Section 1.2) and oppression (Section 1.3), and I'll give preliminary attempts (to be improved on and refined in later chapters) to say how we might understand epistemic injustice and epistemic oppression literally, rather than as hyperbole or metaphor. Before wrapping up, I'll also say something to clarify how the term 'epistemic injustice' is being used in this book (Section 1.4).

1.2 INJUSTICE

For the purposes of this book, let's say that a person or group is subject to an injustice if they are harmed, and this harm is undeserved and due to an unfairness or inequality. When we hear the word 'harm,' we might immediately think of ways that people can be *physically* harmed; they might be injured or killed, for example. However, we'll think of harm much more broadly here, so that it includes other ways that people can be made worse off by the conduct of others. The general idea is that for one person to harm another is for the first to do something that results in a significant setback to the second's interests. We'll leave what counts as a 'significant' setback vague and perhaps dependent on the circumstances; it would be absurd to try to say once and for all how much money someone has to lose for a theft or bad investment to count as harmful to them, for example, and the point generalises.

Most (perhaps all) of us have an interest in being healthy, and so significant setbacks to staying healthy are harmful to us. Often, these setbacks aren't due to unfairness or inequality, in which case they won't count as injustices given what I wrote in the previous paragraph; sometimes we get better evidence about which food choices are healthy than we used to have at an earlier time, but it needn't be an injustice that people were given bad advice so long as those giving the advice did so on the basis of the best evidence available at the time. Of course, sometimes setbacks to staying healthy *are* due to unfairness or inequality; the water crisis in Flint, Michigan that began in 2014 has had a severe impact on the health of the city's largely Black and poor population, and it wasn't a coincidence that this already disadvantaged population's health was sacrificed in the name of saving money (Stanley 2016; Doan 2017).

Believers in corporal and capital punishment will think that imposing some physical harms on a person can be deserved, and can be acts of justice rather than unfairness. A driving accident due to unpredictable weather may cause great harm to befall me, but there's no clear sense in which I do or do not deserve this misfortune, nor is it due to unfairness or inequality; so this won't count as an injustice despite how badly I am harmed by it. As these examples suggest, an injustice, as I'm understanding it, involves someone being harmed, but not merely harmed; they must be *wronged*. That's what's missing when I crash in bad weather; I haven't been wronged by anyone or anything. And that's what some will argue is missing in cases of corporal and capital punishment; these involve harms being inflicted on someone, obviously enough, but (some will argue) they are not wronged because they deserve it.

These are all somewhat simplified examples, but hopefully they serve to illustrate the important points; people are harmed in general when they face significant setbacks to their interests, but such harms are only injustices to the extent that they are undeserved and due to unfairness or inequality. An *epistemic injustice*, then, is an undeserved and unfair significant setback to a person or group's interests that is somehow epistemic in nature, or at least is related to the epistemic in some important sense (which I'll clarify in the next section). It short, it involves a person or some people being *wronged epistemically*.

1.3 OPPRESSION

The philosopher Marilyn Frye has influentially argued that we get insight into how we should understand oppression by looking at the etymology of the word:

> The root of the word "oppression" is the element "press". *The press of the crowd; pressed into military service; to press a pair of pants; printing press; press the button.* Presses are used to mold things or flatten them or reduce them in bulk, sometimes to reduce them by squeezing out the gases or liquids in them. Something pressed is something caught between or among forces and barriers which are so related to each other that jointly they restrain, restrict, or prevent the thing's motion or mobility. Mold. Immobilize. Reduce.
>
> (Frye 1983: 2)

The picture this suggests is that a person or group is oppressed when their agency and autonomy are unwarrantedly and persistently curtailed in various ways. Let's unpack this thought a bit.

Most of us think that people should have a large degree of freedom or liberty. We should have space to exercise our capacities for agency and autonomy; that's to say, we should be in control of our own actions (agency), and we should be self-determining, in the sense that we can form our own conception of what is good, valuable, and worthwhile and are able to pursue that vision (autonomy). It's controversial exactly how much liberty individuals and groups should have. J. S. Mill (1859/2006) famously suggested each of us should have as large a helping of liberty as is compatible with everyone else receiving a similarly large portion; I have overstepped when I harm others, but so long as I don't harm anyone else, I am free to act as I wish. This claim, the 'harm principle,' has been controversial, but the general idea that people should have a considerable degree of scope to exercise their agency and autonomy in ways they deem fit is relatively uncontroversial (in theory at least – in practice, people often want to reserve agency and autonomy for themselves and others like them, as we'll discuss in a moment).

The difference between agency and autonomy is quite subtle, and so it's worth saying a little bit more about these. A person's agency is their capacity to perform actions, rather than merely to be acted on and animated by external forces, such as other people. A person's autonomy is their capacity to be self-determining: to act in accordance with their own will, rather than merely in ways that others want them to act. In various ways and with various motivations (good or bad), we can limit people's opportunities to exercise those capacities. We might give them 'knock-out' drugs or lock them up, but we might instead exercise power or threaten violence to coerce them to do things we want them to do (as we say) against their will.

We can now better understand what is meant when, inspired by Frye, we take oppression to be people facing unwarranted and persistent infringements and restrictions on their ability to exercise their capacities for agency and autonomy. Notice that this way of thinking about oppression doesn't involve thinking that curtailing people's agency and autonomy is oppressive in and of itself; it has to be unwarranted and persistent. Young children, or those who are incarcerated because they have harmed others, may be given limited options and opportunities for exercising agency and autonomy for many years of their lives, but they are typically not thought of as oppressed on that basis since this is not generally taken to be unwarranted. Moreover, oppression is more than just facing the occasional unwarranted setback. I might be unfairly turned away from a nightclub on my birthday by a bouncer on a power trip, ruining my plans to celebrate by tripping the light fantastic, but I'm not oppressed by this misfortune if this isn't part of any broader pattern of mistreatment or discrimination. As Frye implies in the passage quoted above, oppression involves individual obstacles, barriers, and forces forming a structure that works to persistently 'restrain, restrict, or prevent' people from exercising agency and autonomy. This brings us to the striking and influential image that Frye offers to help us picture how she takes oppression to function, that of the bird cage:

> Cages. Consider a birdcage. If you look very closely at just one wire in the cage, you cannot see the other wires. If your conception of what is before

you is determined by this myopic focus, you could look at that one wire, up and down the length of it, and be unable to see why a bird would not just fly around the wire anytime it wanted to go somewhere. Furthermore, even if, one day at a time, you myopically inspected each wire, you still could not see why a bird would have trouble going past the wires to get anywhere. There is no physical property of any one wire, *nothing* that the closest scrutiny could discover, that will reveal how a bird could be inhibited or harmed by it except in the most accidental way. It is only when you step back, stop looking at the wires one by one, microscopically, and take a macroscopic view of the whole cage, that you can see why the bird does not go anywhere; and then you will see it in a moment. It will require no great subtlety of mental powers. It is perfectly *obvious* that the bird is surrounded by a network of systematically related barriers, no one of which would be the least hindrance to its flight, but which, by their relations to each other, are as confining as the solid walls of a dungeon.

(Frye 1983: 4–5)

Patriarchy is a system of oppression; it is a system at work in a society like ours to oppress certain people, primarily women, on the basis of gender. Feminism is the social and political movement to end gendered oppression: that is, to dismantle patriarchy (hooks 2000). Likewise, white supremacy is a system of oppression on the basis of race, a system which oppresses (in various ways and to various degrees, depending when and where we focus on) people who are not white, to the advantage of those who are white (e.g. Mills 1997); anti-racist movements are those that attempt to dismantle this system of oppression.

One thing now widely acknowledged is that it's somewhat artificial to treat these as two distinct systems of oppression, since they work together in an interlocking manner, giving rise to complex and distinctive forms of oppression that are likely to be overlooked or misunderstood if we look at gendered oppression and racialised oppression separately. Kimberley Crenshaw (1989) introduced the term 'intersectionality' to denote the unique forms of oppression faced by Black American women in a white supremacist patriarchy.

There are many other forms of oppression, including oppression on the basis of class, sexuality, disability, age, weight, religion, whether someone is trans or cis (which shows that there's further complexity in the notion of 'gendered oppression' than was previously recognised), and so on. Intersectionality is now often used as a label to cover the myriad ways that all of these different axes of oppression interact with each other.

At this point, you might wonder whether the notions of injustice and oppression are all that distinct from each other. One difference is that oppression, as we're understanding it, is persistent in nature, while injustices *can* be persistent, but seem like they can also be one-offs. As is all-too familiar, a wrongful conviction might be part of a wider pattern of discrimination on the basis of factors like race, but it need not be; it may be instead that someone has bribed the jurors to secure their preferred outcome, and this could be an injustice even if there's no oppression. Still, it seems like injustices are often examples of systems of oppression in operation, and we might be tempted to suggest that oppression is just persistent injustice.[5]

I think that's a misunderstanding of the notion of oppression, at least as I conceive of it (following Frye's lead). Part of the point of the metaphor of the cage is that a single piece of wire in isolation may not offer any real obstacle to the bird. Likewise, a single unwarranted obstacle to a person exercising their agency and autonomy taken in isolation need not count as an injustice. Consider Frye's example of a woman being told by a male colleague at work that she should smile more often as it would make her seem friendlier and more approachable (1983: 2). As Frye notes, this isn't just to be dismissed as a mild annoyance. Rather, it places the woman in a 'double-bind'; she can no longer just be herself, but is faced with the unwelcome choice of acquiescing to someone else's request about what to do with her own face, or being perceived in negative ways as unfriendly and uncooperative. Is this an *injustice*? We could argue the point, but I think many of us will say no, or perhaps that it doesn't really matter. Rather, the reason that the colleague's request is a proper object of moral (and specifically feminist) concern is the one suggested by Frye's cage metaphor, namely the way it fits into a broader persistent pattern of controlling women's behaviour and bodies; it's an aspect of the oppression women face, even if a specific episode doesn't always rise to the level of an injustice.

It is worth recognising a related feature of Frye's metaphor which we may feel less comfortable with. As noted in the previous paragraph, Frye stresses that no single wire by itself impedes the bird's freedom, and one aspect of this, in nonmetaphorical terms, is the point made in the previous paragraph: that the particular ways that women have their agency and autonomy held in check may be relatively innocuous considered in isolation. However, Frye also seems to imply that this is true of *every single wire*, or to get beneath the metaphor again, that each aspect of the structures and forces that collectively curtail the agency and autonomy of oppressed people will trouble us no more when considered in isolation than a request to smile. We can see this implication if we pick out a couple of the sentences from Frye quoted above for closer inspection:

> [E]ven if, one day at a time, you myopically inspected each wire, you still could not see why a bird would have trouble going past the wires to get anywhere. There is no physical property of any one wire, *nothing* that the closest scrutiny could discover, that will reveal how a bird could be inhibited or harmed by it except in the most accidental way.

In other words, the harmfulness of any wire lies *entirely* in its part in the wider structure and is only revealed when we zoom out and consider the cage—the structure of wires—as a whole. However, oppression often seems to take less subtle and more brutal forms. Feminist theorists have long pointed to the role that sexual harassment, sexual violence, domestic abuse, and femicide, as well as the almost omnipresent threat of these forms of violence and control, play in upholding women's oppression; likewise, the oppression of Black people in the United States, particularly Black men, crucially involves actual or potential entanglements with the police, with the accompanying threat of incarceration or death. It's not clear how these overtly controlling, harmful, and violent aspects of oppression are meant to fit into Frye's cage metaphor. That need not be a problem, so long as we are clear about the limitations of this metaphor; metaphors are almost always imperfect, but they can still be useful in understanding and communicating ideas and theories so long as we take care not to read too much into them.

Feminist philosophers and theorists after Frye have had more to say about oppression, much of it building on and refining her account and some of it, predictably enough, exploring other approaches. This isn't our main topic here, and so we can rest content with what we have on the table so far (though see the further suggested readings at the end of the chapter for guidance on what else to read on this topic). The question left for us now is: what could *epistemic* oppression be?

Given the account of oppression I've inherited from Frye, a natural suggestion is that epistemic oppression involves people facing persistent and unwarranted obstacles and constraints when trying to exercise their epistemic agency and autonomy. So far, that's not very helpful; we've reverted back to where we started in this chapter, just sticking 'epistemic' in front of other words. However, we can elaborate on this general idea.

We engage in various epistemic activities and practices: deciding what to investigate; making observations and gathering evidence; drawing conclusions and forming beliefs; discussing and sharing our findings with others in the hope that we can pool our knowledge and understanding to form a more comprehensive and comprehensible picture of the world; uncovering and attempting to resolve disagreements (or 'agreeing to disagree'); and much more besides. You might think that what I'm describing is *scientific* practice, but we engage in all of these things informally all the time. Think about the steps you might take to plan a holiday with other people: you might investigate options and prices for travel and accommodation; choose what kinds of activities you and the others might want to engage in and look into the available options; present your findings to the others, only to find that they have reached different conclusions about how your time and money is best spent, and that you need to work through those differences; and so on. These are all epistemic activities, in that they involve trying to get and share evidence, justification, knowledge, and other epistemic goods, and attempting to remove barriers to these, such as disagreement, when they arise.

We are active participants in these activities and practices—we display epistemic agency. We also exercise some degree of choice and freedom, choosing what to investigate and what to ignore (given that we only have a finite amount of time and energy to spend), how best to pursue our inquiries, how best to respond to disagreement, and so on—we exercise epistemic autonomy. To be sure, we aren't typically given a totally free hand in these things. Particular contexts such as scientific research or legal proceedings may constrain us in specific ways; only certain research methods are allowed in scientific work and often only certain kinds of evidence are taken to be a good basis for reaching a judgement in legal contexts. Even outside of these special contexts, we're almost never completely unconstrained in how we conduct ourselves in our epistemic lives. This observation doesn't seriously challenge our self-conception as epistemically autonomous agents, though, since our actions in general are similarly constrained; we are invariably subject to various laws and formal and informal rules, or bound by the expectations and demands of others, yet we still think that we often act autonomously. By the same lights, we should think that we often exercise epistemic agency and autonomy even though we are not completely unconstrained.

Above I suggested that epistemic oppression can be thought of as involving people facing persistent and unwarranted obstacles when they try to exercise their capacities for epistemic agency and autonomy. I hope that this suggestion has more substance to it, now that we have some sense of what exercising those capacities looks like. I similarly hope that it's clearer what's involved in epistemic injustice, understood in the way I suggested in the previous section; to a first approximation, we can think of epistemic injustice as someone being wronged when engaging in epistemic activities and practices of the sort just outlined. This way of understanding what epistemic injustice and epistemic oppression could be, and how these might be more than just hyperbole or metaphor, will help us understand what it is that the particular, more theoretically developed accounts of epistemic injustice and epistemic oppression discussed in later chapters are trying to capture.

Finally, I hope that it has also become clearer why we might think that epistemic injustice and epistemic oppression are worth worrying about—at least if they're real phenomena. That takes us back to our leading questions, stated above, and in particular, the questions of whether there are any real cases of epistemic injustice or epistemic oppression, and if so, what they're like; those are the questions we'll begin to take up in the next chapter, though it will take most of the rest of the book to properly answer them.

1.4 A TERMINOLOGICAL INTERLUDE

I need to offer a quick note on how I'm going to use terminology moving forward. The term 'epistemic injustice' is sometimes used broadly, as a label for the topic and set of issues brought into the spotlight by Fricker's book of that name, and sometimes more narrowly for the particular notion that Fricker introduces when theorising about that topic (which will examine in Chapter 3). On the former usage, epistemic injustice encompasses the notion of epistemic oppression, while on the latter, epistemic oppression is part of an alternative—possibly a rival—theoretical approach. It's crucially important not to confuse these two uses of the label, or else you might struggle to see how there can be genuine alternatives to Fricker's approach. After all, if the topic under consideration is epistemic injustice, surely we should be talking about epistemic injustice; those who are instead discussing epistemic oppression have (from this perspective) simply changed the subject. Any apparent tension here dissolves once we recognise these two uses of 'epistemic injustice,' so that someone advocating the notion of epistemic oppression over that of epistemic injustice still counts as contributing to discussions of epistemic injustice in the broad, general sense.

I will use the term 'epistemic injustice' in both of these ways; sometimes I'll use it to pick out the broad topic of this book (as in its title), and sometimes I'll mean more specifically the notion that Fricker is offering an account of in her work. I'll try to be very clear which usage is intended at a given time, so we can avoid any potential confusions lurking here. In some ways, it might be less confusing to come up with a new term altogether for the more general topic, but I suspect it's too late for that; if I were to come up with such a term and make it my book title, nobody would know what I was writing about. I'll let familiarity win the day here, even if the result isn't ideal. With that all said, let's turn our attention in the next chapter to apparent examples of epistemic injustice in the broad sense (and perhaps also the narrow sense).

1.5 SUMMARY

I opened this chapter, by looking at the recent proliferation of labels used by contemporary philosophers that prefix something relatively familiar with 'epistemic'. Some of these looked to be hyperbolic or metaphorical on close inspection, but I identified two which seemed both highly suggestive and like they might be worth taking not just seriously, but literally: epistemic injustice and epistemic oppression. Much of this book from Chapter 3 onwards will be occupied with clarifying these two notions, but I've offered a start by saying something about how I'm going to understand injustice and oppression, and by gesturing at how we might understand the notions of epistemic injustice and epistemic oppression. What I've said about these two key notions falls far short of any kind of fully precise characterisation of them, and I'll turn to the task of offering more developed and refined characterisations in Chapters 3 and 4, after we've examined some illustrative examples in the next chapter.

1.6 SUGGESTED FURTHER READING

On what 'epistemic' means, see Hazlett (2016).

Mason (2022) offers a very useful introduction to many of the topics and concepts in feminist philosophy that come up in this chapter, including objectification, oppression, intersectionality, and the idea that feminism is a political movement to end gendered oppression.

For the classic discussion of harms and wrongs, see Feinberg (1987: Chapter 1). I have drawn on Feinberg's discussion in this chapter, particularly his suggestion that one sense of 'harm' involves setbacks to a person's interests, but I don't attribute the position taken in the text to him. For more on the distinction between harms and wrongs in the context of discussions of epistemic injustice, see Dunne and Kotsonis (forthcoming).

For classic discussions of oppression that draw on or dispute elements of Frye's account, see Young (1990/2011) and Cudd (2006), and for a detailed discussion of oppressive double binds inspired by Frye's treatment, see Hirji (2021).

The idea that violating and infringing on a person's agency or autonomy are forms of objectification comes from Martha Nussbaum's classic paper on the topic (1995); Cahill (2011) offers an alternative perspective inspired by Simone de Beauvoir's notion of the Other in *The Second Sex* (Beauvoir 1949/2009). The rival accounts of the moral significance of agency and autonomy offered by Nussbaum and Cahill will prove to be important in Chapter 11.

For an overview of J. S. Mill's moral and political philosophy, including discussion of his controversial harm principle, see Brink (2022).

I explore the tendency to conflate the phenomena under discussion in the literature on epistemic injustice with Fricker's distinctive theoretical descriptions and treatments of those phenomena in more detail in McGlynn (2025) (and this will continue to be a theme throughout this book).

Hänel (2024) is a recent introduction to epistemic injustice in German, including coverage of Fricker and Dotson's accounts.

NOTES

1 These are all taken from the recent literature: epistemic infringement (Leydon-Hardy 2021, 2025); epistemic apprenticeship (Churcher 2025); epistemic oppression (e.g. Fricker 1999; Dotson 2012, 2014); epistemic failure (e.g. Baysan 2018; McLeod 2024); epistemic vices (e.g. Cassam 2019; Tanesini 2021); epistemic atonement (Woodard 2023); epistemic weaponry (Pettigrew 2022); epistemic injustice (e.g. Fricker 2007); epistemic phariseeism (Dormandy 2023); epistemic slurs (Patterson 2020); the epistemic

apocalypse (Habgood-Coote 2023); epistemic health and epistemic inoculation (Piovarchy and Siskind 2023); epistemic complicity (Boult 2023); epistemic dehumanisation (Smith forthcoming); epistemic appropriation (Davis 2018); epistemic trespassing (Ballantyne 2019); epistemic violence (Spivak 1998; Dotson 2011); epistemic rights (e.g. Watson 2018, 2021; Lackey 2022; McGlynn 2023); epistemic death (Medina 2017); epistemic exploitation (Spivak 1999; Berenstain 2016); epistemic redlining (Doan 2017); epistemic reparations (Lackey 2022, 2025; Altanian 2024); epistemic sanity (Dantas 2023); the epistemic IKEA effect (Tiehen 2022); epistemic apathy (Schwengerer and Kotsonis 2025); epistemic shamelessness (Chappell 2023); epistemic utopia (Davis 2021); and epistemic exhaustion (Satta 2024).

2 Of course, there have always been *some* analytic philosophers who have had these kinds of ambitions. See, for example, Stebbing (1939/2022). This is something we're in danger of missing if we focus too much on the 'fathers' of analytic philosophy.

3 Emmalon Davis (2021) argues that the exclusion of certain topics within the discipline of philosophy is in part due to a kind of epistemic injustice.

4 As you might expect from this, there is also a much smaller but still significant trend of identifying different and perhaps unexpected varieties of injustice since Fricker's book: for example, affective injustice (e.g. Srinivasan 2017), aesthetic injustice (e.g. Fraser 2024; McIver Lopes 2024), and ontic injustice (e.g. Jenkins 2020). In noting these trends, I don't mean to be at all dismissive of the work that has been done; on the contrary, much of it is excellent and important.

5 This seems to be how Fricker understands the relationship between injustice and oppression in Fricker (1999): see also Toole (2019: 608).

REFERENCES

Altanian, Melanie. 2024. 'Rethinking the Right to Know and the Case for Restorative Epistemic Reparation.' *Journal of Social Philosophy* 55 (4): 728–745. https://doi.org/10.1111/josp.12492

Ballantyne, Nathan. 2019. 'Epistemic Trespassing.' *Mind* 128 (510): 367–395. https://doi.org/10.1093/mind/fzx042

Baysan, Umut. 2018. 'Memory, Confabulation, and Epistemic Failure.' *Logos & Episteme* 9 (4): 369–378. https://doi.org/10.5840/logos-episteme20189430

Beauvoir, Simone de. 1949/2009. *The Second Sex*. Translated by Constance Borde and Sheila Malovany-Chevallier. London: Random House, Inc.

Berenstain, Nora. 2016. 'Epistemic Exploitation.' *Ergo* 3 (22): 569–590. https://doi.org/10.3998/ergo.12405314.0003.022

Brink, David. 2022. 'Mill's Moral and Political Philosophy.' In Edward N. Zalta and Uri Nodelman, eds. *The Stanford Encyclopedia of Philosophy* (Fall 2022 Edition), https://plato.stanford.edu/archives/fall2022/entries/mill-moral-political/

Boult, Cameron. 2023. 'Epistemic Complicity.' *Episteme* 20 (4): 870–893. https://doi.org/10.1017/epi.2024.6

Cahill, Anne. 2011. *Overcoming Objectification: A Carnal Ethics*. New York and Oxon: Routledge.

Cassam, Quassim. 2019. *Vices of the Mind: From the Intellectual to the Political*. Oxford: Oxford University Press.

Chappell, Sophie Grace. 2023. 'Political Fanaticism and Epistemic Shamelessness.' In Paul Katsafanas, ed. *Fanaticism and the History of Philosophy*: 313–327. Oxon and New York: Routledge.

Crenshaw, Kimberlé. 1989. 'Demarginalizing the Intersection of Race and Sex: A Black Feminist Critique of Antidiscrimination Doctrine, Feminist Theory and Antiracist Politics.' *University of Chicago Legal Forum* 1: 139–167.

Cudd, Ann. 2006. *Analyzing Oppression*. Oxford and New York: Oxford University Press.

Churcher, Millicent. 2025. 'Designing for Epistemic Injustice: Epistemic Apprenticeship as an Institutional Commitment.' *Philosophy and Social Criticism* 51 (3): 501–526. https://doi.org/10.1177/01914537231184493

Dantas, Danilo Franga. 2023. 'Epistemic Sanity or Why You Shouldn't Be Opinionated or Skeptical.' *Episteme* 20 (3): 647–666. https://doi.org/10.1017/epi.2022.43

Davis, Emmalon. 2018. 'On Epistemic Appropriation.' *Ethics* 128 (4): 702–727. https://doi.org/10.1086/697490

Davis, Emmalon. 2021. 'A Tale of Two Injustices: Epistemic Injustice in Philosophy.' In Jennifer Lackey, ed. *Applied Epistemology*: 215–250. New York: Oxford University Press.

Doan, Michael. 2017. 'Epistemic Injustice and Epistemic Redlining.' *Ethics and Social Welfare* 11 (2): 177–190. https://doi.org/10.1080/17496535.2017.1293120

Dormandy, Katherine. 2023. 'Epistemic Phariseeism.' *Religious Studies* 59 (3): 515–532. https://doi.org/10.1017/S003441252200035X

Dotson, Kristie. 2011. 'Tracking Epistemic Violence, Tracking Practices of Silencing.' *Hypatia* 26 (2): 236–257. https://doi.org/10.1111/j.1527-2001.2011.01177.x

Dotson, Kristie. 2012. 'A Cautionary Tale: On Limiting Epistemic Oppression.' *Frontiers: A Journal of Women Studies* 33 (1): 24–47. https://doi.org/10.1353/fro.2012.a472779

Dotson, Kristie. 2014. 'Conceptualizing Epistemic Oppression.' *Social Epistemology* 28 (2): 115–138. https://doi.org/10.1080/02691728.2013.782585

Dunne, Gerry and Alkis Kotsonis. Forthcoming. 'Carving at the Joints: Distinguishing Epistemic Wrongs from Epistemic Harms in Epistemic Injustice Contexts.' *Episteme*. https://doi.org/10.1017/epi.2023.62

Feinberg, Joel. 1987. *The Moral Limits of the Criminal Law Volume 1: Harm to Others*. Oxford: Oxford University Press.

Fraser, Rachel. 2024. 'Aesthetic Injustice.' *Ethics* 134 (4): 449–478. https://doi.org/10.1086/729708

Fricker, Miranda. 1999. 'Epistemic Oppression and Epistemic Privilege.' *Canadian Journal of Philosophy* 29 (1): 191–210. https://doi.org/10.1080/00455091.1999.10716836

Fricker, Miranda. 2007. *Epistemic Injustice: Power and the Ethics of Knowing*. Oxford: Oxford University Press.

Frye, Marilyn. 1983. *The Politics of Reality: Essays in Feminist Theory*. New York: Crossing Press.

Habgood-Coote, Joshua. 2023. 'Deepfakes and the Epistemic Apocalypse.' *Synthese* 201: 1–23. https://doi.org/10.1007/s11229-023-04097-3

Hänel, Hilkje Charlotte. 2024. *Epistemische Ungerechtigkeiten*. Berlin and Boston, MA: Walter de Gruyter GmbH.

Hazlett, Allan. 2016. 'What Does "Epistemic" Mean?' *Episteme* 13 (4): 539–547. https://doi.org/10.1017/epi.2016.29

Hirji, Sukaina. 2021. 'Oppressive Double Binds.' *Ethics* 131 (4): 643–669. https://doi.org/10.1086/713943

hooks, bell. 2000. *Feminist Theory: From Margin to Center* (Second Edition). London: Pluto Press.

Jenkins, Katharine. 2020. 'Ontic Injustice.' *Journal of the American Philosophical Association* 6 (2): 188–205. https://doi.org/10.1017/apa.2019.27

Lackey, Jennifer. 2022. 'Epistemic Reparations and the Right to Be Known.' *Proceedings and Addresses of the American Philosophical Association* 96: 54–89.

Lackey, Jennifer. 2025. 'The Case for Epistemic Reparations.' In Jennifer Lackey and Aidan McGlynn, eds. *The Oxford Handbook of Social Epistemology*: 394–419. New York: Oxford University Press.

Leydon-Hardy, Lauren. 2021. 'Predatory Grooming and Epistemic Infringement.' In Jennifer Lackey, ed. *Applied Epistemology*: 119–147. Oxford and New York: Oxford University Press.

Leydon-Hardy, Lauren. 2025. 'Epistemic Infringement.' In Jennifer Lackey and Aidan McGlynn, eds. *The Oxford Handbook of Social Epistemology*: 328–356. New York: Oxford University Press.

Mason, Elinor. 2022. *Feminist Philosophy: An Introduction*. London and New York: Routledge.

McGlynn, Aidan. 2023. 'Epistemic Rights Violations and Epistemic Injustice.' *Asian Journal of Philosophy* 2 (29): 1–14. https://doi.org/10.1007/s44204-023-00087-x

McGlynn, Aidan. 2025. 'Epistemic Injustice: Phenomena and Theories.' In Jennifer Lackey and Aidan McGlynn, eds. *The Oxford Handbook of Social Epistemology*: 295–327. New York: Oxford University Press.

McIver Lopes, Dominic. 2024. *Aesthetic Injustice*. Oxford and New York: Oxford University Press.

McLeod, Lisa. 2024. 'Heedless Comportment and Epistemic Failure: W. E. B. Du Bois's Diagnosis of Whiteness as Irrevocable License.' *Social Theory and Practice* 50 (2): 257–284. https://doi.org/10.5840/soctheorpract202438212

Medina, José. 2017. 'Varieties of Hermeneutical Injustice.' In Ian James Kidd, José Medina, and Gaile Pohlhaus Jr., eds. *The Routledge Handbook of Epistemic Injustice*: 41–52. Oxon: Routledge.

Mill, John Stuart. 1859/2006. *On Liberty*. Reprinted in John Stuart Mill, *On Liberty and The Subjugation of Women*. London: Penguin Classics.

Mills, Charles. 1997. *The Racial Contract*. Ithaca, NY: Cornell University Press.

Nussbaum, Martha. 1995. 'Objectification.' *Philosophy and Public Affairs* 24 (4): 249–291. https://doi.org/10.1111/j.1088-4963.1995.tb00032.x

Patterson, Adam. 2020. 'Epistemic Slurs: A Novel Explication and Adequacy Constraint for Slur Theories.' *Erkenntnis* 87 (4): 2029–2046. https://doi.org/10.1007/s10670-020-00288-3

Patterson, Orlando. 1982. *Slavery and Social Death: A Comparative Study*. Cambridge, MA and London: Harvard University Press.

Pettigrew, Richard. 2022. 'Radical Epistemology, Structural Explanations, and Epistemic Weaponry.' *Philosophical Studies* 179: 289–304. https://doi.org/10.1007/s11098-021-01660-x

Piovarchy, Adam and Scott Siskind. 2023. 'Epistemic Health, Epistemic Immunity, and Epistemic Inoculation.' *Philosophical Studies* 180 (8): 2329–2354. https://doi.org/10.1007/s11098-023-01993-9

Satta, Mark. 2024. 'Epistemic Exhaustion and the Retention of Power.' *Hypatia* 39 (3): 510–529. https://doi.org/10.1017/hyp.2024.1

Schwengerer, Lukas and Alkis Kotsonis. 2025. 'On the Intellectual Vice of Epistemic Apathy.' *Social Epistemology* 39 (1): 77–90. https://doi.org/10.1080/02691728.2024.2356574

Smith, Leonie. Forthcoming. 'Poverty and Epistemic Dehumanisation.' In Leonie Smith and Alfred Archer, eds. *The Moral Psychology of Poverty*. Dordrecht and New York: Springer Nature.

Spivak, Gayatri Chakravorty. 1998. 'Can the Subaltern Speak?' In Cary Nelson and Lawrence Grossberg, eds. *Marxism and the Interpretation of Culture*: 66–111. Champaign: University of Illinois Press.

Spivak, Gayatri Chakravorty. 1999. *A Critique of Postcolonial Reason: Toward a History of the Vanishing Present.* Cambridge, MA: Harvard University Press.

Srinivasan, Amia. 2017. 'The Aptness of Anger.' *Journal of Political Philosophy* 26 (2): 123–144. https://doi-org.eux.idm.oclc.org/10.1111/jopp.12130

Stanley, Jason. 2016. 'The Emergency Manager: Strategic Racism, Technocracy, and the Poisoning of Flint's Children.' *The Good Society* 25 (1): 1–45.

Stebbing, Susan. 1939/2022. *Thinking to Some Purpose.* Oxon and New York: Routledge.

Tanesini, Alessandra. 2021. *The Mismeasure of the Self.* Oxford and New York: Oxford University Press.

Tiehen, Justin. 2022. 'The IKEA Effect and the Production of Epistemic Goods.' *Philosophical Studies* 179 (11): 3401–3420. https://doi.org/10.1007/s11098-022-01840-3

Toole, Briana. 2019. 'From Standpoint Epistemology to Epistemic Oppression.' *Hypatia* 34 (4): 598–618. https://doi.org/10.1111/hypa.12496

Watson, Lani. 2018. 'Systematic Epistemic Rights Violations in the Media: A Brexit Case Study.' *Social Epistemology* 32 (2): 88–102. https://doi.org/10.1080/02691728.2018.1440022

Watson, Lani. 2021. *The Right to Know: Epistemic Rights and Why We Need Them.* Oxon and New York: Routledge.

Woodard, Elise. 2023. 'Epistemic Atonement.' In Russ Shader-Landau, ed. *Oxford Studies in Metaethics*, vol. 18: 163–190. Oxford and New York: Oxford University Press.

Young, Iris Marion. 1990/2011. *Justice and the Politics of Difference.* Princeton and Oxford: Princeton University Press.

2
CRYING FOR THE MOON
Examples of Epistemic Injustice

2.1 INTRODUCTION

In discussions of epistemic injustice, examples are usually presented *as* illustrations of particular theories, concepts, definitions, and so on. A real-life or fictional example, of the sort we'll look at soon, is laid out in some detail, and we're then given a label that tells us what the example is an example of: 'this is a case of what I'll call testimonial injustice/testimonial smothering/willful hermeneutical ignorance/etc.' (don't worry, I'll introduce all of these labels properly in later chapters). We're then given a general definition which tells us what that label means, and often that definition needs to then be refined or defended as we encounter other examples of what seem like the same phenomena which don't quite fit our initial characterisation.

This is a natural way to proceed, but it can have some serious drawbacks. Presenting an example to you *as* an example of some particular phenomenon tends to shape how you'll interpret that example; it makes you concentrate on certain features, making those salient and significant, while backgrounding others. By itself, this isn't a worry, since this is in the nature of theoretical descriptions of phenomena, including those offered by philosophers. A theory of knowledge, to return briefly to epistemology's traditional concerns, tries to spell out what (if anything) is essential to all instances of knowledge: what

DOI: 10.4324/9781003281863-3

they have in common and so what unifies them, despite all of the ways that they differ from each other at the level of fine detail. A theory of this sort is an attempt to say what can be said about knowledge *in general*, over and above detailed descriptions of particular instances of knowledge. Rival theories will offer rival conceptions of which the key features of particular examples to focus on are. Given all this, it's hardly surprising that a philosopher interested in theorising about epistemic injustice would draw your attention to certain features of the examples they present; that's their job.

That point acknowledged, problems arise when you aren't ever given a neutral description of the example; it is from the start presented to you already clothed in the theoretical descriptions preferred by the theorist doing the presenting, and so you only ever see the example as it looks according to their theory. This can be hard to spot. Perhaps neither you nor the theorist recognises the way that the gap between the phenomena illustrated by the examples and their preferred theoretical treatment of those phenomena has been narrowed or even closed entirely; after all, the theorist may never have considered their examples in any other terms and from any other perspective either. Whether it's deliberate or not, the effect is the same: proper consideration of alternative theoretical descriptions and accounts is made difficult, since it can seem tantamount to dismissing the reality of the examples themselves.

As I have already hinted in the previous chapter, my view is that much of the philosophical discussion of epistemic injustice is guilty of precisely this kind of failure to carefully distinguish the phenomena that we're interested in understanding better from particular theories of those phenomena. There's now a stock of examples, some of which we're about to meet, which are standardly and rather uncritically treated *as* examples of various theoretical notions, both in the literature on epistemic injustice and when the topic is taught to students.[1] Examples like these will be crucially important in this book, but if we're to make proper use of them, we need to guard against the concerns I've just outlined. Now, there's no sure-fire way to go about this. Perhaps there isn't really a fully neutral description of the examples that we'll be focusing on; maybe the only way to convey the features of them that make them important and interesting is to describe them in terms that already pick a theoretical side, at least to an extent. Even if there are ways to describe the examples that are neutral between all the different theories philosophers might have of them, nobody (least of all me) has any guarantee that I'll be the one who manages to find those descriptions.

Still, I'm going to try. In this chapter, after briefly offering some context (Section 2.2), I'm going to lay out a long series of the kinds of examples that have given philosophers interested in epistemic injustice their subject matter, without yet attaching them to any particular philosophical theory or terminology (Section 2.3). I'll try to describe the examples as neutrally as I am able, avoiding drawing particular attention to features that perhaps only some of the accounts we'll look at later will treat as the important ones. I'll then offer an initial discussion of some of the ways that different examples resemble each other or differ from each other (Section 2.4), focusing in on the particular distinction that explains how the rest of the book is arranged (Section 2.5). In the final section (Section 2.6), I'll reflect on the place of the examples within philosophy's recent applied turn. I'll leave it to subsequent chapters to examine more theoretical, elaborated accounts of the examples and what to make of them.

I ended the previous chapter by noting that the term 'epistemic injustice' sometimes means whatever the topic of this book is, and sometimes picks out Fricker's particular theoretical notion and framework for theorising about it (a good example of the kind of worries I've just been describing). Throughout this chapter, I'll only have the former usage in mind; whether these examples should be theorised about in terms of epistemic injustice, as Fricker understands that label, is a substantive question to be addressed in subsequent chapters, not something we can tell just by looking at the examples themselves.

2.2 SHOW AND TELL

Before presenting the examples, I want to offer a bit of context for thinking about them and their significance. It's very often in our interests to be able to influence what other people think. We have a number of ways open to us to do this. I can *show* you something, drawing your attention to something you might not have noticed or appreciated before, as when I pull back the curtains to reveal that it's currently raining. But given that humans have evolved language, I don't need to do this; I can simply *tell* you things. My motives in doing so can vary. I may want to share some knowledge or information or beliefs I have with you. I may, in contrast, wish to deceive or misinform you: to get you to believe something that I don't believe, and perhaps that I know to be false.

Language is a powerful tool for influencing others, for good or for ill; this much hardly needs saying. My ability to influence a particular audience, though, is limited in various ways. Whether my aim is to inform you or deceive you, I'll only be able to influence what you think if you understand what I am saying, and you take me to be believable or trustworthy on the topic at issue. Let's suppose I tell you that it's raining outside at the moment. You express scepticism, pointing out that I've tried to prank you by getting you to wear clothes that are inappropriate for the weather in the past. At this point, I can pull back the curtain and gesture at the downpour happening outside the window, and under normal circumstances how trustworthy you take me to be is no longer relevant: unless you suspect I might have somehow swapped the window for a flat-screen TV, you'll take this to settle the matter. We are able to tell people things rather than having to show them when, but only when, they take us to be speaking believably. Relatedly, it's often the case that the only way I can convey something to a person is by telling them, since it concerns what happened far away, or in the past, or what's going on inside my head, or it is theoretical and abstract rather than concrete and locatable; in these cases, there may be no practical equivalent of pulling back the curtain and letting you inspect for yourself, and so the only chance I have of persuading you is to impress you as credible on the subject in question.

What is it to take someone to be believable when they are speaking on some topic? This has two different sides. First, to regard me as believable on some subject, you'll need to take me to be competent: to be speaking from knowledge, or at least with a high chance of being right. Second, regarding me as believable involves taking me to be sincere, rather than as trying to deceive my audience. You shouldn't treat my pronouncements about physics as believable because I'm clearly clueless on this subject, and so even if I don't intend to mislead you, you will nonetheless be misled if you believe me on this topic due to my lack of competence. You also shouldn't treat me as believable on the weather outside, since you know I like to prank you by getting you to wear inapt outfits. In this second example, you don't need to think that I'm incompetent; indeed, you may know that I take a lot of care to learn the true state of the weather, to better lead you astray.

These reflections on the importance of an audience taking a speaker to be believable become relevant for the issues we discussed in Chapter 1 when we reflect on the fact that people often don't get treated as believable to the degree that they are rightly due; they make an assertion—a claim about how the world is—with the intention of sharing their beliefs (or perhaps their knowledge) with some audience, but their audience doesn't take their claim as seriously as they ought to, perhaps flat-out disbelieving or dismissing it. This can happen for relatively innocent reasons. Sometimes this is just a result of the audience having misleading evidence that conflicts with what the speaker is saying or which tells against the speaker's trustworthiness. It can also be due to carelessness or oversight; I might mishear you, or read a report you have written too quickly, and dismiss what you are telling me by mistake. Mistakes of this kind seem ubiquitous and banal, and at least on the face of it, they don't seem like they involve any kind of injustice.

In this chapter, we'll start looking at a range of examples in which it seems like speakers aren't treated as believable in the way they ought to be, and where this *does* seem to be a form of injustice, rather than the kind of thing we can chalk up to carelessness, oversight, or misleading evidence. Moreover, to pre-empt Section 2.5 a little, in some of the examples this inability of the speakers to be found believable seems to trace back to difficulties in being understood in the first place: perhaps even in making sense of things themselves.

2.3 THE EXAMPLES

Philosopher of Physics:
A philosopher of physics with significant training in physics and an appreciation of cutting-edge research in the field attends a conference where all of the other participants have affiliations in departments of physics rather than philosophy (Fricker 2007: 28–29). The philosopher engages with the research presentations throughout the conference, asking questions and making constructive suggestions about how to interpret various results, but these contributions are received with a dismissive attitude; she is 'just a philosopher,' and so nobody takes any of her points seriously, even though they are grounded in her training and in her understanding of both the general background and the specific issues and results under discussion at the conference.[2]

Miss Triggs:
Miss Triggs is a character in a well-known comic by Riana Duncan, published in *Punch* in 1988. She sits in a meeting, the only woman surrounded by five very similar looking middle-aged men. The man at the head of the table is saying 'That's an excellent suggestion, Miss Triggs. Perhaps one of the men here would like to make it.'

Miranda Fricker reports encountering real-life examples much like this (Fricker 2007: 46–47). She gives a number of examples of women who had to give up most or all of the credit for their best ideas if they wanted to see those ideas taken seriously and perhaps implemented. These women had adopted conscious strategies much like the one ludicrously suggested by the chair of Miss Triggs's meeting; one of them would write her suggestions on slips of paper, which she would then discreetly pass to a sympathetic male colleague who would present them as his own. Such strategies enabled these women to have an impact on decision- and policy-making. However, this impact came at the cost of being disadvantaged in their careers due to a lack of recognition of their successes; typically, the men would receive the credit and the resulting professional advantages.

Patricia Williams:
The Black legal scholar Patricia Williams recalls being racially profiled and denied entry to a Benetton store when out looking for a birthday present for her mother (1991: 44–51). A white shop assistant refused to allow her entry, signalling that the store was closed, despite the fact it was the middle of the afternoon and Williams could clearly see other—also white— shoppers milling around. Recounting the story later, Williams found that many people didn't believe her, or were inclined to question the role of race in the episode, suggesting that Williams was exaggerating or being overly sensitive, or failing to see things from the perspective of the shop assistant.

Marge Sherwood:
In Anthony Minghella's film adaption of Patricia Highsmith's novel *The Talented Mr. Ripley*, the eponymous Tom Ripley has killed Dickie Greenleaf during an argument. Dickie's fiancé, Marge Sherwood, doesn't exactly know what has happened to him, but she has well-founded suspicions that Ripley is somehow involved in his disappearance and that he may be dead. However, when she voices these suspicions to Herbert Greenleaf, Dickie's father and her would-be father-in-law, he is dismissive: 'Marge, there's female intuition, and then there are facts' (Minghella 2000: 130).

Tom Robinson:
In Harper Lee's *To Kill a Mockingbird* (1960), a disabled Black man, Tom Robinson, is on trial for the rape of a younger white woman, Mayella Ewell. Not only is Robinson innocent, his lawyer, Atticus Finch, has decisively demonstrated his innocence to the courtroom, showing that Robinson couldn't have attacked Ewell in the manner she has claimed, and making it probable that the injuries she has sustained were in fact the result of her father, Bob

Ewell, beating her for attempting to kiss Robinson. Throughout his trial, Robinson does his best to give an honest and complete account of his relationship with Mayella Ewell and what happened on the day he is claimed to have assaulted her. None of this is to any avail, though; his testimony in the courtroom gains little traction with most of his audience, and the all-white jury convict him. Robinson is sent to jail, and although Finch is hopeful he will win an appeal, he is instead shot dead (allegedly while trying to escape), leaving behind a wife and three children.

Carmita Wood:
Carmita Wood was, as we would now describe it, sexually harassed by one of the professors in the Cornell University Laboratory of Nuclear Studies. However, this expression did not yet exist when she was targeted in this way. Following Cornell's failure to act or to move Wood to a different department, she eventually quit her position, but needing money to raise her family, she applied for unemployment benefit. Forced to say why she had left her job, she wrote 'health reasons.' The Department of Labor denied her application, deeming these 'non-compelling personal reasons.' Wood appealed, this time offering a detailed account of the professor's behaviour towards her, backed by witnesses who had seen some of this behaviour first-hand. The Department of Labor simply repeated their earlier verdict that Wood had only produced 'non-compelling person reasons' (e.g. Baker 2007: 28; Traister 2018: 167). The term 'sexual harassment' was introduced by a group of feminists at Cornell in April 1975 to enable women like Wood to recognise the commonalities in their experiences, and to join together to in the fight for social, legal, and political reforms.[3]

Wood's application for unemployment benefit was unsuccessful, and her accusations against her harasser were never taken seriously by her employer or the Department of Labor. However, Wood's case was a watershed moment in the (sadly ongoing) movement against sexual harassment, particularly workplace sexual harassment.

"Marie":
In 2008, an 18-year-old woman, known pseudonymously as Marie, reported to police that she had been bound, gagged, and raped at knife-point by a man who took considerable care not to leave any physical evidence (such as D.N.A. evidence). The police interrogated Marie (despite this violating their own procedures), gave undue weight to the unfounded suspicions of one of her foster parents that she was making the story up, uncovered (minor) inconsistencies

in her account, and ultimately successfully applied pressure to get her to confess she had made a false report. Not content with having utterly failed Marie, the police proceeded to file a false-reporting charge against her in 2009. It would take two years for the perpetrator, Marc Patrick O'Leary, to be apprehended by a more competent investigation into a serial rapist in Colorado; they found images O'Leary had taken of his assault of Marie on his hard drive, proving that her initial report had been entirely truthful.

Marie's story was the subject of a Pulitzer Prize winning article by Ken Armstrong and T. Christian Miller, 'An Unbelievable Story of Rape,' jointly published by The Marshall Project and ProPublica in 2015 (and from which I have taken the details about the case). Armstrong and Miller later wrote a book about the case, *A False Report: A True Story of Rape in America* (Armstrong and Miller 2018), and their reporting became the basis of an episode of the radio show *This American Life* in 2016 and a TV miniseries, 'Unbelievable,' in 2019.

Joe Rose:

In Ian McEwan's novel *Enduring Love* (1997), Joe Rose and Jed Parry meet by chance when they are both involved as would-be rescuers during a freak hot-air balloon accident, in which a third member of their impromptu rescue team is horribly killed. Parry immediately forms the impression that Rose is in love with him, and starting later that same day, tracks Rose down and begins a campaign of increasingly unsettling and threatening phone calls, answerphone messages, and letters. Soon Parry stations himself outside Rose's house for large portions of the day when Rose is there, and sometimes follows Rose through London when he leaves. Rose struggles to know what to make of Parry's behaviour and how seriously to take it, and while he increasingly finds Parry threatening, he fails to convince either his fiancé Clarissa or the policemen he talks to that there is anything to worry about. All Parry seems to want is for Rose to admit his love for Parry, abandon Clarissa, find God, and come live with Parry in the large house that he has recently inherited following his mother's death: odd, but not threatening. Rose recognises patterns in Parry's behaviour that eventually and correctly lead him to the conclusion that Parry has de Clérambault's syndrome (erotomania), a disorder which involves delusions that another person is in love with you, but even with this diagnosis in hand, Rose struggles to persuade the police to see Parry as a threat, allowing the situation to escalate until Parry turns violent.

Harriet McBryde Johnson:
Harriet McBryde Johnson was disability rights lawyer and activist who met, corresponded, and debated with the philosopher Peter Singer, and she wrote up her account of their exchanges and interactions in a well-known essay, 'Unspeakable Conversations,' published in the *New York Times Magazine* in 2003. Singer notoriously holds that parents should have the right to euthanise children with disabilities like Johnson's, and in her essay, Johnson described her unsuccessful attempts to convince him that she led a worthwhile life, enjoyed a relatively high level of well-being, and that there were things about her disabilities and her experiences of them that she valued: that more generally 'the presence or absence of a disability doesn't predict quality of life,' and that disabled lives can be 'lived well.' Though Singer engaged with Johnson's points and arguments, they seem to have had little to no impact on his views; the same magazine that carried Johnson's 'Unspeakable Conversations' later published Singer's (2008) obituary for Johnson, which they titled 'Happy Nevertheless.' As Elizabeth Barnes writes:

> McBryde [Johnson] went to great lengths—including her famous essay in the same paper that published the obituary—during her life to explain that she was not happy *nevertheless*. She was just happy, like so many other flourishing disabled people. But she wasn't believed, just as she predicted—in the very same paper—she wouldn't be believed and just as she had so often been disbelieved in the past.
> (Barnes 2016: 138)

Tressie McMillan Cottom:
In her essay 'Dying to be Competent,' sociologist Tressie McMillan Cottom recounts her attempts to get her reports of excruciating pain and bleeding taken seriously by nurses and doctors four months into her pregnancy (McMillan Cottom 2019: 81–86). Medical staff told her it was likely just constipation, or that she had just eaten something that disagreed with her. When they finally agreed to perform an ultrasound, they discovered that McMillan Cottom had been in labour for days, and they found two tumours. She was taken to a delivery room, but was still denied adequate pain medication. When her daughter was born prematurely, the hospital declined to provide any assistance, and her daughter soon died. As McMillan Cottom held her daughter's body, a nurse felt compelled to chastise her: 'Just so you

know, there was nothing we could have done, because you did not tell us you were in labor' (2019: 85).

Amongst all the injustices and torments here, we can note that the medical professionals McMillan Cottom dealt with refused to take her as speaking with authority about her own pain or its significance. As McMillan Cottom writes:

> Everything about the structure of trying to get medical care had filtered me through assumptions of my incompetence.
>
> (2019: 85)

"KV":

Dini Nayeri's (2023) book *Who Gets Believed? When the Truth Isn't Enough* opens with the horrifying story of a man known as KV (sometimes K), who was brutally tortured by the Sri Lankan government because he was suspected to be a member or collaborator of the rival militants, the Liberation Tigers of Tamil Eelam (LTTE). What started as 'routine torture' (2023: 6) involving physical beatings escalated into something else when KV's captors became convinced he had information concerning the whereabouts of gold hidden by the LTTE. His side and back were badly burned when he was branded with a heated metal rod, before they poured gasoline all over the wounds, prolonging the recovery time required by the burns. After months of agony, with a total lack of proper medical attention and countless further beatings, KV made a risky escape from the army camp he was being held in, and eventually made it to the United Kingdom, where he applied for asylum, 'unable to fathom the ordeal just beginning, the mighty, pitiless foe up ahead' (2023: 9). The UK Home Office rejected KV's application for asylum and ordered him to return to Sri Lanka, writing 'You are a fit and healthy young male who it is considered suffered no problems in Sri Lanka' (2023: 24), and plunging him into a nightmarish eight-year-long legal process to appeal their original decision.

You might think this would be an open-and-shut case. After all, the kinds of injuries KV claimed to have sustained would leave distinctive marks and scars; if he lacked those scars, small wonder the Home Office would reject his claims about the suffering he had endured. As you may have already guessed, KV *had* precisely the scars that would substantiate his account of torture. Rather than simply take this compelling evidence at face value (or trust the experts they commissioned to evaluate that evidence, who pronounced it valid), the Home Office decided that they couldn't conclusively rule out a bizarre alternative theory which had KV inflicting the horrific injuries on himself, or choosing to allow himself to be so injured with the help of a medical professional, all in the hope of fooling the Home Office and unjustifiably gaining asylum in the United Kingdom.

Michael Ledford:
In 2000, the state of Virginia found firefighter Michael Ledford guilty of first-degree murder and arson after he confessed to starting a fire that killed his one-year-old son and badly injured his (then) wife. Despite a dearth of forensic evidence and lack of any coherent motive, Ledford, who was just 23 at the time and was recognised to have an undiagnosed mental health disorder—and, we should remember, who had literally just lost his son—was interrogated by police for four hours without a lawyer. Drawing parallels to the way immigration services treat asylum seekers like "KV," Dini Nayeri (2023: 14–20) offers a detailed description of the police's interrogation, picking out the ways that they misled or outright lied to Ledford (including pretending they had evidence they in face didn't have, and promising him help for his then-undiagnosed autism that they had no authority or capacity to offer as part of 'rehabilitation' once he confessed). Despite Ledford's initial—and subsequent—adamance that he could not and would not have endangered his family, the interrogators managed to extract a confession from him, based on a spurious and bizarre motivation that they themselves had suggested to Ledford, and this confession was then treated as decisive evidence of his guilt. At the time of writing, Ledford remains incarcerated in Virginia, less than halfway through his 50-year prison sentence.

2.4 SIMILARITIES AND DIFFERENCES

These examples give a taste of the kinds of concerns philosophers have when they talk about epistemic injustice, and why they take the topic to be of such significance. Reading them all together like this is rather overwhelming, but we'll be returning to many of them across this book in different chapters in a more piecemeal and manageable manner (and without any presumption the reader will remember all of them or their details).

That said, I do want to offer a few preliminary remarks about some of the main points of comparison and contrast between the examples in the remainder of this chapter, while we've got them all assembled together. These remarks will motivate focusing more on some of the examples and less on others, and they will also partly explain why I group the examples and the issues they raise together in particular ways in the chapters that follow.

When introducing the examples above, I noted that they all involve someone trying to convey something of significance to an audience, but facing barriers to being taken as seriously as they should, either because they are seen as personally lacking credibility or because what they are saying is somehow difficult for their audience to understand. While I hope it's clear how each of the examples fits this common description, we shouldn't let that hide that there are also various significant dimensions of contrast across them.

Let's start by observing that the dismissive treatment of our Philosopher of Physics in the first of the examples seems liable to be localised to more or less the specific circumstances detailed. While the philosopher may have a hard time being taken seriously by the scientists at the conference, she is unlikely to encounter the same sceptical attitudes when talking to other audiences on other matters; she needn't worry about being dismissed as a mere philosopher when applying for promotion at her university, or when she talks to her doctor, or when she applies for a mortgage, or when she gets pulled over by the police. That's not to say that her mistreatment at the conference need be inconsequential. She may miss out on professional recognition and opportunities that she deserves, causing her life to go worse that it would have done had her contributions been taken more seriously; she may be considerably harmed, in the terminology of Chapter 1. Still the prejudice she faces as a philosopher is likely to be isolated to the conference (or at least to conferences of this particular kind). Related to this point, we can note that philosophers are not typically a marginalised or oppressed group in a society; her unjust mistreatment at the conference is not an aspect of a wider pattern of injustice faced by philosophers.

In this respect, the first example contrasts with *all* of the other examples I've sketched, since those all seem much less local and circumscribed. I've already noted that Miss Triggs has real-life counterparts, and the historian Mary Beard (2017) argues that the cartoon raises a general question, which she calls the Miss Triggs question: how can we become aware of and tackle the prejudices that often make us not listen to women when they contribute to the public sphere? Some of the other examples also involve all-too familiar tropes about women (that they are merely intuitive rather than rational or objective, that they are prone to misinterpret innocent acts of flirtation, and that they frequently falsely accuse men of sexual violence). Others involve widespread prejudices against Black women in particular (for example, that they lack intelligence or that their reports of pain or of experiences of discrimination are not to be taken seriously), or Black men (that they are habitual liars and rapists who cannot be trusted) or disabled people (that they have a distorted picture of their own predicaments, and are to be pitied rather than believed), or refugees (that they are merely lying to access benefits they do not deserve and which are paid for by those who really belong), or those suspected of having committed crimes (that they will say anything to avoid admitting their guilt, and that the truth can only be forced out of them through interrogation). And in contrast to Philosopher of Physics, the way that the people in most of the other examples are belittled or dismissed when trying to speak does seem to be just one aspect of broader injustices and oppression that they face: oppression on the basis of gender, or race, or disability, and so on, not to mention the complex interaction between all of these.

Second, the examples confirm a point made in Section 2.2 of this chapter, namely that a person's credibility can be called into question either by painting them as epistemically incompetent—as incapable of getting to the truth of the matter—or as mendacious. For example, Herbert Greenleaf silences Marge Sherwood in a way that very clearly indicates that he thinks that her gender is an obstacle to her getting to the truth about what has happened to her fiancé, while Tom Robinson is clearly regarded as knowing fine well what happened between himself and Mayella Ewell, but as unwilling or incapable of telling the truth about it.

We should note, though, that it's not always obvious which of these ways of questioning someone's credibility is in play in a particular example. Take Marie, whose account of being raped at knife-point was found so 'unbelievable' by the police. Did they think that her story was unbelievable because she was incompetent or mendacious? Well, they seem to have tried out both grounds for disbelieving her at different times, at one point suggesting that she had mistaken a vivid dream for a real experience (incompetence) and later that she had lied for the attention (mendacity). Moreover, while epistemic incompetence and lack of sincerity tend to pull in different directions when we focus on particular things a person has said (after all, it's hard to lie about what you don't know), the prejudices against some groups may paint them as exhibiting a blend of incompetence and insincerity. Black men such as Tom Robinson are often treated as both intellectually deficient in general and as untrustworthy on certain topics. Kristie Dotson (2012: 27) interprets Patricia Williams's account as involving being dismissed as both 'paranoid' (and so incompetent) and as 'a liar' when writing and speaking about her experience of being racially profiled. Likewise, Kate Manne has suggested that women who accuse men of sexual assault are sometimes depicted as both epistemically and morally deficient simultaneously—as 'being delusional and a liar' (2018: 218), as opposed to being at most one or the other, as the police took Marie to be.

A third contrast we can draw is that some of the examples are real-life examples involving real people and, to the extent that my descriptions above are accurate, real events, while others are fictions involving fictional characters and events. Carmita Wood was a real person, and the events described above did, to the best of my knowledge, happen much as I have laid them out. Marge Sherwood, on the other hand, is a product of Patricia Highsmith's imagination (further shaped by Anthony Minghella in his adaption for the screen, and by Gwyneth Paltrow in her performance of the character), and we know that the exchange with the equally fictional Herbert Greenleaf described above never took place.

The significance of the use of real-life and fictional examples is both unclear and disputed. One thing we can note is that, in contrast to the kinds of thinly described and abstract thought experiments that analytic philosophers often favour, all of the fictional examples are relatively grounded and realistic. There are no malevolent and all-powerful demons, or Matrix-style supercomputers, or regions full of fake barns, or runaway trams with people tied to the tracks here. That seems important, since these fictional examples are meant to illustrate phenomena that are not merely possible in principle, but widespread and all-too common and familiar (Fisher forthcoming). Miranda Fricker, whose use of the examples drawn from *The Talented Mr. Ripley* and *To Kill a Mockingbird* has made them staples of philosophical discussions of epistemic injustice, has noted that she quite deliberately picked examples drawn from works of fiction since she thought they would be richer, more interesting to read, and more engaging than the usual examples philosophers concoct (Fricker and Law 2023: 20). On the other hand, the use of merely fictional examples might give the impression that the phenomena they're meant to illustrate are equally fictional, or that the historical, situated details of real injustices aren't important (e.g. Berenstain 2020: 755 n30). It will become apparent over the course of this book that there are distinctive advantages and disadvantages associated with each of the different kinds of examples that feature on our list above; for now, let us content ourselves with having noted this distinction within the examples.

Fourth, most of the examples involve speech, and indeed, they involve what we might call interpersonal speech; there's a speaker who addresses themselves to a particular audience, rather than performing a soliloquy or making a more public announcement. In some of the examples, this audience has a single member (as when McEwan's character Joe Rose finds his concerns about Jed Parry dismissed by his fiancé Clarissa), but most of them involve audiences made up of several people (for example, the Maycomb County jurors that Tom Robinson is forced to address in *To Kill a Mockingbird*). However, Harriet McBryde Johnson describes written rather than verbal communication, addressed to an individual, Peter Singer. We might also imagine cases in which a person writes something for an impersonal audience and receives an unjustly dismissive reaction (perhaps without ever knowing about it).[4] For instance, perhaps some readers of Johnson's description in 'Unspeakable Conversations' of the ways that she valued her disability and found her life fulfilling had the same sceptical reaction as Singer. So despite most of the examples involving speech, it doesn't seem like this should be regarded as an essential feature of epistemic injustice of the sort illustrated by those examples. It's not, on the face of it, tied to any particular medium of communication.

Fifth, notice that the examples vary in terms of the stakes involved. Many of them describe situations that are quite literally life and death, and some of them concern how the survivors of sexual violence are treated in its aftermath, while the examples of Miss Triggs (and her real-life counterparts who spoke to Miranda Fricker) and the scepticism faced by Patricia Williams when she told people about being racially profiled seem to involve lower stakes. There's a danger of overstating this point, and minimising the impact that such sexist and racist episodes can have on an individual, or missing the cumulative effect of facing such episodes again and again across a lifetime; we might think again here of Marilyn Frye's observation that inspecting a single wire of a bird cage up close may leave it mysterious how it impedes the bird's movements, discussed in the previous chapter. It nonetheless seems worth observing that some of the cases seem to involve imminent or more serious dangers and risks which others do not (even if we are clear that we should be concerned with harms across this whole spectrum).

Another difference we can observe is that some of the examples involve true reports of rape being unjustly dismissed, as when Marie's account of her ordeal was deemed 'unbelievable,' while others depict truthful denials in the face of false accusations of rape being similarly found unbelievable, as when Tom Robinson fails to convince the jurors of his innocence even when Finch offers them conclusive evidence against the account offered by his accusers. This contrast reiterates a point already clear from the examples involving Black women's word being disregarded, namely that we need to be very careful to pay attention to the complex interplay between different social hierarchies and systems of oppression: in these examples, gender, race, and disability. Women's reports of the sexual violence of men being treated dismissively is a very real and ongoing problem, but there is also a long history of white women falsely accusing racialised men, particularly Black men, of rape (Curry 2017a, 2017b); philosophers studying and applying the notion of epistemic injustice have often sought to acknowledge and address both of these deeply troubling dynamics (e.g. Yap 2017; Manne 2018: Chapter 6; Tilton 2024).

2.5 BELIEVABILITY AND INTELLIGIBILITY

A final distinction we can draw when looking at our examples gestures at what has often struck philosophers as a significant division within the category of epistemic injustice. In some of the examples, what seems of primary concern are questions about *who* gets believed: Miss Triggs can't get credit for her contributions, but the men in the meeting can; Herbert Greenleaf's gendered put-down of Marge Sherwood ('there's female intuition, and then there are facts') makes plain that he distrusts her because she's a woman; Tressie McMillan Cottom faced particularly difficult and consequential obstacles to having her pain addressed, and more generally being seen as competent, due to being a Black woman, and so on. On the other hand, the problems faced by Carmita Wood when she tried to communicate with Cornell University and the Department of Labor seem primarily about *what* she was attempting to convey, rather than who she was. Lacking the notion of 'sexual harassment' which we can so easily retrospectively apply to the behaviour she had to endure, we might think that she faced barriers to making her experiences intelligible to others, and perhaps even struggled to make them intelligible to herself. Importantly, no one else had the notion of sexual harassment at that point in history either, and so others would be similarly impeded in any attempts they made to make Wood's experiences intelligible.

One picture of what's going on in such cases emerges from feminist theorising in the 20th century. It runs, in essentials, as follows. In order to be able to think certain thoughts, and hence to know certain things, a person needs the right conceptual resources. I'll have a little more to say about concepts in Chapter 8, but for now we can think of them as mental representations that we can use to describe, pick out, and classify things in thought, as when I classify objects according to our shared scheme of colour concepts. Likewise, in order to perspicuously express and communicate certain thoughts to others, a person needs to not only have the right concepts, but also suitable expressive resources: linguistic expressions in a language that they share (at least to a degree) with those they are trying to communicate with. The feminist thought now is that some social groups have an outsized influence on whether certain terms and concepts are introduced and gain wide currency in a society, and this has consequences for what members of more marginalised groups are able to grasp and communicate about their own lives and experiences, since those with power tend to use it to skew the available resources in ways that serve their interests. In a retrospective piece added to later editions of Betty Friedan's *The Feminine Mystique*, she put the idea as follows:

> All the terms in every field and profession were defined by men, who were virtually the only full professors, the law partners, the CEOs and company executives, the medical experts, academicians, the hospital heads and clinic directors. [...] It was only after we broke through the feminine mystique and said women are *people*, no more no less, and therefore demanded our human right to participate in the mainstream of society, to equal opportunity to earn and be trained and have our own voice in the big decisions of our destiny, that the problems of women themselves became visible, and women began to take their own experience seriously.
>
> (Friedan 1963/2013: 487)[5]

We can make the general idea here clearer by thinking about how it might apply to the example of Carmita Wood. As a woman, Wood was a member of a group who were mostly excluded from the professions and influential roles within institutions that could exercise influence over her society's communal stock of expressive and conceptual resources, and so the available resources were skewed away from her interest in making her experiences of harassment intelligible, and in favour of her harasser's interest in keeping them poorly understood by Wood and others.

Whether this is the right account of this particular example is something we'll consider in some detail in Chapter 8. For now, it serves to illustrate the way that some of our starting examples seem to be primarily about whether people can make certain things about themselves intelligible rather than whether they can convince their audience that they are a trustworthy speaker. This distinction is often treated as a fundamental one in discussions of epistemic injustice, and I have organised the main division within this book accordingly: Part 2 concerns a speaker's credibility when offering testimony, while Part 3 concerns obstacles some subjects face when trying to make themselves understood.

A few of the examples seem hard to classify within this dichotomy, though, either because we feel unsure which of the two categories is the best fit, or because they seem to involve elements of both. Take Harriet McBryde Johnson's affirmation that a disabled person's life can be a life 'lived well.' Were the challenges she faced persuading her critics like Peter Singer due to those critics dismissing her word because she's disabled (and so unable to make a competent, objective assessment of the worth of disabled lives), or is there a sense in which her audiences really couldn't grasp the message she was trying to convey by putting together the notions of 'disabled' and 'good life,' given their understanding of disability as inherently incompatible with living a good life? It's not clear to me how to answer this question.[6]

If we dig into some of the other examples in even a little more detail, similar issues pop up, as the philosopher José Medina has pointed out (2013: Chapter 2). Take the dismissal of Tom Robinson's account of his relationship with Mayella Ewell by the jurors in *To Kill a Mockingbird*. In a much-discussed interaction, Robinson is pressed by the prosecutor, Mr Gilmer, to explain why he, by his own telling, regularly spent time at the Ewell farm helping Mayella with her work. Robinson replies that he felt sorry for her, an answer which Mr Gilmer pounces upon:

> '*You* felt sorry for *her*, you felt *sorry* for her?' Mr Gilmer seemed ready to rise to the ceiling.

> The witness realised his mistake and shifted uncomfortably in the chair. But the damage was done. Below us, nobody liked Tom Robinson's answer. Mr Gilmer paused a long time to let it sink in.
>
> (Lee 1960: 218)

It's perhaps not immediately obvious what Robinson's mistake here is, and why it's so damaging to his defence, but it seems clear that it goes beyond a suspicion that he is lying. Medina suggests that what Robinson says here has been 'rendered *incredible* (in fact, almost unintelligible), in that culture' since it is ruled out by the dominant shared conception of what's so much as imaginable:

> The interrogation stumbles upon something that falls outside the social imaginary: a Negro feeling sorry for a white girl. What lacks all credibility is not so much Tom Robinson as a knower and informer, but the idea of black pity for white subjects in Jim Crow Alabama.
>
> (Medina 2013: 67)[7]

That Robinson says something so 'incredible' to much of his audience in turn calls his personal credibility further into question (Medina 2013: 96; Yap 2017: 3). If this analysis is on the right track (an issue I'll discuss in Chapter 10), then thinking through this example also indicates that there isn't a clean separation between unjust obstacles to being found believable and unjust obstacles to being understood. It may be useful to artificially separate these, as I will in this book, but we need to bear in mind that ultimately there may not be a sharp distinction here.

2.6 THE SIGNIFICANCE OF THE EXAMPLES

Looking at these kinds of examples helps explain why epistemic injustice as a concept and topic has been taken up widely outside of philosophy and even outside of academia, in a manner that strikingly contrasts with the level of wider influence philosophical ideas and theories typically enjoy. Discussions of epistemic injustice, explicitly drawing on terminology and ideas from Fricker and other philosophers, are found in the domains of healthcare, law, education, politics, and many others, and part of this appeal is surely that the widespread relevance of these ideas is made vivid by the kinds of examples that philosophers have taken as their starting point; they are compelling, troubling, and unnervingly familiar.

Starting from these kinds of examples also makes it very easy to see why academic philosophers view epistemic injustice as a significant topic to focus their collective attention on. I hope there will always be a place in philosophy for serious attempts to answer more abstract and detached questions about ourselves and our place in the wider world, but little urgency seems to attach to whether Smith, Edmund Gettier's character in his influential thought experiments (Gettier 1963), really knows some contrived claim in equally contrived circumstances.[8] The philosopher H. P. Grice once wrote of those looking for an application of their contributions to philosophy that would 'help one to solve the world's problems or one's own problems, or both':

> To them I feel inclined to reply *in the end*: "You are crying for the moon; philosophy has never really fulfilled this task, though it may sometimes have appeared to do so (and the practical consequences of its appearing to do so have not always been very agreeable). It is no more sensible to complain that philosophy is no longer capable of solving practical problems than it is to complain that the study of the stars no longer enables one to predict the course of world events."
>
> (Grice 1989: 179–180)

To many epistemologists, and philosophers more generally, discussions of epistemic injustice have seemed to offer the moon: a domain where the skills, concepts, distinctions, theories, and patterns of thinking that they have developed and cultivated might be applicable to topics with real and clear practical significance. Small wonder there's been such a rush to write, publish, and teach on this topic; moreover, as I noted in Chapter 1, this explosion of interest in epistemic injustice is a central example of a broader trend in epistemology and analytic philosophy, sometimes called 'the applied turn.' Of course, part of Grice's point in the passage just quoted is that philosophers are sometimes prone to delusions (perhaps harmful delusions) of the practical relevance of their work, and so we need to carefully consider whether philosophical discussions of epistemic injustice illustrate or undermine the kind of scepticism expressed by Grice.

Some readers may share a version of Grice's worry, at least as regards the kind of philosophical theorising about the examples that the philosophical literature on epistemic injustice (including this book) engages in. These are readers who recognise the importance of the kinds of examples laid out earlier in Section 2.3 of this chapter, but are sceptical that the philosophical project of attempting to articulate theoretical categories that carve things up in the right way is how to do justice to that importance.

I think a degree of this kind of scepticism is healthy. Philosophers have a much better track record of muddying waters than clearing them; indeed, this often seems to be their goal. In the opening chapter of his classic introduction to the subject, *The Problems of Philosophy*, Bertrand Russell described how the philosopher can take an ordinary, familiar object, such as a table, and raise deep questions about it that render it mysterious and perplexing, thereby showing 'the strangeness and wonder lying just below the surface even in the commonest things of daily life' (1912/2001: 6). Less lyrically, but no less memorably, he once quipped that 'the point of philosophy is to start with something so simple as not to seem worth stating, and to end with something so paradoxical that no one will believe it' (Russell 1956/2025: 166). This picture of philosophy as revealing what is strange, paradoxical, and sometimes wonderous in the everyday, the familiar, and the common sensical is an attractive one, and I think it has its place. However, it has also led to a lot of detached, technical, and hellishly complicated theorising in esoteric jargon about seemingly simple topics; the tradition in epistemology that attempts to say what knowledge is a case in point. Bluntly put: given this track record, why trust philosophy, and particularly the analytic tradition in philosophy that Russell heavily influenced, with examples as meaningful, delicate, and significant as those introduced in Section 2.3?

This book was not written to reveal 'the strangeness and wonder lying just below the surface even in the commonest things of daily life.' If there is wonder to be found beneath the surface of the examples introduced in this chapter, I have no interest in finding it; these are examples filled to the brim with unfairness and unnecessary suffering and horror, and *that's* where our attention should be. My hope is that this book will instead contribute to vindicating those philosophers who hold that philosophy can help us to dissect and understand the workings of certain kinds of injustices, illustrated by our examples, that are all too often part of some people's daily lives. I don't think there's any reassurance I can offer at the outset that this is something that philosophical analysis can achieve, or should be trusted to try, but the remaining chapters will constitute a case that such theorising has its place. We need to be able to pick out the most important features of examples like those presented in this chapter, so that we can identify new instances of such injustices when they arise and better understand how they relate to other kinds of injustice, with the ultimate goal of figuring out how we can most effectively work towards epistemic justice. Moreover, we'll find that the theories offered by philosophers often *do* lead to improved understanding of the various kinds of dynamics involved in the examples—or so I hope to persuade you.

2.7 SUMMARY

Let's take stock. In this chapter, I have approached epistemic injustice via a series of examples, many of which will receive much more detailed treatment in later chapters. I offered a preliminary discussion of some of the main similarities and differences between these examples, and I picked out one contrast as being particularly significant for understanding how philosophical discussions of epistemic injustice have developed, and hence for how this book is organised; on the one hand, we have examples involving a speaker struggling to be found believable, and on the other, examples where a speaker struggles to be understood (perhaps even to understand herself). As useful as that distinction will prove in what follows, we have also noted that these two broad forms of epistemic injustice may interact with each other, and are sometimes difficult to distinguish at all. Finally, I have discussed the significance of the examples for philosophy, and made a plea to those sceptical that philosophy has much to offer consideration of such examples to read on with an open mind.

What this example-focused approach hasn't produced, so far at least, is a more direct, theoretical answer to the question that frames Part 1 of this book: what is epistemic injustice? It's all very well to point to our starting examples and say 'this sort of thing' (and then to whisper 'and probably much more besides'). As I have just indicated, we want to know what (if anything) unifies the examples: what *makes* them examples of epistemic injustice. Let's turn to that question in the next chapter.

2.8 SUGGESTED FURTHER READING

Chapter 5 of Manne (2020) looks at gendered inequalities in access to healthcare and the related dismissals of women's reports of pain, particularly the way that Black women like McMillan Cottom are presumed to be incompetent. Wiggleton-Little (forthcoming) draws attention to the way that the pain reports of Black women are often not taken as calling for any action, so that even when they manage to convince others that they are in pain, this conviction isn't accompanied by any sense of practical urgency (though Wiggleton-Little is sceptical that this dynamic can be fully understood as a form of epistemic injustice).

Havi Carel and Ian James Kidd have done much to kick-start debates on epistemic injustice in medicine and healthcare in general (e.g. Carel and Kidd 2014; Carel and Kidd 2017; Kidd and Carel 2017), and the literature on this is now vast.

Jennifer Lackey's recent work (e.g. Lackey 2020, 2023) attempts to characterise the kind of epistemic injustice faced by people like Michael Ledford who are forced to confess and then find that their protestations of innocence are forever taken to be undermined by that confession. We'll look at some aspects of her discussion in Chapter 6.

Puddifoot and Sandelind (2025) introduce the notion of 'mnemonic epistemic injustice' in order to account for the mistreatment of asylum seekers like KV.

Versions of the feminist picture of the ways women are disempowered when it comes to finding fitting concepts and names for things outlined in Section 2.5 of this chapter are also found in Marilyn Frye's Friedan-inspired essay 'The Problem That Has No Name' (in Frye 1983), and in Andrea Dworkin's remarks on men having the 'great and sublime power' of naming in her discussion of power and pornography (1979: 17). We'll see similar themes emerge when we explore Patricia Hill Collins, Miranda Fricker, and Kristie Dotson's theories in later chapters.

Alex Fisher (forthcoming) offers a recent and, to my mind, plausible defence of the use of fictional examples in defence of philosophical claims, taking Marge Sherwood and Tom Robinson as his main examples.

In Section 2.6, I pushed back on a conception of the task of analytic philosophy as revealing the wonder lying beneath the surface of what's everyday and familiar. I certainly don't mean to suggest philosophers shouldn't concern themselves with wonder and the wonderful: see, for example, De Cruz (2024).

NOTES

1 This is how I treated the examples when writing about and teaching epistemic injustice for many years, and so this is as much a criticism of myself as anyone else. In the preface I describe how I came to see things differently.

2 Fricker notes that this example is only semi-fictional, since it is based on experiences recounted to her. A historical instance of this kind of example is perhaps the treatment of the philosopher Henri Bergson's discussions of scientific theories such as evolution and special and general relativity by scientists such as Albert Einstein: see Herring (2024: Chapter 20).
3 This account of Carmita Wood's story differs in important ways from how the example is standardly described in the literature on epistemic injustice, following Fricker. I'll return to this point in Chapter 8.
4 Ishani Maitra (2010) has argued, contrary to what I suggest here, that there must be some kind of interpersonal relationship in genuine cases of epistemic injustice of this sort.
5 The limitations of and problems with Friedan's book—for example, its focus on the situation of middle-class white women, its rather casual invocation of comparisons to chattel slavery, the Holocaust, and genocide, as well as its abysmal discussion of gay and lesbian relationships (for which Friedan later apologised)—are well known and I won't dwell on them here.
6 I'll return to examples like this in Chapter 5.
7 Medina understands the social imaginary as follows: 'The repository of images and scripts—the so-called *social imaginary*—constitutes the representational background against which people tend to share their thoughts and listen to each other in a culture' (2013: 67 fn4). For criticism of Medina's discussion of Tom Robinson, see Curry (2017b).
8 I offer a brief overview of the so-called 'Gettier problem' for attempts to offer an analysis of what it takes to have knowledge in McGlynn (2014: Chapter 1).

REFERENCES

Armstrong, Ken and T. Christian Miller. 2015. 'An Unbelievable Story of Rape.' *ProPublica*. https://www.propublica.org/article/false-rape-accusations-an-unbelievable-story

Armstrong, Ken and T. Christian Miller. 2018. *A False Report: A True Story of Rape in America*. New York: Crown Publishing Group.

Baker, Carrie. 2007. *The Women's Movement against Sexual Harassment*. Cambridge and New York: Cambridge University Press.

Barnes, Elizabeth. 2016. *The Minority Body: A Theory of Disability*. Oxford: Oxford University Press.

Beard, Mary. 2017. *Women and Power: A Manifesto*. London: Profile Books.

Berenstain, Nora. 2020. 'White Feminist Gaslighting.' *Hypatia* 35 (4): 733–758. https://doi.org/10.1017/hyp.2020.31

Carel, Havi and Ian James Kidd. 2014. 'Epistemic Injustice in Healthcare: A Philosophical Analysis.' *Medical Healthcare and Philosophy* 17: 529–540. https://doi.org/10.1007/s11019-014-9560-2

Carel, Havi and Ian James Kidd. 2017. 'Epistemic Injustice in Medicine and Healthcare.' In Ian James Kidd, José Medina, and Gaile Pohlhaus Jr., eds. *The Routledge Handbook of Epistemic Injustice*: 755–777. Oxon and New York: Routledge.

Curry, Tommy J. 2017a. *The Man-Not: Race, Class, Genre, and the Dilemmas of Black Manhood*. Philadelphia, PA: Temple University Press.

Curry, Tommy J. 2017b. 'This N*****'s Broken: Hyper-masculinity, the Buck, and the Role of Physical Disability in White Anxiety toward the Black Male Body.' *Journal of Social Philosophy* 48 (3): 321–343. https://doi.org/10.1111/josp.12193

De Cruz, Helen. 2024. *Wonderstruck: How Wonder and Awe Shape the Way We Think*. Princeton, NJ and Oxford: Princeton University Press.

Dotson, Kristie. 2012. 'A Cautionary Tale: On Limiting Epistemic Oppression.' *Frontiers: A Journal of Women Studies* 33 (1): 24–47. https://doi.org/10.1353/fro.2012.a472779

Dworkin, Andrea. 1979. *Pornography: Men Possessing Women*. New York: Plume.

Fisher, Alex. Forthcoming. 'In Defence of Fictional Examples.' *The Philosophical Quarterly*. https://doi.org/10.1093/pq/pqaf036

Fricker, Miranda. 2007. *Epistemic Injustice: Power and the Ethics of Knowing*. Oxford: Oxford University Press.

Fricker, Miranda and Stephen Law. 2023. '*Think* Interview: Epistemic Injustice.' *Think* 22 (64): 15–21. https://doi.org/10.1017/S1477175623000040

Friedan, Betty. 1963/2013. *The Feminine Mystique*. London and New York: W. W. Norton and Company.

Frye, Marilyn. 1983. *The Politics of Reality: Essays in Feminist Theory*. New York: Crossing Press.

Gettier, Edmund. 1963. 'Is Justified True Belief Knowledge?' *Analysis* 23 (6): 121–123. https://doi.org/10.1093/analys/23.6.121

Grice, H. P. 1989. *Studies in the Way of Words*. Oxford: Oxford University Press.

Herring, Emily. 2024. *Herald of a Restless World: How Henri Bergson Brought Philosophy to the People*. New York: Basic Books.

Kidd, Ian James and Havi Carel. 2017. 'Epistemic Injustice and Illness.' *Journal of Applied Philosophy* 34 (2): 172–190. https://doi.org/10.1111/japp.12172

Lackey, Jennifer. 2020. 'False Confessions and Testimonial Injustice.' *The Journal of Criminal Law and Criminology* 110 (1): 43–68.

Lackey, Jennifer. 2023. *Criminal Testimonial Injustice*. Oxford and New York: Oxford University Press.

Lee, Harper. 1960. *To Kill a Mockingbird*. London: Arrow Books.

Maitra, Ishani. 2010. 'The Nature of Epistemic Injustice.' *Philosophical Books* 51 (4): 195–211. https://doi.org/10.1111/j.1468-0149.2010.00511.x

Manne, Kate. 2018. *Down Girl: The Logic of Misogyny*. Oxford: Oxford University Press.

Manne, Kate. 2020. *Entitled: How Male Privilege Hurts Women*. London: Penguin.

McBryde Johnson, Harriet. 2003. 'Unspeakable Conversations.' *The New York Times Magazine*. https://www.nytimes.com/2003/02/16/magazine/unspeakable-conversations.html

McEwan, Ian. 1997. *Enduring Love*. London: Jonathan Cape.

McGlynn, Aidan. 2014. *Knowledge First?* Basingstoke: Palgrave MacMillan.

McMillan Cottom, Tressie. 2019. *Thick: And Other Essays*. New York: The New Press.

Medina, José. 2013. *The Epistemology of Resistance: Gender and Racial Oppression, Epistemic Injustice, and Resistant Imaginations*. Oxford: Oxford University Press.

Minghella, Anthony. 2000. *The Talented Mr. Ripley—Based on Patricia Highsmith's Novel*. London: Methuen.

Nayeri, Dina. 2023. *Who Gets Believed? When the Truth Isn't Enough*. New York: Vintage.

Puddifoot, Katherine and Clara Sandelind. 2025. 'Knowing Your Own Past: Trauma, Stress, and Mnemonic Epistemic Injustice.' *Journal of Social Philosophy* 56 (2): 261–281. https://doi.org/10.1111/josp.12557

Russell, Bertrand. 1912/2001. *The Problems of Philosophy*. Oxford and New York: Oxford University Press.

Russell, Bertrand. 1956/2025. *Logic and Knowledge*. London and New York: Routledge Classics.

Tilton, Emily. 2024. 'Rape Myths, Catastrophe, and Credibility.' *Episteme* 21 (2): 408–424. https://doi.org/10.1017/epi.2022.5

Traister, Rebecca. 2018. *Good and Mad: The Revolutionary Power of Women's Anger*. New York: Simon and Schuster.

Wiggleton-Little, Jada. Forthcoming. 'Pain Dismissal and the Limits of Epistemic Injustice.' *Hypatia*. https://doi.org/10.1017/hyp.2025.8

Williams, Patricia J. 1991. *The Alchemy of Race and Rights: Diary of a Law Professor*. Cambridge, MA: Harvard University Press.

Yap, Audrey. 2017. 'Credibility Excess in the Social Imaginary in Cases of Sexual Assault.' *Feminist Philosophy Quarterly* 3: 1–24. https://doi.org/10.5206/fpq/2017.4.1

3

THE NATURE AND SCOPE OF EPISTEMIC INJUSTICE

3.1 INTRODUCTION

The examples laid out in Chapter 2 give a good impression of what this book is about; in the broad sense of 'epistemic injustice' used in the book's title, epistemic injustice is the phenomenon or phenomena illustrated by examples of this sort. Still, as I noted at the end of the previous chapter, philosophers want to be able to say something more precise: we want an account of what, if anything, unifies these examples, together with any others we want to group together with them.

This task is harder than it might first appear. It's not enough to come up with a way of understanding what epistemic injustice is that covers all of the examples, since by itself this probably won't tell us what unifies the examples. Relatedly, we want an account that can cast illumination on the differences we observed in the previous chapter between some of the examples and others, helping us to understand these differences and their significance. Let me illustrate both of these points by looking at a proposal that clearly *doesn't* meet these requirements.

Let's suppose we understood the notion of epistemic injustice really broadly, so that it applied anywhere where we see epistemic dimensions to unjust behaviour or unjust social systems and arrangements. Such a broad conception of what 'epistemic injustice' covers will surely include all of the examples in Chapter 2, but it doesn't offer any hope of saying something informative about what might unify these particular kinds of examples, since it's really vague and it also scoops up a lot of other phenomena that seem markedly different in character.

For example, one issue that has received a lot of attention from legal epistemologists is the treatment of merely probabilistic (statistical) evidence as insufficient for finding a person or company responsible. If all we know is that a bus caused an accident on Main Street and that 90% of buses that drive down Main Street are operated by the Red Bus company, it seems like we'd be remiss to hold the Red Bus company responsible and sanction them on that basis (even if we're privately pretty sure they're responsible). If a court falsely convicted the Red Bus company of negligence on the basis of such probabilistic evidence, without any other collaborating evidence (such as eyewitness testimony), we might say that this was an epistemic injustice of sorts; it's a legal injustice, but one that's due to the sort of evidence appealed to, which is unquestionably an epistemic consideration. Still, this example feels importantly different to any of those that we looked at in Chapter 2, even those (like the examples of Tom Robinson and Michael Ledford) that similarly take place in a legal context. We need a characterisation of epistemic injustice that's more discriminating than this. This is exactly what we're offered in Miranda Fricker's work, and I'll explore her account in the remainder of this chapter.

I'll begin with Fricker's characterisation of epistemic injustice (Section 3.2), before introducing the two subspecies she identifies, testimonial injustice and hermeneutical injustice (Section 3.3). Lastly, I'll consider some notable examples that Fricker's characterisation leaves out, and which have led her and others to draw an important further distinction between different kinds of epistemic injustice (Section 3.4).

3.2 FRICKER'S CHARACTERISATION OF EPISTEMIC INJUSTICE

As just mentioned, the natural starting point here is the characterisation of epistemic injustice offered by Miranda Fricker. As I noted in Chapter 1, Fricker's work kick-started the recent wave of attention on epistemic injustice, and many of the examples introduced in Chapter 2 were taken from her discussion. She also coined the term 'epistemic injustice,' which would seem to give her a reasonable claim to say what it means, up to a point at least.

Fricker starts her book by characterising epistemic injustice as a harm done to one in one's capacity as a knower (2007: 1). Let's say that one acts in one's capacity as a knower when one engages in inquiry or reasoning with the aim of coming by new knowledge, or one reflects and interprets the experiences one has had, or when one shares one's knowledge through testimony or teaching, and so on: in short, when one engages in activities involving the acquisition, production, and sharing of knowledge. Our examples in Chapter 2 seem to fit this characterisation of epistemic injustice neatly. Tom Robinson is prevented from sharing his knowledge of both his innocence and of what really happened between him and Mayella Ewell, while we might suggest that Carmita Wood was prevented from having, let alone sharing, certain pieces of knowledge about herself (for example, that she was sexually harassed). Miss Triggs, in contrast, is able to share her knowledge of how her group should proceed, but she can only do so long as she isn't credited for that knowledge, and so she is still harmed in her capacity as a giver of knowledge. In the cartoon, this is openly acknowledged in a way that's paradoxical and humorous, while her real-life analogues face a similar predicament that is pernicious and isolating because it is left unsaid and unrecognised.

Reassuringly, the injustice faced by the Red Bus company doesn't fit Fricker's characterisation; neither the company nor any of its employees are being harmed in their capacities as knowers, at least as we've described the example above. Rather, they are mistakenly found negligent in their role as a bus service provider on the basis of suggestive but insufficiently conclusive evidence; we can recognise there's an epistemic element to this injustice, without classing it as an epistemic injustice in the sense that interests us here.

At first glance, then, Fricker's account seems pretty promising. That said, there are some features of her characterisation that might catch our attention, and which seem to call for clarifications and revisions.

First, we might find it striking that Fricker uses the term 'harm'; epistemic injustice is a *harm* done to one in one's capacity as a knower. She doesn't say much about how she understands these terms and she often seems to use 'harm' more or less interchangeably with 'wrong,' but given what I said in Chapter 1, we might think that the latter has a subtly different meaning and one that seems more appropriate when trying to pick out epistemic injustices. Recall that I suggested in that earlier discussion that we understand wrong as a more morally loaded notion than harm, since harms can be deserved or undeserved, fair or unfair, and I reserved the notion of a wrong for those harms which are undeserved and unfair.

Given this, it would be better to say that epistemic injustice is a *wrong* done to one in one's capacity as a knower, since this would make clearer why this is a form of injustice. A harm done to a person in their capacity as a knower might turn out to be justified, but we're focusing on cases where that's not the case; we're focusing on wrongs. Now, Fricker does sometimes formulate her characterisation of epistemic injustice in terms of someone being wronged specifically in their capacity as a knower (e.g. 2007: 20), but she's not consistent in this. I'll try to be more consistent in this book, though we'll find that it's tricky when Fricker's use of terminology is so pervasive in discussions of epistemic injustice.[1]

A second striking feature of Fricker's characterisation is the role it accords the notion of knowledge. Knowledge is a central, perhaps (though this is somewhat more controversial) *the* central epistemic notion, but it is not the only one. Epistemology also concerns itself with notions like evidence, justification, certainty, wisdom, warrant, entitlement, credibility, understanding, and so on. Why aren't these mentioned when we're characterising epistemic injustice?[2]

Moreover, when we look at our examples from Chapter 2 again, it's not clear that the notion of knowledge, or of a person's role as a knower, is always the one we need.[3] Take Marge Sherwood. It's not at all obvious, despite her increasingly frantic claims to this effect, that she *knows* that Tom Ripley killed her fiancé Dickie Greenleaf. She has well-founded suspicions, based on evidence; Dickie's rings are in Ripley's possession, and she's sure (and correctly so) that Dickie wouldn't have given them away. Still, it's not even clear we would say she knows he is dead, let alone that Ripley has killed him. But even if she doesn't have knowledge that Ripley has killed Dickie, her suspicions that this is what has happened are ones that Dickie's father Herbert Greenleaf should take seriously, and he manifestly fails to do that. Now, it's true that there are other things Sherwood knows that Greenleaf fails to give her recognition for (for example, that Dickie would not give away his rings), but the general point remains that Greenleaf's failure to heed what Sherwood is telling him doesn't seem best described in terms of how he treats her in her role as a *knower*; that's at most only part of the dynamic we're interested in.

What these considerations suggest is that we should generalise the characterisation of epistemic injustice that Fricker offered in her book, and this is a step Fricker herself has taken in her more recent work; an epistemic injustice occurs when one is wronged in one's capacity as an *epistemic agent* (e.g. Fricker 2013: 1320, 2017: 53). To do something in one's capacity as an epistemic agent is to exercise one's epistemic agency. This avoids focusing too much on knowledge, or on any other particular epistemic notion, but clearly it's not all that informative until more is said about what epistemic agency involves. Fricker doesn't have much to say about this, and in general, the notion of epistemic agency needs more attention from philosophers. However, I already spelled out how I want to understand epistemic agency in Chapter 1, taking it to be agency exercised with respect to our epistemic activities and practices. These will include the activities and practices of acquiring, swapping, and sharing knowledge listed above, but they will also include gathering evidence, gaining understanding, sharing wisdom, acquiring justification for one's beliefs then sharing that justification with others, formulating and testing theories, uncovering and attempting to resolve disagreements with others, figuring out who the experts are on a given topic, and much more besides. The revised proposal, as I understand it, is that epistemic injustice occurs when one is wronged in the course of one playing (or trying to play) one's role within any of these epistemic activities and practices. To return to Marge Sherwood, even if she's not trying to share *knowledge*, she is trying to share well-founded suspicions with Greenleaf, and it's not difficult to see how his dismissive response to this attempt wrongs her in her capacity as an epistemic agent in this sense.

A third distinctive feature of Fricker's characterisation (and the revised versions of it we have considered so far) is that it's *individuals* who are subject to epistemic injustice in the first instance; epistemic injustice occurs when a person is wronged in their capacity as an epistemic agent. This fits with the examples introduced in Chapter 2. Each of them involves a particular person (or small group of people) who seems to be the victim of an epistemic wronging: Miss Triggs; Marge Sherwood; Carmita Wood; Tom Robinson; Marie; and so on. In other kinds of cases, though, we might think that it's primarily entire social groups or communities that are subject to epistemic injustice, rather than individual epistemic agents. Consider two examples. First, we have the notion of *epistemicide*, found in the work of decolonial scholars (e.g. Santos 2014), which involves the destruction of entire systems of knowledge as an aspect of colonial conquest, as when Indigenous knowledge about medicine or about the natural world is suppressed. Second, we have the phenomenon of genocide denial (e.g. Altanian 2021, 2024), where genocidal incidents are denied outright, or given names and descriptions that minimise the violence involved (as when the Armenian genocide becomes 'the Armenian massacre') or entirely sanitise it ('the Armenian tragedy').

On the face of it, these examples involve epistemic wrongs committed against entire societies, cultures, or social groups. Trying to understand them in Fricker's terms, as involving wrongs to individuals in their role as epistemic agents, looks like it engages them at the wrong scale. We can perhaps think of epistemicide as countless instances of individual members of a particular society being epistemically wronged, but that seems to miss what makes epistemicide distinctive (and distinctively devastating and dangerous), namely that the body of knowledge and epistemic practices of an entire society or culture are systematically destroyed. Similar points seem to apply to the example of genocide denial; it's the undermining of the collective memory of an entire people that should trouble us first and foremost, and the epistemic wrongs done to individuals always need to be understood in that larger context.

I'm not trying to criticise Fricker's account by bringing up these examples.[4] It may be that her account of epistemic injustice can illuminate the epistemic wrong involved in cases of epistemicide and genocide denial, or can at least illuminate important aspects of that wrong. Nothing I've said here rules this possibility out. Alternatively, we might take examples of this sort to simply fall outside of the scope of an account of epistemic injustice that starts from the kinds of examples offered in Chapter 2; perhaps we need different epistemological concepts, theories, and resources if we're to do justice to these kinds of macro-scale epistemic wrongs, but a theory isn't mistaken or useless just because it has limited scope.

However things pan out with respect to these issues, the point I want to make here is that Fricker's definition quietly directs our focus to the wrongs faced by individual epistemic agents, and there's room to wonder whether this should really be our starting point in discussions of epistemic injustice. As we'll see in later chapters, this is symptomatic of a general worry that philosophers have had with Fricker's account of epistemic injustice and the influence it has exerted, namely that it seems too focused on the level of just and unjust interactions between individual agents, to the neglect of issues that arise when we instead focus on groups, institutions, cultures, and other larger social units and structures. Whether this criticism is fair is a question we'll leave for later chapters, but it's worth noting the way that this individualistic focus is already built into Fricker's characterisation of epistemic injustice itself, in a way that rarely gets noticed when people introduce the topic.

Let's stick with Fricker's characterisation for now. Bearing in mind our earlier points, we'll say that an epistemic injustice occurs when *someone is wronged in their capacity as an epistemic agent*. This seems to encompass most, perhaps all, of the examples we encountered in Chapter 2 (though we'll revisit this point in later chapters), and it does so in a way that plausibly spells out what's distinctive about those examples. Moreover, Fricker develops her account of epistemic injustice further, so that it can help us to understand some of the differences between the examples we already noted in Chapter 2.

3.3 TESTIMONIAL AND HERMENEUTICAL INJUSTICE

In her book, Fricker identifies two different varieties of epistemic injustice, and these map onto the main distinction within the examples that we looked at in the previous chapter. There I noted that some of the examples seem to primarily involve injustices in who gets believed, while others involve injustices concerning who and what is understood. Corresponding to each of these, we have Fricker's categories of *testimonial injustice* and *hermeneutical injustice*. Testimony is, roughly, making claims about how things are to try to share one's beliefs or knowledge with others, while hermeneutics is the study of interpretations. With this in mind, these names convey the point that some epistemic injustices arise primarily in relation to a speaker's attempts to offer testimony to an audience, while others primarily involve a lack of suitable shared interpretive resources that people can employ to make themselves understood. I'll have a considerable amount to say about how best to characterise both of these varieties of epistemic injustice in later chapters, but some preliminary definitions will be helpful at this stage.

Testimonial injustice involves a speaker receiving less credibility than they deserve when offering testimony due to prejudices held by their audience, typically prejudices against the speaker's social identity. We met the examples Fricker uses to illustrate testimonial injustice in Chapter 2: recall the Philosopher of Physics failing to be taken seriously at a science conference (Fricker 2007: 28–29); Patricia Williams's account of being racially profiled being met with undue scepticism (Williams 1991, Fricker 1998); Herbert Greenleaf's manifestly gendered dismissal of Marge Sherwood's suspicions about Tom Ripley in *The Talented Mr. Ripley* (Minghella 2000, Fricker 2007: 1);

and the jurors at Tom Robinson's trial being unmoved by his protestations of innocence and his account of his interactions with Mayella Ewell in *To Kill a Mockingbird* (Lee 1960, Fricker 2007: 23–26). Each of these features a speaker offering testimony to an audience, but failing to have their testimony accepted due to prejudices held by that audience. It also seems clear that several of the other examples in Chapter 2 might be understood along these lines. For instance, Miss Triggs's inability to have her contributions to the meeting taken seriously when she voices them herself, the police's dismissal of Marie's account of her rape, and the doctors and nurses treating McMillan Cottom's reports of her pain as reflecting her incompetence all plausibly involve speakers getting less credibility than they should due to prejudices held by their audiences.

Hermeneutical injustice occurs when there are barriers to subjects making their experiences intelligible, to themselves or to others, where these barriers are due to these subjects belonging to social groups which tend to be excluded from the kinds of institutions and practices which have the most significant role in shaping a community's shared hermeneutical resources. We have also encountered two of Fricker's examples she uses to illustrate this form of epistemic injustice in Chapter 2. In the first of these, women's marginalisation prior to the 1970s meant society lacked suitable conceptual and expressive resources to render experiences of what we now call sexual harassment intelligible, leading to the kind of unjust episodes faced by women like Carmita Wood in the early 1970s (Fricker 2007: 149–151). In the second, Ian McEwan's character Joe Rose struggles to convey his experiences and fears to others when he is stalked by Jed Parry in the novel *Enduring Love* (McEwan 1997, Fricker 2007: 156–158).

Like her definition of epistemic injustice, Fricker's characterisations of testimonial and hermeneutical injustice and the examples she uses to illustrate them raise a host of questions, but we'll save those for Parts 2 and 3 of this book.

3.4 DISTRIBUTIVE EPISTEMIC INJUSTICE

As I noted in Chapter 2, the number and nature of the examples we introduced there can seem rather overwhelming. However, you might also have a quite different (though perfectly compatible) reaction to the array of examples presented so far; you may feel that it's radically *incomplete*. The point is not that we can think of further real-life or fictional cases which haven't been mentioned yet. Of course, we can keep expanding our initial stock of examples in this fashion, but completeness in that sense presumably isn't something to aspire to, since the study of epistemic injustice isn't a matter of trying to exhaustively list examples we should be concerned about; we'd never be done, and we'd never make any progress on answering the philosophical and theoretical questions that this book is about. Rather, the reason that a nagging sense that there's something missing is significant is that we might feel that there are certain kinds of examples that belong under the heading of epistemic injustice, but which so far are nowhere to be seen.

There are a couple of obvious candidates for what these missing categories of epistemic injustice might be. One observation we might make is that none of the examples in Chapter 2 seem, on the surface at least, to concern class and classism. This reflects a general tendency in the literature on epistemic injustice; issues about class are usually neglected. Some recent work has tried to address this imbalance and to get philosophers to reflect on why class and classism have been so left behind (e.g. Archer and Smith 2020; Spiegel 2022), but as things stand, the examples I offered in Chapter 2 are representative of the kinds of examples that have arrested the attention of philosophers.

Relatedly, and perhaps even more obviously, there's been no mention so far of a host of phenomena that might immediately come to mind when you first think about what epistemic injustice might look like. Access to educational opportunities, well-funded schools, well-stocked libraries, fast and reliable internet, expert advice, and so on are not evenly distributed, but can depend heavily on a person's gender, race, class, whether or not they are disabled, where they are located in the world, and other features of a person's identity and situation. You might have thought that examples of this sort would be paradigm cases of anything worth calling 'epistemic injustice,' yet they again aren't represented in the examples introduced in Chapter 2.

Issues about access to education seem like a particular oversight here, given the role that control over the provision and content of education has long played in sexist, racist, and classist oppression. One of the earliest works of feminist philosophy, Mary Wollstonecraft's *A Vindication of the Rights of Woman* (1792), was in large part a defence of the claim that women should have the same educational opportunities as men. Moreover, many of the most influential discussions of epistemic dimensions of oppression came from thinkers reflecting on the limited or distorting educations offered to Black Americans during the Reconstruction and post-Reconstruction eras that followed the Civil War and the formal end of slavery (Du Bois 1903/1996; Woodson 1933/2009), or to the oppressed in post-colonial South America in the middle of the 20th century (Freire 1933/2018). Why are these all-too-familiar kinds of epistemic inequalities absent from the examples I've used to illustrate what's meant by epistemic injustice?

Part of the explanation may be that this neglect is part of a larger pattern in epistemology as studied within analytic philosophy. You might have thought that epistemologists would be interested in topics like the availability and quality of education, but with a few notable exceptions, you'd be wrong.[5] Even social epistemology—the approach to epistemology that studies the ways that our relations and interactions with both other people and with larger groups and social structures affect what and how we know—has rather puzzlingly neglected the topic of education (Watson 2025). With this wider perspective in mind, it's perhaps not so surprising that issues raised by education and related phenomena have loomed less large in discussions of epistemic injustice than you might have expected.

I suspect a much bigger factor, though, is the heavy influence of Miranda Fricker on discussions of epistemic injustice, as already described in Chapter 1 and earlier in this chapter. On page 1 of her book *Epistemic Injustice*, Fricker addresses unjust and unequal access to epistemic goods and opportunities, such as education, and writes:

> When epistemic injustice takes this form, there is nothing very distinctively epistemic about it, for it seems largely incidental that the good in question can be characterized as an epistemic good.
>
> (2007: 1)

Wealth, power, access to healthcare, housing, job opportunities, bodily safety and autonomy, and many more goods and properties are deeply unequally distributed, and such unequal distributions are clearly of the utmost importance; Fricker isn't denying this (Dieleman 2012: 258). But Fricker's claim is that to the extent that unequal distributions of *epistemic* goods can be assimilated to these other kinds of injustice, there's no special reason for epistemologists to take an interest. Our focus should instead be on *distinctively epistemic* injustices.

We need to be careful to understand what's meant by describing an injustice as 'distinctively epistemic' correctly here. It doesn't mean that the injustices that interest Fricker are *purely* epistemic in character. As we have seen, one of Fricker's main examples of epistemic injustice is Tom Robinson in *To Kill a Mockingbird*, and his inability to convince the jurors of his innocence results in him being falsely imprisoned, and ultimately killed. The epistemic injustice Robinson faces is clearly and crucially tied up with all-too material, non-epistemic forms of injustice and violence; it's not distinctively epistemic, if this is equated to being purely epistemic. So this can't be what Fricker means. Rather, the distinction she is drawing in the passage quoted above is between injustices involving epistemic goods and properties which are *due* to their epistemic nature, and those where understanding how they arise doesn't require any special attention to their epistemic nature (but rather a general theory of how unjust distributions of goods and opportunities arise).

Given this understanding of what Fricker means by 'distinctively epistemic' injustices, it seems very plausible that these should be of special interest to epistemologists, since understanding how they arise and what makes them injustices requires attention to their epistemic character. Still, you may have misgivings about the way that Fricker relies on this point to steer discussions of epistemic injustice away from topics like unjustly unequal access to education. For one thing, it's not clear why Fricker thinks these injustices aren't distinctively epistemic in her sense; she doesn't offer an argument for this claim, and it doesn't strike me as obviously correct. Moreover, even if it turned out that she's right that unjust distributions of educational opportunities aren't a distinctively epistemic form of injustice, we might be more inclined to conclude that we shouldn't focus too narrowly on distinctively epistemic forms of injustice in this sense, than to think that discussions of epistemic injustice can afford to leave such issues aside.

Fricker's exclusion of unjust distributions of epistemic goods and opportunities in her book attracted criticism (e.g. Coady 2010), and to Fricker's credit, she has taken the point, and in more recent work has suggested treating epistemic injustice as an 'umbrella concept' (Fricker 2013: 1318). The examples and kinds of epistemic injustice she focused on in her book would find room under this umbrella, of course, but Fricker means to concede that there's room to include much else. In particular, she draws a distinction between *discriminatory* epistemic injustice, which includes testimonial and hermeneutical injustice, and *distributive* epistemic injustice, which includes phenomena such as unjust differences in access to education and other epistemic goods, resources, and opportunities.

It's worth noting that adopting this 'umbrella' conception of epistemic injustice doesn't mean giving up or revising Fricker's characterisation of epistemic injustice as a wrong done to one in one's capacity as an epistemic agent, since arguably instances of distributive injustice also meet this criterion. When educational opportunities are unfairly distributed, then some people will be prevented from accessing the education they *should* have had, and it seems plausible that these people have thereby been wronged in their capacity as epistemic agents; the same goes for other unequal and unfair distributions of epistemic goods and opportunities. Fricker (2017: 53) explicitly makes this point:

> In this kind of epistemic injustice too, after all, someone is indeed *wronged in their capacity as an epistemic subject*, and so it fits the generic definition originally given.
>
> (Fricker 2007)

Holding on to this characterisation of epistemic injustice allows Fricker to be concessive here without also being saddled with including the example of the Red Bus company. The crucial difference is that, as we noted earlier, the Red Bus company example doesn't seem to involve anyone being wronged in their capacity as an epistemic agent.

Even though Fricker has expanded her conception of epistemic injustice in this way, the literature inspired by her work has almost entirely taken its cue from her original discussion, and has focused on the kinds of examples she directed our attention to there: that is, the kinds of examples that featured in Chapter 2. This book will follow the literature in this respect. Redirecting people's attention to the kinds of examples and phenomena that have been neglected in the existing discussions of epistemic injustice would be an extremely worthwhile project, but it's not my project here. Instead, I want to keep our focus on the kinds of examples presented in Chapter 2, and to examine what kinds of philosophical tools and theories we should appeal to if we're to shine light on them. We shouldn't forget, though, that in narrowing our focus in this manner, we may be only looking at a portion of what falls under the umbrella of epistemic injustice.

3.5 SUMMARY

We started out this chapter by considering the kind of balancing act that a satisfactory account of epistemic injustice needs to perform, neither including too much nor too little. Fricker's characterisation of epistemic injustice seems to offer a reasonable attempt to say what's distinctive about the examples in Chapter 2, at least once it has been refined a little. However, some of the ways it demarcates what counts as an epistemic injustice need careful consideration: for instance, it directs our focus away from phenomena that happen primarily at the level of entire societies and communities rather than individuals, and it seems to leave room open for examples of epistemic injustice that weren't represented in Chapter 2, in particular those involving classism, and those involving unequal distributions of epistemic goods and opportunities. We've considered how we might accommodate such examples within Fricker's account, though I have indicated that my focus in this book will remain the kind of examples that the previous chapter introduced.

3.6 SUGGEST FURTHER READINGS

Fricker presents her work on epistemic injustice as in part a response to Michel Foucault's views on knowledge and power (1998, 2007: Chapter 1): for discussion of Foucault and epistemic injustice, see Allen (2017) and Lorenzini (2022).

Anttila and Dutilh Novaes (2024) examines epistemological themes in Paulo Freire's work on education and oppression, and relates these to contemporary discussions of epistemic injustice.

Byskov (2020) offers a rare discussion of what makes an epistemic injustice a kind of injustice, and it proposes starting from Fricker's focus on discrimination and prejudice and adding further conditions. Another way to approach this question is to look at the relationship between epistemic injustices and violations of epistemic rights, as discussed in Watson (2018, 2021); a natural proposal, floated in McGlynn (2023), is that epistemic injustices count as injustices because they invariably involve violations of individuals' epistemic rights.

In the chapter, I mentioned that Coady has impressed on Fricker that she should pay more attention to what she has come to call distributive epistemic injustice, but in more recent work, he has argued for the stronger conclusion that all epistemic injustice is distributive rather than discriminatory (Coady 2017: see also Simion 2019). See Irzik and Kurtulmus (2024) for some recent work on distributive epistemic injustice, as it arises in science. Fricker's own views on this distinction seem to have shifted since her 2007 book, and at present, she takes the line that distributive and discriminatory epistemic injustices are not two distinct kinds, but rather two different 'theoretical lenses' we can adopt when looking at different examples. One lens might be more illuminating than the other in a given case, and she still holds that a discriminatory lens is better for helping us understand the points she wanted to make about the examples she discussed in her book, but in principle, one could instead adopt a distributive lens to theorise about those examples (see Fricker 2017: 59 n1 and Nikolaidis, Thompson, and Fricker 2023: 793). I return to this idea in Chapter 10.

For a discussion of epistemic injustice in education, see Kotzee (2017) and the papers collected in Dunne (2022) and Nikolaidis and Thompson (2023).

The complaint that the notion of epistemic agency is under-theorised given its importance to discussions of epistemic injustice is made in Catala (2020 and 2025). Catala argues that this isn't just an oversight that needs to be addressed; it has allowed ableist implicit conceptions of epistemic agency to take root in the literature, which reduce epistemic agency to the acquisition of *propositional* knowledge (knowledge that something is the case) and to the attempted sharing of this kind of knowledge via testimony. By implicitly narrowing our conception of epistemic agency in this fashion, we shrink the forms of epistemic injustice that we acknowledge, and Catala worries that we may find ourselves unable to recognise many of the epistemic injustices faced by intellectually disabled people. Hawley (2012) is an early criticism of the epistemic injustice literature's focus on propositional knowledge, and she explores what epistemic injustice about knowledge *how* would look like; see Cath (2025) for discussion. (Kristie Dotson has her own, distinctive characterisation of epistemic agency, which will be introduced in the next chapter.)

NOTES

1   See in particular Chapter 11.
2   See McGlynn (2014) for an opinionated overview of the debate about the centrality of knowledge in epistemology.
3   See Gerken (2019) for related points.
4   For such criticism, see Doan (2018).
5   I don't mean to ignore the work done within the subfield of philosophy of education; the point is rather that epistemologists tend not to be philosophers of education (again, with notable exceptions).

REFERENCES

Allen, Amy. 2017. 'Power/Knowledge/Resistance: Foucault and Epistemic Injustice.' In Ian James Kidd, José Medina, and Gaile Pohlhaus Jr., eds. *The Routledge Handbook of Epistemic Injustice*: 187–194. Oxon and New York: Routledge.

Altanian, Melanie. 2021. 'Remembrance and Denial of Genocide: On the Interrelations of Testimonial and Hermeneutical Injustice.' *International Journal of Philosophical Studies* 29 (4): 595–612. https://doi.org/10.1080/09672559.2021.1997397

Altanian, Melanie. 2024. *The Epistemic Injustice of Genocide Denial*. Oxon: Routledge.

Anttila, Solmu and Catarina Dutilh Novaes. 2024. 'Critical Social Epistemology and the Liberating Power of Dialogue.' In Waldomiro J. Silva-Filho, ed. *The Epistemology of Conversations: First Essays*: 239–262. ChamSpringer Nature.

Archer, Alfred and Leonie Smith. 2020. 'Epistemic Injustice and the Attention Economy.' *Ethical Theory and Moral Practice* 23 (5): 777–795. https://doi.org/10.1007/s10677-020-10123-x

Byskov, Morten Fibieger. 2020. 'What Makes Epistemic Injustice an "Injustice"?' *Journal of Social Philosophy* 52 (1): 116–133. https://doi.org/10.1111/josp.12348

Catala, Amandine. 2020. 'Metaepistemic Injustice and Intellectual Disability: A Pluralist Account of Epistemic Agency.' *Ethical Theory and Moral Practice* 23: 755–776. https://doi.org/10.1007/s10677-020-10120-0

Catala, Amandine. 2025. *The Dynamics of Epistemic Injustice: Situating Epistemic Power and Agency*. Oxford and New York: Oxford University Press.

Cath, Yuri. 2025. 'Social Epistemology and Knowing-How.' In Jennifer Lackey and Aidan McGlynn, eds. *The Oxford Handbook of Social Epistemology*: 580–599. Oxford and New York: Oxford University Press.

Coady, David. 2010. 'Two Concepts of Epistemic Injustice.' *Episteme* 7 (2): 101–113. https://doi.org/10.3366/epi.2010.0001

Coady, David. 2017. 'Epistemic Injustice as Distributive Injustice.' In Ian James Kidd, José Medina, and Gaile Pohlhaus Jr., eds. *The Routledge Handbook of Epistemic Injustice*: 61–68. Oxon and New York: Routledge.

Dieleman, Susan. 2012. 'An Interview with Miranda Fricker.' *Social Epistemology* 26 (2): 253–261. https://doi.org/10.1080/02691728.2011.652216

Doan, Michael. 2018. 'Resisting Structural Epistemic Injustice.' *Feminist Philosophy Quarterly* 4 (4): 1–23. https://doi.org/10.5206/fpq/2018.4.6230

Du Bois, W. E. B. 1903/1996. *The Souls of Black Folk: Essays and Sketches*. New York: Penguin Classics.

Dunne, Gerry (ed.). 2022. 'Special Issue on Epistemic Injustice and Education.' *Educational Philosophy and Theory* 55 (3).

Freire, Paulo. 1933/2018. *The Pedagogy of the Oppressed* (50th Anniversary Edition). Translated by Myra Bergman Ramos. London: Bloomsbury.

Fricker, Miranda. 1998. 'Rational Authority and Social Power: Towards a Truly Social Epistemology.' *Proceedings of the Aristotelian Society* 98 (2): 159–177. https://doi.org/10.1111/1467-9264.00030

Fricker, Miranda. 2007. *Epistemic Injustice: Power and the Ethics of Knowing*. Oxford: Oxford University Press.

Fricker, Miranda. 2013. 'Epistemic Justice as a Condition of Political Freedom?' *Synthese* 190: 1317–1332. https://doi.org/10.1007/s11229-012-0227-3

Fricker, Miranda. 2017. 'Evolving Concepts of Epistemic Injustice.' In Ian James Kidd, José Medina, and Gaile Pohlhaus Jr., eds. *The Routledge Handbook of Epistemic Injustice*: 53–60. Oxon: Routledge.

Gerken, Mikkel. 2019. 'Pragmatic Encroachment and the Challenge from Epistemic Injustice.' *Philosophers' Imprint* 19 (15): 1–19. https://hdl.handle.net/2027/spo.3521354.0019.015

Hawley, Katherine. 2012. 'Knowing How and Epistemic Injustice.' In John Bengson and Marc Moffett, eds. *Knowing How: Essays on Knowledge, Mind, and Action*: 283–299. Oxford and New York: Oxford University Press.

Irzik, Gürol and Faik Kurtulmus. 2024. 'Distributive Epistemic Justice in Science.' *British Journal for the Philosophy of Science* 75 (2): 325–345. https://doi.org/10.1086/715351

Kotzee, Ben. 2017. 'Education and Epistemic Injustice.' In Ian James Kidd, José Medina, and Gaile Pohlhaus Jr., eds. *The Routledge Handbook of Epistemic Injustice*: 324–335. Oxon and New York: Routledge.

Lee, Harper. 1960. *To Kill a Mockingbird*. London: Arrow Books.

Lorenzini, Daniele. 2022. 'Reason versus Power: Genealogy, Critique, and Epistemic Injustice.' *The Monist* 105 (4): 541–557. https://doi.org/10.1093/monist/onac016

McEwan, Ian. 1997. *Enduring Love*. London: Jonathan Cape.

McGlynn, Aidan. 2014. *Knowledge First?* Basingstoke: Palgrave MacMillan.

McGlynn, Aidan. 2023. 'Epistemic Rights Violations and Epistemic Injustice.' *Asian Journal of Philosophy* 2 (29): 1–14. https://doi.org/10.1007/s44204-023-00087-x

Minghella, Anthony. 2000. *The Talented Mr. Ripley—Based on Patricia Highsmith's Novel*. London: Methuen.

Nikolaidis, A. C. and Winston C. Thompson (eds.). 2023. 'Special Issue on Epistemic Injustice: Complicity and Promise in Education.' *Journal of Philosophy of Education* 57 (4–5).

Nikolaidis, A. C., Winston C. Thompson, and Miranda Fricker. 2023. 'Education, Epistemic Injustice, and Truthfulness: Miranda Fricker Interviewed by A. C.

Nikolaidis and Winston C. Thompson.' *Journal of Philosophy of Education* 57 (4–5): 791–802. https://doi.org/10.1093/jopedu/qhad075

Santos, Boaventura de Sousa. 2014. *Epistemologies of the South: Justice against Epistemicide*. Oxon and New York: Routledge.

Simion, Mona. 2019. 'Hermeneutical Injustice as Basing Failure.' In Patrick Bondy and J. Adam Carter, eds. *Well-Founded Belief: New Essays on the Epistemic Basing Relation*: 177–89. New York and Oxon: Routledge.

Spiegel, Thomas. 2022. 'The Epistemic Injustice *of* Epistemic Injustice.' *Social Epistemology Review and Reply Collective* 11 (9): 75–90.

Watson, Lani. 2018. 'Systematic Epistemic Rights Violations in the Media: A Brexit Case Study.' *Social Epistemology* 32 (2): 88–102. https://doi.org/10.1080/02691728.2018.1440022

Watson, Lani. 2021. *The Right to Know: Epistemic Rights and Why We Need Them*. Oxon and New York: Routledge.

Watson, Lani. 2025. 'What Can Social Epistemology Learn from Educational Theory?' In Jennifer Lackey and Aidan McGlynn, eds. *The Oxford Handbook of Social Epistemology*: 633–655. New York: Oxford University Press.

Williams, Patricia J. 1991. *The Alchemy of Race and Rights: Diary of a Law Professor*. Cambridge, MA: Harvard University Press.

Wollstonecraft, Mary. 1792. *A Vindication of the Rights of Woman: with Strictures on Political and Moral Subjects*. London: J. Johnson.

Woodson, Carter G. 1933/2009. 'The Mis-Education of the Negro.' *The Journal of Pan African Studies* eBook. https://www.jpanafrican.org/ebooks/3.4eBook-The%20Mis-Education.pdf

4

SITUATING EPISTEMIC OPPRESSION

4.1 INTRODUCTION

This chapter has three purposes. The first is to introduce *standpoint epistemology*, an approach to epistemology which is explicitly or implicitly part of the background against which discussions of epistemic injustice take place. While contemporary standpoint epistemology has roots in Marxism, I want to instead look at how some of its central ideas emerge in the work of W. E. B. Du Bois, in particular in his best-known work *The Souls of Black Folk* (Section 4.2). Second, I want to take a look at some epistemological themes in Black feminist writings in the 20th century (Section 4.3), leading to a detailed look at the standpoint epistemology in Patricia Hill Collins's now classic book *Black Feminist Thought: Knowledge, Consciousness, and the Politics of Empowerment* (Section 4.4). By focusing on the epistemological aspects of Collins's views, we'll be able to see that she is a successor of Du Bois's approach in certain ways; moreover, this discussion will support recent contentions that in key respects, Collins is illuminatingly thought of as offering an important precursor to Miranda Fricker's work and other contemporary discussions of epistemic injustice. Third, and finally, I want to return to the notion of epistemic oppression introduced in Chapter 1, this time to look at a particular account of epistemic oppression developed by the philosopher Kristie Dotson, which explicitly builds on ideas from Collins's epistemology (Section 4.5).

DOI: 10.4324/9781003281863-5

A persistent criticism of Fricker's work in recent years has been that there were many precursors to her work, particularly but not exclusively within the Black feminist tradition throughout the 20th century, that she failed to mention, let alone give any attention to. The point can be overstated. To my knowledge, there's no evidence to suggest Fricker intentionally or unintentionally appropriated the ideas of any particular theorists (a point I'll return to briefly later in this chapter). Moreover, I think it's simply a mistake to suggest that Fricker simply added catchy labels to things that were already well understood prior to her work. In my view, this involves the kind of conflation between the phenomena we're concerned with and Fricker's quite distinctive theories about those phenomena that I've been trying to warn against (see also McGlynn 2025). This conflation involves a failure to get appropriate perspective on Fricker's contribution to this topic, but more importantly, it flattens our sense of the theoretical possibilities available to us by failing to recognise the importantly distinct and different contributions that others have made.

That all said, as I have observed already in this book, there's a basic criticism of Fricker here that is correct; there was relevant work in the literature, much of it by marginalised scholars, that for whatever reason, Fricker's work overlooked or ignored entirely. There's no excuse for making the same mistake now. However, doing better can't just involve dropping a few citations to earlier literature, while failing to treat that work as genuinely adding to our collective understanding of epistemic injustice. Crucially, this chapter gives us resources that we will appeal to again in several later chapters; in particular, we'll return several times to Collins's discussion of Black feminist thought, which is one reason her work looms so large in this chapter.

4.2 LIFTING THE VEIL

In the opening chapter of *The Souls of Black Folk*, W. E. B. Du Bois introduces two closely related ideas that have had a important influence on contemporary epistemology, and on discussions of epistemic injustice in particular. The first is the *veil*, which Du Bois recounts becoming aware lies between him and the other, white children around him when a white girl refuses to take the card he has offered her during a childhood game:

> Then it dawned on me with a certain suddenness that I was different from the others; or like, mayhap, in heart and life and longing, but shut out from their world by a vast veil.
>
> (Du Bois 1903/1996: 2)

It's important to stress that this veil isn't wholly, or even primarily, an epistemological metaphor. The veil marks, first and foremost, racialised differences in opportunities: for action; interactions with others; to excel; to exercise autonomy in one's life choices; and so on. Du Bois first becomes aware of the veil when he is made aware that there is something that the other children can do that he can't, namely gift his card freely, and he goes on to discuss his growing awareness as he gets older that 'the worlds' he longed for and the 'dazzling opportunities' all go to white people rather than to himself. In short, the veil symbolises the system of racial segregation as put in place following the failures of the Reconstruction era, both as that system was formulated into law during the Jim Crow period and as it was informally and socially enforced.

Still, there is an epistemic thread present in the metaphor of the veil, as Du Bois presents it; the veil runs between Du Bois's reality and those of his white counterparts, but it also prevents the latter from truly seeing him, his reality, and how and why that reality differs from their own. Once he becomes aware of the veil, Du Bois, in contrast, is able to see both sides; moreover, he knows how *he* appears from the other side of the veil (and the degree to which he is often rendered invisible). Du Bois explores these epistemic themes in the second of the ideas I want to bring out, his celebrated notion of *double consciousness*:

> After the Egyptian and Indian, the Greek and Roman, the Teuton and Mongolian, the Negro is a sort of seventh son, born with a veil, and gifted with second-sight in this American world,—a world which yields him no true self-consciousness, but only lets him see himself through the revelation of the other world. It is a peculiar sensation, this double-consciousness, this sense of always looking at one's self through the eyes of others, of measuring one's soul by the tape of a world that looks on in amused contempt and pity. One ever feels his twoness,—an American, a Negro; two souls, two thoughts, two unreconciled strivings; two warring ideals in one dark body, whose dogged strength alone keeps it from being torn asunder.
>
> (1903/1996: 2)

Du Bois's remarks have often been taken as a source of inspiration for epistemologies that maintain that there can be some kind of epistemic advantage associated with social positions that are socially, economically, and politically disadvantaged (and that there are epistemic disadvantages associated with being relatively privileged in these other respects). Perhaps the most developed and widely held approach of this kind is *standpoint epistemology*. I don't mean to suggest that Du Bois's remarks on double consciousness were the only, or even the primary, source of inspiration for standpoint epistemology. In particular, certain interpretations of Marxism were a heavy influence on early versions of feminist standpoint epistemology, and this influence is reflected in some of the terminology still employed by its proponents, as we'll see in this book (for example, see the discussions of 'consciousness-raising' later in this chapter and in Chapter 8). That acknowledged, it will be more helpful for the purposes of this book to have a sense of how standpoint epistemologies have drawn on Du Bois's notion of double consciousness and other aspects of his views (though the interested reader should refer to the suggested further readings at the end of this chapter for where to read about their Marxist origins).

Standpoint epistemology is often called 'standpoint theory,' particularly by philosophers of science, but it bears emphasising that it isn't a single theory, but rather a family of theories unified by a commitment to certain core theses—though which claims are non-optional for standpoint epistemologists is a somewhat disputed matter. Perhaps the most clearly central claims are, first, that knowledge is *socially situated*, at least in the sense that your social location—your class, gender, race, whether or not you are disabled or trans, and so on—shapes what you are likely to know or to be ignorant about, and second, the *epistemic advantage* thesis, according to which the standpoints associated with oppressed social locations are epistemically advantaged or privileged in some way. Alison Wylie (2003) helpfully describes the epistemic advantage thesis as the *inversion* thesis, which nicely captures the way it pictures the epistemic order inverting the usual social and political hierarchies. One reason that standpoint epistemology is really a family of views rather than a single view is that, even restricting our attention to these two theses, there's scope for very different understandings of what they claim: different accounts of the ways that social location shapes the possibilities for knowledge, and the precise nature and scope of the epistemic advantage being claimed.

We'll see some examples of ways these details have been filled out later in this chapter, but another source of variation between different versions of standpoint epistemology concerns how they supplement the first two theses. A third thesis that seems central to at least contemporary versions of standpoint epistemology is that a standpoint is a collective achievement: following the literature, we'll call this the *achievement thesis*. In a recent paper, Briana Toole spells out what this involves as follows:

> The process of acquiring situated knowledge first requires the achievement of a standpoint from which such knowledge is made available. A standpoint is not reduced to an individual's social location but emerges through a collective process of political struggle with those who are more or less similarly situated. Thus, a standpoint is not given but must be achieved through a process known as consciousness-raising.
>
> (2021: 341)

There are a few ideas packed in here. One is that achieving a standpoint requires consciousness-raising, which involves collective reflection on the experiences and conditions of members of a disadvantaged social group, as well as collective struggle to change those conditions.[1] Toole also takes it to follow from the achievement thesis that a standpoint is not just to be equated with a social location; you don't occupy a feminist standpoint, for example, just in virtue of being a woman or having particular experiences of gender-based oppression, as well-known examples such as Phyllis Schlafly and Mary Whitehouse demonstrate all too vividly.

You might have noticed that I've said rather a lot about standpoint epistemology without saying anything explicit about what a *standpoint* is supposed to be. The term is clearly metaphorical, in much the same way as the notion of a social location is metaphorical, relying on an implicit analogy with spatial location (Young 2006: 112). So the task is to give the notion of a standpoint some non-metaphorical content. I think the best approach to this task is to think through what standpoints must be like if they're to play the role accorded to them by standpoint epistemology, as characterised by the three theses already stated; I don't think we can understand what a standpoint is independently of the theory. In particular, I think it's helpful to consider the kind of achievement a standpoint is, according to the achievement thesis. In this vein, the passage from Toole quoted above continues with her statement of what a standpoint is:

> A standpoint thus emerges as a critical perspective on the social world that takes as its starting the point the social location of some particular group. For instance, women, and the experiences of women qua women, form the basis of a feminist standpoint.
>
> (2021: 342)

Similarly, I've tried to sum up what I take standpoints to be, as the notion appears within standpoint epistemology, as follows:

> First, standpoints are sometimes distinguished from viewpoints or sets of distinctive experiences, which may be shared by all or most members of given social group. Experiences of a certain sort may provide the raw materials for developing a standpoint (an idea we'll return to), but the standpoint itself is an epistemic vantage point that's achieved through a combination of collective intellectual labour and social and political struggle. In addition to having experiences which differ from those of members of dominant groups, this may involve: collective reflection on these differences and disparities; seeing the relevant experiences in the light of feminist values and projects; noticing their prevalence and significance for members of the oppressed group in question; developing apt conceptual and expressive resources for interpreting and communicating the experiences in question; and putting these epistemic resources to work in political struggle. The paradigm examples here are the consciousness-raising 'speak-outs' of second-wave feminism.
>
> (McGlynn 2019: 263–264)

Notice that these quotes from both Toole and myself suggest that the starting point for the kind of knowledge made available from a standpoint is the experiences of members of the social group in question; these are the 'raw materials,' as I put it. Not just any experiences are relevant. In Charles Mills's suggestive terminology, members of oppressed social groups tend to be more likely to have 'alien' experiences, which he characterises as experiences that sit outside of, or even tell against, the dominant picture of social reality; they 'lie outside the normal trajectory through the world of members of hegemonic groups' (Mills 1988: 28).[2] But to reiterate, for the standpoint theorist, having such alien experiences isn't sufficient to occupy the relevant standpoint. To pick up the example Toole offers, having 'experiences of women qua women' can 'form the basis of a feminist standpoint,' but only the basis: the standpoint is a collective achievement that starts from such experiences, but requires collective consciousness-raising and engagement in political struggle.

Returning to Du Bois, although his remarks have been influential on standpoint epistemology, there's not much basis for thinking that he is a standpoint epistemologist in this sense. Part of what's involved in his coming to see the veil and how things look from both sides of it surely is that he has alien experiences in Mills's sense; his experience of being singled out during the children's card-swapping game is one significant example. However, he doesn't just *have* such experiences. He reflects on them and recognises their significance: by his own telling, from quite an early age. What's missing in Du Bois's account is the standpoint epistemologist's insistence that what's key is *collective* reflection, discussion, and struggle. In any case, whatever Du Bois's own views, his notion of double consciousness has proved influential on many of the philosophers we'll look at throughout this book.[3]

Du Bois's *The Souls of Black Folk* raises another issue which is worth mentioning, before we move on. When describing the situated knowledge thesis of standpoint epistemology above, I wrote that it claims that your social position 'shapes' what kinds of things you will tend to know or to remain ignorant about. However, standpoint epistemology is sometimes associated with a stronger claim, namely that your social position imposes limits on what you *can* know; Emily Tilton has recently called this the *strong epistemic disadvantage thesis* (2024: 1). On such versions of standpoint epistemology, the 'experiences of women qua women' aren't merely the basis of a feminist standpoint; they are also experiences you *must* have had if you're to acquire the knowledge associated with that standpoint. Du Bois's project in his book suggests that he would be sceptical of anything like this stronger claim. In his 'Forethought,' he describes his book as lifting the veil, and the implication seems to be that he expects his readers, including his white readers, to get a glimpse of what things are like on, and how things appear from, the other side:

> Leaving the world of the white man, I have stepped within the Veil, raising it that you may view faintly its deeper recesses, — the meaning of its religion, the passion of its human sorrow, and the struggle of its greater souls.
>
> (1903/1996: v)

Du Bois seems to think he can communicate at least something important about social reality, as seen from behind the veil, to a reader who has been ignorant of this up until that point; indeed, that seems to be one primary goal of his book. This is an aspect of Du Bois's project we'll find echoed later in this chapter.[4]

4.3 MISSING WORD-SHAPES AND THE NECESSITY OF POETRY

When discussing the examples in Chapter 2, we encountered the idea that one form epistemic injustice can take is that some people lack the words and even the concepts needed to make sense of, and communicate, their own experiences. This is a significant theme in the Black feminist tradition in the 20th century, and in this section, I want to briefly survey a few key thinkers and ideas in this tradition, before turning to Patricia Hill Collins in the next section.

This theme finds poignant expression in Toni Morrison's description of her characters Sethe and Paul D in *Beloved* as discussing the aspects of their past histories which were 'bearable' with each other, but being unable to share 'the things neither had word-shapes for' yet (1987/2005: 116). A few years after the publication of Morrison's novel, she edited a landmark volume of Black feminist writers responding to the Clarence Thomas hearings in 1991, when his confirmation process was rocked by Anita Hill's allegations of sexual harassment. In her contribution to Morrison's volume, Kimberlé Crenshaw examined in detail the way in which Hill was silenced as a Black woman in the context of the hearings due to 'the lack of available and widely comprehended narratives to communicate the reality of her experience as a black woman to the world' (1992: 404). This lack of apt and accessible resources is also a running theme in Audre Lorde's hugely influential essays collected as *Sister Outsider*, though Lorde pays particular attention to the way that these lacks can be circumvented or surmounted. In a justly famous passage in 'The Transformation of Silence into Language and Action,' Lorde calls for her audience not to let fear silence them, and instructs them to seek the words they need to express themselves:

> What are the words you do not yet have? What do you need to say?
> (Lorde 1984/2007: 41)

This process of seeking out the words you need is not one that Lorde expects individuals to do alone; it involves engaging with others and, as Nancy K. Bereano puts it in her introduction as editor of *Sister Outsider*, Lorde asks that 'we pay attention to those voices we have been taught to distrust' (Lorde 1984/2007: 12).[5]

Lorde also discusses the process of putting names to things in order to begin to understand them in her 'Poetry is Not a Luxury.' Poetry, as Lorde understands it in this essay, is 'a revelatory distillation of experience,' and 'the way we help give name to the nameless so it can be thought' (1984/2007: 37). It's clear that Lorde's conception of poetry as 'a revelatory distillation of experience' is broader than what we might usually associate with the term, though its exact boundaries are unclear and disputed. Matthew Cull takes it to cover 'a broad category of autobiographical descriptive work that closely engages and describes our experiences' (2021: 238–239), though in an attached footnote they note that there 'may be good reason to gravitate towards artistic mediums here.'[6] A narrower interpretation of what Lorde has in mind here takes Cull's point in their footnote more seriously, and focuses entirely on *artistic* attempts to capture and express certain experiences. This still encompasses much more than our ordinary conception of poetry, since it will include songs, paintings, novels, sculptures, and so on, in addition to written and spoken verse, but unlike Cull's 'broad category,' it doesn't include things like academic texts. On either interpretation, Lorde is suggesting that poetic expression, broadly construed, is essential for allowing experiences to be named, thought, and communicated, and so is an essential aspect of how experiences can ultimately lead to action.

4.4 CONTROLLING IMAGES AND SUBJUGATED KNOWLEDGE

Perhaps the most significant and influential contribution to our understanding of epistemic injustice in the Black feminist tradition comes from Patricia Hill Collins, particularly in her book *Black Feminist Thought*. I lack space to give a complete summary of Collins's views, and so here I will just pick out some key, interrelated themes which are both worthy of attention in their own right, and which are crucial for understanding more recent philosophical work that builds on Collins, as we will see in the next section and in later chapters.

First, Collins notes that an aspect of Black women's oppression is that they have a number of 'controlling images' placed on them. The controlling images are stereotypes of Black women that have three main functions. They are meant to be punitive, punishing Black women for the ways that they challenge white supremacist, capitalist patriarchy (2000: 69). Their second function is that they serve to place the responsibility and blame for the disadvantages faced by Black women, and by Black families more generally, onto Black women themselves (and particularly onto Black mothers), rather than onto discriminatory and oppressive institutions, practices, and policies. They act as legitimising myths which are 'designed to make racism, sexism, poverty, and other forms of social injustice appear to be natural, normal, and inevitable parts of everyday life' (2000: 76–77).[7] For example, the controlling images depict Black women as emasculating in ways that drive away Black men, leading to high numbers of single-parent households, a story which diverts our attention away from the staggering numbers of Black men, including fathers, caught up in America's ongoing experiment in mass incarceration (see e.g. Alexander 2010 and Coates 2015).

The final and most central function of these images—their 'controlling' function—is to pressure Black women to behave in certain ways deemed more acceptable to a white-patriarchal society. They achieve this in a number of different ways. The images ensure that Black women face a number of double-binds, of the sort we encountered in Chapter 1 when discussing Frye's characterisation of oppression. For example, they leave Black women in an impossible situation when it comes to balancing the competing pressures of earning sufficient income to support their families while being sufficiently engaged in child-rearing and domestic labour to avoid being stigmatised as having failed their families.[8] A notable feature of the system of controlling images that Collins discusses is that all but one of them are stigmatising, but the remaining image, the 'Mammy,' is cast as positive. The Mammy is the 'faithful, obedient domestic servant,' naturally inclined to domestic labour and service jobs, and who can be relied on to instil deference to white people in Black children (Collins 2000: 80–81). Since this is the only acceptable image for Black women to present to those in more powerful social positions, there is considerable pressure on Black women to conform to it, or at least to appear to do so.[9] Collins stresses that this system of images is dynamic, changing in response to the particular ways in which Black women are to be controlled in a given era (2000: 72, 88): for example, whether they are to be pressured into having lots of children (during the era of chattel slavery) or few children (in the post-civil rights era, which officially recognises the entitlement of Black Americans to welfare and other forms of benefits).[10]

Second, Collins attributes the prevalence of these controlling images at least in part to the fact that Black women are marginalised within and excluded from certain institutions and practices which play a dominant role in shaping and spreading the dominant conception of Black women. Here Collins mentions the news, media, schools and universities, governmental agencies, media such as television, films, radio, and music, and those who exercise control over what people consume online (2000: 85).[11] Importantly, Collins thinks that 'African-American institutions also perpetuate these same controlling images' (2000: 86), or more precisely, that institutions like African-American churches can be sites of 'negotiation,' where the controlling images can be reproduced but where they can also be contested (2000: 87). The ubiquity of the controlling images, and the fact that they can be reproduced even in institutions organised and led by Black people, raises the worry that Black women themselves will internalise the images. However, Collins thinks that Black women are largely able to resist this internalisation.

Third, Collins theorises Black women's oppression under this system of controlling images as a kind of objectification; Black women are 'objectified as the Other.' Collins characterises this notion in terms of what she calls 'binary thinking,' which is our tendency to think of diversity in terms of oppositional binaries, which typically involve one side being regarded as derivative and lesser in some sense:

> Objectification is central to this process of oppositional difference. In binary thinking, one element is objectified as the Other, and is viewed as an object to be manipulated and controlled.
>
> (2000: 70)

Objectification of this sort is contrasted with being able to *self-define*. Black women can resist this form of oppression by replacing the externally imposed controlling images with a self-defined and authentic conception of themselves, one that is grounded in their knowledge of their own experiences and their own lives. The body of knowledge and wisdom produced by Black women that enables them to resist being objectified in this way—what Collins calls Black feminist thought—is the product of a Black feminist *standpoint*, in the sense discussed earlier in this chapter. I stressed there that a standpoint is a collective achievement, and here, this means that the Black feminist standpoint is not merely the sum of the experiences and perspectives of Black women, but the product of collective intellectual labour which takes these experiences and perspectives as raw material and subjects them to discussion, scrutiny, and reflection, with an eye towards resisting objectification as the Other.

The sites of this collective intellectual endeavour are what Collins calls 'safe spaces,' places where Black women can share their experiences with each other and reflect on them in relative freedom from dismissal, misunderstanding, interference, or retaliation.[12] Collins observes that '[e]xtended families, churches, and African-American community organizations are important locations where safe discourse potentially can occur' (2000: 100–101), though as we've already seen, these can also be spaces where the controlling images of Black women are sometimes reproduced. Nonetheless, when things go well, '[t]hese spaces are not only safe—they form prime locations for resisting objectification as the Other' (2000: 101). This enables Black women to resist these externally imposed controlling images, at least within the 'hidden space' of their own consciousness (2000: 98), even if they lack the social power to effectively contest the controlling images in more public spheres. It also offers spaces in which Black women can develop the conceptual and expressive resources they need to understand, articulate, and share their experiences (2000: 118, 123–124).

That last point brings us to the final key aspect of Collins's account, namely that the knowledge produced from this Black feminist standpoint, Black feminist thought, is *subjugated knowledge*. It's not recognised as knowledge, because Black women are largely excluded from the kinds of institutions that are tasked with evaluating what counts as knowledge and what doesn't—the paradigms here are academic institutions. These are institutions dominated by 'elite white men,' and Collins argues that as a result, the epistemological standards that operate in them reflect the interests of that group, and are skewed against the claims to knowledge made by Black female academics, and Black women more generally (2000: 251). This is partly due to these institutions and standards implicitly granting the controlling images of Black women the status of common knowledge, so that any claims made by Black women that conflict with the controlling images are thereby liable to be seen as inherently implausible (2000: 253). Associated with the Black feminist standpoint is an alternative set of processes and standards for validating Black women's claims to knowledge (2000: 254)—a Black feminist epistemology, in Collins's terms—but because this alternative epistemology isn't taken seriously in institutions like academia, Black feminist thought remains unrecognised as knowledge:

> I present Black feminist thought as subjugated knowledge in that African-American women have long struggled to find alternative locations and epistemologies for validating our own self-definitions.
>
> (2000: 269)

Black feminist thought is produced by Black feminist intellectuals, but Collins is adamant that 'intellectuals' in the relevant sense shouldn't be equated with academics or so-called 'public intellectuals' (2000: 14–16). bell hooks, Collins herself, and several of the philosophers we'll discuss in this book count as Black feminist intellectuals by Collins's lights, but so does Toni Morrison, though her contributions mostly took the form of works of fiction, and so do other contributors to Black feminist thought who may not have any academic credentials or published writings to their names; the paradigms, for Collins, are blues musicians, and Black women like Sojourner Truth and Maria Stewart who made influential speeches. This point about who counts as doing intellectual work is related to Black feminist thought's status as subjugated knowledge, since this body of knowledge has often had to be developed outside of academic contexts:

> Historically, much of the Black women's intellectual tradition occurred in institutional locations other than the academy.
>
> (2000: 15)

What Collins offers, then, is a tightly interconnected set of ideas and theses that explain how Black women's lack of social power and their underrepresentation in certain key institutions and practices leave them unable to effectively contest the controlling images that proliferate throughout society, and unable to have the knowledge they produce widely recognised *as* knowledge. This last point in turn keeps the whole system of exclusion self-perpetuating, since if research done by Black feminist academics is not epistemically validated and valued, that will make it harder for them to enter and progress in academic institutions. In this sense, these controlling images can leave Black women silenced (2000: ix). However, Collins also explains how Black women have carved out marginalised but essential spaces in which they are able to resist these controlling images and to develop the conceptual and epistemological resources needed to produce knowledge and to articulate a self-conception rooted in Black women's own experiences and values.

As promised, there's at least one further important respect in which Collins's project in her book echoes Du Bois's, as I laid that out earlier in the chapter. Recall that Du Bois presents *The Souls of Black Folk* as pulling back the veil, to enable those on the other side of it to see and understand something of what social reality is really like. Similarly, Collins sees her book as laying out some of the body of knowledge available from a Black feminist standpoint—the product of Black women's collective intellectual labour that she refers to as Black feminist thought—with the aim of contesting and replacing the widespread controlling images of Black women with their own self-defined images, and of undoing Black feminist thought's relegated status as subjugated knowledge.

4.5 EPISTEMIC OPPRESSION REVISITED

We're now well placed to look more closely at the notion of epistemic oppression. Miranda Fricker (1999) has used this term to name the way that oppressed groups tend to lack the conceptual and expressive resources needed to make certain of their experiences intelligible; we might again follow Mills in describing the relevant experience as 'alien,' in the sense introduced earlier in this chapter. Fricker then uses this understanding of epistemic oppression to give a particular kind of explanation of how we should understand standpoint epistemology's claim that oppressed groups are associated with epistemically privileged standpoints; these will be standpoints that can generate the needed resources to render the relevant experiences intelligible, allowing new knowledge to be produced.

So understood, epistemic oppression is relevant to some of the examples we looked at in Chapter 2. Take Fricker's own example of Carmita Wood. One way to describe that example is that women were epistemically oppressed in the early- to mid-1970s, and lacking a suitable concept or expression to name instances of sexual harassment was one aspect of this oppression. However, they were also well placed to rectify this lack, as demonstrated by the success of Wood and the other women who began to hold speak-outs on this issue.[13]

Fricker's proposal about how to think about epistemic oppression in effect has it name a background condition to one of the two forms of epistemic injustice that she identified in her book, namely hermeneutical injustice. It doesn't pick out anything all that distinctive and, as we'll see in later chapters, she mostly switched to different terminology in her book.[14]

A much more interesting and influential account of epistemic oppression is offered in more recent work by Kristie Dotson (2012, 2014). As Dotson proposes understanding it, epistemic oppression involves persistent and unwarranted infringements on the epistemic agency of knowers that prevent them from contributing to the production of knowledge (2014: 115). Epistemic agency here refers to the ability to use, contribute to, and revise shared epistemic resources. These epistemic resources will include the shared conceptual and linguistic resources of the community, of the kinds we've already discussed in relation to the example of Carmita Wood, but it will include other things too. For example, the shared epistemic resources of a community will include certain standards for evaluating whether someone knows or not. Here we might be reminded of Patricia Hill Collins's account of how Black feminist thought is 'subjugated knowledge' due to the imposition of inapt processes of knowledge validation by more dominant social groups, and this is no coincidence, since Dotson takes this to be a paradigmatic form of epistemic oppression (2014: 116).

We can make this more concrete by thinking about some instances of what Collins has in mind when she writes about different standards and processes for knowledge validation. Here are two kinds of cases suggested by Collins's discussion; she is mostly thinking here of academic research conducted in her home discipline of sociology, but I take her points to have much more general applicability. First, different standards for evaluating whether someone's claim represents knowledge can employ different principles for explaining and interpreting any empirical data that has been gathered. If the standards we are using includes no recognition of or commitment to intersectionality—the idea, introduced in Chapter 1, that Black women face distinctive kinds of oppression that cannot be reduced to or understood in terms of that faced by Black men together with that faced by white women—then they may demand that we explain and interpret data in ways that tell against the claims made by Black women about their own lives, leading to those claims being dismissed rather than validated as knowledge (Collins 2000: 252).

Second, we can (and in scientific contexts, are encouraged to) employ standards for whether a claim that someone has made represents knowledge that place a premium on that claim being an instance of a statistically robust generalisation, and that correspondingly devalue claims made on the basis of lived experience.[15] Collins argues that this too leads to Black feminist thought being subjugated, since Black women often treat lived experience as significant even in the absence of quantitative evidence of a broader pattern. Moreover, as Collins clearly sees, this will affect not only which claims are validated as knowledgeable, but also which kind of inquiries are seen as worth pursuing in the first place; only the kinds of questions that can be in principle answered by research methods that will produce evidence of the favoured sort are likely to be supported and undertaken. Questions which we could only answer by trusting Black women's reports of their own lived experiences are likely to simply never be asked by researchers.

Returning to Dotson's account of epistemic agency, we hopefully have a better sense now of what she means in claiming that one of the ways that Black women's epistemic agency is persistently and unwarrantedly infringed upon is that they are prevented from contributing to the epistemic standards that prevail. As observed in our discussion of Collins in the previous section, this dynamic can be self-perpetuating; for instance, the dominant epistemic standards in academia are used to dismiss the intellectual products of Black female scholars, who then often fail to find academic employment, let alone to ascend the ranks within academia to positions of influence which would allow them to exercise sway over the prevailing epistemic standards.

Dotson doesn't explicitly draw on Marilyn Frye's conception of oppression (Frye 1983) in developing her account of epistemic oppression, but the approach I took in Chapter 1 of starting with some Frye-influenced ideas about oppression and seeing how we could make sense of epistemic oppression on that basis landed us pretty close to the conception Dotson offers. There are two apparent differences. The first is that Dotson offers her own, seemingly more specific conception of epistemic agency. Whereas I included any engagement in epistemic activities and practices, Dotson is focused on contributions to the production of knowledge. Second, the conception of epistemic oppression I extracted from Frye's account looked at infringements of both epistemic agency *and* epistemic autonomy. It's unclear how deep either of these differences really is. It may be that they prove to be pretty superficial; for instance, it might turn out, upon reflection, that Dotson's notion of epistemic agency includes key elements of what I called epistemic autonomy in Chapter 1, so that we're talking about more or less the same things in slightly different terms. Even if there are some genuine differences, they seem relatively minor, and in general, Dotson's account of epistemic oppression seems recognisable as a development and elaboration of the notion we identified in Chapter 1.

What does epistemic oppression, understood as Dotson proposes, have to say about the examples laid out in Chapter 2? Up to a point, nothing all that different from what Fricker will say; Dotson takes testimonial and hermeneutical injustice to be subsumed under her own category of epistemic oppression (Dotson 2012, 2014), and so for many of the examples she can offer more or less the same account as Fricker. However, there *are* examples which Fricker's account of epistemic injustice and Dotson's account of epistemic oppression differ on. We'll return to these differences, and the question of how compatible or incompatible Fricker and Dotson's frameworks for theorising about these issues really are, in Chapter 10; by then, we'll have a much better grasp of each philosopher's respective theory, as well as their strengths and weaknesses and their main points of overlap and contrast.

4.6 SUMMARY

This chapter has covered a lot of ground. We started with Du Bois's notion of double consciousness and looked at how it has influenced contemporary standpoint epistemologists, before surveying some of the contributions Black feminists have made to our understanding of epistemic injustice, with a focus on Collins's *Black Feminist Thought*. This set the scene for Dotson's account of epistemic oppression, and we began to bring out what's at stake between this account and Fricker's account of epistemic injustice.

4.7 SUGGESTED FURTHER READING

The criticism that Fricker failed to acknowledge and discuss earlier discussions of epistemic injustice by Black feminists and others has been made by a number of people, but most forcefully in Dotson (2012), Ivy (2016), and Berenstain (2020). They also offer a number of references to other philosophers and thinkers that I haven't attempted to cover in this chapter: see Dotson (2011: 252 and 2012: 29, 44 n24), Ivy (2016: 438–439), and Berenstain (2020: 755 n29). Medina (2021: 409–411) discusses other precursors to Fricker and the contemporary debate, while Ward (2023) looks at epistemic themes in Audre Lorde's work that are different but related to those we briefly touched on in the chapter, focusing on her notion of 'the erotic.'

For discussion of the epistemic themes in Du Bois, see Mills (2007: 18) and Medina (2013: 153–154). Mills draws a parallel between the moment Du Bois becomes aware of the veil and Descartes's realisation that much of what he has taken for knowledge lacks a secure basis; I discuss what we should make of this comparison in McGlynn (2019: Section 5). For criticism of Medina's development of Du Bois's notion of double consciousness, see Hawkins and Davis (2024). For a recent development of some of Du Bois's ideas as a version of standpoint epistemology, see Bright (2024), and for criticism of Bright, see Milanovich (forthcoming).

As briefly mentioned in the chapter, contemporary standpoint epistemology evolved out of early feminist standpoint epistemology, which in turn has its roots in certain developments of Marxist philosophy. If you are interested in this history, two good places to start are Tanesini (1999: Part VI) and Potter (2006: Chapter 5).

There is also an important tradition of feminist standpoint epistemology in the philosophy of science; see Saul (2003: Chapter 8), Potter (2006: Chapter 5), Intemann (2010), and Intemann (2025) for useful overviews, and Crasnow and Intemann (2024) for a comprehensive introduction to feminist epistemology and feminist philosophy of science.

For a very helpful guide to the differences between epistemic injustice and epistemic oppression, see Catala (2024); we will return to this issue in Chapter 10.

NOTES

1 I'll have more to say about what consciousness raising involves later in this chapter when we discuss Patricia Hill Collins, and we will examine an example in detail in Chapter 8.
2 Alison Jagger has offered a related but different idea as part of a defence of the claim that emotions play an essential role in the acquisition of knowledge. Women and members of other oppressed groups have what she calls 'outlaw' emotions; they sometimes respond to situations with emotions which differ from the 'conventionally acceptable' ones, as when a person of colour feels angry rather than amused at a racist joke, or a woman feels uncomfortable and perhaps threatened rather than flattered by sexual attention from men (Jagger 1989: 166).
3 Hawkins and Davis observe that double consciousness functions as a metaphor for 'the collective political struggle of Black Americans, produced through their orientation in a particular racio-historical conflict' (2024: 74–75), and the way I have put things in the text is in danger of interpreting the notion too literally as a claim about Du Bois as an individual. The worry that contemporary epistemologies inspired by Du Bois interpret double consciousness too literally and too individualistically is relevant to Hawkins

and Davis's criticism of Medina's notion of 'kaleidoscopic consciousness,' which is an aspect of Medina's view that we will look at in detail in the final chapter.

4 Harding (1992: 456–457) and Toole (2021: 342) both accept the claim that people who are not members of an oppressed social group, and so who haven't had any experiences from the perspective of that group, may nevertheless occupy the associated standpoint. Indeed, both seem open to the idea that someone who occupies a relatively privileged social position, and so who has no first-hand experiences of oppression, can still attain the knowledge available from an epistemically privileged standpoint; in Harding's memorable example, J. S. Mill can be part of a feminist standpoint. For recent discussions, see Tilton 2024 and Hannon (forthcoming). A related issue has recently received a lot of discussion. This is whether we should practice a 'deferential' epistemology, whereby we should always defer to members of a disadvantaged social group on issues concerning the lives and experiences of that group. In recent work, Olúfẹ́mi Táíwò (2020 and 2022) has argued that deferential epistemology doesn't serve the interests of a remotely radical politics, though he also argues that (contrary to what seems to be sometimes supposed) it's a mistake to think of deferential epistemology as a commitment of standpoint epistemology; rather, it's a misguided way to attempt to put standpoint epistemology into practice. See Tilton and Toole (2025) for further discussion, and Alcoff (1991) for the classic discussion of the problem of 'speaking for others.'

5 Similar themes also appear in Hortense Spillers's essay 'Interstices: A Small Drama of Words' (1984), particularly relating to Black women's sexuality. Berenstain claims on this basis that we should see Fricker's account of hermeneutical injustice as a case of what Emmalon Davis has termed 'epistemic appropriation,' where hermeneutical resources are divorced from their origins, and employed in ways that disproportionately serve the interests of socially dominant groups (Davis 2018), but this seems overstated, and it's not clear on what basis Berenstain picks out Spillers's writing in particular. The less specific claim that Fricker failed to acknowledge and discuss relevant work in the Black feminist tradition that has been done on the issues that she has labelled hermeneutical injustice (and epistemic injustice more generally) is much more plausible, as I have noted already; indeed, I think it's pretty obviously correct, given what I have said in this chapter.

6 This would make the category of poets close to Patricia Hill Collins's broad class of intellectuals; we'll consider Collins's views in detail very shortly.

7 I borrow the notion of a legitimising myth from Christopher Lebron (2015: 57). These are myths designed to mask or justify inequalities, and to present

social hierarchies as part of the natural order of things. Examples of such myths are all too familiar: women are weak and irrational, best suited to domestic labour and child-rearing and require men's protection and income; indigenous populations are lawless, childlike, and savage, and require the rule, guidance, and religion of their colonisers; Jewish people and Black people are lazy and so it's in their own interests, as well as the interests of the society on which they are 'parasitic', to be forced to work; and so on.

8 This particular double-bind is one that many women (and some men) face, regardless of race, but I think Collins would argue that the controlling images make it particularly difficult for Black women to navigate; in particular, the image of the 'welfare mother' or 'welfare queen' who is content to be entirely dependent on the state rather than working is meant to particularly stigmatise Black mothers who accept such state support (despite their being no less entitled to such assistance than white mothers).

9 'The Black Lady', an image of successful Black women professionals, can also appear positive. However, as Collins notes (2000: 80–81), it's not really; according to this image, the success of such women is due to unjust affirmative action programmes rather than genuine achievement (since these are taken to be mutually exclusive), and it is also meant to be 'emasculating', driving away Black men who might otherwise be potential partners, and so it too is an image shot through with sexist, racist, classist, and heteronormative prejudices.

10 A controlling image that may have recently emerged is the so-called 'angry Black women' (Berenstain 2016: 576), which has been wielded against the Williams sisters and Michele Obama, among others.

11 This list overlaps considerably with that offered by Betty Friedan in the passage I quoted in Chapter 2 (and also with those offered more recently by Fricker and other philosophers, as we'll see in later chapters).

12 This differs somewhat from the contemporary use of the term 'safe space' to signal spaces in which people can rely on not encountering certain forms of triggering material or judgemental reactions (or to parody or mock this usage). Derek Anderson (2021) introduces an epistemological conception of safe spaces—spaces which try to neutralise imbalances in 'epistemic power' between differently socially positioned subjects—and discusses how this relates to this more standard conception, though his epistemological conception is slightly different to what Collins has in mind.

13 I'll offer a much more thorough discussion of this example in Chapter 8.

14 I say 'mostly' here because as Amandine Catala has observed (2024: 4), Fricker does occasionally refer to epistemic oppression in her book (e.g. Fricker 2007: 59).

15 The notion of lived experience is familiar, but often found mysterious. I take it to pick out first-personal, first-hand, and embodied experiences. There's a sense in which I have experienced racism; I have witnessed racist behaviour. I don't have lived experience of racism, however, and it's this that's usually meant when people talk about having experienced racism. There's much more to be said about this notion (particularly as it emerges out of the phenomenalist tradition in philosophy, as in the title of the second half of Simone de Beauvoir's *The Second Sex*), but these brief remarks will suffice for my purposes here.

REFERENCES

Alcoff, Linda. 1991. 'The Problem of Speaking for Others.' *Cultural Critique* 20: 5–32. https://doi.org/10.2307/1354221

Alexander, Michelle. 2010. *The New Jim Crow: Mass Incarceration in the Age of Colorblindness*. New York: The New Press.

Anderson, Derek. 2021. 'An Epistemological Conception of Safe Spaces.' *Social Epistemology* 35 (3): 285–311. https://doi.org/10.1080/02691728.2020.1855485

Berenstain, Nora. 2016. 'Epistemic Exploitation.' *Ergo* 3 (22): 569–590. https://doi.org/10.3998/ergo.12405314.0003.022

Berenstain, Nora. 2020. 'White Feminist Gaslighting.' *Hypatia* 35 (4): 733–758. https://doi.org/10.1017/hyp.2020.31

Bright, Liam Kofi. 2024. 'Duboisian Leadership through Standpoint Epistemology.' *The Monist* 107: 82–97. https://doi.org/10.1093/monist/onado32

Catala, Amandine. 2024. 'Epistemic Injustice or Epistemic Oppression?' *KULA: Knowledge Creation, Dissemination, and Preservation Studies* 7 (1): 1–11. https://doi.org/10.18357/kula.294

Coates, Ta-Nehisi. 2015. 'The Black Family in the Age of Mass Incarceration.' Reprinted in Ta-Nehisi Coates. 2017. *We Were Eight Years in Power: An American Tragedy*: 223–281. New York: Penguin Random House.

Collins, Patricia Hills. 2000. *Black Feminist Thought: Knowledge, Consciousness, and the Politics of Empowerment* (Second Edition). New York and Oxon: Routledge.

Crasnow, Sharon and Kristen Intemann. 2024. *Feminist Epistemology and Philosophy of Science*. Oxon and New York: Routledge.

Crenshaw, Kimberlé. 1993. 'Whose Story is it Anyway? Feminist and Antiracist Appropriations of Anita Hill.' In Toni Morrison, ed. *Race-ing Justice, En-Gendering Power: Essays on Anita Hill, Clarence Thomas, and the Construction of Social Reality*: 402–436. London: Chatto and Windus.

Cull, Matthew. 2021. 'Engineering Is Not a Luxury: Black Feminists and Logical Positivists on Conceptual Engineering.' *Inquiry* 64 (1–2): 227–248. https://doi.org/10.1080/0020174X.2021.1883476

Davis, Emmalon. 2018. 'On Epistemic Appropriation.' *Ethics* 128 (4): 702–727. https://doi.org/10.1086/697490

Dotson, Kristie. 2011. 'Tracking Epistemic Violence, Tracking Practices of Silencing.' *Hypatia* 26 (2): 236–257. https://doi.org/10.1111/j.1527-2001.2011.01177.x

Dotson, Kristie. 2012. 'A Cautionary Tale: On Limiting Epistemic Oppression.' *Frontiers: A Journal of Women Studies* 33 (1): 24–47. https://doi.org/10.1353/fro.2012.a472779

Dotson, Kristie. 2014. 'Conceptualizing Epistemic Oppression.' *Social Epistemology* 28 (2): 115–138. https://doi.org/10.1080/02691728.2013.782585

Du Bois, W. E. B. 1903/1996. *The Souls of Black Folk: Essays and Sketches*. New York: Penguin Classics.

Fricker, Miranda. 1999. 'Epistemic Oppression and Epistemic Privilege.' *Canadian Journal of Philosophy* 29 (1): 191–210. https://doi.org/10.1080/00455091.1999.10716836

Fricker, Miranda. 2007. *Epistemic Injustice: Power and the Ethics of Knowing*. Oxford: Oxford University Press.

Frye, Marilyn. 1983. *The Politics of Reality: Essays in Feminist Theory*. New York: Crossing Press.

Hannon, Michael. Forthcoming. 'Social Identity, Understanding, and Deference.' *Philosophical Studies*. https://doi.org/10.1007/s11098-025-02364-2

Harding, Sandra. 1992. 'Rethinking Standpoint Epistemology: What Is "Strong Objectivity"?' *The Centennial Review* 36: 437–470. https://www.jstor.org/stable/23739232

Hawkins, Orlando and Emmalon Davis. 2024. 'The Future of Double Consciousness: Epistemic Virtue, Identity, and Structural Anti-Blackness.' *Ergo* 11 (3): 62–95. https://doi.org/10.3998/ergo.5708

Intemann, Kristen. 2010. '25 Years of Feminist Empiricism and Standpoint Theory: Where Are We Now?' *Hypatia* 25 (4): 778–796. https://doi.org/10.1111/j.1527-2001.2010.01138.x

Intemann, Kristen. 2025. 'Feminist Epistemology as Social Epistemology: The Role of Diversity in Epistemic Communities.' In Jennifer Lackey and Aidan McGlynn, eds. *The Oxford Handbook of Social Epistemology*: 545–561. New York: Oxford University Press.

Ivy, Veronica. 2016. 'Epistemic Injustice.' *Philosophy Compass* 11/8: 437–446. Originally published as Rachel McKinnon. https://doi.org/10.1111/phc3.12336

Jagger, Alison. 1989. 'Love and Knowledge: Emotion in Feminist Epistemology.' *Inquiry* 32 (2): 151–176.

Lebron, Christopher. 2015. *The Color of Our Shame: Race and Justice in Our Time*. Oxford and New York: Oxford University Press.

Lorde, Audre. 1984/2007. *Sister Outsider: Essays and Speeches*. Berkeley, CA: Crossing Press.

McGlynn, Aidan. 2019. 'Redrawing the Map: Medina on Epistemic Vices and Skepticism.' *International Journal for the Study of Skepticism* 9 (3): 261–283. https://doi.org/10.1163/22105700-20191386

McGlynn, Aidan. 2025. 'Epistemic Injustice: Phenomena and Theories.' In Jennifer Lackey and Aidan McGlynn, eds. *The Oxford Handbook of Social Epistemology*: 295–327. New York: Oxford University Press.

Medina, José. 2013. *The Epistemology of Resistance: Gender and Racial Oppression, Epistemic Injustice, and Resistant Imaginations*. Oxford: Oxford University Press.

Medina, José. 2021. 'Feminism and Epistemic Injustice.' In Kim Q. Hall and Ásta (eds.), *The Oxford Handbook of Feminist Philosophy*: 408–417. New York and Oxford: Oxford University Press.

Milanovich, Kai. Forthcoming. 'Distinguishing Situated Knowledge and Standpoint Theory: Defending the Achievement Thesis.' *Hypatia*. https://doi.org/10.1017/hyp.2025.10021

Mills. Charles. 1988. 'Alternative Epistemologies.' Reprinted in Charles Mills. 1998. *Blackness Visible: Essays on Philosophy and Race*. Ithaca: Cornell University Press.

Mills, Charles. 2007. 'White Ignorance.' In Shannon Sullivan and Nancy Tuana, eds. *Race and Epistemologies of Ignorance*: 13–38. Buffalo: SUNY Press.

Morrison, Toni. 1987/2005. *Beloved*. London: Vintage.

Potter, Elizabeth. 2006. *Feminism and Philosophy of Science: An Introduction*. Oxon and New York: Routledge.

Saul, Jennifer. 2003. *Feminism: Issues and Arguments*. Oxford: Oxford University Press.

Spillers, Hortense. 1984. 'Interstices: A Small Drama of Words.' Reprinted in Hortense Spillers. 2003, *Black, White, and in Color: Essays on American Literature and Culture*. Chicago, IL and London: University of Chicago Press.

Táíwò, Olúfémi. 2020. 'Being-in-the-Room Privilege: Elite Capture and Epistemic Deference.' *The Philosopher* 108 (4). https://www.thephilosopher1923.org/post/being-in-the-room-privilege-elite-capture-and-epistemic-deference

Táíwò, Olúfémi. 2022. *Elite Capture: How the Powerful Took over Identity Politics (and Everything Else)*. London: Pluto Press.

Tanesini, Alessandra. 1999. *An Introduction to Feminist Epistemologies*. Oxford: Blackwell Publishers.

Tilton, Emily. 2024. '"That's Above My Paygrade": Woke Excuses for Ignorance.' *Philosophers' Imprint* 24 (8): 1–19. https://doi.org/10.3998/phimp.2796

Tilton, Emily and Briana Toole. 2025. 'Standpoint Epistemology and the Epistemology of Deference.' In Kurt Sylvan, Matthias Steup, Jonathan Dancy, and Ernest Sosa, eds. *The Blackwell Companion to Epistemology* (Third Edition) 584–594. Hoboken, NJ: Wiley-Blackwell.

Toole, Briana. 2021. 'Recent Work in Standpoint Epistemology.' *Analysis* 81 (2): 338–350. https://doi.org/10.1093/analys/anab026

Ward, Caleb. 2023. 'Audre Lorde's Erotic as Epistemic and Political Practice.' *Hypatia* 38 (4): 896–917. https://doi.org/10.1017/hyp.2023.76

Wylie, Alison. 2003. 'Why Standpoint Matters.' In Robert Figueroa and Sandra Harding, eds., *Science and Other Cultures*: 26–48. Oxon and New York: Routledge.

Young, Iris Marion. 2006. 'Responsibility and Global Justice: A Social Connection Model.' *Social Philosophy and Policy* 23 (1): 102–130. https://doi.org/10.1017/S0265052506060043

Part 2

BEING BELIEVED

5

THE CENTRAL CASE OF TESTIMONIAL INJUSTICE

5.1 INTRODUCTION

In Chapter 2, I noted that the kinds of examples that motivate discussions of epistemic injustice can be roughly separated into those that primarily concern speakers struggling to be found believable when making claims to an audience, and those that seem to involve obstacles to a person being understood. The chapters in Part 2 of this book are going to focus on the former, while those in Part 3 will focus on the latter. We'll start in this chapter by looking at the form of epistemic injustice that has received by far the most attention, both from Miranda Fricker and in the subsequent literature: testimonial injustice.

Testimonial injustice, as Fricker characterises it, occurs when a speaker receives a credibility deficit due to prejudices held by their audience—we already encountered this definition, as well as some of the examples Fricker offers to illustrate it, in Part 1 of this book. There's a great deal to unpack and discuss in Fricker's definition, as simple as it can seem at first, and we will spend much of the present chapter and the next engaged with this task. First, however, I want to briefly introduce the notion of testimony and to look at how, on Fricker's picture, testimonial injustice arises more or less inevitably from our testimonial practices (Section 5.2). We'll then turn our attention properly to Fricker's account of testimonial injustice, focusing on

DOI: 10.4324/9781003281863-7

what she calls the 'central case,' taking a close look at the two examples she offers (Sections 5.3 and 5.4), and making more explicit some of the notable and distinctive features of the account Fricker provides of them (Section 5.5). Finally, we'll consider a variant account of how testimonial injustices can arise, particularly against disabled people, and we'll examine how this variant relates to Fricker's own account and examples (Section 5.6).

5.2 TESTIMONY, STEREOTYPES, AND PREJUDICES

In C. A. J. Coady's influential book *Testimony: A Philosophical Study*, he draws a distinction between *formal* and *natural* testimony. Formal testimony is what might first spring to mind when you hear the word 'testimony,' involving statements delivered in a particular kind of legal setting, paradigmatically a courtroom, typically with unusually strict conditions in place for when you can speak and what you can say (perhaps with statements being given under oath, for example) which allow it to have the status of evidence in the relevant legal proceedings. Natural testimony occurs outside that particular setting, in everyday interactions, and typically involves no special demands (though if challenged or if the stakes are particularly high, we may promise that what we're saying is true). Coady offers some utterly banal examples to illustrate the category of natural testimony; it can mean 'giving someone directions to the post office, reporting what just happened in an accident, telling someone the result of the last race or the latest cricket score' (1992: 39).

Often, discussions of the epistemology of testimony focus on natural testimony, leaving formal testimony as a matter for philosophers of law or legal epistemologists.[1] The same is somewhat true of the literature on testimonial injustice; it's mostly natural testimony that's at issue, and so by 'testimony' in what follows I'll mostly have this in mind. That said, one of the examples in Chapter 2—indeed, one of Fricker's own main examples, to be discussed in this chapter—takes place in a courtroom, so we won't entirely ignore formal testimony.

The examples of natural testimony offered by Coady suggest that testifying is just a matter of *telling*; it's using language, broadly construed, to share your beliefs or knowledge. Testimonial beliefs are those formed on the basis of someone telling you things, and testimonial justification and testimonial knowledge are justification and knowledge gained by being told something by someone else. This conception of testimony as telling is not entirely uncontroversial (e.g. Lackey 2008: 21–22), but it's plausible and will serve our purposes here. We should note that testimony isn't achieved by any particular medium for communicating with others; I'll often write as if the recipient of testimony is always a 'hearer,' but you can testify using the written word, or braille, or Morse code, just as readily as you can with the spoken word.[2]

Turning from the nature of testimony to its epistemology, the main question here is how we are able to get testimonial knowledge and justification by being told something by someone else. Here we return to a point made in Chapter 2, namely that in order to accept someone's testimony, you need to find them believable, where this involves taking them to be both competent on the subject matter at hand and sincere rather than lying. In cases where you know a person well, there's no puzzle about this; you'll likely have a reasonable, albeit fallible, sense of the kinds of topics they know something about and how trustworthy they tend to be. Often, though, we lack that kind of relationship with someone who is offering us testimony, and so we'll have little specific information about their competence and sincerity. How do we figure out which speakers to believe, and which not to?

Well, often we don't. To be sure, we sometimes do try to figure out whether to believe someone, particularly if the costs of being wrong are unusually high. This isn't how things typically go, though; usually, in the absence of reasons to distrust someone, we just accept what they tell us without seeming to think about it all that much. There's little to no 'figuring out' involved. Isn't this totally irresponsible? How can this possibly be a way of gaining justification or even knowledge?

Different theories in the epistemology of testimony split from each other largely over how they respond to these questions. Traditionally, there have been two camps in this debate. One of these holds that accepting someone's testimony in the absence of good reasons to judge they're likely to tell the truth is indeed irresponsible. We can't get knowledge or justification by believing something just because someone told us so; we need reasons that speak in favour of judging that their say-so is to be trusted before we can conclude that what they have said is true. The opposed camp insists that we *can* responsibly believe something just on someone's say-so, so long as there are no red flags, and that this can be a route to knowledge. If what a person is saying conflicts with things you already know, or you know that they've a track-record of making mistakes or lying (as in the fable of The Boy Who Cried Wolf), or they're acting shifty, then of course you should be on your guard, but the default response to someone telling you something is just to believe it. This second camp contends that their picture fits better with our actual testimonial practices, and that demands that hearers always have positive independent reasons to think a speaker is believable would make testimonial knowledge implausibly hard to get.[3]

Fricker thinks that's what's needed is an epistemology of testimony which finds middle ground between these two extreme views. On the picture Fricker outlines and defends, accepting testimony always involves, at some level, making a judgement about how believable—in her preferred terminology, how *credible* or *trustworthy*—the speaker is: the first camp gets that much right. However, they're wrong about what's involved in forming such judgements and the way that they influence whether we'll accept a given piece of testimony or not. We're able to reach judgements about how credible a speaker is effortlessly and quickly, without having to start digging into their past record as a testifier, since the gaps in our knowledge about them can be filled in by relying on *stereotypes* about the social group(s) they belong to.

We often talk of stereotypes and any reliance on them as inherently criticisable: for example, to describe someone as engaging in 'stereotyping' is typically to charge them with doing something epistemically and perhaps also morally suspect. Crucially, though, this isn't how Fricker is thinking about stereotypes. Instead, she offers a neutral definition, according to which 'stereotypes are *widely held associations between a given social group and one or more attributes*' (2007: 30). This conception allows that stereotypes can be reliable, can be based on good evidence, and can be operating in the formation of your credibility judgement about a person without this being in the slightest problematic; for instance, consider the association between French people and the appreciation of fine food. Stereotypes can function to cover over some of the gaps in our knowledge about the reliability of individual speakers, and when things go well, as they often do, this contributes to the smooth, effortless operation of our testimonial practices, even when we are receiving testimony from people we don't know very well.

It's worth noting that though Fricker talks about credibility *judgements*, that term is misleading here to the extent that it suggests that hearers form *beliefs* about how trustworthy each speaker is. Sometimes we might form a belief like this, but as Fricker is thinking about these judgements, more often than not they are ways of *perceiving* people. You often *see* other people as more or less trustworthy, based on their appearance, how they behave, how they express themselves, and so on: 'a hearer's sensitivity to the many prompts and cues that bear on trust is his capacity for a certain sort of social perception' (2007: 71). Fricker suggests we're born with innate capacities of this sort, which then get shaped and honed as we interact with other people and communities throughout our lives.

A moment ago, I said that stereotypes allow our testimonial practices to function smoothly when things go well. Unfortunately, of course, things don't always go well. We're prone to relying on stereotypes which are *prejudicial*, where prejudices are false associations between a social group and a (typically) negative attribute, such as being lazy, being mendacious, being incompetent, being naive, being prone to crime or to violence, and so on. Moreover, as Fricker conceives of them, prejudices aren't just poorly supported by evidence, but they're also stubbornly difficult to correct with evidence that shows them to be mistaken. You might be completely unaware that you're relying on a prejudice in judging other people, and since prejudices are stereotypes and so often operate at the level of how we perceive people rather than what we believe about them, your credibility judgements about a particular social group can be prejudicially low even if you sincerely believe that members of that group are as trustworthy as anyone else. Just as being a sincere avowed anti-racist doesn't inoculate you against seeing Black men as lazy or dangerous, and Black women as hypersexualised or bad mothers, it doesn't inoculate you against seeing them as less credible than you ought to when they are trying to share their knowledge with you. On the picture of testimony that Fricker offers, testimonial injustice is a near inevitable side-product of the normal operation of our testimonial practices, which requires us to somehow compensate for our lack of information about the competence and sincerity of many of the people who offer us testimony; testimonial injustice is the price we pay for allowing stereotypes to 'oil the wheels of testimonial exchange' (2007: 32).

5.3 THE 'CENTRAL CASE' OF TESTIMONIAL INJUSTICE

According to Fricker's characterisation, a testimonial injustice occurs when a testifier receives a credibility deficit due to prejudices held by their audience (2007: 17). For example, a scientist may try to convey her findings to a group of her peers, only to find that they don't give her testimony as much credibility as they ought, due to prejudices they have against the research methodology she employed to produce them (2007: 27). However, Fricker focuses our attention on testimonial injustices that arise due to particular kinds of prejudices, illustrated by the example of the Philosopher of Physics we encountered in Chapter 2, whose contributions to a physics conference are dismissed out of hand because she is, as the other participants might put it, 'just a philosopher' (2007: 28–29). In this example, the credibility deficit that the speaker receives is due to an *identity* prejudice—a prejudice against people who share a particular social identity—and it's such prejudices that interest Fricker.

What makes the both the scientist using a disfavoured methodology and the Philosopher of Physics distinctive is that the prejudices involved are relatively local and idiosyncratic to the group and setting described, and so the testimonial injustice they contribute to is, as Fricker puts it, *incidental* (2007: 27). Other prejudices, particularly other identity prejudices, are not like this; instead they "track' the subject through different dimensions of social activity—economic, educational, professional, sexual, legal, political, religious, and so on' (2007: 27). Identity prejudices of this sort include prejudices against people of particular genders, races, and sexualities, against disabled people, trans people, fat people, and older people, against people of particular socio-economic classes, and against those who practice or identify with certain religions, to give some familiar examples.[4] Testimonial injustices based on such prejudices are *systematic*. The 'central case' of testimonial injustice, for Fricker, is a *systematic identity-prejudicial credibility deficit* (2007: 28). It's the central case, in this sense, that is the focus of Fricker's discussion (so much so that the subsequent literature often overlooks or forgets about non-central cases of testimonial injustice, especially those that don't involve identity prejudices).

In the paper in which Fricker first introduced the notion of testimonial injustice (Fricker 1998), the main example she used to illustrate it was Patricia Williams's account of telling people she had been racially profiled when out shopping for a Christmas gift for her mother, only to face sceptical responses from people determined to insist that it didn't happen as she told it, or that race couldn't have been a factor.[5] However, by her 2007 book, Fricker had shifted to her two well-known fictional examples, Marge Sherwood and Tom Robinson. I have already introduced and discussed these examples in earlier chapters, but a quick recap is in order. In Anthony Minghella's screenplay of Patricia Highsmith's *The Talented Mr. Ripley*, Marge Sherwood has well-founded suspicions that Tom Ripley is involved in the disappearance of her fiancé, Dickie Greenleaf. She voices these suspicions to Dickie's father, Herbert Greenleaf, only to be summarily dismissed: 'Marge, there's female intuition, and then there are facts' (Minghella 2000: 130). In Harper Lee's *To Kill a Mockingbird* (1960), a disabled Black man, Tom Robinson, testifies truthfully that he is innocent of the crime he has been accused of, that of raping a younger white woman, Mayella Ewell. Robinson's lawyer, Atticus Finch, conclusively demonstrates Robinson's innocence to the court, but despite this, Robinson finds it impossible to get the all-white jurors to accept his testimony, and they find him guilty, with what ultimately prove to be lethal consequences.

Both Sherwood and Robinson are awarded less credibility than they should have been due to identity prejudices held by their audience. Moreover, the prejudices in question are the kind that 'track' subjects through different contexts of their lives; in Sherwood's case, these are largely prejudices against women (particularly young, not-yet-married women), while in Robinson's, his testimony is dismissed because he is a Black man. The two examples differ not just in the particular identity prejudices in play, but also in how those prejudices work to call into question the speaker's credibility. As we noted in Chapter 2, Greenleaf's prejudices target Sherwood's credibility by painting her as epistemically incompetent, while the jurors' prejudices against Tom Robinson target his credibility by painting him as insincere.[6] While recognising this difference between the examples, Fricker argues that both can be seen as exemplifying a unified species of epistemic injustice:

> ...despite the possibility that a prejudice might separate the twin components of epistemic untrustworthiness, I suggest that the experience of testimonial injustice remains unified enough to warrant a unified ethical characterisation in terms of being wronged *qua* giver of knowledge.
>
> (2007: 45)

We can see here why Fricker takes testimonial injustice to be a species of epistemic injustice, at least according to her initial characterisation of epistemic injustice in her book; in testimonial injustice, one is wronged in one's capacity as a knower by being wronged in one's capacity as a giver of knowledge. In Chapter 11, we'll see how she develops this thought and offer some objections, but we can let it stand for now.

5.4 DISTINCTIVE FEATURES OF FRICKER'S ACCOUNT

In the rest of this chapter, I want to clarify some key points about Fricker's account and consider some of the distinctive claims she makes about her examples of the central case of testimonial injustice, particularly the two she focuses on in her book. As a starting point, it's worth noting that there are alternative interpretations of at least some of Fricker's examples which downplay or contest the epistemic aspect that Fricker's notion of testimonial injustice is meant to capture. Consider Tom Robinson's conviction by the jurors. As Fricker presents the example, it's a battle between evidence and prejudice, and prejudice wins out, with the result that the jurors come to believe that Robinson is guilty despite the clear proof of his innocence (2007: 23). She is very clear that this is how she is interpreting the example:

> ...when it comes to the verdict, the jurors go along with the automatic distrust delivered by the prejudices that structure their perception of the speaker. They find him guilty. And it is important that we are to interpret the novel so that the jurors really do find him guilty. That is to say, they do not privately find him innocent yet cynically convict him anyway.
>
> (2007: 25)

It's not clear why we have to read the novel this way.[7] An alternative interpretation sees Tom Robinson's trial as a sham in which evidence is meaningless; it's nothing more than a legal veneer for finishing the attempted lynching that Finch's daughter Scout has inadvertently foiled earlier in the novel, before the trial has even begun. The jurors may genuinely see Robinson as a rapist, due to their prejudices, but the import of this might be less that this outweighs the evidence that Robinson is speaking the truth about his encounter with Mayella Ewell, and more that it renders it utterly irrelevant; if they see Black men as untrustworthy rapists in general, then whether or not Robinson raped this particular woman doesn't really matter for whether he is an appropriate target of violence.[8] Perhaps the jury actually accepted that Robinson couldn't have attacked Ewell in the manner she describes, given his disability, and so they believed much of his story; such details may simply have mattered no more to the jurors than to the lynch mob.

It's not my aim to defend this interpretation of Lee's novel here, nor is it obvious that this kind of account of the example generalises to the other examples Fricker presents as illustrations of testimonial injustice. For instance, Herbert Greenleaf really does seem to think that Tom Ripley has acted commendably towards his son, and that Marge Sherwood can't see this because, as a woman, she doesn't understand the situation. Still, Tom Robinson may have been the victim of, not testimonial injustice, but total *indifference* to his testimony; his life may have been forfeit before he ever had a chance to speak. I'm mostly going to leave this alternative interpretation aside here, since the literature I'm engaging with almost universally follows Fricker's interpretation. I don't think it's obviously incorrect, though, and it points to something that in general we should be guard on against, namely being too quick to look for a subtle epistemological story of what's happening in examples of injustice and violence better understood in primarily non-epistemic terms (see Táíwò 2022).

A second observation is that even when a speaker is offering testimony to a prejudiced audience, only some of their testimony is likely to be subject to a credibility deficit. The Philosopher of Physics whose contributions to discussions of science are dismissed out of hand may be regarded as an expert by the very same audience as soon as the conversation drifts to more overtly philosophical matters. Herbert Greenleaf would presumably take Marge Sherwood's word on many subjects; she's not regarded as epistemically incompetent across the board, but only where she needs to rely on 'female intuition' (Fricker 2007: 135). And as Fricker writes:

> …it is clear that, for instance, Tom Robinson might have been relied on and trusted epistemically on certain matters even by the more thoroughly racist white citizens of Maycomb County—matters relating to his daily work, no doubt, and indeed many everyday matters of practical import, so long as there was no challenge to a white person's word, no perceived implication of non-inferiority of intellect, nothing about the subject matter that might be seen to imply that this Negro was getting above himself.
> (Fricker 2007: 131)

There are at least a couple of factors that determine what kinds of topics a particular person will be found credible when testifying about. The first of these factors is suggested in the passage just quoted from Fricker. Tom Robinson's testimony challenges that of those positioned in his society as his racial superiors, in particular Mayella and Bob Ewell, and it seems to be in part this feature of his testimony that triggers a credibility deficit. Kate

Manne observes that in general, examples of testimonial injustice tend to involve a speaker's word being pitted against that of someone ranked above them in some relevant social hierarchy, as when Sherwood's charge that Ripley is responsible for Dickie Greenleaf's disappearance conflicts with Ripley's own account (Manne 2018: 195).[9]

The other factor is the content of the prejudices in play. As we've already noted, Herbert Greenleaf sees Sherwood as a woman, but more than that, as a young, unmarried, and so naive woman whom he presumes, wrongly, to lack insight into what his son Dickie is really like (Fricker 2007: 87–88). Similarly, the prejudices confronting Tom Robinson are part of a familiar package that construct Black men as inherently criminal, as rapists, as unable to control themselves around white women in particular, and so on. In general, the content of the prejudices operating in a particular instance of testimonial injustice shape which topics certain kinds of people can and can't speak about credibly.

The third observation I want to make is that while Fricker's examples involve a speaker receiving a prejudicial credibility deficit when offering testimony, she does also acknowledge a variant in which the prejudices against the competence or sincerity of a particular social group are so strong, members of that group simply aren't consulted on certain topics at all, calling this *pre-emptive* testimonial injustice (2007: 130). Fricker is keen to stress that a version of the previous point holds here too, observing that 'it would be stretching the pessimistic social imagination too far to imagine a society (original or historical) that contained social groups whose members' knowledge or opinions were *never* solicited on *any* subject matter' (2007: 130–131).

Fourth, to return to a point already made in Chapter 2, it's not clear that either of Fricker's two main examples are *pure* cases of testimonial injustice, since each might be thought to contain elements of hermeneutical injustice.[10] When Marge Sherwood voiced her suspicions about Ripley to Greenleaf, was it just scepticism about 'female intuition' that was playing a role, or did he find the manner in which she expressed those suspicions too intuitive or too 'hysterical' to regard her as even making sense? When Tom Robinson testified to the court that he helped Mayella Ewell out with her work because he felt sorry for her, was he mistrusted because he's a disabled Black man, or did he express a thought that his audience, in some sense, just couldn't understand?[11] To the extent that it's tempting to think that the answer to each of these questions is 'both!', it looks like we're open to the idea that there's an element of hermeneutical injustice present in these examples. Given that these are paradigm cases of testimonial injustice, we might suspect that this will prove to be a general feature of any realistic examples of testimonial injustice.

Fifth, testimonial injustice is typically something which *particular people* do to other people. Herbert Greenleaf and the jurors at Tom Robinson's trial are *perpetrators* or *culprits* of testimonial injustice, as Fricker puts things; they have each committed testimonial injustice against the respective speakers.

Now, Fricker doesn't deny that there might be cases of testimonial injustice that happen even though no one in particular perpetrates them, and both she and Elizabeth Anderson have suggested that pre-emptive testimonial injustice, of the sort I introduced a moment ago, may illustrate what this could look like. Here's an example, adapted from one that Anderson offers (2012: 166). Consider an academic journal that publishes cutting-edge peer-reviewed work in logic, but only ever solicits referee reports from men on the work that is submitted. One way this could happen is that the editors are prejudiced against women when it comes to logic, taking them to be unable to make a competent assessment of the kind of technical work submitted to the journal. This would be an example of pre-emptive testimonial injustice of the kind already discussed.

We might suppose instead, though, that the editors have no such prejudice, but are operating with a database that stores details about possible referees and, as a hangover from an earlier, more sexist age, all of the entries are men. Not realising that the database hasn't been updated recently, the editors rely on it and end up only soliciting the opinion of men on the papers they receive. So long as the editors are reasonable in supposing that the system would suggest a qualified woman to referee a given paper if there was one, it may not seem right to say that *they* are perpetrating a testimonial injustice against women logicians; rather, the injustice stems from an unfairness in how the systems they rely on have been set up. We might try to point the finger at the people who set up the database of potential referees in the first place, suggesting that they are the culprits here, but this may not be any more plausible. It may be that the database was compiled gradually by a large group of people, none of whom ever saw the complete list, and during a period when women gaining relevant qualifications in logic was even rarer than it is today. None of these individuals need have been any more prejudiced than our present-day editors; still, women are being systematically excluded from contributing their expertise to the peer-review practices of the journal due to their gender.[12]

Even if we accept this kind of case as illustrating testimonial injustice, it clearly differs from the examples of the central case that Fricker offers, and from most of the other examples of testimonial injustice offered in the literature, since these *do* involve perpetrators. One reason this is worth noting is that it offers a stark, surprising, and controversial point of contrast with Fricker's views about the other variety of epistemic injustice she identifies; hermeneutical injustice, according to Fricker, is a 'purely structural' form of injustice (2007: 159), meaning it *never* has perpetrators. We'll give this contrast due consideration in Chapter 10.

5.5 ADAPTIVE PREFERENCES AND TESTIMONIAL INJUSTICE

The examples of the central case of testimonial injustice presented by Fricker all involve identity prejudices which bear fairly directly on the credibility of certain groups of people when they offer testimony on particular topics; for example, the prejudices encountered by Marge Sherwood paint her as unable to coolly assess the evidence about the kind of man her fiancé was, while the prejudices at work in the Maycomb County courtroom construct Tom Robinson as a rapist and liar, and so incapable of telling the truth about his interactions with Mayella Ewell. However, Elizabeth Barnes (2016) has proposed an alternative, less immediate way that identity prejudices can give rise to systematic testimonial injustices.[13]

Barnes's proposal comes in the context of a debate concerning how much weight we should give what she calls disability-positive testimony: first-person testimony from disabled people who report that they value their disabilities; that they enjoy high levels of well-being and that this is in part due to, rather than in spite of, their disabilities; that they wouldn't want to cease being disabled if that were somehow an option; that their disability is something worthy of celebration and pride; and so on.[14] Recall that we looked at a particular example of this sort in Chapter 2, when we considered the disability-rights activist Harriet McBryde Johnson trying to persuade the philosopher Peter Singer that she led a meaningful and fulfilling life, in an attempt to get him to give up his controversial view that it should be permissible for parents to euthanise infants with certain disabilities (a view Singer's critics have described as a form of eugenics).[15]

Barnes takes disability-positive testimony to be strong evidence for the thesis that having a disability does not mean that you are living a life of less value, or that you cannot enjoy a high degree of well-being. However, she notes that this testimony is frequently dismissed, being treated as of little or no relevance by those who want to insist that being disabled is inherently bad for you, and she's keen to examine and undermine the best argument that can be made in favour of this kind of dismissal.

She takes the strongest case of this sort to claim that disability-positive testimony expresses *adaptive preferences*, and so can be safely ignored. Adaptive preferences, in the relevant sense, are preferences you have for something that makes you worse off, in response to a restriction to your range of options.[16] For example, many women may report preferring to occupy traditional, submissive gender roles, but if we have grounds for thinking this would be a preference for something that makes a person worse off, we can discount such reports:

> Thus the presence of her preference for submissive gender roles does not by itself give us any evidence that a life that coheres to submissive gender roles is just as good as a life that does not. Because her preferences are adaptive—formed towards something suboptimal in light of a severely diminished set of options—they cannot serve as such evidence.
>
> (Barnes 2016: 127)

Applied to disability, the suggestion is that disability-positive testimony can be dismissed because it merely expresses the adaptive preferences of disabled people; we might regard such sentiments as understandable and admirable, but we shouldn't think they tell us anything about the value or desirability of disabled lives. In response, Barnes argues that this dismissal of disabled people's testimony is a kind of testimonial injustice. The reason is that classifying the preferences expressed by disability-positive testimony as adaptive, in the relevant sense, involves taking them to be preferences for something which makes a person worse off. In the absence of independent reasons for this claim, it amounts to a prejudice that a disability makes a person's life go worse than it would otherwise, and so that disability-positive testimony is mistaken or misguided. Moreover, Barnes identifies a number of prejudices about disabled people and their experiences and lives that are both commonplace and in tension with the kinds of affirmations of the value of disabilities and the lives led by disabled people found in disability-positive testimony:

> Disability is tragedy. Disability is loss. Disability is misfortune.
> (2016: 168)

Disabled people are those who lost the 'body lottery'; they're just really unlucky (and so we shouldn't think too deeply about ways in which society, institutions, and physical spaces might be responsible for any disadvantages disabled people face).[17] When disabled people seem to be thriving, that's because they've heroically overcome the odds; they're thriving *despite* their disability, never in virtue of it. These are the identity prejudices which Barnes thinks underwrite the particular kinds of testimonial injustices faced by disabled people when testifying about their own disabilities, lives, and well-being.[18]

Is the complex dynamic that Barnes identifies really a kind of testimonial injustice? It seems to fit Fricker's definition, at least if we agree with her claim that there are no independent reasons to think that being disabled inherently makes a person worse off; that's to say, it seems to involve speakers receiving credibility deficits because of prejudices held by their audiences.[19] On the other hand, the phenomenon Barnes describes does seem somewhat different to Fricker's own examples of testimonial injustice, and it's worth trying to pin down what's distinctive about it.

One contrast is in the way that the prejudices involved function to undermine the credibility of the speaker. As I noted at the outset of this section, in Fricker's central examples, the identity prejudices bear rather directly on the speaker's credibility on the subject matter at hand. The content of the prejudices about disabled people identified by Barnes seems to call their credibility into question via a somewhat different route. The prejudices don't explicitly paint disabled people as insincere or epistemically incompetent, but rather concern the link between disability and well-being. These prejudices then drive a dismissal of disability-positive testimony, by seemingly justifying the claim that such testimony merely reports adaptive preferences.

Relatedly, in Fricker's examples, we'd expect that the same testimony coming from someone with a different social identity wouldn't be dismissed so readily. After all, if the credibility deficit is due to an identity prejudice, then those who aren't in the scope of that prejudice should be able to testify without that loss of credibility. In *The Talented Mr. Ripley*, Dickie Greenleaf's friend Freddie Miles figures out Ripley's role in Dickie's disappearance rather too late for his own good, but let's suppose he had come to appreciate Sherwood's evidence at an earlier point in the story, and he had laid his own suspicions about Ripley out to Herbert Greenleaf: would Greenleaf have dismissed Miles as similarly out of touch with the facts? That seems unlikely.[20] In contrast, it seems like *anyone* who made claims that conflict with the prejudices about disabilities identified by Barnes would be likely to find their testimony widely met with scepticism.

There are a number of possible explanations of this apparent difference between Barnes's examples and Fricker's. One natural thought is that if I am prejudiced against the testimony of a particular social group on a particular topic—I take them to be epistemically incompetent, or as liable to lie—then I will reject testimony from anyone that reports something that could only be known by taking the testimony of members of that group seriously. To take an oversimplified example, suppose that I prejudicially think that women know nothing about different models of car; I baselessly think that all cars look more or less alike to all women. I'm likely to regard my friend's report that a mutual acquaintance drives a BMW with suspicion, as soon as I learn that his only evidence is that his wife recently saw our acquaintance driving a car that *she* identified as a BMW. If I prejudicially regard her testimony on this particular issue as worthless, I'll be likely to regard any testimony purely based on her testimony as equally worthless, regardless of whether I would have trusted my friend's own independent judgement. We might describe this as a form of *second-hand* testimonial injustice, and suggest that this is what's going on when disability-positive testimony is rejected even when it comes from nondisabled people.[21]

Another idea, which has been explored in the literature, is that there can be forms of testimonial injustice that are due, not to prejudices against the identity of the speaker, but rather against the *content* of what the speaker is saying (Davis 2021; Dembroff and Whitcomb 2022). This is plausibly part of what is going on in Barnes's examples of rejected disability-positive testimony, and it again explains why certain audiences are liable to reject such testimony even if it comes from a nondisabled person. A related suggestion is that there is an element of hermeneutical injustice in these examples. The thought is that a person who says that disabled people need not lead tragic lives is saying something that doesn't really make sense to their audience, given the way they conceptualise disability, and that this effect is independent of any identity prejudices that the audience may have against disabled people in particular. This might remind us of an observation made in Chapter 2 and in the previous section of this chapter, namely that when Tom Robinson says (for instance) that he felt sorry for Mayella Ewell, he may be struggling to make himself understood, rather than merely struggling to come across as credible, due to the flawed interpretive schemas that the jurors bring to the courtroom.[22]

I won't attempt to decide which of these three proposals best explains why disability-positive testimony is liable to be regarded with suspicion even when it is offered by nondisabled people. For our purposes here, it's enough to note that although Barnes's examples plausibly do meet Fricker's definition of the central case of testimonial injustice, they seem importantly and interestingly different to Fricker's own examples in ways that aren't fully understood yet.

5.6 SUMMARY

This chapter has introduced Fricker's account of testimonial injustice, locating it within broader issues in the epistemology of testimony, and seeing how it accounts for features of various examples, in particular her two main illustrations of the 'central case' of testimonial injustice. We ended the chapter by clarifying some aspects of Fricker's account and her treatment of these examples, and by looking at a different, less direct way that examples meeting Fricker's definition can arise pointed out by Barnes.

Fricker's account of testimonial injustice as prejudicial credibility deficit has been very widely adopted. It's not hard to see why; it seems to offer a simple but illuminating picture of what is going on not just in Fricker's examples, but in a wide range of others involving speakers failing to be taken seriously in various significant domains of human interaction.

However, Fricker's account isn't as straightforward or as clear as it might appear at first glance, and a number of philosophers have argued that it needs to be made more precise and opened up in various ways, or perhaps replaced altogether. In the next chapter, we'll start by asking several relatively simple questions about the key notions that figure in Fricker's definition, and we'll find that doing so lands us in uncertainty and controversy more quickly than you might expect, while the final chapter of Part 2 of the book, Chapter 7, looks at an alternative way of theorising about these issues.

5.7 FURTHER SUGGESTED READINGS

Fricker often frames testimonial injustice as involving a prejudicial lack of trust in a speaker. She takes this to be interchangeable with her official definition in terms of a credibility deficit, but one strand in the literature on epistemic injustice that has not been covered in this chapter concerns the relationship between testimonial injustice and trust, if we start conceiving of the latter not as synonymous with credibility, but as involving rich interpersonal relations. For discussions of this topic, see the papers collected in Altanian and Baghramian (2023), as well as Hawley (2017 and 2019) and McGlynn (2024). Carter (2025) is a helpful recent overview of the role that trust plays in social epistemology in general.

A second reason it's significant that Fricker takes testimonial injustice to have perpetrators, in addition to the one mentioned at the end of the chapter, is that it opens up questions about whether such perpetrators are always or ever responsible or blameworthy for the injustices they perpetrate. Fricker's own controversial views on this issue are laid out in Fricker (2007: Chapter 4 and 2016), and have been extensively criticised in Piovarchy (2020) and McKenna (2023: Chapter 7); see Riggs (2012) for an alternative account.

Issues concerning responsibility and blameworthiness have also been extensively debated in the literatures on topics related to testimonial injustice, and epistemic injustice more generally. Many of the chapters in Brownstein and Saul (2016) and Beeghly and Madva (2020) discuss whether we are responsible and blameworthy for our implicit biases. There has also been a very active debate within the literature on epistemic vices concerning whether we are responsible for those, including vices that have been claimed to produce epistemic injustices; for a representative sample, see Medina (2013: Chapter 4), Battaly (2019), Cassam (2019: Chapter 6), Tanesini (2021: Chapter 8), and McKenna (2023: Chapter 7). See Chapter 12 of this book for further discussion of epistemic virtues and vices.

Tremain (2017) and Curry (2017) both argue that Fricker and others fail to do justice to the role played by Robinson being a *disabled* Black man; Robinson's disability is typically deemed relevant only insofar as it's the key piece of evidence of his innocence, aside from his own testimony, but Tremain and Curry call for more reflection on the ways that his disability contributes to the prejudices he confronts and perhaps also how they bear on the reception of his testimony.

Barnes's discussion raises a general and important issue; avowals—first-person attributions of certain mental states to oneself, as when one reports on one's own pains, beliefs, happiness levels, preferences, or well-being—have typically been regarded by philosophers as authoritative and immune to doubt, in a way that contrasts with ordinary testimony and which cries out for philosophical explanation (e.g. Wright 1998). However, one implication of Barnes's discussion is that avowals about one's own well-being can be subject to testimonial injustice, which seems to sit poorly with the traditional picture. I lack space to do this topic justice here, but see Borgoni (2019, 2025, forthcoming) for insightful and interesting discussion.

For critical discussions of aspects of Barnes's discussion of disability and disability-positive testimony, see Hiller (2023), Carter (2023), and Nadelhoffer (2022), and for an overview of the relevance of disability to social epistemology in general, see Reynolds and Timpe (2025).

For discussions of whether and how testimonial injustice might 'deepen' political disagreements, making them more difficult to resolve, see Lagewaard (2021) and McGlynn (2023). Hannon and Woodard (2025) is a comprehensive introduction to these kinds of issues in political epistemology.

NOTES

1 Coady is, in some ways at least, an exception to this. He approaches his account of natural testimony indirectly, by giving an account of formal testimony and then removing or relaxing the conditions which seem like they no longer apply when we move away from legal settings (1992: 39–42). The resulting accounts of formal and natural testimony are not all that plausible, though, as has been pointed out by Elizabeth Fricker (1995: 396–397) and Jennifer Lackey (2008: 15–19).
2 Or so I'll assume; this last claim has been recently disputed (van Woudenberg 2021).
3 The first camp is usually called reductionism, as it holds that 'the knowledge-providing power of testimony can be reduced to the knowledge-providing power of other sources' (Nagel 2014: 77). The second camp, which holds that a person's say-so can be sufficient to believe something, and perhaps even to give you knowledge, is usually known as antireductionism or non-reductionism. Fricker instead uses the labels inferentialism and noninferentialism, but otherwise her conception of the debate is much as I have sketched it in the text; see Goldberg (2010) for criticism of this understanding of the debate and Fricker's views on testimony.

4 It will no doubt not be lost on the reader that this list overlaps with the familiar forms of oppression mentioned in Chapter 1.
5 Fricker takes this example from Code (1995). Code's notion of 'rhetorical spaces' in that work is an often-overlooked precursor to Fricker's discussion of epistemic injustice, as is her suggestion that 'ethical-political questions and epistemological questions are inextricably intertwined' (1995: xiii: see also 63–64): see Fricker (1998: 169–170) for discussion of Code and this example.
6 As noted in Chapter 2, Williams's example is a somewhat tricky one to classify in this respect, since as Dotson (2012: 27) reads it, it involved elements of both imputed incompetence and imputed insincerity.
7 See Curry (2017). Fricker observes that this is how Atticus Finch seems to understand the jurors' psychology (2007: 25–26), which is one point to take into account, but doesn't settle the matter by itself.
8 See Smith (2020: Chapter 23) and McGlynn (forthcoming: Section 4) for discussion of the way that viewing certain groups as inherently criminal and violent leads to the treatment of members of that group as interchangeable when it comes to punishment for particular (alleged) crimes.
9 However, this doesn't seem to be a feature of all cases of testimonial injustice; for example, there are plausibly cases of 'intra-group' testimonial injustice (see Grabelsky 2023 and Tobi 2023).
10 Recall that this is the second species of epistemic injustice Fricker identifies, involving speakers facing obstacles to making themselves understood, due to a lack of fitting shared interpretive resources.
11 See Medina (2013: Chapter 2) and Pohlhaus (2012); I discuss their points (and some differences between them) in detail in Chapter 10.
12 See Doan (2017) for a real-life example of structural testimonial injustice, though Doan argues that it doesn't quite conform to Fricker or Anderson's accounts.
13 Readers who want to stay focused on Fricker's account can skip over Section 5 to the end of this chapter.
14 I follow Barnes (2016: 5–6) in using 'disabled people' and avoiding 'person-first' language such as 'people with disabilities,' though I'm aware not everyone has the same preferences on this.
15 Singer defends this view in Singer (1979), amongst other places.
16 There are various competing conceptions of adaptive preferences; Barnes (2016: 123–128) surveys these, and argues that the one given in the text, due in essentials to Amartya Sen and Martha Nussbaum, underwrites the strongest version of the argument against taking disability-positive testimony seriously.

17 Recall Collins's observation, discussed in Chapter 4, that the controlling images of oppressed groups make pervasive forms of injustice 'appear to be natural, normal, and inevitable parts of everyday life' (2000: 76–77).
18 Barnes doesn't deny that disabled people also face more straightforward kinds of testimonial injustice that pattern more clearly with Fricker's examples, of course.
19 I'm not clear on whether we should think of the prejudices Barnes identifies as identity prejudices in Fricker's sense; that strikes me as an interesting but tricky question.
20 It's less clear that this point holds for the example from *To Kill a Mockingbird*, since it is not just Robinson's testimony that is found incredible, but also Atticus Finch's related conjectures and accusations (Pohlhaus 2012: 725). I'll come back to this example very shortly.
21 Thanks to Matthew Cull. There's a question here about who the injustice is done to, in such cases; is it my friend's wife, or my friend's wife and my friend who repeats what he has learned from his wife? I won't try to settle this here.
22 In fact, Barnes is committed to there being hermeneutical injustice involved in the rejection of disability-positive testimony, though she doesn't explicitly recognise this point. She argues that the prejudices about disability and disabled people mentioned in the text (for example, that disability is tragic) are aspects of the 'dominant understanding of disability,' and since this understanding is distorting, 'the experience of thriving disabled people becomes obscured and difficult to understand' which amounts to 'hermeneutical injustice for disabled people' (2016: 180). By Barnes's own lights, then, disability-positive testimony is an attempt to express something that will not be fully intelligible to those in the grip of the dominant understanding of disability, and this is a form of hermeneutical injustice.

REFERENCES

Altanian, Melanie and Maria Baghramian (eds.). 2023. *Testimonial Injustice and Trust*. Oxon: Routledge.

Anderson, Elizabeth. 2012. 'Epistemic Justice as a Virtue of Social Institutions.' *Social Epistemology* 26 (2): 163–173. https://doi.org/10.1080/02691728.2011.652211

Barnes, Elizabeth. 2016. *The Minority Body: A Theory of Disability*. Oxford: Oxford University Press.

Battaly, Heather. 2019. 'Vice Epistemology Has a Responsibility Problem.' *Philosophical Issues* 29 (1): 24–36. https://doi.org/10.1111/phis.12138

Beeghly, Erin and Alex Madva (eds.). 2020. *An Introduction to Implicit Bias: Knowledge, Justice, and the Social Mind*. London: Routledge.

Borgoni, Cristina. 2019. 'Authority and Attribution: The Case of Epistemic Injustice in Self-Knowledge.' *Philosophia* 47 (2): 293–301. https://doi.org/10.1007/s11406-018-0002-x

Borgoni, Cristina. 2025. 'First-Person Authority and the Social Aspects of Self-Knowledge.' In Jennifer Lackey and Aidan McGlynn, ed. *The Oxford Handbook of Social Epistemology*: 679–696. New York: Oxford University Press.

Borgoni, Cristina. Forthcoming. 'First-Person Authority and Epistemic Injustice.' *Journal of Philosophical Research*.

Brownstein, Michael and Jennifer Saul (eds.). 2016. *Implicit Bias and Philosophy Volume 2: Moral Responsibility, Structural Injustice, and Ethics*. Oxford and New York: Oxford University Press.

Carter, J. Adam. 2025. 'Trust and Its Significance in Social Epistemology.' In Jennifer Lackey and Aidan McGlynn, eds. *The Oxford Handbook of Social Epistemology*: 182–200. New York: Oxford University Press.

Carter, Matilda. 2023. 'Minority Minds: Mental Disability and the Presumption of Value Neutrality.' *Journal of Applied Philosophy* 40 (2): 358–375. https://doi.org/10.1111/japp.12636

Cassam, Quassim. 2019. *Vices of the Mind: From the Intellectual to the Political*. Oxford: Oxford University Press.

Coady, C. A. J. 1992. *Testimony: A Philosophical Study*. Oxford: Oxford University Press.

Code, Lorraine. 1995. *Rhetorical Spaces: Essays on Gendered Locations*. New York: Routledge.

Collins, Patricia Hills. 2000. *Black Feminist Thought: Knowledge, Consciousness, and the Politics of Empowerment* (Second Edition). New York and Oxon: Routledge.

Curry, Tommy J. 2017. 'This N*****'s Broken: Hyper-masculinity, the Buck, and the Role of Physical Disability in White Anxiety toward the Black Male Body.' *Journal of Social Philosophy* 48 (3): 321–343. https://doi.org/10.1111/josp.12193

Davis, Emmalon. 2021. 'A Tale of Two Injustices: Epistemic Injustice in Philosophy.' In Jennifer Lackey, ed. *Applied Epistemology*: 215–250. New York: Oxford University Press.

Dembroff, Robin and Dennis Whitcomb. 2022. 'Content-Focused Epistemic Injustice.' In Tamar Szabó Gender, John Hawthorne, and Julianne Chung, eds. *Oxford Studies in Epistemology*, vol. 7: 48–70. New York: Oxford University Press.

Doan, Michael. 2017. 'Epistemic Injustice and Epistemic Redlining.' *Ethics and Social Welfare* 11 (2): 177–190. https://doi.org/10.1080/17496535.2017.1293120

Dotson, Kristie. 2012. 'A Cautionary Tale: On Limiting Epistemic Oppression.' *Frontiers: A Journal of Women Studies* 33 (1): 24–47. https://doi.org/10.1353/fro.2012.a472779

Fricker, Elizabeth. 1995. 'Telling and Trusting: Reductionism and Anti-Reductionism in the Epistemology of Testimony.' *Mind* 104 (414): 393–411. https://doi.org/10.1093/mind/104.414.393

Fricker, Miranda. 1998. 'Rational Authority and Social Power: Towards a Truly Social Epistemology.' *Proceedings of the Aristotelian Society* 98 (2): 159–177. https://doi.org/10.1111/1467-9264.00030

Fricker, Miranda. 2007. *Epistemic Injustice: Power and the Ethics of Knowing*. Oxford: Oxford University Press.

Fricker, Miranda. 2016. 'Fault and No-Fault Responsibility for Implicit Prejudice: A Space for Epistemic 'Agent-Regret'.' In Michael Brady and Miranda Fricker, eds. *The Epistemic Life of Groups: Essays in the Epistemology of Collectives*: 33–50. Oxford and New York: Oxford University Press.

Goldberg, Sanford. 2010. 'Comments on Miranda Fricker's *Epistemic Injustice*.' *Episteme* 7 (2): 138–150. https://doi.org/10.3366/epi.2010.0004

Grabelsky, Dana. 2023. 'Intra-Group Epistemic Injustice: Jewish Identity, Whiteness, and Zionism.' *Social Epistemology* 37 (6): 810–823. https://doi.org/10.1080/02691728.2023.2245773

Hannon, Michael and Elise Woodard. 2025. *Political Epistemology: An Introduction*. Oxon and New York: Routledge.

Hawley, Katherine. 2017. 'Trust, Distrust, and Epistemic Injustice.' In Ian James Kidd, José Medina, and Gaile Pohlhaus Jr., eds. *The Routledge Handbook of Epistemic Injustice*: 69–78. Oxon and New York: Routledge.

Hawley, Katherine. 2019. *How to Be Trustworthy*. Oxford: Oxford University Press.

Hiller, Avram. 2023. 'How Does Disability Affect Wellbeing? A Literature Review and Philosophical Analysis.' *Journal of Philosophy of Disability* 3: 7–46. https://doi.org/10.5840/jpd2023101823

Lackey, Jennifer. 2008. *Learning from Words: Testimony as a Source of Knowledge*. Oxford: Oxford University Press.

Lagewaard, Thirza. 2021. 'Epistemic Injustice and Deepened Disagreement.' *Philosophical Studies* 178 (5): 1571–1592. https://doi.org/10.1007/s11098-020-01496-x

Lee, Harper. 1960. *To Kill a Mockingbird*. London: Arrow Books.

Manne, Kate. 2018. *Down Girl: The Logic of Misogyny*. Oxford: Oxford University Press.

McGlynn, Aidan. 2023. 'Hidden Depths: Testimonial Injustice, Deep Disagreement, and Democratic Deliberation.' *International Journal of Philosophical Studies* 31 (3): 361–381. https://doi.org/10.1080/09672559.2023.2263710

McGlynn, Aidan. 2024. 'Making Life More Interesting: Trust, Trustworthiness, and Testimonial Injustice.' *Philosophical Psychology* 37 (1): 126–147. https://doi.org/10.1080/09515089.2022.2133695

McGlynn, Aidan. Forthcoming. 'Epistemic Objectification in Pornography.' *The Philosophical Quarterly*. https://doi.org/10.1093/pq/pqaf032

McKenna, Robin. 2023. *Non-Ideal Epistemology*. Oxford: Oxford University Press.

Medina, José. 2013. *The Epistemology of Resistance: Gender and Racial Oppression, Epistemic Injustice, and Resistant Imaginations*. Oxford: Oxford University Press.

Minghella, Anthony. 2000. *The Talented Mr. Ripley—Based on Patricia Highsmith's Novel*. London: Methuen.

Nadelhoffer, Thomas. 2022. 'Chronic Pain, Mere-Differences, and Disability Variantism.' *Journal of Philosophy of Disability* 2: 6–27. https://doi.org/10.5840/jpd20223110

Nagel, Jennifer. 2014. *Knowledge: A Very Short Introduction*. Oxford: Oxford University Press.

Piovarchy, Adam. 2020. 'Responsibility for Testimonial Injustice.' *Philosophical Studies* 178: 597–615. https://doi.org/10.1007/s11098-020-01447-6

Pohlhaus Jr., Gaile. 2012. 'Relational Knowing and Epistemic Injustice: Towards a Theory of *Willful Hermeneutical Ignorance*.' *Hypatia* 27: 715–735. https://doi.org/10.1111/j.1527-2001.2011.01222.x

Reynolds, Joel Michael and Kevin Timpe. 2025. 'Disability and Social Epistemology.' In Jennifer Lackey and Aidan McGlynn, eds. *The Oxford Handbook of Social Epistemology*: 513–531. New York: Oxford University Press.

Riggs, Wayne. 2012. 'Culpability for Epistemic Injustice: Deontic or Aretetic?' *Social Epistemology* 26 (2): 149–162. https://doi.org/10.1080/02691728.2011.652210

Singer, Peter. 1979. *Practical Ethics*. Cambridge: Cambridge University Press.

Smith, David Livingstone. 2020. *On Inhumanity: Dehumanization and How to Resist It*. New York: Oxford University Press.

Táíwò, Olúfẹ́mi. 2022. *Elite Capture: How the Powerful Took over Identity Politics (and Everything Else)*. London: Pluto Press.

Tanesini, Alessandra. 2021. *The Mismeasure of the Self*. Oxford: Oxford University Press.

Tobi, Abraham. 2023. 'Intra-Group Epistemic Injustice.' *Social Epistemology* 37 (6): 798–809. https://doi.org/10.1080/02691728.2023.2182653

Tremain, Shelley. 2017. 'Knowing Disability, Differently.' In Ian James Kidd, José Medina, and Gaile Pohlhaus Jr., eds. *The Routledge Handbook of Epistemic Injustice*: 175–184. Oxon: Routledge.

van Woudenberg, René. 2021. *The Epistemology of Reading and Interpretation*. Cambridge: Cambridge University Press.

Wright, Crispin. 1998. 'Self-Knowledge: The Wittgensteinian Legacy.' In Crispin Wright, Barry Smith, and Cynthia MacDonald, eds. *Knowing Our Own Minds*: 13–46. Oxford: Oxford University Press.

6

TESTIMONIAL INJUSTICE, PREJUDICES, AND CREDIBILITY DEFICITS AND EXCESSES

6.1 INTRODUCTION

Miranda Fricker's account of testimonial injustice has been hugely influential, to the point that there often seems to be little room for disagreement. To reject Fricker's notion of testimonial injustice and the philosophical framework she embeds it in can often seem tantamount to denying that examples like the three we looked at in the previous chapter—Patricia Williams, Marge Sherwood, and Tom Robinson—illustrate any genuine phenomenon. The examples are often simply presented *as* examples of testimonial injustice in Fricker's sense, with little to no discussion. Alternative accounts of the kind of phenomenon illustrated by the examples seem to be treated as merely offering slightly different labels to pin to things.

Given what I've said in Part 1 of this book, it will come as little surprise to the reader that I think that way of approaching the study of testimonial injustice is a mistake. We can accept that the kinds of examples of testimonial dysfunction we've been discussing are significant and illustrate a relatively unified phenomenon without thereby adopting Fricker's particular account of testimonial injustice as involving a speaker receiving a prejudicial credibility deficit.

My aim in this chapter isn't to try to demonstrate that Fricker's characterisation of testimonial injustice is mistaken, or to convince you that you shouldn't accept it. Rather, the point is that her account isn't just a neutral description of those examples. It needs to be recognised as a piece of philosophical theorising that makes certain decisions and assumptions about what it is about those examples that we should draw attention to and take to be the basis of a theoretically important category, and what are irrelevant details that we can abstract away from. These choices and assumptions can be disputed, and they may have consequences that we find implausible, even if we remain convinced that the examples deserve our attention. In the remainder of this chapter, I will bring this out by raising four deceptively simple-looking questions about Fricker's definition:

- What is a credibility deficit? (Section 6.2)
- Should we pay so much attention to credibility deficits? (Section 6.3)
- Can credibility *excesses* also be testimonial injustices? (Section 6.4)
- Should we pay so much attention to prejudices? (Section 6.5)

Looking at how Fricker answers these questions will bring out some of the most distinctive and controversial aspects of her account of testimonial injustice, aspects that have too often been overlooked when people have discussed, applied, and taught it. In the following chapter, we'll look at Kristie Dotson's alternative theoretical framework, which answers many of the questions quite differently; that's one reason to think that it's a mistake to take Doston to be offering essentially the same philosophical framework with different labels.

6.2 WHAT IS A CREDIBILITY DEFICIT?

Section 5.2 of the previous chapter said something about what prejudices are for Fricker, and how they infiltrate our testimonial practices, giving rise to testimonial injustice. The other aspect of Fricker's definition that we need to understand is what a credibility deficit is. This can seem obvious enough; it's when a speaker receives less credibility or trust than they ought to when offering testimony to an audience. On second thoughts, though, this raises an obvious question. What determines how much credibility a speaker ought to get on a given occasion? Or put differently, when a speaker receives a credibility deficit, what is it a deficit with respect to? As Jennifer Lackey observes, it is helpful to know what a proper assessment of a speaker's credibility looks like if we're trying to understand what an improper assessment involves (Lackey 2023: 10).

The answer to this question is frequently left implicit or metaphorical in discussions of testimonial injustice, including in Fricker's work; for example, Fricker often writes that in testimonial injustice, the speaker receives a 'deflated' degree of credibility (e.g. 2007: 1), which is both metaphorical and leaves open the question 'deflated from what?'. Less metaphorically she also characterises a prejudicial credibility deficit as when 'prejudice on the hearer's part causes him to give the speaker less credibility than he would otherwise have done' (2007: 4). This suggests that a credibility deficit is a deficit relative to the amount of credibility the hearer *would* have given the speaker if, counterfactually, he hadn't relied on a prejudice in coming to a credibility judgement about her: but by itself this still doesn't give us any sense of what determines how much credibility a speaker ought to receive in a given case.

Here's a natural thought. In Chapter 2, we separated challenges to how credible a subject is into doubts about how competent the speaker is and how sincere they are, and we've seen in the previous chapter that Fricker also makes this separation. We might suggest, then, that what fixes how believable a subject is are facts about how competent and sincere they actually are on the question at hand. A speaker who is in fact mistaken or has only gotten the right answer by sheer luck, or who is in fact attempting to mislead their audience, merits a low degree of credibility. A speaker who has in fact been both epistemically responsible in forming their belief and sincere when reporting it to their audience merits a high degree of credibility, even if they happen to have gotten things wrong on this occasion. Another way to put the idea here is that a speaker is credible on some particular topic to the degree that they reliably speak the truth about it. A credibility deficit can then be understood as a speaker being taken to be less reliable than they *in fact* are when offering testimony to an audience on a particular occasion.

We find an account of this sort in a predecessor to Fricker's discussion of testimonial injustice. Trudy Govier (1993) points out the possibility of mismatches between a person's 'normative credibility'—how worthy they in fact are of being believed when testifying—and their 'rhetorical credibility,' which is the degree to which their audience regards them as worthy of being believed. Govier notes that such mismatches can be due to stereotypes and prejudices against certain groups of people (1993: 94–95), and she offers as her central example of this the dismissal of Anita Hill's testimony during the Hill-Thomas hearings in 1991, which came up in Chapter 4. On Govier's analysis, Hill had a very low degree of rhetorical credibility when testifying that she had been sexually harassed by Clarence Thomas, despite her high degree of normative credibility, and this gap opened up due to the predominant prejudices against Black women circulating in America in the early 1990s; think back to the system of 'controlling images' of Black women that Patricia Hill Collins analysed and criticised, as we discussed in that earlier chapter.

It's crucial to understanding Fricker's account of testimonial injustice to realise that this is not at all how she is thinking of credibility deficits. As I've already complained, Fricker is prone to leaving the notion vague and unspecified, but she does commit herself to a more substantive account in a passing remark in her book:

> Unlike those goods that are fruitfully dealt with along distributive lines (such as wealth or health care), there is no puzzle about the fair distribution of credibility, for credibility is a concept that wears its proper distribution on its sleeve. Epistemological nuance aside, the hearer's obligation is obvious: she must match the level of credibility she attributes to her interlocutor to the evidence that he is offering the truth.
>
> (Fricker 2007: 19)

For a speaker to receive a credibility deficit, on this view, is for her to receive less credibility from her audience than is supported by the evidence that the audience has concerning whether the speaker is telling the truth. Following the literature, let's call this Fricker's *evidentialist* account of credibility deficits.[1] It's important to recognise that 'evidence' is being used rather expansively here. It includes specific information you have about the speaker and what they are saying, background information you have about the topic which their testimony might cohere with or make improbable, information about the track-record of the speaker as a testifier on this topic or in general, information about their degree of relevant expertise or lack thereof, what they've said on previous occasions, observations you have made about their current appearance and mood (whether they seem nervous, angry, calm and collected, suspicious, focused, or distracted), and so on. However, the relevant evidence can't only include such information, since as we've already discussed, Fricker thinks that we often find ourselves weighing up testimony with only limited information of this sort. So the 'evidence' that hearers should match their credibility judgements to needs to include the kinds of stereotypes discussed in Section 5.2 of the previous chapter, since we saw that the role of such stereotypes is to fill in the gaps in the evidence we frequently have about particular speakers. However, *prejudicial* stereotypes don't count as evidence, since they distort our credibility judgements away from where our evidence says those judgements ought to be. Testimonial injustice occurs when some of the stereotypes a hearer relies on are prejudicial and lead to the hearer lowering their confidence in the truth of what they are told below where it ought to be in light of the evidence, so understood.

An example will help to bring out the difference between this evidentialist account of what a credibility deficit involves and the kind of account I attributed to Govier above. Consider a scrupulously honest used-car salesman, who draws on his vast knowledge about cars to offer expert and well-meaning advice to all of his potential customers, but who finds himself frequently accused of trying to trick people into buying vehicles which are unsafe, overpriced, or otherwise against their interests (Fricker 2007: 42). Supposing that the stereotype that used-car salesmen are unscrupulous and dishonest really is generally reliable, and so not a mere prejudice, should we say that our exception to that rule receives a credibility deficit when his advice is dismissed? Understood along the lines suggested by Govier, the answer is plausibly affirmative; his degree of rhetorical credibility is much lower than it ought to be, as given by his degree of normative credibility. However, Fricker's evidentialist account gives the opposite verdict; those who regard his advice with suspicion based on the stereotype about his profession are judging his credibility as they ought, in line with the evidence they have (assuming that they don't have any specific evidence about his honesty that should make them rethink the applicability of the stereotype in this instance). More generally, the two accounts will differ in cases in which the available evidence about how reliable someone's testimony is is misleading; in such cases, Fricker holds that the hearer judges as they ought even if they give the speaker far less credibility than their degree of normative credibility in Govier's sense would suggest they are owed.

Fricker clearly takes her evidentialist conception of credibility deficits to be obviously correct, which perhaps explains why she barely mentions it in her book, and doesn't argue for it beyond the somewhat cryptic quoted remark that 'credibility is a concept that wears its proper distribution on its sleeve' (2007: 19). To try to see what Fricker means by this, we might draw an analogy to the concept of being funny. To be funny is partly a matter of getting a certain reaction or response to your attempts to be humorous; someone who is never found funny by anyone isn't funny—they are, we'd say, just 'trying to be funny.' While being funny isn't just a matter of getting a certain response—we typically allow that people can laugh inappropriately at something that's 'not funny'—the response does seem to be a crucial component. Being funny can't come radically apart from being found funny. I think in saying that credibility wears its proper distribution on its sleeve, Fricker is making a similar point: that being credible involves not just being competent and sincere, but also inducing a certain response in one's audience, that of finding the speaker credible. Being credible and being found credible can't come radically apart either. If that's right, it's an objection to anything in the vicinity of Govier's notion of normative credibility (since it does seem like you can have a high degree of normative credibility in this sense even if no one ever recognises this), and it's perhaps a relatively short step to the conclusion that what determines how much credibility a hearer should give a speaker is the evidence they have to go on, rather than on potentially inaccessible facts about how reliably competent and sincere the speaker in fact is.

Still, this all seems a bit more involved and potentially controversial than Fricker's brief claims about what's 'obvious' might justify. Moreover, her evidentialist account of credibility deficits has attracted a significant amount of criticism from other philosophers, suggesting that she was too quick to conclude that there's no puzzle concerning how to understand how much credibility a hearer ought to give a speaker (and so what counts as a deficit).

Several philosophers have objected to Fricker's evidentialist conception on the grounds that it fails to accommodate cases in which a speaker receives a degree of credibility that accords with the evidence that they are telling the truth, and yet in which there is (it is contended) still testimonial injustice present. For example, suppose that I give a speaker the level of credibility that my evidence suggests they should receive on some topic. However, I simultaneously give someone else (myself perhaps) considerably more credibility that my evidence warrants; I award them a *credibility excess*. While it's true that I've matched the credibility I give the speaker to the evidence I've got, I've unfairly left them at a comparative disadvantage when it comes to credibility on the topic in question. Have I really satisfied my epistemic obligations to the speaker? Jennifer Lackey (2018) argues that I have not, but that Fricker's account of credibility deficits lacks the resources to say what I've done wrong.[2]

Another problem for Fricker's evidentialist account was originally identified by Katherine Hawley, though the version of it I'll present here is my own modification.[3] Let's assume that it's a reliable stereotype that Americans are not dependable sources about the pronunciation of Scottish place names. Suppose now that you hear an American telling some people to pronounce 'Glasgow' as 'Glaz-go.' You don't have independent evidence that would settle the matter one way or the other, and you also don't have much information about the particular American speaking; from what you can tell, he seems well-intentioned and well-educated and his testimony on other aspects of Scotland and Scottish life demonstrates some familiarity with it. Still, it seems like Scottish-place-name-pronunciation could be something of an Achilles' heel, given what you know about Americans in general. The evidence doesn't clearly support either a favourable or an unfavourable credibility judgement, but there also doesn't seem to be a single right way for you to weigh up these different pieces and types of evidence.[4] In such cases, it seems permissible to give more weight to the fact that he's American and to withhold judgement, but also permissible to give the speaker the benefit of the doubt, given that you have no evidence that's specific to this speaker to think he's wrong, and he impresses as knowledgeable about related matters. Your evidence leaves some leeway concerning how much credibility to give his testimony on this matter; you can satisfy Fricker's evidentialist requirement in different ways, each of which seems epistemically responsible and permissible.

However, let's further suppose that you are disposed to *always* weigh the fact that a person is American heavily against their testimony in cases in which it would be permissible to give them the benefit of the doubt, while you are disposed to give people of other nationalities the benefit of the doubt whenever you can. In reaching an unfavourable credibility judgement on this basis, you might not rely on any stereotypes that are themselves prejudiced, but there seems to be a kind of prejudice manifested by your dispositions nonetheless. It's tempting to say that there's a sense in which you have given this particular American less credibility than you ought to have, due to prejudice, but this isn't to be understood in terms of you giving a lower degree of credibility than fits the evidence you have, since as we described the example the low degree of credibility you give them *does* fit your evidence. It's just that there was a more generous way to comply with Fricker's evidentialist account open to you, one that would be more consistent with how you would judge a non-American in similar circumstances, and you didn't take that option.[5]

Both Lackey's examples and this one are, on the face of it, rather abstract and hypothetical. That said, they are not particularly far-fetched, and so there's reason to think they describe genuine forms that credibility deficits can take. Indeed, Lackey has more recently argued that many of the actual instances of testimonial injustice generated by features of the criminal justice system take these forms (Lackey 2023: Chapter 1).[6] Given this, these kinds of examples do serve to put pressure on the evidentialist account that Fricker offers. While the notion of a credibility deficit may seem clear and unproblematic enough when it is left vague, the problems raised for Fricker's particular evidentialist understanding of it raises concerns about whether it can really be a central notion in our understanding of testimonial injustice.

6.3 SHOULD WE PAY SO MUCH ATTENTION TO CREDIBILITY DEFICITS?

Perhaps the notion of a credibility deficit can be clarified in a way that avoids the problems raised in the previous section, or perhaps those problems can be explained away without forcing any modification to Fricker's evidentialist conception. Rather than address those issues in more detail, I want to turn to our second question: should we be paying so much attention to credibility deficits in the first place? Should they really be part of the definition of testimonial injustice?

It seems hard to question that the examples from Chapter 2 that Fricker takes to illustrate testimonial injustice involve speakers receiving less credibility than they are due (however exactly we understand that), where this is because their audiences harbour identity prejudices. That said, that this description fits the examples doesn't show that this is the right feature of those examples to pick out as theoretically important; this is another instance of a general point about theorising that I stressed in Chapter 3.

An alternative proposal is that the key feature of the examples is that they involve an audience prejudicially failing to recognise a speaker as speaking from knowledge. For instance, Tom Robinson tries to share his knowledge concerning his relationship with Mayella Ewell and what really happened on the day she claims he raped her, and while the jurors presumably take Robinson to know the truth about these things, they don't regard his testimony as expressing that knowledge because they prejudicially take him to be lying. They fail to recognise him as a knower with respect to the testimony he offers to them. In cases in which it's the speaker's competence, rather than their sincerity that's called into question, the hearer won't recognise the speaker as having relevant knowledge they could share.

It's important to recognise that this isn't merely an alternative way to describe what happens when a speaker receives a prejudicial credibility deficit, though my impression is that the literature is not always clear on this point. There will be considerable overlap between cases in which a speaker prejudicially receives less credibility that they are due and cases in which a speaker tries to share their knowledge via testimony and their audience prejudicially fails to recognise the speaker as speaking from knowledge, but these aren't merely superficially different formulations of the same basic idea, and they don't always agree on whether a particular example involves testimonial injustice (Luzzi 2016). There are a number of different kinds of cases which bring this out, but let's briefly consider two.

The first starts from Fricker's own observation that a speaker can receive a prejudicial credibility deficit even if her testimony is accepted by her prejudiced audience (2007: 17).[7] Such cases will involve a speaker receiving a relatively high degree of credibility when testifying, but not as much as they are due. This points to the possibility of cases involving hearers who correctly recognise a testifying speaker as expressing their knowledge, and who accept that testimony, but who nonetheless prejudicially lower their confidence in that speaker's testimony (Piovarchy 2020: 610; McGlynn 2021: 163). For instance, a sexist might grudgingly accept the testimony of a woman on a topic typically regarded as a masculine domain—football, or engineering, or philosophy for that matter—failing to recognise that her testimony reflects her expertise concerning the subject matter at hand. He recognises her testimony as expressing her knowledge, but were it not for his sexist prejudices, he would rightly be even more confident than he is that she is right.

The second kind of case involves a speaker making true claims on the basis of evidence that clearly isn't sufficient for her to have knowledge, but receiving a credibility deficit due to the hearer's prejudices (Gerken 2019: 2; McGlynn 2021: 163). In the previous chapter, I suggested that Marge Sherwood may be an example of this type. It's really not always clear that Sherwood is expressing knowledge when she voices her suspicions about Tom Ripley concerning her fiancé's disappearance. When she says to Ripley, with her fiancé's father Herbert Greenleaf listening, 'You killed Dickie! I know it was you!,' we needn't take her self-ascription of knowledge to be correct in order to think that Greenleaf commits a testimonial injustice by dismissing what she says entirely on the basis of sexist prejudices. She is voicing a reasonable and well-founded suspicion, and Greenleaf fails to take her as seriously as he should—he fails to give her as much credibility as she is due—even if he would be right to deny she has knowledge. So it's a mistake to think that a speaker receiving a credibility deficit from an audience is just the same as their audience failing to recognise them as speaking from knowledge; these are distinct proposals. Moreover, it looks like the second proposal doesn't comfortably fit one of Fricker's principal examples—indeed, the very example that she uses to introduce the notion of testimonial injustice in her book (2007: 7)—which seems like a significant strike against it. We'll return to this issue in the next chapter.[8]

6.4 CAN CREDIBILITY EXCESSES ALSO BE TESTIMONIAL INJUSTICES?

Credibility deficits involve a person getting less credibility than they ought when testifying (though we've already seen there are issues hiding in the idea of 'getting less than they ought' here). The opposite can also happen, as we've already noted; a person can receive a credibility *excess*, where their audience awards them an undeservedly high degree of credibility. Suppose that someone receives a credibility excess, perhaps due to prejudices held by their audience. Could this be a case of testimonial injustice? Fricker's characterisation rules this out; as we have seen, testimonial injustices involve, by definition, credibility deficits. This is no accident or oversight. When Fricker first introduced the notion of testimonial injustice (Fricker 1998), she was explicitly open to the possibility that credibility excesses might count as cases, and she deliberately distances herself from that prior position in her book. Her reason for ruling out credibility excesses as testimonial injustices is that they typically attach to people in positions of relative privilege, and tend to benefit those people even further. Fricker does acknowledge that someone who is rarely doubted or challenged may be epistemically harmed in the long term; the cumulative effect may be that they develop a kind of arrogance, for example. Moreover, Fricker is willing to accept that this may be a 'special case' of testimonial injustice (2007: 20–21). However, she wants to reserve the label for cases in which there is an *immediate* wrong done to the speaker in their role as an epistemic agent, and she takes this to mean that only credibility deficits really count as testimonial injustices.[9]

Much of the subsequent literature has suggested that Fricker grants too little significance to credibility excesses, and that her initial position on this issue may have been more defensible than the one she adopts later in her 2007 book. There are two different versions of this point, which need to be carefully distinguished. According to the first version, Fricker restricts her definition of testimonial injustice to credibility deficits because she always locates the injustice in the speaker's situation at a particular instant, failing to sufficiently acknowledge the way that testimonial injustice really involves a series of related judgements across a range of different speakers within a testimonial exchange that is extended over time. The second version alleges that there are cases in which a particular speaker faces a testimonial injustice *by being given a credibility excess* (and not merely because we have broadened our gaze beyond an individual speaker at a particular instant). Let's take each version in turn.

When Fricker weighs up whether to include credibility excesses as testimonial injustices, she focuses on how receiving such an excess bears on the situation and character of the person who receives it, 'the speaker.' Part of her reason for this focus stems from her rejection of a distributive model of injustice for credibility. As discussed in Chapter 3, Fricker doesn't think that the epistemic injustices she focuses on should be thought of as involving an unjust distribution of goods or opportunities. At a given moment, there is only so much food, water, shelter, medicine, and only so many hospital beds, doctor appointments, spots at universities, etc. to go around, so that if one person or group gets too much—more than their fair share—that means that others will get too little. Fricker (2007: 19–20) argues that in various respects, credibility isn't like this. It's not a finite good that we need to puzzle over how to divide up fairly; we just need to ensure everyone gets their due (which, as discussed earlier in this chapter, Fricker conceives of as the amount of credibility that matches the available evidence that each person is telling the truth). It's this picture of unjust credibility deficits that leads Fricker to think that we can zoom in on what's going on with the speaker and the prejudices their audience hold about them to determine whether there's a testimonial injustice or not.

Medina agrees with Fricker that credibility isn't a finite good or opportunity that we need to find a fair way to share out, like food or doctor appointments. However, he thinks it's a mistake to draw the conclusion from this that Fricker does, that we can focus in on a single speaker and the evidence available to her audience that she is telling the truth and figure out just from that whether there's an testimonial injustice. Although credibility isn't a finite good, Medina holds that assigning it justly involves offering the different speakers in an exchange a *proportionate* share of credibility. We can illustrate what he means by considering one of Jennifer Lackey's examples that we discussed earlier in the chapter. Let's fill out the example a little, along the lines indicated by Lackey (2018). Suppose I'm party to a conversation about a subject that's typically regarded as a masculine domain with five other men and one woman. When the woman speaks, I listen attentively to what she has to say, and I'm careful to guard against the possibility that I have unduly dismissed her contributions or prejudicially regarded them with suspicion, and my efforts pay off—the degree of credibility I give what she says matches my evidence she is speaking truly. However, I systematically inflate the amount of credibility I award to the men, including myself, when we speak. Her contributions are good; ours are ingenious, mind-blowing, game-changing, and so on.[10] In such a case, Lackey invites us to share the judgement that I have not done as I should by the woman in this group, even though I met the evidentialist criterion that Fricker offers.

Medina's diagnosis of what's gone wrong in examples like this is that I have given the men in the exchange a disproportionately high degree of credibility, while the woman is getting a disproportionately small degree given her 'epistemic capacities and assets' (Medina 2013: 62), and this is a testimonial injustice. Medina and Lackey both maintain that even though credibility isn't a finite resource, it's still the case in a particular communicative setting that the way that the contributions of some speakers are overly esteemed is linked to the way that those of others are relatively under esteemed, and that Fricker doesn't properly reckon with this point. Moreover, it leads her to mistakenly think that we can determine whether there's a testimonial injustice in a given case just by looking for a mismatch between the credibility given to a particular disadvantaged speaker and the evidence she is telling the truth.

Medina illustrates his alternative picture by re-examining some details of Fricker's own example, the courthouse scenes in To Kill a Mockingbird. He argues that Tom Robinson's difficulties in being perceived as credible are partly due to the credibility excess that the white jurors (and the courtroom more generally) grants to his principal accuser, Mayella Ewell, not to mention the prosecutor, Mr Gilmer (2013: 65–66). Medina's claim that credibility assessments are implicitly relational in this fashion has been influential, particularly on feminist philosophers who have appealed to the notion of testimonial injustice to explain some of the dynamics that often occur when women accuse relatively privileged and powerful men of sexual assault. In stark contrast to a disabled, poor Black man like Tom Robinson, such men are frequently given, not just the benefit of the doubt, but outsized levels of sympathy and credibility—what Kate Manne (2018) calls 'himpathy.' The credibility excesses received by such men when they are accused of sexual misconduct contributes to the corresponding credibility deficits experienced by their accusers (Yap 2017; Manne 2018: Chapter 6).

As already noted, there is room for a quite different challenge to Fricker's downplaying of credibility excesses. Medina's response implicitly concedes a key point to Fricker, namely that an individual speaker who receives a credibility excess doesn't thereby experience a testimonial injustice. It's only by broadening out to include other speakers, those caught up in an audience's comparative assessments of credibility, that Medina is able to make the argument that credibility excesses can be a form of testimonial injustice. A less concessive challenge to Fricker would make the case that a speaker receiving a credibility excess can be a testimonial injustice *for that very speaker*: that receiving a credibility excess can harm a speaker in their capacity as an epistemic agent there and then (and not merely cumulatively, as in the kinds of examples Fricker treats as 'special cases' of testimonial injustice).

Is this possible? Several philosophers have argued that it is, so let's look at some of the examples they've offered. The first comes from Emmalon Davis.

> Math Help: A group of American high-school students struggle to complete a difficult algebra question during their lunch period. After several failed attempts to solve the problem among themselves, the students decide to seek outside help. The students have heard that Asian-Americans are particularly good at math, so they ask an Asian-American student seated nearby for help with the problem.
>
> (Davis 2016: 487)

In this example, a so-called 'positive stereotype' associated with a particular social group means that particular speakers who belong to that group are treated as overly authoritative on certain subjects.[11] Davis also offers examples in which one person is wrongly treated as a kind of 'spokesperson' for the whole group; consider the phenomenon pointed out by bell hooks, whereby the testimony of one Black person is taken to be representative of Black people as a whole:

> All too often in our society, it is assumed that one can know all there is to know about black people by merely hearing the life story and opinions of one black person.
>
> (2015: 11)[12]

There may be contingent and cumulative epistemic harms associated with this kind of treatment; for example, the student may lose confidence in her own mathematical abilities, due to being unable to live up to the unfairly elevated expectations being imposed on her. But Davis's point is that there seems to be an immediate and inherent harm done to the speaker in her role as an epistemic agent. Exactly how to characterise this harm is a matter of some dispute (as we'll see in Chapter 11), but Davis's discussion suggests one plausible answer. The speakers in her examples are not treated as having anything distinctive to contribute by their testimony. Rather, they're treated as representative of a group of people who're regarded as homogeneous rather than as individuals with distinctive contributions to share; they're treated as epistemically *fungible* (Davis 2016: 488; McGlynn 2020, 2021).

A second, related kind of case of credibility excess that has been argued to be an instance of testimonial injustice requires us to think again about the controlling images of Black women that were introduced in our discussion of Patricia Hill Collins in Chapter 4. As we saw, Collins laid out and criticised an entire system of prejudicial stereotypes about Black women that function to limit their choices in life, to place the responsibility for any social disadvantages that they and their families face onto Black women themselves rather than onto prejudice or unjust social arrangements, and to prevent them from being seen as knowers on certain topics.[13] As in Davis's cases, such as Math Help, a flipside of these kinds of prejudices can be that Black women's testimony on particular topics might sometimes be given a credibility excess rather than a credibility deficit.

In a recent paper, Catalina Carpan (2022) looks at some cases that are particularly concerning, involving the 'adultification' of Black girls: the treatment and perception of them as older and more experienced and mature then they in fact are. This adultification interacts disastrously with the controlling image of Black women as hyper-sexual, leading to Black girls—teens and pre-teens—being prejudicially regarded and treated as sexually experienced and knowledgeable by law enforcement officers, lawyers, jurors, and others. This can lead to Black girls being given a credibility excess in legal contexts; their false testimony about matters relating to sex—rape, consent, trafficking, and so on—is given more weight that it ought to be, with the result that perpetrators of sexual violence may be given less severe punishments than they merit (2022: 797).

Finally, recall one of our initial examples of epistemic injustice in Chapter 2, Michael Ledford. As I write, Ledford is serving a 50-year prison sentence for first-degree murder and arson, following a fire that killed his one-year-old son. Ledford confessed to intentionally setting the fire, but as documented by Dina Nayeri (2023: 14–20), the confession was forced out of him through a variety of manipulation techniques, including interrogating him for hours longer than recommended, lying about having other evidence that incriminated him, exploiting his then-undiagnosed autism, including falsely promising him help for it if he confessed, and so on. Crucially, Ledford's interrogation is not an isolated case, but rather represents standard practice for American police; indeed, all of these practices, including lying about having other evidence and making false promises, are *legally permissible* in the United States.

In recent work, Jennifer Lackey (2020, 2023) has argued that these kinds of extracted confessions are then given a credibility excess. Confessions are often regarded as conclusive in legal contexts—as the 'gold standard' in evidence—and this means that they're treated as outweighing other physical evidence (however reliable), eye-witness testimony by others, and, most crucially here, the protestations of innocence by the same suspect before, during, and after the interrogation. Indeed, a confession on a single occasion can be treated as outweighing decades—sometimes an entire lifetime—of recantations of that confession. Lackey takes this to illustrate a form of testimonial injustice rather different to that characterised by Fricker. While Davis and Carpan's examples of credibility excess still turn on the role that identity prejudice is playing (even though this prejudice is producing an excess rather than a deficit of credibility), for Lackey, the key in her examples of forced confession is rather the way that the speaker's epistemic agency is 'denied or subverted in the obtaining of their testimony' (2020: 45). Lackey calls this *agential testimonial injustice*. As she notes, there is an injustice done to the confessor when their subsequent recantations are given less credibility than they deserve (2020: 59–60), but her thought is that they also face agential testimonial injustice when their confession is given a credibility excess. This is an injustice, on her account, because their testimony is only treated as having so much force because it has been extracted from them in conditions under which their epistemic agency has been denied or subverted.

Here's one way to see Lackey's thought. Why is it that confessions under interrogation are treated as so compelling? There's no single answer. Partly, it's because such confessions are self-incriminating, and there's an (entirely false) assumption that innocent people would never incriminate themselves in this fashion (2020: 65). But another important aspect of this is that interrogations are thought of as situations which strip away the suspect's capacity to exercise their epistemic agency in order to mislead their interrogators about what has happened and what they've done. The suspect's attempts to lie their way out are systematically shut down, until they have *no option* but to tell the truth. So their testimony is treated with suspicion until it is produced in a way that denies or subverts their epistemic agency, at which point is it treated as incontrovertible evidence of guilt. A credibility excess awarded to a speaker in this way disrespects and harms the speaker in their capacity as an epistemic agent:

> [O]ne is epistemically wronged by virtue of being regarded as a testifier—a giver of knowledge—only when one's testimony is extracted and is thus the product of a process that subverts one's epistemic agency.
>
> (Lackey 2020: 61)[14]

Davis, Carpan, and Lackey's examples suggest that not only was Fricker wrong to revise her characterisation of testimonial injustice to exclude credibility excesses, but that some of the most important applications of the notion of testimonial injustice may require us to adopt a more expansive conception. Of course, I don't mean to suggest that these examples from the literature are unchallengeable; no doubt, some philosophers will want to dispute whether they really count as instances of testimonial injustice.

Still, the examples collectively make a strong case for revising Fricker's definition to include *any* unjust mismatches between how much credibility a speaker receives from their audience and how much credibility they ought to receive, not just deficits.

6.5 SHOULD WE PAY SO MUCH ATTENTION TO PREJUDICES?

Lackey's discussion of agential testimonial injustice neatly brings us our fourth and final question for this chapter; should we really build it into our definition of testimonial injustice that it is due to prejudice? Lackey is not the first philosopher to downplay this aspect of Fricker's characterisation, and Fricker herself discusses a potential counterexample in her book that she credits to Penelope Mackie. Suppose that a speaker is offering an audience testimony, and the speaker doesn't belong to any social groups which their audience harbours prejudices towards. The speaker really has the knowledge he claims to have, and he's sincerely trying to share that knowledge. However, his audience fail to take him to be a credible testifier, due to the way he is acting; the speaker won't make eye contact with the audience, keeps pausing as if to figure out how best to spin a yarn, and generally comes across as insincere (2007: 41). In fact, this behaviour is a manifestation of discomfort at speaking to this audience rather than insincerity; nonetheless, since these really *are* often signs of insincerity, we might not think the audience's hesitation to accept the speaker's testimony is prejudicial.

This appears to be a case of testimonial injustice that doesn't involve any prejudice on the part of the speaker's audience, since we stipulated there are no identity prejudices at work, and the interpretation of the speaker as insincere seems to be reasonable rather than prejudicial, even though it's mistaken. However, Fricker denies that this is a case of testimonial injustice; the speaker is just subject to 'epistemic bad luck.' In such cases, the audience did all that anyone could ask of them—the audience 'has not put a foot wrong' (2007: 42)—but sometimes evidence is misleading. The speaker might still be harmed by having their testimony dismissed, but there's no wrong or injustice: harm, but no foul.

A number of philosophers have raised concerns about Fricker's willingness to chalk up these kinds of examples as ones of bad luck rather than epistemic injustice. For instance, Ishani Maitra offers an example which is a variant of the one discussed by Fricker, and which should remind the reader of 'Marie' from Chapter 2, the real-life case of a young woman who eventually confessed that her perfectly truthful account of being raped at knifepoint was false after being subject to a critical interrogation by two policemen.[15] In Maitra's variant,

> the speaker is a victim of a crime—say, a rape victim—and the hearer is a police officer to whom she is reporting her ordeal. Even granting that the stereotype here is genuinely reliable and nonprejudicial, if this police officer dismisses the victim merely because of her shifty manner, without making any further effort to check whether she is really lying, he (intuitively speaking) seems to commit a wrong against the victim.
>
> (2010: 203)

If we accept both Maitra's description of the example and her verdict about it, that suggests that some of the kinds of examples that Fricker would have us class as just epistemic bad luck in fact involve a speaker being wronged (not merely unluckily harmed) by their audience.

We might respond on Fricker's behalf by noting that even if 'shifty' behaviour is a reliable sign of lack of trustworthiness in the general population, it's not when we focus on survivors of sexual violence in particular, in which case the stereotype isn't 'genuinely reliable.' We might also worry that features of this particular example make this issue about reliability rather moot. A police officer who dismisses a rape victim's testimony on this kind of basis 'without making any further effort to check whether she is really lying' simply hasn't done their job; they have failed to discharge their role in even the most minimal sense. That means we should be cautious here, since our sense that the police officer has done badly by the speaker might be linked to their professional role, rather than indicating that they have wronged the speaker in a distinctively epistemic sense. Perhaps in certain professional or legal contexts, epistemic bad luck carries more significance and so failing to eliminate it counts as an injustice to the speaker, without this necessarily being an epistemic injustice of the kind that interests Fricker.

Still, the example does serve to put some pressure on Fricker's picture. I suspect the verdict that the speaker in Maitra's example has been wronged remains even if we replace the police officer with an audience who doesn't have any professional obligations or duties in that context. Moreover, while it's true that we can debate whether the audience in the example ignorantly employs a reliable stereotype that fails to apply to the particular speaker in question or employs a prejudicial stereotype, there seems to be something odd about attaching as much significance to this distinction as Fricker's view has us do. Even if there are no prejudices of the sort Fricker discusses at work, the credibility deficit received by the speaker in such cases seems to be an aspect of the broader package of injustices faced by speakers belonging to a particular disadvantaged group (survivors of rape, in Maitra's example); that's why we should be wary of too quickly classifying these as just epistemic bad luck, involving harms but no wrongs.[16]

6.6 SUMMARY

Fricker's characterisation of testimonial injustice seems relatively straightforward, which no doubt has contributed to the widespread uptake it has enjoyed. However, this chapter has tried to show that there is considerable underlying complexity and controversy, which emerges as soon as we start to ask some fundamental questions about the different elements of the account. I have raised four of those questions here, focusing on the key role that credibility deficits and prejudice play in Fricker's account, and I think it's fair to say that these questions raise some genuine and tricky problems. As familiar and popular as Fricker's definition of testimonial injustice has become, there remains considerable work to be done to pin-down what it actually means and commits us to, and to show that these commitments are defensible. In the next chapter, we'll consider Kristie Dotson's alternative way to theorise about the kinds of examples of testimonial dysfunction that motivated Fricker.

6.7 SUGGESTED FURTHER READING

Marušić and White (2018) and Goldberg (2022) offer further criticisms of Fricker's 'evidentialist' account of credibility deficits beyond those discussed in the chapter.

Lackey (2023) is a book-length treatment of particular kinds of testimonial injustice, and more specifically kinds of prejudicial credibility excess, that arise within the criminal justice system in the United States (though, sadly, much of Lackey's discussion is likely to generalise to other places). McKinney (2016) offers an excellent discussion of false confessions as 'extracted speech.'

Luzzi (2024) makes an interesting case for the initially odd claim that there can be cases of testimonial injustice that involve a speaker receiving the amount of credibility they are due, due to their audience simultaneously giving them a prejudicial credibility deficit and a prejudicial credibility excess which cancel each other out.

NOTES

1 Evidentialism about justification is the view that what you have epistemic justification to believe is determined by (or more precisely, in the technical jargon, 'supervenes' on) your evidence; two epistemic subjects with exactly the same evidence will have the same degree of justification for the same propositions. The classic defense of evidentialism in this sense is Conee and Feldman (1985). Fricker's remark doesn't commit her to evidentialism about justification, but she is offering a related account of what determines how much credibility you ought to give a speaker: hence the label. In contemporary epistemology, evidentialism about justification is primarily contrasted with reliabilism, according to which a justified belief is one formed via a reliable belief-forming mechanism (e.g. Goldman 1979); we might therefore, again with a little poetic license, call the alternative account of credibility deficits considered in the previous paragraphs a *reliabilist* account, given that it says that how much credibility you ought to get is determined by your track-record of competence and sincerity when offering testimony, though this terminology isn't standard.

2 As Lackey is aware, her argument here is related to points made by Medina concerning the significance of credibility excesses that we will discuss in the next section of this chapter. Lackey also presents cases in which a hearer has limited and so unfavourable evidence about how credible a speaker is due to the hearer's own failures to be epistemically responsible—had they engaged in gathering evidence as they ought to, their evidence would support awarding a far higher degree of credibility to the speaker—and she argues that these too are cases of credibility deficits that Fricker's evidentialist picture can't recognise: compare Maitra (2010: 205–206). See Matheson (2025) for responses to Lackey's objections.

3 See Hawley (2014: 2043–2044 and 2017: 76–77), and McGlynn (2024). See also Pettigrew (2025).

4 Fricker expressly rejects the idea that there's a 'precise science' when it comes to reaching credibility judgements (2007: 18).

5 Fricker does write: 'What is the basic mechanism in testimonial exchange whereby prejudice corrupts hearers' judgements of speaker credibility?

Prejudice can insinuate itself in a number of ways, but I shall pursue the idea that its main point of entry is via stereotypes that we make use of as heuristics in our credibility judgements' (2007: 30, emphasis added). This clearly suggests that she doesn't wholly rule out other ways in which prejudice can 'corrupt' a hearer's credibility judgements. Still, she defines testimonial injustice in terms of credibility deficits, and proposes the evidentialist account of what the latter involves that we've been discussing in this section, and so it's not obvious that she has left herself much room to accommodate this possibility without revising key elements of her account.

6 We will discuss some of Lackey's examples, which are similar to that of Michael Ledford from Chapter 2, later in this chapter.
7 See also Pettigrew (2025).
8 We should note that Luzzi (2016) has constructed cases which break the tie between prejudicial imputed ignorance and prejudicial credibility deficits in the other direction—they involve an audience unjustly failing to recognise that a speaker is speaking from knowledge while giving that speaker exactly the degree of credibility that they deserve—and he has argued, not without plausibility, that these are cases of testimonial injustice. See McGlynn (2025) for discussion.
9 The epistemic wrong or harm must be 'primary,' in Fricker's terminology: see Chapter 11 for discussion.
10 Those readers familiar with the literature on biases in the letters of support written for job candidates will perhaps not find this example far-fetched.
11 For discussion of these so-called 'positive' stereotypes and how they can be harmful, see Oluo (2018: Chapter 14).
12 See also the preface to the first edition of Collins (2000).
13 We'll return to that last thought in the next chapter, when we look at Kristie Dotson's development of it.
14 Though Lackey doesn't think agential testimonial injustice is grounded in prejudice in the way testimonial injustice as Fricker characterises it is, it's important to note that Lackey does accept that prejudice will often be in the mix, and in particular that racial prejudices can feed into agential testimonial injustice, making it more likely that certain people will face such an injustice than others (Lackey 2020: 64–67).
15 Maitra bills her example as suggesting that there can be cases of testimonial injustice that don't involve identity prejudices (2010: 202, 205), but I stressed in the previous chapter that Fricker's account doesn't in fact require identity prejudices for testimonial injustice. I take the interesting question to be rather whether Maitra has offered a plausible case of testimonial injustice which doesn't rest on *any* relevant prejudices. Kristie Dotson has offered a

quite different account of the significance of this example; I'll come back to this in Chapter 10.

16 Compare Dotson (2012): I'll spend the next chapter on Dotson's views and how they differ from Fricker's.

REFERENCES

Carpan, Catalina. 2022. 'The Adultification of Black Girls as Identity-Prejudicial Credibility Excess.' *Ethical Theory and Moral Practice* 25: 793–807. https://doi.org/10.1007/s10677-022-10324-6

Collins, Patricia Hills. 2000. *Black Feminist Thought: Knowledge, Consciousness, and the Politics of Empowerment* (Second Edition). New York and Oxon: Routledge.

Dotson, Kristie. 2012. 'A Cautionary Tale: On Limiting Epistemic Oppression.' *Frontiers: A Journal of Women Studies* 33 (1): 24–47. https://doi.org/10.1353/fro.2012.a472779

Feldman, Richard and Earl Conee. 1985. 'Evidentialism.' *Philosophical Studies* 48 (1): 15–34. https://doi.org/10.1007/BF00372404

Fricker, Miranda. 1998. 'Rational Authority and Social Power: Towards a Truly Social Epistemology.' *Proceedings of the Aristotelian Society* 98 (2): 159–177. https://doi.org/10.1111/1467-9264.00030

Fricker, Miranda. 2007. *Epistemic Injustice: Power and the Ethics of Knowing.* Oxford: Oxford University Press.

Fricker, Miranda. 2016. 'Epistemic Injustice and the Preservation of Ignorance.' In Rik Peels and Martijn Blaauw, eds. *The Epistemic Dimensions of Ignorance*: 160–177. Cambridge: Cambridge University Press.

Fricker, Miranda. 2017. 'Evolving Concepts of Epistemic Injustice.' In Ian James Kidd, José Medina, and Gaile Pohlhaus Jr., eds. *The Routledge Handbook of Epistemic Injustice*: 53–60. Oxon: Routledge.

Gerken, Mikkel. 2019. 'Pragmatic Encroachment and the Challenge from Epistemic Injustice.' *Philosophers' Imprint* 19 (15): 1–19. https://hdl.handle.net/2027/spo.3521354.0019.015

Goldberg, Sanford. 2022. 'What Is a Speaker Owed?' *Philosophy and Public Affairs* 50 (3): 375–407. https://doi.org/10.1111/papa.12219

Goldman, Alvin. 1979. 'What is Justified Belief?' In George S. Pappas, ed. *Justification and Knowledge: New Studies in Epistemology*, 1–25. Dordrecht: Reidel.

Govier, Trudy. 1993. 'When Logic Meets Politics: Testimony, Distrust, and Rhetorical Disadvantage.' *Informal Logic* 15 (2): 93–104. https://doi.org/10.22329/il.v15i2.2476

Hawley, Katherine. 2014. 'Partiality and Prejudice in Trusting.' *Synthese* 191: 2029–2045. https://doi.org/10.1007/s11229-012-0129-4

Hawley, Katherine. 2017. 'Trust, Distrust, and Epistemic Injustice.' In Ian James Kidd, José Medina, and Gaile Pohlhaus Jr., eds. *The Routledge Handbook of Epistemic Injustice*: 69–78. Oxon: Routledge.

Lackey, Jennifer. 2018. 'Credibility and the Distribution of Epistemic Goods.' In Kevin McCain, ed. *Believing in Accordance with the Evidence*: 145–168. New York: Springer.

Lackey, Jennifer. 2020. 'False Confessions and Testimonial Injustice.' *The Journal of Criminal Law and Criminology* 110 (1): 43–68.

Lackey, Jennifer. 2023. *Criminal Testimonial Injustice*. Oxford and New York: Oxford University Press.

Luzzi, Federico. 2016. 'Testimonial Injustice without Credibility Deficit (or Excess).' *Thought* 5: 203–211. https://doi.org/10.1002/tht3.212

Luzzi, Federico. 2024. 'Testimonial Injustice from Countervailing Prejudices.' *Social Epistemology* 38 (5): 607–618. https://doi.org/10.1080/02691728.2023.2291765

Maitra, Ishani. 2010. 'The Nature of Epistemic Injustice.' *Philosophical Books* 51 (4): 195–211. https://doi.org/10.1111/j.1468-0149.2010.00511.x

Marušić, Berislav and Stephen White. 2018. 'How Can Beliefs Wrong?—A Strawsonian Epistemology.' *Philosophical Topics* 46 (1): 97–114. https://www.jstor.org/stable/26529452

Matheson, Jonathan. 2025. 'Evidentialism and Social Epistemology.' In Jennifer Lackey and Aidan McGlynn, eds. *The Oxford Handbook of Social Epistemology*: 820–839. New York: Oxford University Press.

McGlynn, Aidan. 2020. 'Objects or Others? Epistemic Agency and the Primary Harm of Testimonial Injustice.' *Ethical Theory and Moral Practice* 23: 831–845. https://doi.org/10.1007/s10677-020-10078-z

McGlynn, Aidan. 2021. 'Epistemic Objectification as the Primary Harm of Testimonial Injustice.' *Episteme* 18 (2): 160–176. https://doi.org/10.1017/epi.2019.9

McGlynn, Aidan. 2024. 'Making Life More Interesting: Trust, Trustworthiness, and Testimonial Injustice.' *Philosophical Psychology* 37 (1): 126–147. https://doi.org/10.1080/09515089.2022.2133695

McGlynn, Aidan. 2025. 'Epistemic Injustice: Phenomena and Theories.' In Jennifer Lackey and Aidan McGlynn, eds. *The Oxford Handbook of Social Epistemology*: 295–327. New York: Oxford University Press.

McKinney, Rachel. 2016. 'Extracted Speech.' *Social Theory and Practice* 42 (2): 258–284. https://doi.org/10.5840/soctheorpract201642215

Nayeri, Dina. 2023. *Who Gets Believed? When the Truth Isn't Enough*. New York: Vintage.

Oluo, Ijeoma. 2018. *So You Want to Talk about Race*. Berkley, CA: Seal Press.

Pettigrew, Richard. 2025. 'What Is the Characteristic Wrong of Testimonial Injustice?' *The Philosophical Quarterly* 75 (4): 1428–1451. https://doi.org/10.1093/pq/pqaf034

Yap, Audrey. 2017. 'Credibility Excess in the Social Imaginary in Cases of Sexual Assault.' *Feminist Philosophy Quarterly* 3: 1–24. https://doi.org/10.5206/fpq/2017.4.1

7

EPISTEMIC VIOLENCE AND SILENCING

7.1 INTRODUCTION

A number of the examples laid out in Chapter 2 involve a speaker offering testimony to an audience, and finding that they are not listened to due to their audience regarding them as incompetent or as lying. We have discussed Fricker's well-known examples from *The Talented Mr. Ripley* and *To Kill a Mockingbird* at length in previous chapters. However, we should also think here of Patricia Williams's account of telling people about being racially profiled and ultimately denied access to a shop, only to find people didn't accept her claim that racism played a role (1991), or Tressie McMillan Cottom's experiences of being deemed incompetent when trying to get help for her unexpected and unexplained pain during pregnancy (2019).

In Chapters 5 and 6, we have examined Miranda Fricker's account of testimonial injustice, which would count all of these as examples of a speaker getting less credibility than they ought due to systematic identity prejudices: in the last two examples, prejudices that associate Black women with epistemic incompetence or tendencies to exaggerate when it comes to racism and their own experiences of pain. However, I've tried to emphasise that this is a particular theoretical account of such examples, not a neutral, pretheoretical description of them. This means that there's room to reject Fricker's account of the examples without thereby suggesting that the examples aren't genuine or significant, and in the previous chapter, we looked at some of the reasons philosophers have offered for being suspicious of various aspects of Fricker's treatment of them. It also means that there's room for alternative theoretical approaches, which may (or may not) improve on Fricker's in these respects.

In this chapter, we're going to look at such an alternative. This is largely due to Kristie Dotson, though Dotson explicitly draws on Patricia Hill Collins's ideas, and (in contrast to Fricker), she also situates herself with respect to a longer tradition in Black feminist theorising. I'll start by looking at how Dotson treats the examples mentioned at the start of this introduction, but also how she brings to light other, less obvious kinds of testimonial dysfunction (Section 7.2). The remainder of the chapter will look at some of the main differences between Dotson's approach and Fricker's, building on some of the distinctions and arguments in the previous chapter. I'll first focus on the central role that ignorance plays in Dotson's account (Section 7.3), before turning to her notion of epistemic violence and how it contrasts with Fricker's notion of epistemic injustice (Section 7.4). It's not my intention to try to decide which of these two approaches is preferable. My aim is the more modest one of helping people see that these are genuinely different approaches and to better understand what separates them. That said, I will float a reconciliatory proposal at the end of the chapter (Section 7.5), one that Dotson herself has already outlined.

7.2 TESTIMONIAL QUIETING, TESTIMONIAL SMOTHERING, AND EPISTEMIC VIOLENCE

In Chapter 4, I sketched various aspects of Patricia Hill Collins's epistemology. These included her dissection of various 'controlling images'—prejudicial stereotypes—of Black woman, and her understanding of the distinctive body of knowledge build up by Black women, *Black feminist thought*, as 'subjugated knowledge' (Collins 2000). Collins argues for the claim that Black feminist thought is subjugated knowledge by looking at the ways that institutions that have the authority to validate (or fail to validate) researchers' theses as knowledge are dominated by white, relatively affluent men. These epistemic gatekeepers tend to uncritically accept the controlling images of Black women, and so to reject any claims made by Black women in academia that conflict with these images. Moreover, they impose epistemological standards for assessing whether a claim counts as knowledge that reflect their own interests, such as maintaining their privileged position in society and perpetuating the fiction that they, and they alone, merit this privileged position.

Collins offers an illuminating account of how Black women are systematically and unfairly denied opportunities to contribute to their society's shared pool of knowledge; we'll come back to this in Chapter 10 when we take a closer look at Dotson's account of epistemic oppression. What Collins doesn't offer is a general account of ways that Black women, and members of other marginalised groups, can face unfair obstacles to sharing their knowledge with others via testimony. This isn't a criticism of Collins—after all, that wasn't something she set out to do. Still, insofar as our interest lies in the kinds of examples I started this chapter with, and more generally, the kinds of examples I laid out in Chapter 2, Collins's discussion of Black feminist thought as subjugated knowledge isn't quite what we're after.

Still, Collins's ideas are extremely suggestive, and Kristie Dotson has drawn on them in identifying two ways in which members of marginalised groups can be 'silenced' in the context of our testimonial practices: two practices of silencing, as Dotson calls them. The first of these is *testimonial quieting*, where the prejudices held about a speaker prevent her from being correctly identified as a knower when she offers testimony. Dotson describes this as 'the kind of silencing illustrated in Patricia Hill Collins's work' (2000: 242). What she has in mind here is the way that the controlling images of Black women discussed by Collins often prevent them from being seen as knowers on a range of topics, including their own lives and experiences. An audience who cannot see past these controlling images will not be able to appropriately *reciprocate* the testimony of Black women. Dotson takes this notion of reciprocating someone's speech from Jennifer Hornsby, and it involves a hearer participating in an exchange of testimony in such a way that they not only hear what the speaker is saying, but understand what it is she is trying to *do* in saying what she does:

> I give the name "reciprocity" to the condition that provides for the particular way in which successful illocutionary acts can be performed. When there is reciprocity among people, they recognize one another's speech as it is meant to be taken: An audience who participates reciprocally does not merely understand the speaker's words but also, in taking the words as they are meant to be taken, satisfies a condition for the speaker's having done the communicative thing she intended.
>
> (Hornsby 1995: 134)[1]

Several of the controlling images that Collins lays out involve the idea that Black women are emasculating, and so drive away Black men as potential partners, and that they are bad, irresponsible mothers. A hearer who views a Black woman through these images will find it difficult to reciprocate her testimony about how to keep a romantic partner interested or how to face parenting challenges, since they will be unlikely to recognise that she can speak from knowledge on these topics. While Collins focuses on controlling images of Black women, Dotson also mentions controlling images of other marginalised social groups, such as Black men (2011: 247).

We can already see a contrast with Fricker emerging, one that echoes differences between Dotson's notion of epistemic oppression and Fricker's notion of epistemic injustice, as discussed in Part 1 of this book. As I mentioned above, Dotson's primary focus isn't on particular instances of silencing, but rather on *practices* of silencing, which involve persistent episodes of silencing of a particular form. The relationship between instances and practices of silencing isn't always clear in Dotson's discussion, which makes it somewhat tricky to apply the account to individual cases. Dotson does discuss some particular examples of Black women being silenced by their audiences (as we'll see in detail very shortly) which suggests that it's not simply a mistake to use the account to understand what's going on in instances of silencing, but some care is needed. We'll come back to some of these issues shortly, but for now, it seems clear enough the kind of dismissal that Tressie McMillan Cottom faced when reporting her pain to medical practitioners can be seen as an instance of a practice of silencing Black women, which is at least in part due to prejudices that conflict with the idea that someone like her could speak competently and authoritatively on these matters (for example, prejudices that Black women tend to be overly emotional and uneducated).

Although Dotson illustrates testimonial quieting with appeal to Collins's controlling images, these kinds of prejudices don't seem to be essential to how she understands this form of silencing. What's crucial to testimonial quieting is that it's a practice of silencing due to what Dotson calls *pernicious ignorance*, where pernicious ignorance is ignorance that is reliable and, in a given context, harmful (2011: 238). Dotson offers a number of seemingly different characterisations of what it is for ignorance to be reliable in the relevant sense, but I take the core idea to be that reliable ignorance isn't mere ignorance of one or two particular truths about some domain, which might be coincidental, but rather involves reliably failing to get things right across that whole domain: it is 'a maladjusted sensitivity to the truth with respect to some *domain of knowledge*' (2011: 241).[2]

To see how reliable ignorance might be different from prejudice, consider different relationships a person can have towards the facts about where the meat they eat comes from, or the pay and lives of those who make the clothes they wear or mine the metals needed to make their phone (McGlynn 2025: 304). They might have convenient misconceptions, not based on any evidence, which they are reluctant to give up even in the face of strong counter-evidence; they might cling to the belief that they only eat animals that have been well-treated, raised in an environmentally conscious fashion, and which are killed with an absolute minimum of suffering, for example. That would be prejudicial thinking. However, another possibility is that they may simply not have given any thought to these matters whatsoever, or to the extent that they have considered them, they've reached no views one way or another. This would be reliable (and perhaps even pernicious) ignorance that doesn't involve any prejudices. As the examples I've chosen suggest, to say that we're not dealing with prejudice here shouldn't be taken to imply that this ignorance is an entirely innocent matter; this kind of (likely motivated) lack of curiosity into the conditions that other creatures and people live in so that you can enjoy a certain lifestyle seems both epistemically and morally problematic.[3]

Pernicious ignorance in this sense is plausibly an aspect of some of the examples that we're concerned with in this chapter. Let's try thinking through the example of Patricia Williams, with Dotson's notion of testimonial quieting in mind. Part of what's going on in this example may well be that the controlling images of Black women in circulation at that time distorted how Williams's audience viewed her when she offered them her description of what had happened. However, we can also imagine, without offering any excuses for her audiences, that their dismissal of her testimony about the racism she faced was due at least in part to reliable ignorance concerning the nature and prevalence of racism in U.S. society during that period in time, as well as the harms done to a person who has to face this kind of discrimination all the time.[4] A person who reliably failed to get at the truth concerning this entire domain of knowledge would be badly placed to reciprocate Williams's testimony about her experiences of being racially profiled; they would be liable to treat her as exaggerating or being overly sensitive.[5] Moreover, this kind of dismissal of experiences of racism will be harmful in some contexts; it can leave victims of racism feeling isolated, makes it harder to combat racism, can break apart friendships and other kinds of valued relationships, and so on.[6] So this example can plausibly be understood as one of epistemic quieting in Dotson's sense, and this is true regardless of whether the controlling images of Black women played a big part in her audience's failure to recognise her as speaking from knowledge. The crucial thing is rather that this kind of dismissal of testimony is rooted in pernicious ignorance.

Testimonial quieting illustrates a more general category that Dotson calls *epistemic violence*, taking a lead from Gayatri Spivak (1988); you might recall that this was on the list we started with back in Chapter 1. Intuitively, epistemic violence refers to the ways that people can try to eliminate the knowledge possessed by marginalised groups, in particular by silencing them when they try to share their knowledge. Dotson offers a more precise definition using the notions we've already laid out when describing testimonial quieting:

> Epistemic violence is a failure of an audience to communicatively reciprocate, either intentionally or unintentionally, in linguistic exchanges owning to pernicious ignorance.
>
> (2011: 242)

Dotson also identifies a second form of epistemic violence, though she's not claiming that these two practices of silencing are the only ones. Rather, she picks two which she takes to illustrate quite different profiles that epistemic violence can present, and in particular, the second is meant to offer an example of a kind of silencing that's very difficult to spot in practice.

This second form of epistemically violent silencing identified by Dotson is what she calls *testimonial smothering*. Testimonial smothering is a particular form of coerced self-silencing. It involves a speaker pre-emptively opting not to offer 'unsafe' or 'risky' testimony to a potential audience due to that audience (typically inadvertently) raising doubts concerning their ability to reciprocate the speaker's potential contribution. The particular doubts Dotson focuses on concern the audience's ability to find a speaker's testimony intelligible, or at least to be sensitive to the limits of their own ability to find it intelligible.[7] A speaker may truncate what she otherwise might have said, due to her would-be audience failing to demonstrate the capacity to be appropriately receptive to testimony that involves information it would be risky for her to divulge, where this lack of capacity is due to (or at least appears to be due to) pernicious ignorance, in the sense characterised above. Dotson offers the following example.

Cassandra Byers Harvin:
> In her article, "Conversations I Can't Have," Cassandra Byers Harvin expresses her reluctance to engage in conversations about race in a U.S. context due to the ways "race talk" has been framed in U.S. public discourse. She expresses her desire to avoid conversations about O. J. Simpson and to avoid speaking candidly about race with her colleagues as a result of the "hurt feelings and surprise and defensiveness" that her audience may take on during such conversations (Harvin 1996: 16). She describes one encounter in a public library with a white woman, "early-50s-looking" who asks Harvin what she is working on. Harvin responds by indicating she is researching "raising black sons in this society" (16). The white woman promptly asks, "How is that any different from raising white sons?" Harvin notes that it is not only the question that is problematic, as it indicates a kind of lack of awareness of racial struggles in the United States, but also the tone of the question that indicated the white woman believed that Harvin was "making something out of nothing" (16). Harvin explains that in response to the question she politely pretended that she was running out of time in order to extricate herself from the situation.
>
> (2011: 247)

As we've already noted, Dotson stresses that testimonial smothering is a particularly pernicious form of silencing, since it's very hard to spot (2011: 254 n13). To say that the speaker has been silenced in this sense shouldn't be taken to suggest that she has fallen silent, so that there's a perceptible gap in the conversation where her contribution should have gone. Rather, speakers engaging in testimonial smothering will make their excuses and leave (as Harvin did), or if that's not possible, they'll find other things to say; they may offer an edited version of what they had originally hoped to say which they deem less risky and unsafe to give to their audience, or they may try to subtly change the topic of the conversation. In either of these latter cases, from the point of view of the audience and the other conversational participants and observers, it may seem as if the speaker has said what they wanted to say; it may only be the speaker who is in any kind of position to tell that they have, in a sense, been silenced.

7.3 EPISTEMIC VIOLENCE AND TESTIMONIAL INJUSTICE

Superficially, Dotson's two forms of silencing may not look all that different from testimonial injustice as Fricker characterises it. As a result, sometimes Dotson is presented as offering no more than a cosmetic change to Fricker's views, albeit a change that better recognises the contributions of earlier theorists like Spivak and Collins to our understanding of these forms of silencing faced by marginalised groups.[8] In particular, someone might suggest that testimonial quieting looks like the central case of testimonial injustice, as illustrated by examples like Tom Robinson in *To Kill a Mockingbird*, while testimonial smothering looks like Fricker's 'pre-emptive' testimonial injustice, discussed in Chapter 5, where '[t]he credibility of such a person on a given subject matter is already sufficiently in prejudicial deficit that their potential testimony is never solicited; so the speaker is silenced by the identity prejudice that undermines her credibility in advance' (2007: 130).

However, the differences are far more significant than the apparent similarities here. While both testimonial smothering and pre-emptive testimonial injustice involve a speaker who is harmed by not being able to contribute their testimony in the first place, rather than by having what they *have* said dismissed, the mechanisms involved are quite different. As we've just seen, Dotson is interested in a form of coerced *self*-censoring speakers engage in with respect to particular topics and audiences, while Fricker is focused on speakers being prejudicially overlooked when they should have been consulted. The two notions aren't even trying to describe roughly the same kinds of cases.

In contrast, testimonial quieting and testimonial injustice are attempts to give a theoretical description of very similar kinds of cases: those involving speakers who do get to offer testimony, but have that testimony dismissed by their audience. Still, they are quite different from each other in a number of key respects, which return us to our discussion of distinctive features of Fricker's account of testimonial injustice in the previous chapter, in particular the centrality that she gives to *credibility deficits* and to *prejudices*. Dotson's account of epistemic violence and the different forms it can take contrasts with Fricker's views in both of these respects. Let me make this more explicit.

First, Dotson's characterisation of testimonial quieting doesn't invoke the notion of a credibility deficit at all. Rather, it involves failure to reciprocate in a testimonial exchange by failing to recognise the speaker as expressing their knowledge: it 'occurs when an audience fails to identify a speaker as a knower' (2011: 242). In the prior chapter I argued (following the lead of Luzzi 2016) that these are genuinely distinct conceptions of the kind of epistemic misevaluation of the speaker we are focused on, applying to distinct, albeit overlapping, sets of cases. Related to this, we should also note that whether a speaker is subject to testimonial quieting seems to depend on whether they in fact express knowledge through the testimony offered to their audience; I'll return to this point later in this chapter.

Second, as I've already argued, although testimonial quieting will very often be due to prejudices, it seemingly need not be. Unlike Fricker's definition of testimonial injustice, it doesn't seem to be built into Dotson's characterisations of testimonial quieting or epistemic violence in general that prejudice must be playing a key role.[9]

A third contrast between testimonial injustice and testimonial quieting is the very different theoretical frameworks in which Dotson and Fricker situate their respective accounts of the testimonial dysfunction illustrated by our examples. For Fricker, testimonial injustice is a variety of epistemic injustice; it's her main illustration of what an injustice involving a person being wronged in their capacity as an epistemic agent looks like. This means that some of the distinctive aspects of Fricker's understanding of epistemic injustice that we picked out in Chapter 3 shape how she approaches testimonial injustice too. Her focus is on individual epistemic agents, which in cases of testimonial injustice will be particular speakers (such as Tom Robinson).[10] She's interested in *wrongs* done to these individuals, not mere harms (where, recall, a harm can be just or unjust, deserved or undeserved, while a wrong is always unjust and undeserved).[11] Finally, this wrong must be distinctively epistemic. In contrast, Dotson's testimonial quieting is one kind of epistemic violence, and epistemic violence is not restricted in *any* of these three respects. Let's look at an example that Dotson offers (2011: 240), which brings this point out very starkly.

Arsonist Toddler:
A three-year-old child is reliably ignorant about the effects of fire and fails to appropriately reciprocate an attempt to teach her about fire safety due to

this ignorance. Moreover, this toddler starts a fire not long after this attempt, since she, understandably enough, finds fire pretty. Unfortunately, the fire she starts quickly gets out of control, resulting in property damage.

Since the toddler's ignorance about the effects of fire is reliable and harmful (given the damage done by the fire), it counts as pernicious ignorance; moreover, she fails to reciprocate testimony due to this ignorance, and so she behaves in an epistemically violent way, by Dotson's lights.[12] Notice, though, that *distinctively epistemic wrongs done to the speaker* don't figure in this analysis of the example. I didn't specify that it was the speaker's property that was damaged, and even if it was, fire damage to your property surely isn't a distinctively epistemic harm: hopefully that much remains uncontroversial, even in our epistemic era (see Chapter 1). Moreover, given that the toddler didn't understand what she was doing and didn't intend the resulting damage, and given that three-year-olds generally aren't regarded as fully responsible for the consequences of their actions, we no more want to say that she wronged the property owner than we would say that they had been wronged if the property had caught fire due to a random bolt of lightning. Still, the child's ignorance was harmful in this context, since the property owner was harmed by them, and that's all Dotson's account of epistemic violence cares about.

7.4 OBJECTIONS TO DOTSON'S ACCOUNT

Dotson offers a detailed and compelling account of two practices of silencing, one of which encompasses many of the examples that we started this chapter with, and she gives an overarching theoretical framework in which to understand these kinds of silencing and their significance. Moreover, her account not only acknowledges, but is rooted in earlier work on the ways that members of marginalised groups can find themselves excluded, dismissed, and silenced: particularly the contributions of Collins and Spivak. Not only is Dotson's picture of testimonial dysfunction quite distinct from Fricker's, the differences allow Dotson to avoid some of the biggest worries with Fricker's account of testimonial injustice, as identified in the previous chapter. For example, Dotson doesn't owe us an account of credibility deficits, nor does she need to draw a sharp contrast between the kinds of examples that interest us in this book and those merely involving epistemic bad luck.

While I think there are undeniably some advantages to Dotson's account, there are, inevitably, concerns we might raise with some of its features. We have in effect already covered many of the relevant points in some detail, and so we can be brief here.

There are a number of ways that Fricker's definition of testimonial injustice has struck people as unnecessarily or problematically restricted and narrow, and Dotson's notions seem broader in precisely those respects: for instance, think about the way that Dotson relaxes Fricker's focus on prejudices. However, the same is also true in reverse; in certain respects, Dotson's notions seem artificially restricted in ways that Fricker's is not. Here's a case in point. Dotson defines testimonial quieting in terms of knowledge—it involves a knower failing to get recognition *as* a knower—and I argued in Chapter 6 that such a definition will miss whole classes of cases which intuitively seem like they illustrate the same phenomenon as our paradigmatic examples of testimonial dysfunction; for instance, recall our observation that Marge Sherwood seems to be unjustly dismissed by Greenleaf even if he'd be right not to credit her with knowledge. It's open to Dotson to reply that although this case (and the others we discussed in the previous chapter) are not instances of testimonial quieting by her lights, they can still be regarded as illustrating some related but slightly different phenomenon. The suspicion will still remain, though, that Dotson has overly restricted her definition by casting it in terms of failure to recognise a knower rather than some other central theoretical notion (such as Fricker's credibility deficits).[13]

Likewise, Dotson's definition of testimonial smothering imposes a very precise structure on genuine instances of this phenomenon. There are a couple of intuitive ideas in the vicinity of testimonial smothering that we can articulate here. One is that sometimes a speaker is forced into truncating their testimony on a given topic when speaking to a particular audience because what they want to say carries risks, and they don't trust their audience enough to be willing to run those risks. Another is that a speaker can be forced to truncate their testimony since their audience doesn't seem like they'll be able to comprehend the testimony the speaker originally wants to give; I suspect that this is often more or less how people in fact interpret testimonial smothering.[14] However, Dotson's definition of testimonial smothering is much more specific and demanding than either of these intuitive thoughts, requiring that the speaker take the hearer to have failed to demonstrate that they're capable of finding that testimony intelligible (or recognising the limits of their understanding), and that this lack of capacity is due to (or is perceived by the speaker to be due to) pernicious ignorance in Dotson's sense. Moreover, Dotson only gives us a couple of examples, and she neither considers alternative theoretical descriptions of those examples, nor shows that the particular features she highlights and so builds into her definition are the relevant ones for understanding the phenomenon here in general rather than just these specific instances.[15]

To make this worry more vivid, let's consider another example that Dotson offers in order to illustrate what she means by 'unsafe' testimony (2011: 244–245).[16] Black women may truncate their testimony about sexual and domestic violence perpetrated by Black men to certain audiences because there's a risk of reinforcing the controlling images of Black men, which picture them as inherently criminal 'superpredators' and rapists (as we've discussed in earlier chapters when examining the jurors' perception of Tom Robinson during his trial). Dotson doesn't claim that Black women are subject to testimonial smothering when they truncate their testimony to certain audiences in this way, but she does write of such cases that 'it is possible that testimonial smothering or some other form of coerced silencing is afoot' (2011: 245).

Notice that in this example, the reason that Black women truncate their testimony isn't that their audiences haven't demonstrated that they'll find such testimony comprehensible, but rather that they can't be trusted not to treat it as reinforcing widespread prejudices against Black men as a group. So this kind of example doesn't meet all of Dotson's criteria for counting as testimonial smothering. Now, in the line I just quoted, she suggests that it might instead illustrate 'some other form of coerced silencing,' but we can again wonder what the motivation might be for understanding the category of testimonial smothering so narrowly, rather than having a broader category which is more relaxed about the precise reason the speaker doesn't want to give risky testimony to a particular audience.[17]

What this suggests is that Dotson's particular theoretical choices can be disputed. Her definitions of both testimonial quieting and smothering are strikingly narrow in particular respects, and it's left unclear what's meant to motivate focusing on the specific features that Dotson's approach treats as key.

Moreover, while it's also true that Dotson's overarching category of epistemic violence is in some ways less constrained than Fricker's conception of epistemic injustice, many people are liable to find it *too* unconstrained. Recall Dotson's example of the Arsonist Toddler from the previous section, involving a three-year-old who fails to reciprocate a lesson about fire safety, and starts a fire that does considerable damage to a building. Dotson acknowledges when she introduces the example that many will take it to show that her understanding of epistemic violence is much too 'consequentialist,' by which she means that her characterisation only cares about whether harm was done, not about whether that harm was unjust, undeserved, intentional, and so on. Dotson's own reaction to her example is different, though:

> I do not find it strange to say that the child in this instance acted in an epistemically violent way by not heeding the words of the speaker who warned her against starting a fire.
>
> (2011: 240)

It's true, Dotson concedes that her characterisation of epistemic violence is in certain respects very broad, meaning that it extends to cases like Arsonist Toddler where we might not have intuitively thought it would apply. However, the lesson she thinks we should take from this is that epistemic violence is a much more ubiquitous phenomenon than we tend to assume. As she puts the point:

> The charge that the definition of epistemic violence is too broad fails to recognize the reality that epistemic violence is a broad practice.
>
> (Dotson 2011: 240)

Despite this, I can't help but feel that a notion of epistemic violence that applies to our young fire-starter is indeed too broad, and I suspect that many will share that sense. Dotson insists that this involves a failure to 'recognise the reality' of how ubiquitous epistemic violence really is, but it's not clear on what grounds she makes this claim, or what she takes to be involved in properly recognising reality here. She is, of course, free to offer a definition of epistemic violence that applies beyond the kinds of examples we started this chapter with to those like Arsonist Toddler, but we perhaps need reassurance that nothing interesting or important gets lost when we draw the boundaries of our theoretical categories so widely.

7.5 PLURALISM

It hasn't been my objective in the previous chapter or this one to make the case for or against any particular treatment of the examples. Rather, my aim has been to show that there are genuinely distinct theoretical approaches that we can take here, and to bring out the most significant differences between these. I do think that there are certain respects in which Fricker's notions and her overall framework for thinking about testimonial dysfunction of the kind illustrated by our examples has advantages over Dotson's, but I'm equally inclined to say the converse is true.

Perhaps it's a mistake to think we need to choose. After all, the point that I've been stressing throughout both Parts 1 and 2 of this book is that the same phenomena can be viewed through different theoretical lenses, where this involves focusing on certain aspects of examples of those phenomena to the exclusion of others. We can insist on seeing these different theoretical approaches as rivals to each other, but an alternative is to suggest that which lens is the best fit can vary across different theorists, and possibly even for one and the same theorist across different times, depending on what project they're engaged in and so what's of most significance to them.

This ecumenical thought can be taken to motivate a form of *pluralism* about theoretical accounts of testimonial dysfunction of the kind illustrated by the examples. Rather than taking Fricker and Dotson's views as competing to be *the* right account, whatever that would mean, each may be articulating one set of theoretical tools which help us to understand certain aspects of what's going on in our examples. Different aspects may be the key ones depending on which projects we're engaging in. A pluralism of this sort has been briefly suggested by Dotson (2012: 42); I won't try to spell out what it might look like in more detail here, but I will have much more to say about this in Chapter 10. For now, the point is just that it may offer a principled reason not to try to pick a winner between the two approaches to testimonial dysfunction we've looked at across Part 2 of this book. Perhaps, when it comes to epistemic injustice, we really can have our cake and eat it.

7.6 SUMMARY

My focus here has been Kristie Dotson's treatment of the kind of testimonial dysfunction illustrated by many of the examples introduced in Chapter 2, and by the examples I laid out at the beginning of this chapter. I traced the way that Dotson's views developed out of Patricia Hill Collins's account of Black feminist thought as a kind of subjugated knowledge and the role Collins accords the controlling images of Black women. Dotson identifies two 'practices of silencing' that occur within testimonial exchanges, testimonial quieting and testimonial smothering, and she offers a characterisation of an overarching category, epistemic violence, which they both fall under. As well as looking at Dotson's definitions of each of these notions, I've spent time in this chapter drawing on points made in the previous one to bring to light the most significant respects in which Dotson's picture differs from Fricker's. I closed by raising some objections to various aspects of Dotson's views, and by briefly floating a pluralist proposal, according to which the different theoretical accounts developed by Fricker and Dotson can each have their place. This last thought is one we'll return to more seriously at the end of Part 3 of this book, after we've had a chance to look at the other main form that epistemic injustice can take, involving obstacles to people making their experiences and other aspects of their lives intelligible.

7.7 FURTHER SUGGESTED READINGS

As Dotson notes, Hornsby's notion of reciprocating another's speech is developed in the context of offering an interpretation and defence of Catharine MacKinnon's claim that pornography silences women (e.g. MacKinnon 1987, 1994). Rae Langton (1993) offers a related account, drawing on J. L. Austin's notion of 'uptake' (Austin 1975); in Langton's terms, pornography creates conditions in which women systematically fail to gain uptake from their audiences when they try to do certain things with their words (such as refusing sex and protesting pornography). Dotson also notes some similarities between her notion of testimonial smothering and certain forms of silencing identified by Langton (Dotson 2011: 253 n12). See Vince (2018) for an interesting attempt to understand the claim that pornography silences women by appealing to Dotson's account of silencing as a form of epistemic violence. Mason (2022: Chapter 13) is a very helpful introduction to all of these issues.

Fricker sometimes uses the language of silencing to describe examples of the central case of testimonial injustice (e.g. 2007: 8, 14–15, 86), but it's left unspecified what she means by this. In Chapter 6 of her book, however, she distinguishes two more specific forms of silencing which she takes to be kinds of testimonial injustice. The first is pre-emptive testimonial injustice, which I introduced in Chapter 5 and which came up again in this chapter. The other is what she describes as 'extreme' testimonial injustice, where people sharing a particular social identity have been so dehumanised that they simply don't register with their audience's 'testimonial sensibility' (understood as in Chapter 5). They're not even given low credibility when speaking; rather *no* credibility judgement is made (2007: 140). Fricker offers this kind of extreme testimonial injustice as an interpretation of the claim that pornography silences women; I argue against this interpretation in McGlynn (2019).

A related notion of silencing is discursive injustice, introduced by Quill Kukla (writing as Rebecca Kukla), which they characterise as occurring

> when members of any disadvantaged group face a systematic inability to produce certain kinds of speech acts that they ought, but for their social identity, to be able to produce—and in particular when their attempts result in their actually producing a different kind of speech act that further weakens or problematizes their social position.
>
> (Kukla 2014: 441)

In one of Kukla's examples, a woman who is a floor manager in a predominantly male factory tries to issue orders to the those under her authority, only to find that they take her utterances to have the force of requests that they are free to ignore if they so wish (2014: 445–448).

A recent debate concerns whether any of these different accounts of silencing can help us to understand certain examples of Indigenous peoples being unjustly silenced when testifying about the impact that industrial activity and resource extraction will have on them and their environment. See e.g. L. Townsend and D. L. Townsend (2020), L. Townsend and D. L. Townsend (2021), Townsend (2021), McGlynn (2021), L. Townsend and D. Townsend (2021), and Vannini (2023). For a more general overview and historical look at the distinctive epistemic injustices faced by Indigenous peoples, see Tsosie (2017).

Spivak's influential and controversial examination of the ways that the 'subaltern' are silenced (e.g. Spivak 1988) is often identified in the literature as an earlier, and until recently uncredited, discussion of epistemic injustice, and of testimonial dysfunction in particular (e.g. Dotson 2012: 44 n24, Ivy 2016: 443 n7, Pohlhaus 2017: 13, Berenstain 2020: 738 and 755 n29). I don't know of any detailed discussion of how Spivak's ideas relate to views in the contemporary philosophical literature on epistemic injustice, though Dotson (2012) makes several relevant points.

Wiggleton-Little (forthcoming) argues that neither Fricker nor Dotson's frameworks can fully do justice to the particular way that the pain reports of Black women are dismissed in medical contexts.

This chapter looked at whether prejudice or ignorance should be the main epistemic notion in our definitions of testimonial dysfunction. Bain (2022) looks more generally at whether the kinds of prejudices responsible for epistemic injustice should be thought of as causally or explanatorily prior to the kind of active ignorance theorised by Mills (e.g. 2007), and concludes that they should not; on the contrary, Bain argues, 'ignorance-first' accounts that see epistemic injustices as secondary phenomena, downstream of ignorance, are more plausible and more explanatorily powerful.

McWilliams (forthcoming) offers an excellent overview of almost all the topics we have covered in Part 2 of this book.

NOTES

1 The terminology of 'illocutionary acts' goes back to J. L. Austin (1975). When a speaker says something, they utter particular words with (in that context) particular meanings, and they do so intending their utterance to have a certain effect on their audience. To give some simple examples, I might say 'Wittgenstein only published one philosophical book in his lifetime,' intending to persuade you of the truth of this claim, or I might say 'The gate is open!', intending you to take action in response, and in particular to run out of the path of the escaped bull. However, Austin observed that there's a level in between these, which is the act the speaker intends to perform *in* making that utterance. I *asserted* that Wittgenstein only published one philosophical book in his life time, with the intention of getting you to share my belief or knowledge, and I *warned* you that the gate was open, with the intention of getting you to run out of the path of the bull that has just been accidentally set loose. Much feminist philosophy of language, including Hornsby's work, has concerned the idea that one way that a person or group can be silenced is in being prevented, not from uttering the words they want to, but from performing the illocutionary act they intent to in uttering those words; their words are robbed of the power to refuse, or protest, or order. See the further suggested readings at the end of this chapter for more on this topic and how it relates to epistemic injustice.

2 As noted in the main text, Dotson offers several different definitions of reliable ignorance in her paper. First, reliable ignorance 'is ignorance that is *consistent* or follows from a predictable gap in cognitive resources' (2011: 238).

Alternatively, reliable ignorance is ignorance that's due to 'a kind of *counterfactual incompetence* with respect to some domain of knowledge' (2011: 241), where counterfactual incompetence involves failing to meet the two 'tracking' conditions that Robert Nozick proposed as necessary conditions on knowing some proposition P: were P not true, one wouldn't believe P, and were P true, one would believe P (Nozick 1981). Nozick proposed the tracking conditions as a way of spelling out the idea that knowing requires not just happening to get things right, but getting things non-accidentally or non-luckily right. Finally, there's the characterisation quoted in the main text. These different characterisations don't seem equivalent, and I find the second, in terms of counterfactual incompetence, rather harder to grasp than the others.

3 Dotson writes that 'reliable ignorance needs to be understood not as a simple lack of knowledge, but as an active practice of unknowing,' drawing a link to Charles Mills's work on active white ignorance (e.g. Mills 2007). Medina (2013: Chapter 1) discusses the way that those in relatively privileged positions in a society will tend to be incurious and close-minded when it comes to truths that would upset their sense that they merit those advantages they enjoy.

4 See the second half of Medina (2013) for a detailed account of how such ignorance can be culpable rather than exculpatory.

5 Dotson's definitions of reliable and pernicious ignorance don't make explicit whether it is individual epistemic agents who can be ignorant in these ways, or only groups of agents, but she does explicitly attribute reliable and even pernicious ignorance to particular individuals in her examples (e.g. 2011: 240); we'll discuss some of these examples shortly.

6 Dotson stresses that reliable ignorance that is harmful in one context may not be in another (2011: 239). Does that mean that we can only say that reliable ignorance is pernicious with respect to those contexts in which it is in fact harmful? Or is it rather that pernicious ignorance is reliable ignorance that is harmful in some-or-other context (so that we can say, overall, that reliable ignorance is pernicious so long as there's at least one context in which it's harmful)? It's not entirely clear to me and some of what Dotson says seems to fit the first picture better, and some seems to suggest she has the second in mind; on the whole, I'm inclined to think her view is closer to the second picture than the first, but I remain unsure. In general, I find it difficult to square Dotson's claims about the importance of looking at particular contexts and circumstances in order to determine if reliable ignorance is pernicious (2011: 239) with her insistence that it's practices of silencing rather than instances of silencing that we're concerned with; I won't attempt to resolve this issue here.

7 Dotson introduces two pieces of technical terminology to capture this dynamic (2011: 245). Testimony that a hearer can understand, or for which they are at least aware of the bounds of their own understanding (so that they won't mistakenly *think* they understand when they don't) is *accurately intelligible* for that hearer. When a speaker positively assesses a hearer's ability to find what they're considering saying accurately intelligible, then she takes them to have demonstrated *testimonial competence*; when a speaker judges that a hearer has failed to demonstrate testimonial competence, she takes them to have manifested *testimonial incompetence*.

8 Relatedly, Medina describes Dotson as 'providing fine-grained distinctions that can be used to develop a sharper and more nuanced understanding of the original categories of testimonial and hermeneutical injustice' (2021: 414). I think this is also a mistake; this misses the extent to which she offers a very different kind of theoretical treatment of these phenomena than Fricker, not a refinement of Fricker's approach.

9 If I fail to recognise a speaker as a knower due to my own ignorance, there is a sense in which I am prejudiced towards her; I am prejudiced concerning whether she is expressing knowledge or not. Given this, how can I say that prejudice might not be involved in epistemic quieting? The point is that this failure to recognise the speaker as a knower, even if it counts as a prejudice, need not be rooted in further prejudices I hold. In contrast, as Fricker defines testimonial injustice, it is a failure to give the speaker as much credibility as she deserves, where this failure is due to prejudices held by the hearer. The difference lies in whether underlying prejudices are playing this role; for Fricker, they are as a matter of definition, while for Dotson, they need not be. Thanks to Jade Fletcher for suggesting I clarify this distinction.

10 We saw in the previous chapter that this is something José Medina (2013: Chapter 3) criticises Fricker for in his discussion of why we should pay more attention to credibility excesses. In most conversations, there is no such figure as *the* speaker; rather, we have a number of different people who typically take it in turns to speak or to make up part of someone's else's audience, and Medina thinks we need to think about whether credibility is portioned out proportionately across all of these people.

11 I noted in Chapter 3 that Fricker's use of terminology is not always clear on this point, and she often uses 'harms' when 'wrongs' seems like it better captures her views.

12 You might question this description of the example. For instance, you might suggest that the child's failure to reciprocate the fire-safety lecture isn't due to her ignorance about fire, but rather her underdeveloped linguistic and cognitive abilities. Since the example is Dotson's own, and she endorses

the claim that it illustrates epistemic violence, I won't pursue such doubts further.
13 A complication here is I noted in the prior chapter that Luzzi (2016) has offered cases suggesting that a definition in terms of credibility deficits is too narrow. That suggests that there's no straightforward winner here, but that doesn't affect the point in the text that Dotson's notion of testimonial quieting seems overly restrictive.
14 This is more or less how Fricker explains Dotson's notion (Nikolaidis, Thompson, and Fricker 2023: 795), and Medina (2021: 414) offers a similar gloss.
15 In addition to Cassandra Byers Harvin, Dotson also discusses Uma Narayan's decision not to participate in conversations about dowry murders in the United States (Narayan 1997) and describes this as 'an example of testimonial smothering' (Dotson 2011: 249). See Medina (2013: 163–176) for an alternative discussion of this example in the context of racialised ignorance and epistemic injustice.
16 Another example we might consider here is people with dementia self-silencing due to the worry that their testimony will be unreliable, where this worry stems from the prevalence of widespread dehumanising prejudices. Sibbald (2023: 807) calls this a case of testimonial smothering in Dotson's sense, but I doubt it meets Dotson's conditions. There's a question, then, about whether this is an example that we want to group together with other, clearer examples of testimonial smothering, or whether we treat is as illustrating a related but distinct phenomenon.
17 Medina (2013: 101–103) offers a discussion of Black women self-silencing about sexual and domestic violence by Black men along these more general lines, though in fact he takes this to be a form of hermeneutical injustice.

REFERENCES

Austin, J. L. 1975. *How to Do Things with Words* (Second Edition). Cambridge, MA: Harvard University Press.

Bain, Zara 2022. 'On the Relationship between Ignorance and Epistemic Injustice: An Ignorance-First Analysis.' In Linsey McGoey and Matthias Gross, eds. *Routledge International Handbook of Ignorance Studies* (Second Edition): 47–60. Oxon and New York: Routledge.

Berenstain, Nora. 2020. 'White Feminist Gaslighting.' *Hypatia* 35 (4): 733–758. https://doi.org/10.1017/hyp.2020.31

Collins, Patricia Hills. 2000. *Black Feminist Thought: Knowledge, Consciousness, and the Politics of Empowerment* (Second Edition). New York and Oxon: Routledge.

Dotson, Kristie. 2011. 'Tracking Epistemic Violence, Tracking Practices of Silencing.' *Hypatia* 26 (2): 236–257. https://doi.org/10.1111/j.1527-2001.2011.01177.x

Dotson, Kristie. 2012. 'A Cautionary Tale: On Limiting Epistemic Oppression.' *Frontiers: A Journal of Women Studies* 33 (1): 24–47. https://doi.org/10.1353/fro.2012.a472779

Fricker, Miranda. 2007. *Epistemic Injustice: Power and the Ethics of Knowing.* Oxford: Oxford University Press.

Harvin, Cassandra Byers. 1996. 'Conversations I Can't Have.' *On the Issues* 5 (2): 15–16.

Hornsby, Jennifer. 1995. 'Disempowered Speech.' *Philosophical Topics* 23 (2): 127–147. https://doi.org/10.5840/philtopics199523211

Ivy, Veronica. 2016. 'Epistemic Injustice.' *Philosophy Compass* 11 (8): 437–446. Originally published as Rachel McKinnon. https://doi.org/10.1111/phc3.12336

Kukla, Rebecca. 2014. 'Performative Force, Convention, and Discursive Injustice.' *Hypatia* 29 (2): 440–457. https://doi.org/10.1111/j.1527-2001.2012.01316.x

Langton, Rae. 1993. 'Speech Acts and Unspeakable Acts.' Reprinted in Langton, Rae. *Sexual Solipsism: Philosophical Essays on Pornography and Objectification*: 25–63. Oxford: Oxford University Press.

Luzzi, Federico. 2016. 'Testimonial Injustice without Credibility Deficit (or Excess).' *Thought* 5: 203–211. https://doi.org/10.1002/tht3.212

MacKinnon, Catharine. 1987. *Feminism Unmodified: Discourses on Life and Law.* Cambridge, MA: Harvard University Press.

MacKinnon, Catharine. 1994. *Only Words.* London: HarperCollins Publishers.

Mason, Elinor. 2022. *Feminist Philosophy: An Introduction.* Oxon and New York: Routledge.

McGlynn, Aidan. 2019. 'Testimonial Injustice, Pornography, and Silencing.' *Analytic Philosophy* 60: 405–417. https://doi.org/10.1111/phib.12152

McGlynn, Aidan. 2021. 'Extreme Testimonial Injustice or Discursive Injustice? A Reply to Townsend and Townsend on Indigenous Peoples in the Inter-American Human Rights System.' *Social Epistemology Review and Reply Collective* 10 (4): 23–30.

McGlynn, Aidan. 2025. 'Epistemic Injustice: Phenomena and Theories.' In Jennifer Lackey and Aidan McGlynn, eds. *The Oxford Handbook of Social Epistemology*: 295–327. New York: Oxford University Press.

McMillan Cottom, Tressie. 2019. *Thick: And Other Essays.* New York: The New Press.

McWilliams, Emily Colleen. Forthcoming. 'Testimonial Injustice and the Nature of Epistemic Injustice.' In Kurt Sylvan, Matthias Steup, Jonathan Dancy, and Ernest Sosa, eds. *The Blackwell Companion to Epistemology* (Third Edition). Hoboken, NJ: Wiley-Blackwell.

Medina, José. 2013. *The Epistemology of Resistance: Gender and Racial Oppression, Epistemic Injustice, and Resistant Imaginations*. Oxford: Oxford University Press.

Medina, José. 2021. 'Feminism and Epistemic Injustice.' In Kim Q. Hall and Ásta, eds. *The Oxford Handbook of Feminist Epistemology*: 408–417. Oxford: Oxford University Press.

Mills, Charles. 2007. 'White Ignorance.' In Shannon Sullivan and Nancy Tuana, eds. *Race and Epistemologies of Ignorance*: 13–38. Buffalo: SUNY Press.

Narayan, Uma. 1997. *Dislocating Cultures: Identities, Traditions, and Third World Feminism*. New York: Routledge.

Nikolaidis, A. C., Winston C. Thompson, and Miranda Fricker. 2023. 'Education, Epistemic Injustice, and Truthfulness: Miranda Fricker Interviewed by A. C. Nikolaidis and Winston C. Thompson.' *Journal of Philosophy of Education* 57 (4–5): 791–802. https://doi.org/10.1093/jopedu/qhad075

Nozick, Robert. 1981. *Philosophical Explanations*. Cambridge, MA: Harvard University Press.

Pohlhaus Jr., Gaile. 2017. 'Varieties of Epistemic Injustice.' In Ian James Kidd, José Medina, and Gaile Pohlhaus Jr., eds. *The Routledge Handbook of Epistemic Injustice*: 13–26. Oxon: Routledge.

Sibbald, Kaitlin. 2023. 'Are Metaphors Ethically Bad Epistemic Practice? Epistemic Injustice at the Intersections.' *Hypatia* 38 (4): 801–821. https://doi.org/10.1017/hyp.2023.90

Spivak, Gayatri Chakravorty. 1998. 'Can the Subaltern Speak?' In Cary Nelson and Lawrence Grossberg, eds. *Marxism and the Interpretation of Culture*: 66–111. Champaign: University of Illinois Press.

Townsend, Dina Lupin and Leo Townsend. 2021. 'Epistemic Injustice and Indigenous Peoples in the Inter-American Human Rights System.' *Social Epistemology* 35 (2): 147–159. https://doi.org/10.1080/02691728.2020.1839809

Townsend, Leo. 2021. 'Discursive Injustice and the Speech of Indigenous Communities.' In Leo Townsend, Preston Stovall, and Hans Bernhard Schmid, eds. *The Social Institution of Discursive Norms: Historical, Naturalistic, and Pragmatic Perspectives*: 248–263. Oxon and New York: Routledge.

Townsend, Leo and Dina Lupin Townsend. 2020. 'Consultation, Consent, and the Silencing of Indigenous Voices.' *Journal of Applied Philosophy* 37 (5): 781–798. https://doi.org/10.1111/japp.12438

Townsend, Leo and Dina Lupin Townsend. 2021. 'Are 'Epistemic' and 'Communicative' Models of Silencing in Conflict? Reply to McGlynn.' *Social Epistemology Review and Reply Collective* 10 (7): 27–32.

Tsosie, Rebecca. 2017. 'Indigenous Peoples, Anthropology, and the Legacy of Epistemic Injustice.' In Ian James Kidd, José Medina, and Gaile Pohlhaus Jr., eds. *The Routledge Handbook of Epistemic Injustice*: 356–369. Oxon and New York: Routledge.

Vannini, Angelo. 2023. 'Towards Epistemic Translatability: On Epistemic Difference and Hermeneutical Injustice.' *Social Epistemology* 37 (6): 839–851. https://doi.org/10.1080/02691728.2023.2188127

Vince, Rosa. 2018. 'Testimonial Smothering and Pornography: Silencing Refusing Sex and Reporting Assault.' *Feminist Philosophy Quarterly* 4 (3): article 5. https://doi.org/10.5206/fpq/2018.3.5784

Wiggleton-Little, Jada. Forthcoming. 'Pain Dismissal and the Limits of Epistemic Injustice.' *Hypatia*. https://doi.org/10.1017/hyp.2025.8

Williams, Patricia J. 1991. *The Alchemy of Race and Rights: Diary of a Law Professor*. Cambridge, MA: Harvard University Press.

Part 3

BEING UNDERSTOOD

8

THE CENTRAL CASE OF HERMENEUTICAL INJUSTICE

8.1 INTRODUCTION

In Part 2 of this book, we have been focused on unjust obstacles to being believed when testifying. It's time now to turn to unjust obstacles to being understood, and we'll approach this topic starting with the notion of hermeneutical injustice. As noted in Chapter 3, hermeneutics is the study of interpretation, and so *hermeneutical injustice* suggests a form of injustice that relates somehow to interpretation or interpretability. Miranda Fricker identifies this as a second species of epistemic injustice, in the sense that it involves a wrong done to a person in their capacity as an epistemic agent. Notably, Fricker's (2007) book gave far less attention to hermeneutical injustice than testimonial injustice, with the latter taking up the first six chapters and the former only appearing in the seventh and final chapter. In a subsequent interview, Fricker explained that this was primarily because she took a shorter treatment of hermeneutical injustice to be feasible due to the way it could build on the longer and more detailed discussion of testimonial injustice (Dieleman 2012: 258). The next few chapters will call this perspective into question, as we'll find that few shortcuts have been opened by our discussion of testimonial injustice in the earlier chapters of this book. In any case, Fricker has often been read as seeing hermeneutical injustice as of secondary importance, and the literature on epistemic injustice has sometimes reflected this prioritising of testimonial injustice.

DOI: 10.4324/9781003281863-11

In recent years, there's been an increasing appreciation of the fact that hermeneutical injustice is as least as complex, interesting, and significant as testimonial injustice, if not more so, leading to a wave of new work and fresh insights. We're going to spend several chapters unpicking some of the most important issues that hermeneutical injustice and related phenomena raise; even so, we won't be able to cover everything that merits our attention.

In this chapter, I'll start by presenting Fricker's characterisation of hermeneutical injustice (Section 8.2), before turning my attention to the main examples she has used to illustrate what she calls, parallel to her treatment of testimonial injustice, the 'central case' of hermeneutical injustice (Section 8.3). I'm going to spend much of the chapter focused on the example of Carmita Wood, which we first encountered in Chapter 2, since the historical details as given by Fricker don't seem wholly accurate in light of what we now know (Section 8.4). Moreover, I'll argue that getting these details right proves to support the claim some philosophers have made that the significance of the example for our understanding of hermeneutical injustice is not what Fricker and most of the subsequent literature takes it to be. I'll suggest that Carmita Wood *did* face a hermeneutical injustice—but not in the way Fricker suggests (Section 8.5).

8.2 DEFINING HERMENEUTICAL INJUSTICE

Let's say that hermeneutical injustice occurs when subjects face difficulties in making their significant social experiences intelligible, either to themselves or to others, where these difficulties are due to belonging to a group that has been *hermeneutically marginalised* (Fricker 2007: 158).[1] There's a lot folded into this definition which we need to unpack before we can apply it to the examples.

Your *significant* social experiences are those that it is in your interests to make intelligible (to yourself or to others). The focus here on experiences in particular might be queried. Nick Clanchy has suggested that we should generalise this so that hermeneutical injustice involves obstacles to making *something significant* about yourself intelligible, where this might include your experiences, or your gender, your race, your sexuality, or some other aspect of your identity or life. I'm sympathetic to this broadening of the definition, but I'll continue to put things in terms of experiences to stay in line with the literature I'll be discussing in these chapters.[2]

For now, we'll understand what it is to be hermeneutically marginalised along the lines suggested in Chapter 2: it's to be excluded from the kinds of roles, institutions, and practices that shape a society's communal hermeneutical resources, which are the resources readily and standardly available to make your experiences intelligible to yourself and to others. These will include resources such as concepts, expressions, and modes of expression (for example, the dialect of a language you speak). A society's communal stock of resources can be thought of as including those hermeneutical resources that have widespread currency throughout that society; it 'contains only meanings that just about anyone can draw upon and expect those meanings to be understood across social space by just about anyone else' (Fricker 2016: 163).[3] Fricker often refers to the practices within a society that have influence over its shared stock of hermeneutical resources as *meaning-making* practices.

As this already suggests, the notion of hermeneutical injustice is a complex one, and there is even more unclarity and disagreement about what it is and what it includes and excludes than there is with testimonial injustice. I'll come back to some of the tricky philosophical issues it raises in the next two chapters; in the remainder of this chapter, I want to engage in a study of Fricker's principal examples.

8.3 THE CENTRAL CASE OF HERMENEUTICAL INJUSTICE

Let's turn to examining Fricker's two main examples meant to illustrate hermeneutical injustice, both of which she takes from Susan Brownmiller's memoir of the second-wave feminist movement, In Our Time: Memoir of a Revolution (1999).[4] The first was one of our initial examples in Chapter 2. It concerns Carmita Wood, who, as we would now put it, sexually harassed by a professor as she worked as a lab-assistant and later as an administrator in the Nuclear Studies Lab at Cornell University in the early 1970s.[5] On Fricker's telling, at the time there was no apt label to classify and communicate her experiences. This led to a number of harms that compounded the original harassment; Wood suffered stress, and had her claim for unemployment insurance rejected after she finally left her job as she couldn't articulate why she had left: she could only write that she had 'personal reasons,' which were deemed insufficient by the Department of Labor (Fricker 2007: 150). Later a group of women at Cornell held a 'speak out' where they attempted to remedy the lack of expressive and conceptual resources, with an eye towards both appealing against Wood's rejected employment insurance claim and raising awareness of the problem more generally. One of the Cornell group present at that event, Karen Sauvigné, describes the key moment as follows:

> We wanted something that embraced a whole range of subtle and unsubtle persistent behaviors. Somebody came up with "harassment." *Sexual harassment!* Instantly we agreed. That's what it was.
> (Brownmiller 1999: 281, quoted in Fricker 2007: 150)

The other example that Fricker takes from Brownmiller's memoir involves a woman, Wendy Sanford, who had been suffering from postpartum depression. However, lacking this concept, Sanford had taken herself to be failing at being a parent due to her own deficiencies (and had been joined in that negative assessment of herself by her husband). During a workshop at MIT on medical and sexual issues facing women, Sanford had come to understand her own experiences, and to recognise that they were shared by many other women and weren't at all her own fault (Brownmiller 1999: 182, discussed in Fricker 2007: 149).

What do these examples have in common, according to Fricker, and what makes them injustices? And what's the significance of the moments in these narratives when someone hits on the expression 'sexual harassment' and the other women present immediately agree 'That's what it was,' or when Sanford is introduced to the term 'postpartum depression' (which she would later describe as 'one of those moments that makes you a feminist forever')? Let's take each of these questions in turn; to pre-empt a little, the second will prove to be surprisingly tricky to answer.

On Fricker's understanding, the women in both examples struggled to interpret their own experiences due to a lack of fitting conceptual resources, and this gave rise to gaps in their self-understanding and self-knowledge.[6] Concepts, as I introduced them in Chapter 2, are mental representations that enable us to think about, describe, and categorise things in thought. For example, our shared system of colour concepts allows us to categorise our colour experiences, keep track of and talk about the colours of various objects, and so on. Someone who entirely lacked the concept turquoise would be severely limited in their capacity to think and communicate about that colour. They wouldn't be able to think the thoughts that we would express as 'turquoise is pretty' or 'turquoise reminds me of the sea' or 'turquoise is closer to blue than to red' or 'I want to paint my living room turquoise.'

The best they could do would be to think of it as *that colour*, gesturing at or focusing on a sample of turquoise in their environment or perhaps in memory, or likening it to nearby colours that they did have concepts for, and this would limit their ability to think about turquoise: for instance, it would make it hard to build up a body of knowledge about it over time.[7] Fricker in effect presents the predicament of both of the women in her examples as analogous in relevant respects to someone missing a colour concept. They each have certain experiences, but they lack a fitting concept to categorise those experiences in a way that makes them intelligible, and allows them to acquire knowledge.

Let's briefly return to our imaginary turquoise-lacker. Without this concept, they wouldn't be able to competently use any linguistic expression that refers to it, and this would mean that their ability to communicate with others would be extremely limited too. They could use the expression 'that colour' in the presence of a sample of turquoise, or when all parties can be relied on to conjure up a sample in memory, and say things like 'I want to paint my living room *that* colour,' but again this is very restricted. In particular, think about the difficulties such a person would have trying to share knowledge about their experiences of turquoise with others who had never encountered that colour.

Again, this offers an (imperfect) analogy for how Fricker presents her examples. The two women also faced obstacles when trying to communicate these experiences and their significance to others, due to the unavailability of apt conceptual and expressive resources; Wood couldn't communicate to others that she had been sexually harassed and Sanford couldn't communicate that she was suffering from postpartum depression, since both they and their audiences lacked the vocabulary I've just used. Moreover, the experiences in question were ones very much in the interests of Wood and Sanford to understand and communicate; they were significant to them, as I used that term above.

That all said, there's still an important question we haven't addressed; what makes these obstacles to being understood *injustices*? Concerning Wendy Sanford, Fricker writes:

> No doubt there is a range of historical-cultural factors that might help explain this particular lack of understanding—a general lack of frankness about the normality of depression, for instance—but in so far as significant among these explanatory factors is some sort of social unfairness, such

as a structural inequality of power between men and women, then Wendy Sanford's moment of truth seems to be not simply a hermeneutical breakthrough for her and for the other women present, but also a moment in which some kind of epistemic injustice is overcome.

(2007: 149)

Fricker introduces the notion of hermeneutical marginalisation as a way to link this background 'social unfairness' to the lack of fitting hermeneutical resources available to Sanford.[8] As we've seen already, the idea is that certain institutions and practices in a society have an outsized role in shaping which hermeneutical resources make it into that society's communal stock—they command the most influence over which kinds of resources are produced in the first place, but also which can gain widespread currency in that society—and women and other oppressed groups are largely excluded from these institutions and practices. The upshot of this hermeneutical marginalisation of certain groups is that the communal resources, those that 'just about anyone can draw upon and expect those meanings to be understood across social space by just about anyone else,' will tend to be skewed in ways that favour the interests of members of more dominant groups. Experiences that may be very significant to marginalised groups, such as sexual harassment and postpartum depression, are ones for which a society may be slow or reluctant to formulate and proliferate suitable hermeneutical resources. That's what makes these examples injustices, for Fricker.

I'm going to return this crucial notion of hermeneutical marginalisation in much more detail in the next chapter, since the way I've been presenting it so far turns out not to fit with important aspects of Fricker's treatment of it. In the remainder of this chapter, I'll leave these complications aside and stay focused on Fricker's examples of the central case of hermeneutical injustice.

A first point to note is that the two examples seem different to each other in some important respects. With Carmita Wood, the crucial step towards remedying the injustice was the introduction of a fitting expression, which on Fricker's interpretation of the example also introduced a fitting concept expressed by that piece of vocabulary.[9] The term 'sexual harassment' and the concept it expressed then started to gain currency as it was used by Lin Farley and other members of the Cornell group in their public speaking and writing which resulted in it getting picked up by *The New York Times*, by the feminist lawyer Catharine MacKinnon, and by others who also propagated it out into the world at large. In contrast, there's no reason to think that Wendy Sanford was witness to the birth of a conceptual or expressive practice. Rather, the natural reading of the account we're offered is that she was inducted into one that already existed; Sanford learning about postpartum depression at the MIT workshop was part of the expression (and so the concept) spreading out to the people who needed it, after it had already been coined.[10] This isn't a difference that Fricker registers as holding any significance, but it seems important for thinking about the sense in which each of these examples illustrates a step towards hermeneutical and epistemic justice.

8.4 SEXUAL HARASSMENT BEFORE 'SEXUAL HARASSMENT'

Fricker's presentation of Carmita Wood's story has been a source of much controversy. In particular, a number of philosophers have argued that Wood's understanding of her own experiences prior to April 1975, when Farley and her group had their breakthrough, wasn't anything like as impoverished as Fricker's discussion suggests. In laying out the ways that the hermeneutical injustice faced by Wood was harmful to her, Fricker writes:

> The cognitive disablement prevents her from understanding a significant patch of her own experience: that is, a patch of experience which it is strongly in her interests to understand, for without that understanding she is left deeply troubled, confused, and isolated, not to mention vulnerable to continued harassment. Her hermeneutical disadvantage renders her unable to make sense of her ongoing mistreatment, and this in turn prevents her from protesting it, let alone securing effective measures to stop it.
>
> (2007: 151)

It's not clear how well any of this describes Carmita Wood's actual situation or her response to it, though.[11] Let's take a closer look, in light of what's now known. First, Wood's harasser, Boyce McDaniel, made it clear to her that he didn't think she should have been appointed to her position in the lab (which she was the first woman to hold), and he had tried to publicly humiliate her and undermine her in various ways since she had been in post; his sexual harassment of Wood was just one way, albeit one particularly serious and harmful way, that he tried to put her, to use the sadly familiar idiom, back 'in her place.'[12] He also behaved inappropriately towards other women in the lab, and Wood was not the only one to complain about him (Baker 2007: 28).

Second, on Brownmiller's telling, quoted by Fricker, Wood applied once for unemployment benefit but couldn't think of anything to write as her reason for having left her job at Cornell, so put 'personal reasons,' only to have her application denied. She then turned to Lin Farley and her group at Cornell, and they worked together to figure out how to appeal the decision. This isn't quite right, though.[13] In Wood's initial application for unemployment benefits, she wrote that she had left her position at Cornell for health reasons, and these were deemed 'personal non-compelling reasons' by the Department of Labor in rejecting it. Wood appealed this decision, prior to meeting Lin Farley's group, this time offering a relatively detailed account of McDaniel's behaviour towards her, how it made her feel, and the way it had impacted her health; she also involved two witnesses who could confirm aspects of her account. Rather dismally, in response to this appeal, the Department of Labor simply repeated their verdict that these were 'personal non-compelling reasons.'

Third, the women involved in the Cornell speak-outs in which the term 'sexual harassment' was coined in 1975 were already heavily engaged in conversations about it, prior to Carmita Wood getting in touch. Lin Farley had taught a class on women and work in the Fall semester of 1974, and issues about sexual coercion in the workplace had come up repeatedly. Farley had even had her class engage in earlier consciousness-raising/speak-out sessions on this issue as part of this course (Baker 2007: 29).[14] Farley came out of these earlier discussions with a diagnosis of why the issue was so difficult to even begin to tackle—they lacked a name for it:

> When I left the class, I thought that we needed to have a name for what this phenomenon was. We all needed to be talking about the same thing.
> (Farley, quoted in Swenson 2017)

> It was something that we all talked about but because it didn't have a name we didn't know we were all talking about the same thing.
> (Farley, quoted in Swenson 2017; Traister 2018: 167)

Given this, it seems implausible that Wood herself, or women more generally, were bereft of conceptual or expressive resources prior to Lin Farley's group coming up with the name 'sexual harassment'; they were talking with each other, and Wood even made what seems like a fair job of communicating with the Department of Labor (even if that didn't have the desired effect). There may not have been a fitting label in their society's communal stock of hermeneutical resources, but this doesn't seem to have had the dire cognitive and communicative consequences that Fricker claims.

Fricker has responded to the objection that she overlooked that women had some resources for thinking and communicating about their experiences of sexual harassment prior to being able to label them as such, seeming slightly bemused and perhaps even a little frustrated that people have treated this as a problem for her discussion of this example. Far from the example showing that she had totally missed the fact that members of marginalised groups can find ways to talk amongst themselves even when their society fails to provide a ready-made and shared label for their experiences, Fricker takes it to illustrate that she was always on board with this possibility:

> [T]he possibility of localised hermeneutical practices is built in to the picture of how Carmita Wood and her fellow consciousness raisers overcame hermeneutical injustice.
>
> (2016: 166)

That's fair enough, as far as it goes.[15] Still, once we have a better sense of the challenges Carmita Wood actually faced, and the ways that she and her contemporaries responded to and discussed their experiences prior to April 1975, it's hard to see this as an example that demonstrates how a hermeneutical gap can leave someone unable to interpret their own experiences, in a state of confusion, or unable to act and communicate in ways it is in their interests to be able to. This doesn't seem like an accurate characterisation of Carmita Wood and her contemporaries at all, in which case the sense in which they succeeded in making progress towards hermeneutical justice can't be as Fricker describes it (if the example's even to be regarded as illustrating hermeneutical injustice in the first place).

Why have we devoted so much time to going through the details of this particular example? Partly, it's to contribute to correcting the record. Carmita Wood was a real person, not a philosopher's abstraction or thought experiment, and so if philosophers want to make this a central example in this debate, there's an onus on us to get things right. There are also more philosophical reasons, though, in addition to this point. In the previous paragraph, I suggested that the example likely doesn't show what Fricker presents it as showing; victims of sexual harassment like Wood seem to have been able to attain a fair degree of understanding of their experiences, and to communicate and act despite the hermeneutical injustice they supposedly faced; that their efforts were often ineffectual seems more to do with running up against a wall of indifference and hostility, rather than lacking the right terminology. If that's so, though, then what was the significance of the moment when someone came up with 'sexual harassment'? Recall how Karen Sauvigné reports the group's reaction: '*Sexual harassment!* Instantly we agreed. That's what it was.' What's happening here? And if—as I think we should—we still share Fricker's sense that this was a hermeneutical breakthrough and a step in the direction of hermeneutical justice, how are we to make sense of this breakthrough?

8.5 HERMENEUTICAL JUSTICE AND POLITICAL SOLIDARITY

I think we get a pointer in the right direction by taking another look at Farley's account of the aims of the group in introducing the term 'sexual harassment,' as expressed in the quotes above. She thought it important to name what she and her students had experienced so that they would all be 'talking about the same thing' and would be able to recognise that they were all talking about the same thing. Notice, though, that there's a perhaps surprising element of choice or intention here. Sexual harassment isn't a natural kind, like water or gold; it doesn't have an underlying nature or essence that gives it unity. What counts as 'the same thing' depends on how things are conceptualised, and this is partly a matter of choice rather than something that is simply given to us by the world. We can see this element of choice quite clearly in the example, if we take a fresh look at it. Farley's Cornell group *wanted* to find a way to conceptualise what Wood and others had endured in a relatively expansive way, so as to include as broad a range of behaviours and experiences as they possibly could. This is an aim they were entirely explicit about—here's the quote from Sauvigné one last time, and it makes this point quite clearly:

> We wanted something that embraced a whole range of subtle and unsubtle persistent behaviors. Somebody came up with "harassment." *Sexual harassment!* Instantly we agreed. That's what it was.

Likewise, in explaining why 'sexual harassment' had seemed apt, Farley said that it covered '[e]verything from phrases that referenced sex to touch, all the way up to forced sexual relations, it runs the whole gamut' (quoted in Swenson 2017). Rebecca Traister puts the point in a recent account of the Cornell feminists and Carmita Wood by writing that 'Farley and her colleagues searched for something all-encompassing' (2018: 167). The moment described by Sauvigné in which someone hit on the term 'sexual harassment' and it immediately resonated with the other women present, then, is a report of finding a term with suitable *generality*, given that this was their explicit goal. Ishani Maitra writes:

> Presumably, something about this label seems to *fit* what happened to Wood in a way that the other labels do not, and this is apparent to all concerned.
> (2018: 348)

But I think this misunderstands what happened. The crucial point is not that 'sexual harassment' was a particularly apt or fitting label for what Wood endured, but that it covered a whole range of experiences, some of them in fact quite different to Wood's; the group were precisely *not* attempting to tailor a label for Wood's experiences in particular, but to cast their net as widely as possible. Moreover, as we've seen, this inclusive approach to conceptualising was deliberate and strategic. Lin Farley further expanded on her motivations for this kind of approach in a 2017 op-ed in *The New York Times*:

> Now women could share stories and strategies. They understood that they weren't alone, that millions of working women shared their experience. It was as if a light had been switched on in a dark room. The solidarity that women felt for one another was contagious; sisterhood in the workplace suddenly seemed doable.
>
> Perhaps we might even see the start of a national working women's union – it is easy to pick off one woman at a time for sexual harassment, but not so easy if women all look out for one another. The enthusiasm with which women embraced the idea of sexual harassment indicated an intense desire to change conditions for themselves at work; our new vocabulary would help.
>
> Or so I thought.
> (Farley 2017)

The motivations for a broad, inclusive concept, then, related to a desire to build shared understanding and solidarity amongst women, as a basis for coordinated activism to change women's situation.[16] To adapt a well-known feminist slogan, Farley and her group aimed to make the personal as political as they possibly could.[17]

If the discussion offered here is on the right track, Fricker's two examples of the 'central case' of hermeneutical injustice in fact illustrate quite different aspects of this kind of injustice from each other. Moreover, it's not clear that either illustrates a community-wide hermeneutical lacuna—gap—being filled for the first time. Wendy Sanford was most likely inducted into an already existing linguistic and conceptual practice, and so while this was a game-changing moment for her and for the other neophytes in her group, the most natural way to think about how this was a step towards hermeneutical justice is that it represents the proliferation of these vital hermeneutical resources out to the people who needed them, rather than the creation of fitting hermeneutical resources. My detailed look at the example of Carmita Wood, on the other hand, has brought us close to Rebecca Mason's conclusion about it:

> By providing a safe space for feminist discussion of the issues and behaviors affecting women's lives, the consciousness-raising group in which Wood participated surely enhanced her understanding of her experiences (by, for instance, helping to articulate the systematic nature of the phenomenon she helped to name). But rather than functioning as "a life changing flash of enlightenment" (Fricker [2007], 98), naming created a hermeneutical environment conducive to organized social activism against one manifestation of sexism.
>
> (2011: 297–298)

Mason nicely captures here the significance of the introduction of a fitting label for sexual harassment; the name helped sexual harassment to be seen as pervasive and systematic, and for its victims to begin to organise against it. It's less clear that Mason is right to contrast this with the thought that naming sexual harassment was a 'life changing flash of enlightenment'; perhaps we do better to see these as two sides of the same coin, in the sense that a 'flash of enlightenment' can accompany hitting on a way of conceptualising something that immediately creates vital connections between the experiences of different people, as in the case of Carmita Wood and the Cornell feminists. Recall Farley's words, quoted above:

> Now women could share stories and strategies. They understood that they weren't alone, that millions of working women shared their experience. It was as if a light had been switched on in a dark room.

8.6 SUMMARY

We started this chapter with Fricker's definition of hermeneutical injustice and began the task of unpacking what it says and what it implies. We then examined Fricker's two examples of the central case of hermeneutical injustice, focusing on the injustice faced by Carmita Wood in the example from Chapter 2. While I've ultimately agreed with Fricker that Wood faced a hermeneutical injustice, and that the introduction of the concept of sexual harassment was an important step towards hermeneutical justice, I have offered a rather different picture of why this is so, based on a more accurate account of the details of the example.

Our focus on Fricker's examples in this chapter has meant that we haven't really dug into the moving parts of her characterisation of hermeneutical injustice, and in particular we haven't given the crucial notion of hermeneutical marginalisation any scrutiny yet. These issues will be our topic in the next chapter.

8.7 SUGGESTED FURTHER READING

It's unclear who exactly coined the term 'sexual harassment.' Lin Farley has claimed that it was her, as in the title of Farley (2017); Clanchy (2024: 705 n4) has argued that things aren't so straightforward.

Strebeigh (2009: Part 4) offers an account of the (fragile) route by which the concept of sexual harassment became embedded in American employment law: Chapter 15 of his book focuses on the period discussed in this chapter.

Catala (2020) and Fürst (2024) both offer further proposals concerning the epistemic and hermeneutical resources available to Carmita Wood and other women prior to the introduction of the concept of sexual harassment.

Fraser (2018) is a fantastic paper, arguing that the widespread use of certain metaphors, such as those drawing comparisons to rape or to the

Holocaust, give rise to hermeneutical injustice. For further interesting discussion of the complicated relationship between metaphor and hermeneutical injustice (and justice), see Sibbald (2023) and Ney (2024).

Arora, Hutchison, and Rogers (forthcoming) offers a fascinating look at the contributions of Dalit feminists to identifying and addressing the kinds of obstacles to being understood that Fricker classifies as hermeneutical injustices, as well as discussing the reasons that Dalit feminism is so neglected in work in Anglophone feminist philosophy.

NOTES

1 In Fricker's own words, hermeneutical injustice is 'the injustice of having some significant area of one's social experience obscured from collective understanding owing to hermeneutical marginalisation' (2007: 158), though she offers various other formulations throughout her work on this.
2 See Clanchy (2023: 814 fn4); Romdenh-Romluc (2017: 3) suggests we understand the notion of 'experiences' broadly, to include the kinds of things Clanchy has in mind. See Preston-Roedder (2024) for a discussion of epistemic injustice and denials of biracial people's self-attributions of race, and Turyn (2023) and Henckel (forthcoming) for similar points concerning trans people's self-attributions of gender.
3 Fricker was less explicit about how she was thinking of collective hermeneutical resources in her 2007 book. This has led to several misinterpretations in the literature; I don't intend to discuss these here, but see Goetze (2018: 75–77) for a useful overview.
4 While familiar, the metaphor of different 'waves' of feminist activism may distort as much as it illuminates: see e.g. Rodrigues (2025).
5 Carmita Wood seems to have reverted to her original name, Carmita Dickerson, prior to her death. However, the literature almost without exception calls her Wood, and so I've stuck with that to avoid confusion. There has been some uncertainty about Wood's race, and how that should factor into discussions of the example and sexual harassment more generally. Wood is in fact white (e.g. Campbell 2017), though as is often observed, it's striking and significant that many of the women to first bring sexual harassment lawsuits against their harassers were not. Thanks to Jenny Saul here, who has helped philosophers get this detail of the example right.
6 See Fraser (2018) for one proposal about how to understand what it is for a concept to be fitting or ill-fitting (though she acknowledges it may not work as a general account).

7 In a recent paper, O'Shaughnessy and Sprevak (2024) propose that we should think of concepts as *containers for knowledge* about a category, which may be a helpful metaphor for thinking about them here.
8 The notion of hermeneutical marginalisation is a successor of Fricker's earlier notion of epistemic oppression, discussed in Chapter 4.
9 Fricker doesn't offer a view on the relationship between concepts and language, as far as I can tell, but it's not clear that there's anything particularly mysterious about this case as Fricker describes it. Introducing an expression into a language surely isn't always a matter of naming a concept that already exists; instead, sometimes conceptual innovation seems to be a direct result of linguistic innovation, when someone coins a fitting expression in some language and it gets a suitable degree of uptake. See Longworth (2013) for a brief, accessible introduction to the general issues here.
10 This is also how Goetze (2018: 77), George and Goguen (2021), and Dougherty (2023: 824) interpret this example.
11 Berenstain (2020: 741) charges Fricker with being over-reliant on Brownmiller's account, which seems plausible.
12 This is a textbook example of misogyny, in Kate Manne's sense. On Manne's influential analysis, misogyny involves the performance of various 'down girl' moves designed to put women back 'in their place' when they threaten the patriarchal order, for example by coming to occupy roles traditionally reserved for men: roles that are 'his for the taking' (e.g. Manne 2018: 113–121).
13 See e.g. Baker (2007: 28), Campbell (2017), and Traister (2018: 167).
14 There is some acknowledgement of this in the account Fricker reproduces; in the fuller version of the quote from Karen Sauvigné that I have focused on in the text, she notes that 'Lin's students had been talking in her seminar about the unwanted sexual advanced they'd encountered on their summer jobs' (Brownmiller 1999: 281, quoted in Fricker 2007: 150).
15 I do think some of the criticisms of Fricker on this point have been rather overstated. Mason complains that on Fricker's picture, the naming of sexual harassment occurs 'ex nihilo' (2011: 298), while Berenstain writes that 'Fricker's methodology reveals a tacit commitment to the assumption that until a group of white women activists at Cornell University came up with the perfect phrase to describe the problem of sexual harassment, the phenomenon had gone not only unrecognized but untheorized' (2020: 739). These claims seem needlessly uncharitable to me. That said, Berenstain's remark is part of a broader worry that Fricker overlooks the work of Black feminists on sexual harassment throughout the 20th century, and Mason is rightly drawing attention to injustices associated with a phenomena that has come to be known as 'hermeneutical dissent', see Chapters 4 and 10 for related discussion.

16 There are trade-offs involved here. A very inclusive concept, as sexual harassment is intended to be, runs the risk of what Rebecca Traister calls 'category collapse' (2018), where very different problematic behaviours, perhaps requiring very different responses, are put under a single label: compare Maitra's notion of an 'internal distortion' (Maitra 2018). There are some important issues here, not just for discussions of second-wave feminist activism against sexual harassment, but also for Traister's main focus, the recent #MeToo movement; unfortunately it would take me too far afield to discuss those in this book, but see Pohlhaus (2020: 245–249) for some insightful relevant remarks.

17 I return to the note of pessimism sounded at the end of this quote from Farley ('Or so I thought') in the suggested readings offered in Chapter 10.

REFERENCES

Arora, Swati, Katrina Hutchison, and Wendy Rogers. Forthcoming. 'Epistemic Exclusion: Theorizing Dalit Feminism.' *Hypatia*. https://doi.org/10.1017/hyp.2025.10019

Baker, Carrie. 2007. *The Women's Movement against Sexual Harassment*. Cambridge and New York: Cambridge University Press.

Berenstain, Nora. 2020. 'White Feminist Gaslighting.' *Hypatia* 35 (4): 733–758. https://doi.org/10.1017/hyp.2020.31

Brownmiller, Susan. 1999. *In Our Time: Memoir of a Revolution*. New York: Random House Publishing.

Campbell, Jessica. 2017. 'The First Brave Woman Who Alleged 'Sexual Harassment'.' *Legacy.com*, December 7, 2017. https://www.legacy.com/news/culture-and-history/the-first-brave-woman-who-alleged-sexual-harassment/

Catala, Amandine. 2020. 'Metaepistemic Injustice and Intellectual Disability: A Pluralist Account of Epistemic Agency.' *Ethical Theory and Moral Practice* 23: 755–776. https://doi.org/10.1007/s10677-020-10120-0

Clanchy, Nick. 2023. 'Whose Hermeneutical Marginalization?' *Episteme* 20: 813–832. https://doi.org/10.1017/epi.2023.16

Clanchy, Nick. 2024. 'Tackling Hermeneutical Injustices in Gender-Affirming Healthcare.' *Hypatia* 39 (4): 688–710. https://doi.org/10.1017/hyp.2024.15

Dieleman, Susan. 2012. 'An Interview with Miranda Fricker.' *Social Epistemology* 26 (2): 253–261. https://doi.org/10.1080/02691728.2011.652216

Dougherty, Emma C. 2023. 'Toward an Agential Conception of Hermeneutical Injustice: Isolation and Domestic Violence.' *Hypatia* 38 (4): 822–838. https://doi.org/10.1017/hyp.2023.75

Farley, Lin. 2017. 'I Coined the Term 'Sexual Harassment'. Corporations Stole It.' *The New York Times*, October 28, 2017. https://www.nytimes.com/2017/10/18/opinion/sexual-harassment-corporations-steal.html

Fraser, Rachel Elizabeth. 2018. 'The Ethics of Metaphor.' *Ethics* 128 (4): 728–755. https://doi.org/10.1086/697448

Fricker, Miranda. 2007. *Epistemic Injustice: Power and the Ethics of Knowing*. Oxford: Oxford University Press.

Fricker, Miranda. 2016. 'Epistemic Injustice and the Preservation of Ignorance.' In Rik Peels and Martijn Blaauw, eds. *The Epistemic Dimensions of Ignorance*: 160–177. Cambridge: Cambridge University Press.

Fürst, Martina. 2024. 'Closing the Conceptual Gap in Epistemic Injustice.' *Philosophical Quarterly* 74 (1): 229–250. https://doi.org/10.1093/pq/pqad024

George, B. R. and Stacey Goguen. 2021. 'Hermeneutical Backlash: Trans Youth Panics as Epistemic Injustice.' *Feminist Philosophy Quarterly* 7 (4): 1–34. https://doi.org/10.5206/fpq/2021.4.13518

Goetze, Trystan. 2018. 'Hermeneutical Dissent and the Species of Hermeneutical Injustice.' *Hypatia* 33 (1): 73–90. https://doi.org/10.1111/hypa.12384

Henckel, S. J. Forthcoming. 'You Think You Know Someone: Trans Identities and Epistemic Injustice.' *Hypatia*. https://doi.org/10.1017/hyp.2025.4

Longworth, Guy. 2013. 'Concepts and Language.' In Harold Pashler, ed. *Encyclopedia of the Mind*: 176–179. Los Angeles, CA: SAGE Publications.

Maitra, Ishani. 2018. 'New Names for Old Wrongs.' *Episteme* 15 (3): 345–362. https://doi.org/10.1017/epi.2018.27

Manne, Kate. 2018. *Down Girl: The Logic of Misogyny*. Oxford: Oxford University Press.

Mason, Rebecca. 2011. 'Two Kinds of Unknowing.' *Hypatia* 26 (2): 294–307. https://doi.org/10.1111/j.1527-2001.2011.01175.x

Ney, Milan. 2024. 'Metaphors and Hermeneutical Resistance.' *European Journal of Philosophy* 32 (1): 159–178. https://doi.org/10.1111/ejop.12839

O'Shaughnessy, Robert and Mark Sprevak. 2024. 'Concepts are Containers.' *Croatian Journal of Philosophy* 24 (72): 333–350. https://doi.org/10.52685/cjp.24.72.1

Pohlhaus Jr., Gaile. 2020. 'Epistemic Agency under Oppression.' *Philosophical Papers* 49 (2): 233–251. https://doi.org/10.1080/05568641.2020.1780149

Preston-Roedder, Erica. 2024. 'You Aren't Really Black, You Aren't Really White: Racial Denials and Epistemic Injustice in the Black-White Multiracial Community.' *Journal of Ethics and Social Philosophy* 27 (1): 34–59.

Rodrigues, Laís. 2025. 'Historically Drowning Othered Voices with a Few Waves.' *Hypatia* 40 (3): 613-632. https://doi.org/10.1017/hyp.2024.80

Romdenh-Romluc, Komarine. 2017. 'Hermeneutical Injustice and the Problem of Authority.' *Feminist Philosophy Quarterly* 3 (3): 1–23. https://doi.org/10.5206/fpq/2017.3.1

Sibbald, Kaitlin. 2023. 'Are Metaphors Ethically Bad Epistemic Practice? Epistemic Injustice at the Intersections.' *Hypatia* 38 (4): 801–821. https://doi.org/10.1017/hyp.2023.90

Strebeigh, Fred. 2009. *Equal: Women Reshape American Law*. New York and London: W. W. Norton & Company.

Swenson, Kyle. 2017. 'Who Came Up with the Term 'Sexual Harassment'?' *The Washington Post*, November 22, 2017. https://www.washingtonpost.com/news/morning-mix/wp/2017/11/22/who-came-up-with-the-term-sexual-harassment/

Traister, Rebecca. 2018. *Good and Mad: The Revolutionary Power of Women's Anger*. New York: Simon and Schuster.

Turyn, Gus. 2023. 'Gender and First-Person Authority.' *Synthese* 201: 1–19. https://doi.org/10.1007/s11229-023-04125-2

9
INCIDENTAL HERMENEUTICAL INJUSTICE AND HERMENEUTICAL MARGINALISATION

9.1 INTRODUCTION

The previous chapter looked at Fricker's examples of the central case of hermeneutical injustice. However, I didn't really spell out the significance of this focus on the *central* case. As we saw in Chapter 5, the central case of testimonial injustice was its *systematic* form, contrasted with its *incidental* form illustrated by the example, first introduced in Chapter 2, of the Philosopher of Physics having their contributions prejudicially dismissed at a science conference. Fricker takes hermeneutical injustice to also have incidental cases, but this proves to be a much less straightforward matter than the parallel claim for testimonial injustice.

On the face of it, this isn't an issue that should require a whole chapter of this book. After all, hermeneutical injustice differs from testimonial injustice in a number of respects: why shouldn't this prove to be one of them? Moreover, it seems like a fairly peripheral issue, given that Fricker and other philosophers are mostly focused on systematic forms of epistemic injustice. Who cares if there are incidental cases of hermeneutical injustice, given that we're mostly going to ignore them anyway?

These are understandable responses, and they probably explain why—with a few notable exceptions to be discussed shortly—most philosophers

DOI: 10.4324/9781003281863-12

working on hermeneutical injustice haven't paid this issue much attention. That's a mistake, though. Thinking about whether and how we can make sense of incidental cases takes us fairly quickly to the most central and important questions concerning hermeneutical injustice, since it bears directly on the relationship between hermeneutical injustice and the key notion of hermeneutical marginalisation, and on how we should think about hermeneutical marginalisation in the first place. Surveying different attempts to make sense of incidental cases, as I will do in this chapter, turns out to be a way of looking at several quite fundamentally different ways of thinking about hermeneutical injustice. There's nothing peripheral about the issue at all.

Let's begin by looking at Fricker's example designed to demonstrate the possibility of incidental cases, and then we'll get clear on why this leads to an issue for her account, and for our understanding of hermeneutical injustice more generally (Section 9.2). We'll then spend the rest of the chapter evaluating various attempts to address this puzzle by rethinking the notion of hermeneutical marginalisation or its relationship to hermeneutical injustice (Sections 9.3–9.6). Unfortunately, none of the existing options seems very satisfactory, and so this issue will remain a challenge for Fricker's account of hermeneutical injustice at the end of the chapter.

9.2 JOE ROSE

The thesis that there can be incidental cases of testimonial injustice seems both uncontentious and relatively philosophically uninteresting. Let's quickly review some key points from Chapter 5. For Fricker, testimonial injustice involves a speaker receiving less credibility than she ought to from her audience due to that audience's prejudices. In Fricker's principal examples, which illustrate what she calls the 'central case' of testimonial injustice, these are prejudices concerning the speaker's identity, and they 'track' the speaker through different spheres of social interactions; in Fricker's terminology, the central case of testimonial injustice is that of *systematic identity prejudicial credibility deficit*. What Fricker spots is that this framework leaves room for testimonial injustices based on prejudices that are relatively local, as in the example of the Philosopher of Physics, first introduced in Chapter 2. Such cases don't raise any obvious problems for Fricker; as we've just seen, they seem to fit entirely comfortably within her framework. You might assume the same would be true of incidental cases of hermeneutical injustice.

INCIDENTAL HERMENEUTICAL INJUSTICE   187

Moreover, Fricker provides us with what she takes to be a case in point. This is Joe Rose, the main character from Ian McEwan's novel *Enduring Love*, whom we also first met in Chapter 2. Rose is white, straight, cis, nondisabled, wealthy, and enjoys a successful career as a science writer, having written numerous bestselling books and published in the best-known magazines and periodicals.[1] He meets the novel's antagonist, Jed Parry, during their joint attempt with three other men to bring down a hot air balloon which has floated out of control with a young boy inside its basket, an attempt in which one of the would-be rescuers is horribly killed. Parry finds Rose's phone number and address, and immediately begins a barrage of calls, voicemail messages, and letters; he also stations himself outside Rose's apartment for much of each day, and sometimes follows Rose around London. Rose finds Parry's behaviour and communications increasingly threatening, but he can't convince his fiancé Clarissa or the policemen he talks to that there's anything to be worried about. Clarissa's dismissal of Rose's concerns leads to the breakdown of their relationship, while the police's inaction allows Parry the opportunity to turn violent, resulting in a badly botched attempt on Rose's life in which a bystander is shot, and a final showdown in which Parry takes Clarissa hostage at knife-point before being shot in the arm by Rose.

This is, Fricker proposes, a fictional illustration of what incidental hermeneutical injustice would look like. Rose doesn't belong to any marginalised group; indeed, in addition to advantages he has generally in virtue of his social identity, he personally commands a lot of influence through his ability to reach large audiences and to be treated as an authority on a range of topics when he does so. Still, Fricker argues, this has the hallmarks of a case of hermeneutical injustice. Rose faces obstacles to understanding his own experiences and their significance, and to communicating the nature and significance of these experiences to others, when it would very much be in his interests to do so. It's less clear why Fricker thinks this should be thought of as an injustice; we'll return to this below.

There's a point about this example I'd like to make, then leave mostly to the side for the remainder of my discussion of it. Fricker's description of Rose's predicament is sparse and selective, and the subsequent literature on the example has tended not to pick up on this. The result has been that virtually none of the claims made about this example in the literature make much sense when we bear in mind key details concerning the plot and characters in McEwan's novel. Jed Parry has de Clérambault's Syndrome (or 'erotomania') which involves delusions that another person is in love with the sufferer, and often that they are trying to send the sufferer secret messages. Rose spends much of the novel unsure of how to interpret Parry's behaviour and how afraid to be of him; however, he *is* familiar with the concept of de Clérambault's Syndrome (an advantage of having one's protagonist be a popular science communicator), and so although it takes him a while to remember the details, he is able to correctly identify Parry as a sufferer relatively quickly. This means that Rose has a period of deep uncertainty about what is happening, followed by a period of relative clarity informed by his correct diagnosis of Parry, and at no point does he seem to lack any relevant concepts or expressions; rather, his memory is just slow to produce the details he needs.[2] Much of the difficulty he has communicating his experiences stems from the fact that the relevant concept, de Clérambault's Syndrome, is relatively esoteric, which means that the police aren't familiar with it and that when Rose explains it to them, they question his standing to diagnose Parry given that he has no formal qualifications to do so. None of this looks like a case of hermeneutical injustice at all.

I think the way Fricker intends her readers to interpret the example is to see Joe Rose as a victim of *stalking*, but one in which Rose and others struggle to see that as a fitting description due to widely held stereotypes and conceptual schema that picture stalking as invariably involving male perpetrators and female victims.[3] So although there is a concept and an expression that *should* be available to Rose to understand and communicate his experiences, these have been rendered unavailable by the gendered patterns which, although not part of the dictionary meaning of 'stalking,' are part of what Fricker calls their 'social meaning.' This is how I'll understand the example in what follows, even where doing so conflicts with my understanding of McEwan's novel.

One reason to proceed in this manner is that the example, so understood, is representative of a class of cases which seem important to engage with when thinking about hermeneutical injustice. These are cases of atypical victims of certain kinds of crimes that are more typically directed at members of marginalised and oppressed social groups, such as male victims of stalking, domestic abuse, and sexual violence, who struggle to understand their experiences and make them understood by others for this reason. This may not be the right way to think about Joe Rose in the novel—for one thing, de Clérambault's Syndrome typically has male victims and female perpetrators, so it's not Rose's gender that makes this an atypical case but rather Parry's—but if we understand the example as Fricker suggests, Rose can go proxy for cases of this general kind. Moreover, we can perhaps see why Fricker is tempted to treat examples of this sort as involving incidental hermeneutical injustice. They share features in common with her examples of the central case of hermeneutical injustice, but unlike in the systematic case, the obstacles they face to making their experiences understood don't seem to be an aspect of a broader pattern of oppression or marginalisation. So let's take Joe Rose as a representative of this kind of example (even if we need to distort details of McEwan's story to make it fit this mould).

We seem to have identified a class of examples, which we're taking Joe Rose to represent, that show that incidental hermeneutical injustice is possible and worth paying attention to (even if we mostly stay focused on systematic cases). However, as I mentioned above, incidental hermeneutical injustice is puzzling and problematic in a way that incidental testimonial injustice isn't. The issue, simply put, is that by Fricker's definition, hermeneutical injustice is (at least in part) due to hermeneutical marginalisation, and hermeneutical marginalisation looks like an inherently systematic and structural phenomenon, relating to which of a society's practices and institutions get to play the largest meaning-making role, together with inequalities in which kinds of people are included in and which excluded from these practices and institutions. There's no clear analogue of the merely local prejudices involved in incidental testimonial injustice, and no obvious way to make sense of the idea that Joe Rose belongs to a hermeneutically marginalised group.

What are our options for resolving this puzzle? On the face of it, there are four main strategies, each of which has been explored in the literature. First, we can give up the part of Fricker's definition that says that hermeneutical injustice is always based on hermeneutical marginalisation, and explore if that helps us to identify more local mechanisms that could give rise to incidental hermeneutical injustice. We then have two apparently less drastic options that allow us to keep Fricker's definition more or less intact; we can reconsider the nature of hermeneutical marginalisation, so that Joe Rose meets this condition despite all of his many privileges, or we can loosen (without breaking entirely) the connection between hermeneutical marginalisation and hermeneutical injustice. Finally, there's the option of denying that incidental hermeneutical injustice is a genuine phenomenon, and finding some other account of Joe Rose's predicament. Over the next four sections, we'll take each of these options in turn.

9.3 HERMENEUTICAL INJUSTICE WITHOUT HERMENEUTICAL MARGINALISATION

One apparently extreme option here is to deny that hermeneutical injustice always needs to be based on hermeneutical marginalisation; even if systematic cases are explained in terms of hermeneutical marginalisation, perhaps incidental cases need not be (e.g. Dougherty 2023: 836 n3). As we've already noted, this involves revising Fricker's definition of hermeneutical injustice, as well as generalising her explanation of what it is that makes cases of hermeneutical injustice count as injustices, which seem like costs; however, there are arguably already other reasons to consider taking these steps. Let's take a look.

As we saw in the previous chapter, Fricker offers a particular account of why the women in her two examples of the central case, Carmita Wood and Wendy Sanford, faced injustices, involving the claim that women were a hermeneutically marginalised group. Presumably, though, nobody (including Fricker) thinks that this describes the *only* way that a person could unjustly face obstacles to making their significant experiences intelligible. For instance, someone could systematically isolate their gay or trans child, preventing them from interacting with their peers, reading websites, or consuming media that would introduce them to concepts and terms that would enable them to understand their own sexuality or gender; this, sadly, is unlikely to impress you as a farfetched scenario.[4] Why does the definition of hermeneutical injustice specify that the injustice must have arisen in one particular way? As Mona Simion writes:

> What is plausibly essential to hermeneutical epistemic injustice is that the relevant form of epistemic failure is unjustly brought about, no matter how this happens, that is, whether as a result of marginalization or not.
>
> (Simion 2019: 180)

Moreover, given that Fricker's specification about the source of the injustice was based entirely on consideration of examples of the central, systematic case, why insist that it's part of the definition of incidental cases too? Perhaps, to return to the suggestion we started this section with, the difference between systematic and incidental hermeneutical injustice is between those which are due to hermeneutical marginalisation and those that are due to more local causes of injustice, as illustrated by the example of the child being isolated away from the hermeneutical resources that would help them.

What this suggests is that breaking the link between hermeneutical injustice and hermeneutical marginalisation perhaps isn't as radical a step as it might initially appear, and it needn't be an ad hoc move in response to Joe Rose; rather, this treatment of the example emerges as part of a general, plausible criticism of how Fricker restricts her account of hermeneutical injustice. That acknowledged, we haven't yet been offered an alternative explanation of why we should think that Joe Rose faces an epistemic injustice. It's all very well to point out that there could in principle be a story here that's quite different to that in terms of hermeneutical marginalisation, but without any details, the proposal is liable to seem like an empty promise. Dougherty writes:

> To make sense of this issue, I argue that Joe was not hermeneutically marginalized, rather his interlocuters were subscribing to harmful dominant narratives about who can be a victim of stalking. The interference of these dominant narratives prevented them from being able to understand Joe's experiences.
>
> (2023: 836 n3)

However, being faced with interlocuters who subscribe to such harmful narratives isn't automatically an injustice; it depends on how and why such narratives have become dominant. Fricker specifies that this is an injustice when the proliferation of these harmful narratives is due to the hermeneutical marginalisation of the victims, but Dougherty offers no alternative to this; they stop exactly at the point when a further, distinct explanation is needed.[5]

This response to the puzzle generated by incidental cases of hermeneutical injustice seems incomplete, then; simply giving up the restriction that hermeneutical injustices must be due to hermeneutical marginalisation isn't sufficient to give an account of Joe Rose and similar cases. Moreover, as we've seen, it embroils us in a much larger discussion about revisions to Fricker's definition of hermeneutical injustice; I've noted that this is a discussion we may want to have anyway, for the reasons given by Simion, but it's worth seeing what options we have for making sense of incidental hermeneutical injustice if we resolve to leave Fricker's definition, including the link it makes to hermeneutical marginalisation, relatively intact.

9.4 'FLEETING' HERMENEUTICAL MARGINALISATION

Fricker's own proposal is that despite all appearances to the contrary, Joe Rose *is* hermeneutically marginalised. It might seem like there's no room for this possibility, but that's because there's a widespread tendency to misinterpret her conception of hermeneutical marginalisation. What can make her conception hard to pin down, encouraging such misinterpretation, is that there seem to be two competing strands of thought in what she writes on this topic. On one strand, hermeneutical marginalisation involves certain social groups being almost entirely excluded from certain professions, roles, organisations, and practices which have an outsized role in determining the shape and contents of a society's communal hermeneutical resources. Fricker mentions journalism, academia, politics, and the law here (2007: 152, 155–156), and this list should seem familiar from our earlier discussions of Betty Friedan in Chapter 2 and Patricia Hill Collins in Chapter 4. Since these kinds of institutions and practices are where the power lies when it comes to shaping a society's communal hermeneutical resources, those resources tend to be skewed in a way that favours the socially dominant. As Fricker points out, marginalisation of this sort isn't the same as non-participation in a society's hermeneutically influential practices; a hermit may have no influence over the hermeneutical resources of the society they nominally belong to, but they haven't thereby been marginalised (2007: 153). Rather, marginalisation involves exclusion that is *discriminatory*; hence Fricker's classification of hermeneutical injustice along with testimonial injustice as a form of discriminatory epistemic injustice, as discussed in Chapter 3.

On this picture of hermeneutical marginalisation, it's natural to think that individuals are marginalised only in a derivative sense; it's social groups who are first and foremost kept out of certain professions and social roles, and individuals are hermeneutically marginalised just in virtue of being a member of at least one marginalised group. This doesn't seem to leave any room for incidental cases of hermeneutical injustice, of the sort Joe Rose is meant to illustrate, since Rose isn't a member of any hermeneutically marginalised social group. Moreover, it's not hard to see why this first conception can seem to capture what Fricker has in mind when she discusses hermeneutical marginalisation. For example, something like this picture is suggested by her elaboration of the kind of background inequality that explains, on her view, why Carmita Wood and Wendy Sanford faced injustices:

> In order to find the deeper source of the intuition that there is an epistemic injustice at stake in the examples from Brownmiller, we should focus on the background social conditions that were conducive to the relevant hermeneutical lacuna. Women's position at the time of second wave feminism was still one of marked social powerlessness in relation to men; and, specifically, the unequal relations of power prevented women from participating on equal terms with men in those practices by which collective social meanings are generated. Most obvious among such practices are those sustained by professions such as journalism, politics, academia, and law—it is no accident that Brownmiller's memoir recounts so much pioneering feminist activity in and around these professional spheres and their institutions. Women's powerlessness meant that their social position was one of unequal hermeneutical participation, and something like this sort of inequality provides the crucial background condition for hermeneutical injustice.
>
> (Fricker 2007: 152)

Perhaps on the basis of passages such as this, the picture I've just outlined is how Fricker's notion of hermeneutical marginalisation is standardly introduced in the literature, and it's more or less how I understood it in the previous chapter.[6] When Fricker explicitly introduces the notion of hermeneutical marginalisation, however, it looks quite different to the picture I've just described. She writes:

> Let us say that when there is unequal hermeneutical participation with respect to some significant area(s) of social experience, members of the disadvantaged group are *hermeneutically marginalized*.
>
> (2007: 153)

The main thing to observe here is that this characterises hermeneutical marginalisation as being disadvantaged when it comes to hermeneutical participation 'with respect to some significant area(s) of social experience' rather than in general. This makes room for the idea that members of a social group might be advantageously placed when it comes to hermeneutical participation with respect to certain significant areas of social experience, but disadvantageously placed with respect to others, and indeed this is a possibility that Fricker explicitly embraces, writing that 'the complexity of social identity means that hermeneutical marginalization afflicts individuals in a differentiated manner; that is, it may afflict them qua one social type, but not another' (2007: 154). Her example of this is a woman who has a well-paid position in a 'large corporation with a macho work ethic':

> [S]he may be entirely unable to frame meanings, even to herself, relating to the need for family-friendly working conditions (such sentiments can only signal a lack of professionalism, a failure of ambition, a half-hearted commitment to the job), and yet she may be in a hermeneutically luxurious position as regards her ability to make sense of other, less gendered areas of her work experience.
>
> (2007: 154)

That individuals might be hermeneutically marginalised with respect to some but not all of their experiences isn't a possibility we'd expect on the first picture of hermeneutical marginalisation we distinguished above. There the idea was that one either is or isn't a member of a group that has been systematically shut out of their society's engines of meaning-making.

Holding that hermeneutical marginalisation happens with respect to particular experiences of individuals is also what creates room for cases of incidental hermeneutical injustice, such as Joe Rose. As Fricker understands such cases, they involve subjects who are hermeneutically marginalised 'only fleetingly, and/or only in respect of a highly localized patch of their social experience' (2007: 154). In the introduction to this chapter, I deferred answering the question of why Fricker thinks that Rose faces an injustice, given that he's not a member of any marginalised group, and we're now better placed to consider what she writes about this:

> [I]f the obscurity of Joe's experience constitutes a kind of hermeneutical injustice, this has nothing to do with any general social powerlessness or any general subordination as a generator of social meaning, for his social identity is that of the proverbial white, educated, straight man. Still, he is none the less up against a one-off moment of hermeneutical

marginalization. The competing and trivializing interpretations coming from Clarissa [Rose's fiancé] and the police respectively mean that Joe's hermeneutical participation is hindered in respect of a significant, if highly localized, patch of his social experience, and for this reason his case qualifies as a hermeneutical injustice.

(2007: 157–158)

I don't find this treatment of the example very plausible, for a number of reasons. On Fricker's interpretation of the novel (in contrast to my own), Rose clearly does face a hermeneutical *disadvantage* due to the relative unavailability of the resources he needs for his purposes, but it's still not clear why we should think that this disadvantage amounts to an injustice. Fricker insists that Rose, despite appearances, is hermeneutically marginalised, but she has to distort the notion of hermeneutical marginalisation beyond recognition in order to make this claim even prima facie plausible. It's simply not clear what it means to be hermeneutically marginalised only with respect to some of one's socially significant experiences and not the rest, and Fricker's descriptions of this as a fleeting or 'one-off moment' don't help me to make sense of this. I also don't find Fricker's description in the passage quoted above of the way that Rose's fiancé and the police both offer alternative, ill-fitting interpretations of his experiences helpful for pinning down a way in which he is hermeneutically marginalised. To say that he is unable to offer them a more fitting characterisation of what is happening that makes his experiences intelligible to them is just to describe the particular hermeneutical disadvantage he faces in these exchanges, without explaining in what sense this counts as unequal hermeneutical participation on this topic; as Romdenh-Romluc writes, 'the supposed marginalisation simply collapses into the supposed injustice' (2016: 600).

It's worth pausing over this point, since it is a crucial one for understanding both how Fricker is thinking about incidental hermeneutical injustice, and why her views on this are implausible. Rose's failed attempt to communicate with the police describes a significant moment in which his hermeneutical disadvantage prevents him from making his experiences intelligible to someone when it's very much in his interests to be able to do so, and on Fricker's picture as it emerges from discussion of cases like Carmita Wood and Wendy Sanford, this is a moment of hermeneutical disadvantage that *would* constitute a hermeneutical injustice if it resulted from a particular kind of background inequality: if 'significant among these explanatory factors [of the lack of understanding] is some sort of social unfairness' (Fricker 2007: 149). That condition simply isn't met in Joe Rose's case. Instead, Fricker keeps referring to the moment of unintelligibility as if it *itself* counts as Rose experiencing a 'fleeting' or 'localised' kind of hermeneutical marginalisation. That's the problem Romdenh-Romluc captures so neatly in the phrase quoted above. In a more recent paper on these issues, Fricker describes Rose as the 'vanishingly minimal case' (2016: 166) of hermeneutical marginalisation. I worry that we're losing any purchase we had on the notion of hermeneutical marginalisation.[7]

A further objection to Fricker's treatment of incidental hermeneutical injustice is that it sits badly with verdicts she offers about other examples.[8] She asks us to contrast her examples of hermeneutical injustice with someone who develops a medical condition affecting their social behaviour that is unnamed and misunderstood by their society. According to Fricker, such a person suffers a hermeneutical disadvantage in being unable to understand and communicate their experiences, but 'they are not subject to hermeneutical injustice; rather, theirs is a poignant case of circumstantial epistemic bad luck' (2007: 152). This verdict has been controversial. Shelley Tremain argues that Fricker simply assumes that having an undiagnosed and unrecognised condition which leads to difficulties in social interactions is not itself a hermeneutically marginalised identity. Against this assumption, Tremain contends that:

> [T]he detrimental consequences that accrue to these people are produced by precisely the sort of background conditions from which Fricker claims that a hermeneutical disadvantage must result in order to qualify as a form of hermeneutical injustice.
>
> (2017: 178)

So while Fricker thinks it's just a matter of bad luck that the condition in this kind of example has gone undiagnosed and unnamed, leading to mere hermeneutical disadvantage, Tremain counters that this lack of hermeneutical resources *is* an aspect of a broader set of injustices faced by people struggling with conditions which are observed but not understood by the wider public. We'll discuss this example in more detail in the next chapter. For now, the point is that Fricker's insistence that this is just bad luck, and so a mere hermeneutical disadvantage, sits badly with her contortions to show that Joe Rose is hermeneutically marginalised and so faces a genuine hermeneutical injustice despite possessing all of the social advantages and influence that we've already noted. In order to try to make it plausible that Rose is nonetheless hermeneutically marginalised, Fricker is willing to say this is 'fleetingly' or in a 'localized' sense. She doesn't, however, extend any of the same considerations to the group suffering from the unnamed illness; rather, for Fricker, they don't count as hermeneutically marginalised at all, not even in a 'localised' manner. It's very hard to see what principle is meant to underwrite Fricker's particular combination of verdicts here about who counts as hermeneutically marginalised, and so subject to genuine hermeneutical injustice rather than merely being the victim of epistemic bad luck.[9] If anything, I have some inclination to say she's judged these cases exactly backwards.

9.5 DISPLACED HERMENEUTICAL MARGINALISATION

Let's try a different approach. Suppose we keep Fricker's definition of hermeneutical injustice in terms of hermeneutical marginalisation, but we concede that Joe Rose isn't hermeneutically marginalised—not even 'fleetingly' or for a 'one-off moment.' It seems to follow that Rose doesn't face a hermeneutical injustice. Still, it can seem implausible to simply chalk Rose's predicament up as just bad luck, since the obstacles he faces seem very much related to the hermeneutical marginalisation of certain disadvantaged social groups; the puzzling thing is that he's not a member of any of them. Along these lines, Medina briefly suggests that Rose's situation is in part due to the hermeneutical marginalisation of 'non-heterosexuals' (2013: 107 fn 8), since this group includes the men most likely to have been stalked by other men, and so who are best able to contribute to making such experiences widely intelligible.[10] And in a recent paper, Nick Clanchy develops the idea that Rose faces a hermeneutical injustice in virtue of a social group that Rose himself doesn't belong to being hermeneutically marginalised, namely women (2023: 826).[11] So unlike Simion and Dougherty, Clanchy retains the connection between hermeneutical injustice and hermeneutical marginalisation, but they weaken it in a manner that makes room for Rose to face an injustice; genuine hermeneutical injustice (as opposed to epistemic bad luck) does need to be explained by background hermeneutical marginalisation, but the victim of the injustice need not be a member of the marginalised group. We can think of this as a kind of *displaced* hermeneutical marginalisation. I'll focus on Clanchy's version of this idea, since their discussion is the most detailed and developed.

What Clanchy offers is a way to make sense of the difference between systematic and incidental hermeneutical injustice while accepting that both varieties by definition result from hermeneutical marginalisation. Moreover, they do so while retaining the first of the two pictures of such marginalisation I distinguished in the previous section, according to which it is a large-scale inequality involving certain social groups being systematically excluded from certain roles, institutions, and practices. The difference between incidental and systematic cases lies rather in the relationship between the victim of the injustice and the social groups that are marginalised in this way:

> Fricker proposes that a hermeneutical injustice is systematic insofar as the hermeneutical marginalization which gives rise to it is symptomatic of a broader relative social powerlessness; otherwise, it is incidental (2007: 156). But on the picture I develop, the hermeneutical marginalization which gives rise to the injustice in Joe's case *is* symptomatic of a broader relative social powerlessness – just not that of a group to which Joe himself belongs. Thus contra Fricker, I propose that a hermeneutical injustice is systematic insofar as the wronged party is themselves a member of the group whose hermeneutical marginalization gave rise to the injustice; otherwise, it is incidental.
>
> (Clanchy 2023: 814)

Clanchy suggests that Rose's hermeneutical disadvantage counts as a kind of 'collateral damage' done by the hermeneutical marginalisation of women, or as I've called it above, a kind of displaced hermeneutical marginalisation, and they claim that this is sufficient for this to count as a genuine instance of hermeneutical injustice.

Giving up the assumption that someone can only experience a hermeneutical injustice if they are a member of a relevant hermeneutically marginalised group avoids the problems that Fricker ran into in making sense of incidental hermeneutical injustice. Still, I don't think we should underestimate the extent to which this proposal also departs from Fricker's explanation of why her two examples of systematic hermeneutical injustice involve genuine injustices. Her idea was that episodes of people struggling with ill-fitting or missing hermeneutical resources were injustices insofar as they were symptomatic of wider (perhaps historical) inequalities faced by their social group; it's quite different to try to explain why a hermeneutical disadvantage is an injustice in terms of the marginalisation of *other* groups of people. I don't think that's a conclusive consideration; indeed, I should acknowledge that it's less of an objection to Clanchy's proposal than a restatement of it with some suggestive italics added. Still, it serves to express my worry that there's something inherently implausible about the idea of displaced hermeneutical marginalisation, due to the way it reconceives of (or, more bluntly, breaks) the link between the supposed victim of an injustice and the background inequalities which are meant to explain why it's an injustice. While I take Clanchy's account to be a big improvement on Fricker's approach, ultimately, I find it unsatisfactory for quite similar reasons.

9.6 BAD LUCK

At this point, it seems like we're pretty much out of options; if we accept that hermeneutical injustice always stems from hermeneutical marginalisation, and that Joe Rose isn't hermeneutically marginalised, and that displaced hermeneutical marginalisation isn't real, then we seem left with the conclusion that Rose doesn't face a hermeneutical injustice. Rather he is subject to a form of epistemic bad luck, since while the communal hermeneutical resources in his society are generally skewed in *favour* of the social group he belongs to, he has the misfortune to be an anomaly, facing situations that members of his social group tend to inflict on others rather than experience themselves. On this view, incidental hermeneutical injustice isn't a genuine phenomenon. That's the fourth and final position in the contemporary literature (McGlynn 2025: 320–322).

Someone who takes this line need not be committed to saying that the obstacles Rose faces when trying to be understood are remotely trivial, or even that they're less serious than they would be if he *had* faced a genuine hermeneutical injustice. Fricker rightly notes that the consequences for Rose are 'life-shattering,' and argues on this basis that incidental hermeneutical injustice 'can be disastrous in someone's life' (2007: 158). There's no reason that the proponent of the line suggested can't simply make the same point, but about the kind of bad luck Rose encounters. It's also completely appropriate to feel sorry for Rose, since he's greatly harmed through no real fault of his own: still, that doesn't show that what he's wrestling with is an epistemic injustice rather than a grievous misfortune.

At this point, though, we do well to remember that we're treating the example of Joe Rose as illustrative of a whole range of cases that includes male victims of stalking, domestic abuse, sexual violence, and more besides. Are we happy extending this treatment of Rose, according to which he faces bad luck rather than an injustice, across this entire range? If we are, the kind of account of Rose outlined in this section may well seem worthy of further elaboration and development. If not—and increasingly this is the camp I'd locate myself in—we'll need to consider whether we have really exhausted all of the options for making sense of incidental hermeneutical injustice, as well as the challenges faced by Joe Rose.[12]

9.7 SUMMARY

In this chapter, I've used the apparently minor question of whether there can be incidental cases of hermeneutical injustice as a frame for discussing a cluster of key issues about this kind of injustice, including the nature of hermeneutical marginalisation, and the kind of link that needs to be present between instances of hermeneutical disadvantage and the background inequality of hermeneutical marginalisation in order for them to qualify as hermeneutical injustices. I've argued that Fricker's picture of hermeneutical marginalisation is (ironically) difficult to make sense of, and so doesn't offer a route to understanding how there can be incidental cases of hermeneutical injustice. Clanchy's attempt to show how incidental cases can arise even if we maintain a more structural conception of hermeneutical marginalisation strikes me as a more plausible strategy, but it reconceives the link between hermeneutical marginalisation and instances of hermeneutical injustice in a fairly radical way, leaving us without a clear explanation of why we should think that such cases involve an injustice rather than mere bad luck. We have also explored the prospects of two more revisionary approaches, one of which relaxes Fricker's definition of hermeneutical injustice so that it no longer requires hermeneutical marginalisation, and the other which refuses to abandon that definition at the cost of denying that there are any genuine cases of incidental hermeneutical injustice. In the end, I haven't found a resolution to the puzzle presented by these issues that I find entirely satisfying. What I do hope to have persuaded the reader of is that making progress towards any such resolution will involve further attention to some of the most fundamental questions about hermeneutical injustice and to the crucial but elusive notion of hermeneutical marginalisation.

The discussion in this chapter has again raised issues about Fricker's contrast between epistemic injustice and epistemic bad luck, and about where she thinks the line between these goes, which we originally encountered when examining her account of testimonial injustice in Chapter 6. It's time to return to those issues, as well as to consider an alternative to Fricker's approach to hermeneutical injustice.

9.8 RECOMMENDED FURTHER READING

In a more recent discussion of Joe Rose, Fricker offers a slightly different treatment of the example than in her book, suggesting that it's a 'minimal' case of hermeneutical injustice in the sense that 'the individual could make perfect sense of [his own experience], and could have communicated it to almost any social other except the particular social others he specifically needed to communicate it to' (2016: 165). I think the objections to Fricker's earlier discussion offered in the chapter carry over, but I won't try to show that here.

Wilhelm (2025) recounts the author's own experiences of having his accounts of sexual assault dismissed or minimised due to being a man, and considers how conversations about sexual violence can be more inclusive. Curry (2017a, 2017b) examine sexual violence against Black men and boys in particular, and the ways that they are represented as perpetrators, never victims, of such violence; Curry (2017b) relates this to discussions of Harper Lee's character Tom Robinson in the literature on epistemic injustice, as discussed in Chapters 5 and 6 (and again in the next chapter).

NOTES

1 This list is based on both things McEwan explicitly states in the text, and natural inferences based on things he could have said about Rose but didn't. See Lewis (1978) for the classic philosophical discussion of how such unstated truths in fiction are determined.
2 The switch occurs in Chapter 14, when Rose remembers the name 'de Clérambault's Syndrome,' and is able to apply it to Parry. Prior to this, many of the difficulties Rose has figuring out how threatened to feel by Parry and in conveying his increasing wariness to the police are due to Parry's motives and intentions appearing baffling and somewhat ridiculous. Parry

doesn't have an apparently sexual motive, and he isn't initially violent; what he seems to want is that Rose leaves Clarissa, renounces his atheism, and comes to live in the large house that Parry has recently inherited after the death of his mother. It's the diagnosis of de Clérambault's Syndrome that starts to make sense of all of this.

3 For instance, Fricker writes of 'Joe's own understanding of his experience of being stalked' (2007: 157), which suggests this interpretation. As we saw in Chapter 3, Fricker uses the term 'stereotype' as a neutral term, such that stereotypes need not be false, prejudicial, or unreliable; I use it in the same way here.

4 A number of philosophers have discussed cases involving this kind of isolation, and the way that it can cut a person off from the hermeneutical resources they need: see Kidd and Carel (2017), George and Goguen (2021), Dougherty (2023), and Cull (2024). Luzzi (2024) describes another dynamic we might consider here, focusing on a distinctive kind of epistemic injustice perpetrated against intersex people.

5 Simion doesn't discuss this issue or Joe Rose at all, so the point in the text is no objection to her.

6 For some clear examples of Fricker's notion of hermeneutical marginalisation being understood this way in the literature, see Mason (2011: 297), Romdenh-Romluc (2016: 595–596 and 2017: 5–6), Byrne (2020: 372), Falbo (2022: 343), and Clanchy (2023: 818) (though importantly Clanchy does recognise that Fricker departs from this conception in her discussion of Joe Rose: see 2023: 822). Three clear exceptions are Jenkins (2017: 197–198), Fraser (2018: 733–734), and Simion (2019: 179–180). Much of the rest of the literature presents the notion in ways that leave it rather unclear how it's being understood.

7 See Clanchy (2023: Section 3) for further arguments for the conclusion that Rose isn't hermeneutically marginalised.

8 Romdenh-Romluc (2016) already points out this tension, and was an important influence on the present discussion.

9 Compare Romdenh-Romluc (2016: 604–605).

10 Clanchy also makes this point in passing (2023: 825).

11 Berenstain (2020: 737) makes similar points, though in contrast to Clanchy, Berenstain isn't trying to make sense of incidental hermeneutical injustice, but rather to argue that Fricker mischaracterises systematic forms of injustice as incidental.

12 I'll briefly mention two directions that have been proposed to me when I have presented the ideas in this chapter. The first, due to Jer Steeger, is that Joe Rose faces a *contributory injustice* of the sort we'll look at in the next chapter

when discussing Kristie Dotson's work; after all, as we'll see, this is a category Dotson places many of the examples that Fricker's account treats as mere epistemic bad luck into, and the thought is we might avoid treating Rose as merely unlucky in the same way. The second suggestion is due to Fed Luzzi, and it involves looking at how certain people or certain groups can be marginalised within a particular institution or meaning-making practice even if they are not a member of a group that's hermeneutically marginalised within their society as a whole; this seems importantly analogous to the predicament of our Philosopher of Physics who is subject to testimonial injustices in a particular context on the basis of prejudices that are local rather than re-emerging in a variety of different social settings. This second proposal strikes me as especially worth exploring, and I do so in as-yet unpublished work with Luzzi; I'm also indebted to discussion with Katharine Jenkins and Filipa Melo Lopes here.

REFERENCES

Berenstain, Nora. 2020. 'White Feminist Gaslighting.' *Hypatia* 35 (4): 733–758. https://doi.org/10.1017/hyp.2020.31

Byrne, Eleanor Alexandra. 2020. 'Striking the Balance with Epistemic Injustice in Healthcare: The Case of Chronic Fatigue Syndrome/Myalgic Encephalomyelitis.' *Medicine, Healthcare, and Philosophy* 23: 371–379. https://doi.org/10.1007/s11019-020-09945-4

Clanchy, Nick. 2023. 'Whose Hermeneutical Marginalization?' *Episteme* 20: 813–832. https://doi.org/10.1017/epi.2023.16

Cull, Matthew. 2024. 'Trans Epistemology and Methodological Radicalism: Un Œuf, But Enough.' *Hypatia* 39 (1): 44–60. https://doi.org/10.1017/hyp.2023.102

Curry, Tommy J. 2017a. *The Man-Not: Race, Class, Genre, and the Dilemmas of Black Manhood*. Philadelphia, PA: Temple University Press.

Curry, Tommy J. 2017b. 'This N*****'s Broken: Hyper-masculinity, the Buck, and the Role of Physical Disability in White Anxiety toward the Black Male Body.' *Journal of Social Philosophy* 48 (3): 321–343. https://doi.org/10.1111/josp.12193

Dougherty, Emma C. 2023. 'Toward an Agential Conception of Hermeneutical Injustice: Isolation and Domestic Violence.' *Hypatia* 38 (4): 822–838. https://doi.org/10.1017/hyp.2023.75

Falbo, Arianna. 2022. 'Hermeneutical Injustice: Distortion and Conceptual Aptness.' *Hypatia* 37 (2): 343–363. https://doi.org/10.1017/hyp.2022.4

Fraser, Rachel Elizabeth. 2018. 'The Ethics of Metaphor.' *Ethics* 128 (4): 728–755. https://doi.org/10.1086/697448

Fricker, Miranda. 2007. *Epistemic Injustice: Power and the Ethics of Knowing.* Oxford: Oxford University Press.

Fricker, Miranda. 2016. 'Epistemic Injustice and the Preservation of Ignorance.' In Rik Peels and Martijn Blaauw, eds. *The Epistemic Dimensions of Ignorance*: 160–177. Cambridge: Cambridge University Press.

George, B. R. and Stacey Goguen. 2021. 'Hermeneutical Backlash: Trans Youth Panics as Epistemic Injustice.' *Feminist Philosophy Quarterly* 7 (4): 1–34. https://doi.org/10.5206/fpq/2021.4.13518

Jenkins, Katharine. 2017. 'Rape Myths and Domestic Abuse Myths as Hermeneutical Injustices.' *Journal of Applied Philosophy* 34 (2): 191–205. https://doi.org/10.1111/japp.12174

Kidd, Ian James and Havi Carel. 2017. 'Epistemic Injustice and Illness.' *Journal of Applied Philosophy* 34 (2): 172–190. https://doi.org/10.1111/japp.12172

Lewis, David. 1978. 'Truth in Fiction.' *American Philosophical Quarterly* 15 (1): 37–46. https://www.jstor.org/stable/20009693

Luzzi, Federico. 2024. 'Deception-Based Hermeneutical Injustice.' *Episteme* 21 (1): 147–165. https://doi.org/10.1017/epi.2021.7

Mason, Rebecca. 2011. 'Two Kinds of Unknowing.' *Hypatia* 26 (2): 294–307. https://doi.org/10.1111/j.1527-2001.2011.01175.x

McGlynn, Aidan. 2025. 'Epistemic Injustice: Phenomena and Theories.' In Jennifer Lackey and Aidan McGlynn, eds. *The Oxford Handbook of Social Epistemology*: 295–327. New York: Oxford University Press.

Medina, José. 2013. *The Epistemology of Resistance: Gender and Racial Oppression, Epistemic Injustice, and Resistant Imaginations.* Oxford: Oxford University Press.

Romdenh-Romluc, Komarine. 2016. 'Hermeneutical Injustice: Blood-sports and the English Defence League.' *Social Epistemology* 30 (5–6): 592–610. https://doi.org/10.1080/02691728.2016.1172363

Romdenh-Romluc, Komarine. 2017. 'Hermeneutical Injustice and the Problem of Authority.' *Feminist Philosophy Quarterly* 3 (3): 1–23. https://doi.org/10.5206/fpq/2017.3.1

Simion, Mona. 2019. 'Hermeneutical Injustice as Basing Failure.' In Patrick Bondy and J. Adam Carter, eds. *Well-Founded Belief: New Essays on the Epistemic Basing Relation*: 177–189. New York and Oxon: Routledge.

Tremain, Shelley. 2017. 'Knowing Disability, Differently.' In Ian James Kidd, José Medina, and Gaile Pohlhaus Jr., eds. *The Routledge Handbook of Epistemic Injustice*: 175–184. Oxon: Routledge.

Wilhelm, Isaac. 2025. 'Disregard: Attitudes about Male Survivors.' *Hypatia* 40 (1): 54–63. https://doi.org/10.1017/hyp.2024.11

10

CONTRIBUTORY INJUSTICE AND EPISTEMIC OPPRESSION

10.1 INTRODUCTION

In Chapter 4, I introduced Kristie Dotson's account of epistemic oppression. She characterises this as involving persistent and unwarranted infringements on the ability of some knowers to use and revise shared epistemic resources. As noted in that earlier chapter, the notion of shared epistemic resources is broader than Miranda Fricker's notion of shared hermeneutical resources. The latter picks out the shared interpretative resources widely available for people to draw upon to make themselves and their experiences intelligible (to themselves or to others), paradigmatically concepts and expressions. A society's shared epistemic resources, in contrast, also includes the principles and standards used to assess whether something is knowledge or not. An epistemic system, as I'll use the term, is an interpretive and evaluative framework of such hermeneutical resources and epistemic principles.[1]

Consider, for instance, the way that our society prizes research that results in statistically significant generalisations across groups and populations, rather than that which reports the lived experience of individuals. Patricia Hill Collins has argued that this is a contributing factor in the knowledge of Black women being 'subjugated': that's to say, in its failure to gain validation as knowledge (2000: Chapter 11). Black women do produce knowledge, on Collins's analysis, but the epistemological criteria used in academia and elsewhere for

DOI: 10.4324/9781003281863-13

evaluating their contributions fails to recognise those contributions *as* knowledge. This is due, in Dotson's terms, to Black women being persistently and unwarrantedly prevented from contributing to the epistemological systems our society recognises as legitimate; this exclusion is a paradigm case of epistemic oppression, as Dotson conceives of it (2014: 116).

However, even if there are types of epistemic resources that aren't hermeneutical resources, hermeneutical resources will typically be epistemic resources in Dotson's sense; contributing to the introduction and revision of conceptual and expressive resources is a way to contribute to creating and sharing knowledge within your society.[2] This suggests that we may be able to offer an alternative account of the phenomena that motivated Fricker's account of hermeneutical injustice, seeing them as illustrating a kind of epistemic oppression.

In fact, as we'll see in this chapter, this isn't quite how Dotson approaches things. Instead of replacing Fricker's account, she adopts it but subsumes it: keeping Fricker's category of hermeneutical injustice but treating it as a form of epistemic oppression. However, by relocating Fricker's account within this alternative broader framework, Dotson hopes to avoid various objections that she and others have raised against Fricker. In particular, Dotson proposes a related but distinct form of epistemic oppression, which she calls *contributory injustice*, and she argues that this new category enables us to accommodate some examples which Fricker's account systematically mishandles. For Dotson, a proper treatment of unjust barriers to being understood requires both the notion of hermeneutical injustice and the additional category of contributory injustice, where these are conceived of as closely related but distinct species of epistemic oppression.

The plan for this chapter is to start by looking at some further features of Fricker's account of hermeneutical injustice that have been found problematic in the literature (Section 10.2), and to see how Dotson's category of contributory injustice (and related notions introduced into the literature by other philosophers around the same time) help with these problems (Section 10.3). That done, we'll turn to the difficult question of whether we should see these proposed additional forms of injustice as genuinely new, or if we can instead view them as subspecies of hermeneutical injustice (Section 10.4–10.6). We'll find that this question is closely tied to the larger issue of whether the problems with Fricker's account of hermeneutical injustice are revealing limitations of her broader account of epistemic injustice, and so motivate a shift to instead approaching these phenomena as

CONTRIBUTORY INJUSTICE AND EPISTEMIC OPPRESSION 207

varieties of epistemic oppression. Finally, we'll return to a proposal put forward by Dotson, and discussed briefly in Chapter 7, that's pluralist in spirit (Section 10.7). This involves treating her theoretical notions and overarching framework and Fricker's less as rivals competing to do the same job, and more as each having their own roles to play in an overarching investigation into the many forms that epistemic injustice, in the broadest sense, can take.

10.2 HERMENEUTICAL DISSENT AND EPISTEMIC BAD LUCK

Let's begin with a brief recap of Fricker's account of hermeneutical injustice, this time emphasising the features of it that will be of most relevance to the discussion of this chapter. Hermeneutical injustices occur when someone faces obstacles to making some of their significant experiences intelligible, either to themselves or to others, where these obstacles are at least in part due to that person being a member of a hermeneutically marginalised group: a group that's excluded from, or isolated within, the institutions and practices that have the biggest sway in shaping their society's shared hermeneutical resources. Those who face the same obstacles to making their experiences intelligible for other reasons are merely subject to epistemic bad luck, according to Fricker; we may say that they suffer from a hermeneutical *disadvantage*, but if that disadvantage isn't due to hermeneutical marginalisation, it's not a hermeneutical injustice. Unlike typical cases of testimonial injustice, Fricker insists that hermeneutical injustice has no perpetrators; it's a 'purely structural' form of injustice (2007: 159).[3]

In order to illustrate the possibility of hermeneutical disadvantage through bad luck, Fricker sketches a schematic example:

> If, for instance, someone has a medical condition affecting their social behaviour at a historical moment at which that condition is still misunderstood and largely undiagnosed, then they may suffer a hermeneutical disadvantage that is, while collective, especially damaging to them in particular. They are unable to render their experiences intelligible by reference to the idea that they have a disorder, and so they are personally in the dark, and may also suffer seriously negative consequences from others' non-comprehension of their condition. But they are not subject to hermeneutical injustice; rather, theirs is a poignant case of circumstantial epistemic bad luck.
>
> (2007: 152)

In the previous chapter, I appealed to this example to show how apparently unprincipled Fricker's verdicts are about who is and isn't hermeneutically marginalised, and so subject to a genuine injustice, since the claim that the group Fricker describes in this quote are not hermeneutically marginalised contrasts so dramatically with her insistence that Joe Rose, the hyper-privileged protagonist of Ian McEwan's novel *Enduring Love*, is hermeneutically marginalised despite all appearances. As I noted in that earlier discussion, Shelley Tremain has contended that Fricker implausibly assumes, rather than shows, that the group she describes is not hermeneutically marginalised (2017: 178). Dotson also criticises Fricker's treatment of this example, but from a rather different angle. For Dotson, the example reveals two closely related limitations of Fricker's account of hermeneutical injustice, both of which we have already encountered in some form in earlier chapters.

First, Dotson takes it to shows that Fricker leaves no room for a phenomenon that, following Goetze (2018), we can call *hermeneutical dissent*. Hermeneutical dissent occurs when a marginalised social group produces their own hermeneutical resources, and uses those resources to understand their own experiences, and to communicate about them within that group. A number of philosophers have charged Fricker with overlooking this possibility, and instead assuming that the communal stock of hermeneutical resources in a society exhausts all of the resources available to anyone in that society. We considered this objection briefly in Chapter 8, since it's closely linked to complaints that Fricker mishandled her main example of the central case of hermeneutical injustice, Carmita Wood. Fricker, we saw, contends that as she understands the example of Wood, it's actually an illustration of hermeneutical dissent; it involves members of a hermeneutically marginalised group creating their own hermeneutical resources to rectify a significant and harmful omission in the communal stock of resources available in their society:

> [T]he possibility of localised hermeneutical practices is built in to the picture of how Carmita Wood and her fellow consciousness raisers overcame hermeneutical injustice.
>
> (2016: 166)

This does suggest that Fricker acknowledged the possibility of hermeneutical dissent and allowed room for it in her discussion of hermeneutical

CONTRIBUTORY INJUSTICE AND EPISTEMIC OPPRESSION 209

injustice, but this quote also gestures towards a respect in which she failed to fully explore its significance. One striking feature of the example of the term 'sexual harassment' and the associated concept is how quickly it proliferated out into wider society, gaining use in legal and employment settings, as well as more generally. This was partly thanks to tactical choices made by the group who created these hermeneutical resources, and partly thanks to the group managing to get the attention of key figures in journalism and in the legal profession, as discussed in Chapter 8. However, we can readily imagine that things didn't go so smoothly: that members of more dominant social groups with more access to influence over their society's communal hermeneutical stock successfully resisted 'sexual harassment' becoming recognised as meaningful. Fricker focuses on examples of relative success, in which a significant step towards epistemic justice seems to have been taken, but in doing so she overlooks, or at least neglects, the point that the attempt to proliferate out hermeneutical resources can also be a site of injustice.

Dotson's objection isn't just that Fricker's characterisation of epistemic injustice is too narrow, but also that it's contrasted with mere epistemic bad luck in a way that leaves her unable to capture the epistemic harms present in cases that don't meet her narrow definitions. This is the second worry with Fricker's account that Dotson thinks is illustrated by Fricker's handling of the case of the group who face a hermeneutical disadvantage due to a lack of a diagnosis that fits their symptoms. Unlike Tremain, Dotson thinks we can concede that Fricker's right to say that it doesn't meet her characterisation of hermeneutical injustice. However, rather than resting content with saying it's a 'poignant case' of bad luck (Fricker 2007: 152), Dotson suggests that we instead view it as a case in which hermeneutical dissent is accompanied by a persistent refusal by dominant groups members to recognise the intelligibility of resources created by the group in question. However, the option of introducing a new category of epistemic injustice to account for such cases is one that Fricker's account, with its dichotomy of injustice and mere bad luck, closes off (Dotson 2012: 25).

This is Dotson's motivation for introducing the category of contributory injustice, mentioned in the introduction to this chapter. Contributory injustice involves speakers struggling to make themselves intelligible because they're using hermeneutical resources—concepts, expressions, and so on—which are not used by or recognised as valid by their broader community, including their audience, and where this refusal to acknowledge and use these resources is the result of that audience's 'situated ignorance': ignorance which 'follows from one's social position and/or epistemic location with respect to some domain of knowledge' (2012: 248).[4] This, Dotson proposes, will be the likely fate of the group described in Fricker's thought experiment, which is why Dotson takes it to involve both hermeneutical dissent and contributory injustice:

> To imagine that the person with the underresearched medical ailment remains in the same state of unawareness as general society is, generally, absurd. Alternative hermeneutical resources often arise in response to circumstances such as these. Though dominant hermeneutical resources may remain behind on conceptualizing his ailment, his knowledge may not be lagging at all, in terms of the ability to render it intelligible. What is barred, then, is gaining the appropriate uptake by those utilizing dominant hermeneutical resources as opposed to the alternative resources he and others in his same position have developed. This failure to gain uptake so as to influence dominant hermeneutical resources is a form of epistemic injustice on my account—contributory injustice.
>
> (2012: 40)

We encountered another example that Dotson thinks fits the profile of contributory injustice back in Chapter 6: Ishani Maitra's example of a rape victim who is disbelieved by the police due to behaving in ways that accord with (supposedly) reliable cues of untrustworthiness (Maitra 2010: 203). If we take the policeman in this example to be invoking reliable stereotypes rather than prejudices and yet still feel that the speaker isn't merely subject to bad luck, this example puts pressure on the centrality Fricker's definition of testimonial injustice as prejudicial credibility deficit accords to prejudice. Another way of looking at the example, though, is as again putting pressure on Fricker's claim that cases of epistemic harm that don't quite fit her characterisation are to be classed as merely involving bad epistemic luck. Dotson offers a treatment of the example along these lines, suggesting that even if we (charitably) suppose that the policeman's assumptions about what the speaker's hesitancy in speaking and body-language indicate are not prejudicial, the stereotype he relies on 'though reliable, does not provide the appropriate conceptual frame with which to understand the testimony of a victim of sexual violence, and as a result the police officer utilizes ill-fitting hermeneutical resources' (2012: 39). As a result, Dotson claims, even if the officer doesn't perpetrate a testimonial injustice in this example, the speaker is subject to a contributory injustice.

It's not clear to me that Maitra's example really does involve contributory injustice, as Dotson characterises it. As I introduced contributory injustice a moment ago, it's a possible consequence of hermeneutical dissent, where a marginalised group within a society creates and uses hermeneutical resources that fit their experiences, but which aren't part of their society's communal stock of such resources. Contributory injustice happens when a member of such a group uses hermeneutical resources that her audience doesn't use or recognise as intelligible. Intuitively, that isn't what's going on in Maitra's example; there's no hermeneutical dissent, it's just that the police officer is applying a (we're supposing) generally reliable stereotype to someone who is an exception to it. Even if we suppose, with Dotson, that this amounts to the police officer using 'ill-fitting hermeneutical resources' (a move I think we should regard with some suspicion), the example still doesn't fit Dotson's characterisation. The speaker in the example isn't using hermeneutical resources that the officer is unfamiliar with or resistant to; she's just behaving and responding in particular ways, such as not holding his gaze, and the officer badly misinterprets these cues.

Still, even if this example isn't one of contributory injustice, there do seem to be plausible cases, including perhaps Fricker's example of the people facing obstacles to making their experiences of an undiagnosed illness intelligible. Moreover, Dotson's complaint that Fricker's dichotomy between testimonial injustice and mere bad luck leaves her poorly placed to give a plausible account of Maitra's example seems well taken, as we noted in Chapter 6, even if we reject the alternative account of the example Dotson provides.

10.3 EPISTEMIC OPPRESSION AND HERMENEUTICAL INJUSTICE

Dotson introduces her notion of epistemic oppression, defined as in Chapter 4 and at the beginning of this chapter, to encompass Fricker's notions of testimonial and hermeneutical injustice as well as her own notion of contributory injustice—plus, presumably, any other forms we identify. Let's start this section by taking a look at Dotson's full, official definition of epistemic oppression.

Epistemic oppression involves persistent and unwarranted infringements on the epistemic agency of knowers that prevent them from contributing to the production of knowledge. Dotson has a very particular notion of epistemic agency in mind here; epistemic agency refers to the ability to 'utilize persuasively shared epistemic resources within a given community of knowers in order to participate in knowledge production and, if required, the revision of those same resources' (2014: 115). As I have stressed already, these epistemic resources will include the shared hermeneutical resources of the community, as conceived by Fricker, but it will include other things too, such as the standards for evaluating which academic research is validated as adding to a society's collective knowledge.

There are a number of questions we might have about how Dotson's categories of contributory injustice and epistemic oppression relate to Fricker's two species of epistemic injustice. One natural question to ask, in light of Part 2 of this book, is why in Dotson's work on epistemic oppression she focuses on testimonial injustice, and doesn't really mention her own notions of testimonial quieting and smothering (Dotson 2011). We examined these in some detail in Chapter 7, and I made a case there that these are quite different to Fricker's notion in several important respects; moreover, these differences were clearly due to deliberate theoretical choices Dotson made in developing her distinctive account of silencing. Why is Dotson concerned to subsume testimonial *injustice* under her account of epistemic oppression, given that she presumably takes her own account of these phenomena to be superior? I don't know the answer to this question; the best I could offer would be pure speculation, and I prefer to simply note that this is a little puzzling.

A more pressing question concerns the relationship between contributory injustice and hermeneutical injustice: why not consider contributory injustice a kind of hermeneutical injustice, rather than a new species of epistemic oppression?[5] After all, it doesn't seem like that much of a stretch to suggest that cases of contributory injustice fit the definition of hermeneutical injustice that we have been working with throughout the past few chapters of this book; we might maintain that they involve people facing obstacles to making their significant experiences intelligible to others, where these obstacles are due to their belonging to a hermeneutically marginalised group. These examples don't quite have the form of Fricker's two examples of the central case of hermeneutical injustice, Carmita Wood's lack of the concept of sexual harassment and Wendy Sanford's lack of the concept of post-partum depression, but we saw already in Chapter 8 that these two cases are quite different from each other in certain respects. More generally, there seems to be a surprising amount of diversity in the forms that hermeneutical injustice, and steps towards hermeneutical justice, can take.[6] Perhaps what Dotson calls contributory injustice is just further proof of that lesson.[7]

There are several things Dotson says that are relevant to responding to this attempted assimilation of contributory injustice to hermeneutical injustice in Fricker's sense. Dotson starts by drawing a number of contrasts between the two. First, contributory injustice involves what we've been calling hermeneutical dissent—the creation and use of hermeneutical resources by marginalised groups that haven't achieved the kind of widespread currency in a society to be part of that society's communal stock—and Dotson takes Fricker to have missed this possibility entirely. Second, by Fricker's own definition, hermeneutical injustice must be due to hermeneutical marginalisation, but contrary to what I suggested in the previous paragraph, contributory injustice need not (2012: 40–41); moreover, this is crucial to finding room for examples like Fricker's patients struggling to understand and communicate their experiences of an unnamed condition to count as a kind of epistemic injustice rather than just a 'poignant' case of bad luck. Third, according to Fricker, hermeneutical injustice is 'purely structural,' involving no individual perpetrators, but contributory injustice is not purely structural:

> Both the structurally prejudiced or biased hermeneutical resources and the agent's situated ignorance are catalysts for contributory injustice. As such, it is located within the gray area between agential and structural perpetuation of epistemic injustice.
>
> (Dotson 2012: 31)

Similarly, around the same time as Dotson proposed contributory injustice as a distinct form of epistemic injustice, Gaile Pohlhaus Jr. influentially introduced a category she calls 'willful hermeneutical ignorance' (Pohlhaus 2012), which involves members of dominant groups refusing to acknowledge and employ hermeneutical resources developed by oppressed groups in order to render their experiences intelligible; she argues that Tom Robinson faces this kind of injustice at his trial in addition to the testimonial injustice highlighted by Fricker (Pohlhaus 2012: 724–731).[8] Despite the label, and the points of similarity with hermeneutical injustice as Fricker understands it, Pohlhaus insists that wilful hermeneutical ignorance is a distinct form of epistemic injustice, and that it may in fact be a particular strain of contributory injustice in Dotson's sense (2012: 734 n3). Pohlhaus's reason for not treating wilful hermeneutical ignorance as a subspecies of hermeneutical injustice is its *wilful* character; it involves particular individuals wilfully refusing to use certain hermeneutical resources when it is open to them to (at least try to) do so, whereas hermeneutical injustice is purely structural (Pohlhaus 2012: 734 n6). Here we can see Pohlhaus drawing attention to precisely the same contrast as Dotson does.

In addition to these points of contrast, Dotson appeals to what she describes as an 'order-of-change' (or 'scope of change') approach to argue that even if testimonial, hermeneutical, and contributory injustice are sometimes difficult to separate and tell apart in practice, we can be sure that they are theoretically distinct. 'Order-of-change' is a metaphor borrowed from organisation theory, the branch of sociology that studies how organisations function, how they are structured, how they interact with each other and with individuals and their environments, and how they change over time. Each successive order of change involves a more radical kind (and not just degree) of alteration, and Dotson's proposal is that the three types of epistemic injustice can be distinguished 'by identifying the kinds of changes each minimally requires for justice' (2012: 26). Testimonial injustice only requires first-order changes, since it can be minimally addressed without us having to question whether credibility is valuable, so long as we work to address unjust misattributions of credibility:

> Because testimonial injustice does not necessarily demand that we jettison the value of credibility for establishing epistemic authority, testimonial injustice can be addressed with first-order changes. That makes it a first-order epistemic injustice. As a result, what is required to address testimonial injustice and faulty credibility assessments are "incremental modifications that make sense within an established framework."
>
> (Dotson 2012: 28, quoting Bartunek and Koch 1987: 484)

In contrast, minimally addressing hermeneutical injustice requires, in an expression Dotson borrows from Rae Langton, a 'conceptual revolution' (Langton 2010: 460, 463). This doesn't merely involve tinkering within a framework, but rather changes to the framework itself, and so hermeneutical injustice is second-order epistemic injustice. Finally, addressing contributory injustice involves not just an ability to make changes to a framework, but to switch between different sets of hermeneutical resources, which Dotson likens to 'world'-travelling as described by the feminist philosophers Maria Lugones (1987) and Mariana Ortega (2006). Dotson quotes Ortega's way of spelling out what this involves:

> "World"-traveling has to do with actual experience; it requires a tremendous commitment to practice: to actually engage in activities where one will experience what others experience; to deal with flesh and blood people not just their theoretical construction; to learn people's language in order to understand them better not to use it against them; to really listen to people's interpretations however different they are from one's own; and to see people as worthy of respect rather than helpless beings that require help.
>
> (Ortega 2006: 69)

This more demanding project of coming to understand multiple sets of hermeneutical resources and to switch to recognising and using resources that stem from people who are quite different to yourself is what third-order change requires. Contributory injustice is therefore third-order epistemic injustice, according to Dotson, and it is 'difficult but not impossible' to address (Dotson 2012: 34).[9]

10.4 IS HERMENEUTICAL INJUSTICE ALWAYS 'PURELY STRUCTURAL'?

We now have two reasons on the table for thinking that contributory injustice (and related notions such as wilful hermeneutical ignorance) are not to be assimilated to Fricker's category of hermeneutical injustice: the former contrasts with the latter since it involves recognition of the phenomenon of hermeneutical dissent and because the latter is due to hermeneutical marginalisation and is 'purely structural' while the former is not; and hermeneutical injustice is second-order epistemic injustice, while contributory injustice is third order, and so we can distinguish them 'by identifying the kinds of changes each minimally requires for justice' (Dotson 2012: 26).

However, each of the points that this case for regarding contributory injustice as distinct rests on is controversial and contestable. As we have noted a number of times, starting back in Chapter 8, Fricker has contended that she always recognised the possibility of what we've been calling hermeneutical dissent: she maintains that on her treatment of the example of Carmita Wood, it illustrates hermeneutical resources being developed by members of a marginalised group. It's true that she doesn't give any attention to examples involving such resources being resisted by members of dominant social groups, and perhaps overlooked the possibility of injustices of this particular form, but that doesn't yet show that there's any principled obstacle to incorporating them into her account of hermeneutical injustice.

Fricker clearly does hold that hermeneutical injustice is due to hermeneutical marginalisation and that it's a purely structural form of injustice, involving no perpetrators, and so Dotson and Pohlhaus can hardly be accused of misrepresenting her views about that. However, philosophers have independently questioned whether Fricker is right to regard these as features of hermeneutical injustice. I already discussed the possibility that there might be forms of hermeneutical injustice that aren't due to hermeneutical marginalisation in the previous chapter, and so I won't consider this again. In any case, it's not obvious that there can be contributory injustice against someone that isn't hermeneutically marginalised. Dotson appeals to Fricker's mystery illness example in drawing this supposed contrast with hermeneutical injustice, but as we've already seen, Tremain (2017) has cast doubt on this interpretation of Fricker's example.

Fricker's claim that hermeneutical injustice never has perpetrators has been even more widely questioned. I'll focus here on José Medina's objections to Fricker, which are particularly influential and, to my mind, compelling.[10] Medina, like Dotson and Pohlhaus, looks at examples involving marginalised subjects who have the concepts necessary to understand their own experiences and the expressive resources needed to communicate amongst members of their own social groups, but where those resources are not shared with members of more dominant social groups: cases of hermeneutical dissent, as we've called them. The injustices in such cases will take the form of speakers belonging to disadvantaged social groups facing obstacles to making themselves intelligible to audience members from outside those groups (Medina 2013: 98–101). Like Pohlhaus, Medina takes this to be part of what is going on during Tom Robinson's trial in *To Kill a Mockingbird*

(Medina 2013: 67–70, 96 n1). He also agrees with both Pohlhaus and Dotson that these examples do not involve a purely structural form of injustice; there are perpetrators, such as the jurors in Tom Robinson's trial. However, unlike Pohlhaus and Dotson, Medina treats such examples as illustrating a kind of hermeneutical injustice, concluding on that basis that Fricker was mistaken to think that hermeneutical injustice is always purely structural.[11]

There are several reasons to favour Medina's argument and conclusion over Pohlhaus and Dotson's introduction of new categories that supposedly contrast with hermeneutical injustice. First, as we have already noted, the examples Medina, Pohlhaus, and Dotson offer plausibly meet the definition of hermeneutical injustice we have been working with since Chapter 8. For example, it's entirely natural to suggest that the struggles Tom Robinson faces when trying to make certain aspects of his relationship with Mayella Ewell intelligible to the jurors are due, in part, to the jury interpreting everything he says using inadequate—indeed, distorting—hermeneutical resources, which embed racist presumptions of Black inferiority, as well as controlling images of Black men as hypersexualised rapists and as deceitful. That there aren't more fitting meanings present in the communal stock of hermeneutical resources is surely related to the fact that disabled Black men were a (doubly) hermeneutical marginalised group. The jurors perhaps could do much more to try to penetrate through the distorting conceptualisations they bring to bear when listening to Robinson, and of course they don't, so the obstacles Robinson faces to making his experiences intelligible perhaps aren't *purely* related to his hermeneutical marginalisation; still, his example seems to meet the definition of hermeneutical injustice as an epistemic agent facing obstacles to making their experiences intelligible, where these obstacles are due to hermeneutical marginalisation.[12]

Relatedly, Medina notes that Fricker herself at times recognises that particular audiences can do better or worse when listening to a speaker who is struggling to make their experiences intelligible due to ill-fitting shared hermeneutical resources. A hearer can be attentive and attuned to the possibility that the speaker is not merely confused but is instead struggling to make something intelligible for this reason, and they can be open to using unfamiliar concepts and expressions or to collaborating with the speaker to try to find a way to frame the speaker's experiences in ways that render them intelligible, thereby mitigating the effect of the inadequacies of their shared hermeneutical resources. On the other hand, they can be (intentionally or unintentionally) close-minded, dismissive, and impatient, thereby compounding the speaker's struggles. Fricker takes the first, more cooperative hearer to be exhibiting what she calls the virtue of hermeneutical justice; we'll come back to this in more detail in the final chapter. However, she has little to say about the second hearer.

Medina asks (2013: 113): given that Fricker is happy to say that the first hearer is responding virtuously, why not say that the second is responding viciously? And if we recognise that some individuals in a situation of hermeneutical injustice are responding viciously, why not hold that they are perpetrating hermeneutical injustice? The hearer is not, of course, responsible for the background conditions which have led to a lack of fitting hermeneutical resources being readily available to the speaker; hermeneutical marginalisation is, we might agree, a purely structural unfairness, rather than something that particular agents perpetrate. It doesn't follow, Medina is suggesting, that hermeneutical injustice has no perpetrators; in particular, in cases in which a hearer responds viciously to a speaker struggling to make herself intelligible, we should regard the hearer as a 'co-perpetrator.'[13]

Fricker has responded to Medina's point, rejecting the idea that such people are co-perpetrators of the hermeneutical injustice, and instead insisting that they only count as a perpetrator of a part of it:

> Failures of virtue are bad in themselves, and when we fail to be appropriately open to the perspectives of others we are doing something bad and may even be wronging them as individuals. But being culpable for one's part in a broader injustice makes one a perpetrator only of that part; it does not make one a perpetrator of the broader injustice itself.
>
> (Fricker 2016: 172 fn16)

However, the moment in which the speaker is wronged as an individual is an instance of hermeneutical injustice, not merely a part of a broader injustice. Consider how Fricker puts this point in her book when arguing for her claim that hermeneutical injustice has no perpetrators:

> No agent perpetrates hermeneutical injustice—it is a purely structural notion. The background condition for hermeneutical injustice is the subject's hermeneutical marginalization. But the moment of hermeneutical injustice comes only when the background condition is realized in a more

or less doomed attempt on the part of the subject to render an experience intelligible, either to herself or to an interlocutor. The hermeneutical inequality that exists, dormant, in a situation of hermeneutical marginalization erupts in injustice only when some actual attempt at intelligibility is handicapped by it.

(Fricker 2007: 159)

This 'moment of hermeneutical injustice,' when injustice 'erupts,' may be only one part of a broader injustice—there may be multiple eruptions—but it is still a hermeneutical injustice in its own right, by Fricker's own lights. If what ultimately 'dooms' the speaker's attempt to make their experiences intelligible to their audience on a particular occasion is not merely that there aren't fitting and shared hermeneutical resources due to hermeneutical marginalisation, but also that their audience is too close-minded or dismissive to make any effort to try to catch the speaker's meaning, or to even pick up on the fact that the speaker is struggling due to a lack of apt shared expressive resources, this kind of 'wronging them as an individual' seems to be a way of perpetrating a hermeneutical injustice, just as Medina suggests.

Of course, there is a lot involved in such a case that the particular hearer isn't responsible for, but the same seems true in cases of systematic testimonial injustice, where Fricker doesn't seem to have the same reservations about thinking there are perpetrators (Maitra 2010: 209). For instance, Herbert Greenleaf isn't responsible for the ubiquitous nature of sexist assumptions in his society, and he may not be responsible for having absorbed them. He's also not responsible for all of the other occasions on which other people channel those same prejudices across different contexts, giving the injustice its systematic character. Nonetheless, Fricker holds that he behaves viciously towards Marge Sherwood when he dismisses her testimony due to sexist prejudices, and that this counts as perpetrating a testimonial injustice; why not make the parallel claims about vicious hearers in instances of systematic hermeneutical injustice?

What this discussion suggests is that it's not clear that hermeneutical injustice contrasts with contributory injustice (or wilful hermeneutical ignorance) in any of the respects emphasised by Dotson and Pohlhaus. Fricker's account of hermeneutical injustice seems to recognise and accommodate the phenomenon of hermeneutical dissent and although Fricker doesn't consider such cases, her definition seems to cover forms of injustice that involve dominantly situated hearers failing or refusing to use resources created as hermeneutical dissent. Moreover, while Fricker does take hermeneutical injustice to be both due to hermeneutical marginalisation and purely structural, the former point has been disputed and is in any case of dubious relevance, and there's a strong case to be made that the latter is an overgeneralisation from the kinds of examples of the central case that she focuses on. Contrasting contributory injustice with hermeneutical injustice, Dotson writes in a passage quoted earlier that the former 'is located within the gray area between agential and structural perpetuation of epistemic injustice' (2012: 31). Medina's arguments suggest that this is in fact an apt description of many cases of hermeneutical injustice too.

10.5 ORDERS OF EPISTEMIC INJUSTICE

What of Dotson's claim that we can distinguish contributory from hermeneutical injustice with an order-of-change model, since the minimal changes required to address contributory injustice are third order, while those for hermeneutical injustice are second order? Here too I think Dotson's points are disputable. For one thing, what counts as 'minimally addressing' a form of injustice isn't pinned down in Dotson's discussion, and it's not clear that it is given a consistent meaning throughout. Pohlhaus elaborates on the relevant question we should be asking as follows:

> Dotson identifies three levels on which systemic exclusion can operate to impede agency by asking the question: when a system is impeding the epistemic agency of a targeted group of knowers, how would the system need to change so that it no longer impedes?
>
> (2020: 235)

As I introduced the notion of an epistemic system earlier in this chapter, it includes various kinds of epistemic resources, such as the hermeneutical resources available for a society to render their social experiences intelligible, as well as epistemic principles, standards, and frameworks that are recognised as determining whether a claim should be counted as part of a society's collective knowledge or not. So Pohlhaus's framing of Dotson's point is that we can distinguish the different levels of epistemic injustice by examining what kinds of changes are needed to address a given epistemic system that's producing a particular kind of epistemic injustice. That's helpful, but I still find the details offered by Dotson puzzling.

For starters, Dotson tells us that minimally addressing systematic testimonial injustice requires incrementally improving our credibility judgements, developing a testimonial sensibility (in the sense discussed in Chapter 5) that is less prone to relying on prejudices (Dotson 2012: 28); she notes that Fricker takes this to be the cultivation of a virtue, the virtue of testimonial justice. We have also just seen that Fricker takes there to be a virtue of hermeneutical justice, which involves becoming adept at working to repair communicative exchanges when the speaker is struggling with ill-fitting hermeneutical resources, or at least being open and alert to the possibility that this is what is going on and perhaps suspending judgement (Fricker 2007: 169–173). We might have expected, given what Dotson says about testimonial injustice, that incremental progress in this direction is what minimally addressing hermeneutical injustice and (at least some cases of) contributory injustice would involve, but instead Dotson insists that these require second-order and third-order changes respectively. Why this apparent contrast in what counts as minimally addressing different forms of epistemic injustice? What principle is at work when Dotson picks out particular steps towards epistemic justice as the relevant minimal ones in each of the three cases? I don't think we've been offered answers to these key questions.

I also worry that at times, Dotson overstates what's involved in the kinds of changes needed at each stage. As noted, she follows Langton in describing what's needed to minimally address hermeneutical injustice as a 'conceptual revolution,' but Langton seems to use this term somewhat hyperbolically to describe processes like those we see in Fricker's example of Carmita Wood, where a single concept and expression was added to a society's shared stock of meanings without all that many other changes being made. Langton writes:

> [Wood] couldn't find an adequate concept to understand her own experience, let alone describe it. This sort of lacuna in someone's conceptual resources can mean that however hard someone tries, they can't make their experiences understood, even to themselves. What was needed, in this case, was a conceptual revolution, filling the lacuna with an entirely new concept—sexual harassment.
>
> (Langton 2010: 460)

As we've seen, Dotson contrasts the framework-wide changes needed to address hermeneutical injustice with the small-scale modifications to an established system that characterise first-order change. However, once we see how unrevolutionary Langton's 'conceptual revolution' really is, it's not clear there's really all that much of a contrast between testimonial and hermeneutical injustice here.[14]

More importantly, a similar point can be made when it comes to third-order changes. Dotson presents these as involving 'world'-travelling, and emphasises just how demanding this can be, involving building deep and genuine relations of trust with people unlike yourself, and then beginning the process of trying to understand the alternative set of resources through which those people understand the social and natural worlds—a process which Dotson points out can take years, even decades (2012: 35). However, it's not clear how helpful reflecting on these kinds of deeply persistent cases is for ascertaining what's involved in minimally addressing contributory injustice in general. Consider once more Fricker's example of a group of sufferers of an as-yet unnamed illness, which Dotson takes to be liable to progress into an instance of contributory injustice as the members of this group learn more about their symptoms and get more adept at recognising them and communicating about them to each other. It's not entirely clear what it would take to address this injustice, but on the face of it, it seems unlikely that a decades-long process of 'world'-traveling is what's required.

I want to pause over this point, since I think Dotson is getting at something important, but it reveals a potential problem with her category of contributory injustice. Dotson's invocation of 'world'-travelling gestures at a class of examples involving groups (or perhaps even whole societies) who have produced and who use conceptual schemes and other hermeneutical and epistemic resources that are very different to our own, and which have been systematically ignored or suppressed.[15] Addressing the injustices involved in such examples may well involve the kind of difficult, long-term commitment to learning your way around a whole new way of thinking about and conceptualising the world that Dotson has in mind. We might think here of Indigenous knowledge of the natural world or of medicine, such as the examples discussed at the very end of Chapter 7. This is an important class of examples, and it's not clear that Fricker's account of hermeneutical injustice, or her proposed remedial virtue, are aptly applied to it.

However, Dotson seems to want to put such examples into a much broader category, contributory injustice, which also includes a number of cases that look much closer to hermeneutical injustice, as understood by Fricker: consider again Fricker's own example of the mystery-illness sufferers if we suppose, with Dotson, that they have engaged in hermeneutical dissent. Remedying the injustice in these latter kinds of cases may require much less; for instance, it may require only the kind of small-scale 'conceptual revolution' envisaged by Langton in cases of hermeneutical injustice, such as a society reluctantly coming to use the label for a medical condition that's already in use amongst those that suffer from it.

Dotson has drawn our attention to two important classes of cases, and both involve marginalised groups creating, not just knowledge, but their own hermeneutical resources (and perhaps more broadly their own epistemic systems, which determine both what they can understand and what they accept as knowledge). However, there are significant differences between them and it's not clear to me whether Dotson's own categories draw the relevant line in the right place. Some of the cases she wants to classify as contributory injustice seem to be plausibly treated as variants of hermeneutical injustice in Fricker's sense, and to require only relatively minor changes to a society's hermeneutical resources to address, while others seem to happen on a much larger scale and to call for the kind of 'world'-travelling Dotson envisions; it's not clear we want a single category, distinct from Fricker's hermeneutical injustice, to cover these two kinds of cases, nor does this seem to be the picture supported by Dotson's orders-of-change model.

10.6 EPISTEMIC INJUSTICE VS. EPISTEMIC OPPRESSION

Where does all this leave us? In the past two sections, we have been considering different arguments for the claim that contributory injustice must be a distinct form of epistemic injustice from hermeneutical injustice, and I've expressed some scepticism about these arguments, since the contrasts that Dotson and others have drawn seem overstated, and in some cases may disappear under close scrutiny. I've also raised some concerns about using orders-of-change as a way to try to taxonomise different kinds of epistemic injustices, and to the extent we can work past these concerns, I don't think such considerations support Dotson's three-way division as she presents it.

What I want to do in this section is consider, in light of the discussion to this point, what each of the notions of epistemic injustice (in Fricker's sense) and epistemic oppression (in Dotson's) is doing for us, and whether we could make do with just one of them. First of all, there are a number of phenomena which Dotson's notion seems to capture really well. To return to our starting point in this chapter, take Patricia Hill Collins's account of how Black feminist thought is subjugated in and by academia. One of Collins's insights is that Black women have been limited in their capacity to contribute to the standards for evaluating what does and does not count as knowledge, and this dynamic is one that Dotson's account of epistemic oppression helps to illuminate; indeed, as we noted above, it is a paradigmatic case of epistemic oppression in Dotson's sense. Fricker offers accounts of ways that members of particular social groups can be persistently prevented from contributing to the pool of knowledge and to the communal stock of hermeneutical resources in their society, but it's not obvious she has much to say about other ways that people can have their epistemic agency systemically curtailed, such as we find in Collins's discussion. I also acknowledged at the end of the previous section that some of the examples that Dotson takes to illustrate contributory injustice, including those involving the systematic suppression of concepts and knowledge produced by Indigenous peoples and other marginalised groups, may not fit comfortably within Fricker's framework, but we can add that it's plausible that they might well count as instances of epistemic oppression in Dotson's sense. Thinking about what unifies these two types of examples, and with a nod to Dotson's orders-of-change model, we might suggest that the notion of epistemic oppression is most clearly applicable when we're dealing with forms of epistemic injustice that require a change of epistemic system, rather than merely a modification (whether small- or large-scale) to an existing system.

Should we, as Dotson suggests, see the two kinds of epistemic injustice identified by Fricker as 'species of epistemic oppression' (2012: 36)? If we focus on systematic cases of each, that seems like a reasonable enough proposal, but as Amandine Catala (2024) has emphasised, to the extent that we recognise forms of testimonial and hermeneutical injustice that lack a persistent and systematic character, there is reason to resist any kind of wholesale replacement of Fricker's notion of epistemic injustice with that of epistemic oppression.

10.7 PLURALISM ABOUT EPISTEMIC INJUSTICE

The proposal I've been building up to here is that we need both notions—epistemic injustice as Fricker understands it and epistemic oppression as characterised by Dotson—if we want to do justice to all of the phenomena that fall under epistemic injustice in the broadest sense (as it appears in this book's title). Perhaps we should adopt a pluralist attitude, recognising that different philosophers are interested in different questions, or even that the same philosopher might be interested in different questions in different contexts. As noted in Chapter 7, Dotson seems attracted to such a pluralism in places, though she stresses that it requires close attentiveness to the limitations of a given approach. It may sometimes be fruitful and legitimate to adopt Fricker's focus on certain epistemic injustices that have particular distinctive features, Dotson concedes. The risk we always need to guard against is slipping into seeing these as the *only* such injustices that are genuine and worth caring about, and so failing to see the need for other resources and theories that can help us understand and address the cases Fricker's account of epistemic injustice misses:

> What Fricker offers is *an* account of epistemic injustice. This indicates that there are strengths and limits to her account. Instead of taking her to task about what she overlooks or what her account cannot track, we can simply acknowledge the strengths and limitations of her position and move on to offer another theory of epistemic injustice that addresses the limitations of her account. Accounts of epistemic injustice, then, can stand side by side, useful for different kinds of analyses in possibly compatible and incompatible sets of hermeneutical resources.
>
> (Dotson 2012: 42)

This strikes me as a tempting picture, in light of the discussion in this chapter, and of this book more generally, but we might wonder whether it's really coherent to think we can have our cake and eat it in this fashion. Suppose that Fricker's theory and Dotson's disagree about a particular example, with the former saying that it's just a case of epistemic bad luck rather than an injustice, and the latter saying it's an injustice of a form not recognised within Fricker's framework. Aren't we going to end up with contradictions if we try to endorse both? How can they stand 'side by side' if, as Dotson suggests, they are aspects of potentially 'incompatible' sets of resources?

To see what I think Dotson has in mind, think of the conception of philosophical theorising that I introduced in Chapters 2 and 3, and have relied on throughout this book. Such theorising involves making some features of examples of the phenomena being studied central and important while abstracting away from other features as noise, and one way to understand Dotson is that she is proposing that there are multiple good ways to do this. Even with respect to the same phenomenon, which features of the examples of this phenomenon are regarded as central and significant by a given theorist and which are backgrounded depends on that theorist's interests, and the particular project they are engaged in; indeed, the very same theorist can approach a particular phenomenon with different theoretical approaches on different occasions.

Pluralism of this sort avoids committing us to contradictory verdicts by seeing theories of epistemic injustice as tools for particular purposes, each with its own strengths and weaknesses. For some projects, our focus may need to be on the systematic and persistent exclusions of certain groups from using or revising their society's epistemic resources to contribute to the production of knowledge, as Dotson's framing has things, while for other projects, we may need to be attentive to the specific ways that particular individuals can be wronged in their capacity as epistemic agents, including in one-off moments of injustice that aren't part of a larger pattern of oppression. These resources are incompatible in the sense that we cannot coherently employ both frameworks for a particular project simultaneously, but that doesn't seem all that worrying or limiting.

In fact, understanding pluralism about theories of epistemic injustice this way fits well with Fricker's recent suggestion that we should think of the distinction between distributive and discriminatory epistemic injustice (discussed in Chapter 3) not as different classes of epistemic injustices, but as different theoretical lenses we can adopt depending on what project we're engaged in:

> As regards these two approaches, I take the view that for almost any unfair inequality you could come at it theoretically either through a distributive conception or a discriminatory one. That is to say, in general, you can look at injustices through either lens. Each will deliver its own perspective, and highlight different aspects. A theorist therefore has a choice, to be determined by which frame you think is going to be most revealing or explanatorily powerful for your purposes.
>
> (Nikolaidis, Thompson, and Fricker 2023: 793)

Fricker here articulates precisely the kind of pluralist attitude I take Dotson to be proposing with respect to Fricker's overall theory and her own. There remains much more to be said about the details of this approach to epistemic injustice (again, in the broadest sense), and in particular, it remains unclear what kinds of different projects we might engage in and how we go about determining which theoretical framework is the best tool for the job in a given instance. Still, Dotson's ecumenical proposal seems like an attractive and potentially plausible way to respond to the observation that while both her theory and Fricker's seem to have limitations, they also each seem to have the power to illuminate aspects of the unjust obstacles that can face us when we try to exercise our epistemic agency.

10.8 SUMMARY

This chapter has considered whether some of the apparent limitations of Fricker's account of hermeneutical injustice motivate introducing further categories of epistemic injustice to sit alongside testimonial and hermeneutical injustice. We have also weighed up whether we should take a more dramatic step, and shift from Fricker's account of epistemic injustice to an overarching framework in terms of epistemic oppression, of the sort we saw Dotson laying out in our discussion in Chapter 4. To both of these questions, I have offered mixed answers. I take Dotson's notion of contributory injustice (and Pohlhaus's related notion of wilful hermeneutical ignorance) to pick out genuine phenomena which Fricker overlooked. However, while Dotson argues that Fricker's account of epistemic injustice renders her in principle incapable of recognising contributory injustice, I don't think that's been demonstrated; rather, I think it remains a live option to consider contributory injustice a particular variety of hermeneutical injustice. Exploring this question has given us a chance to take a close look at Fricker's claim that hermeneutical injustice is a purely structural form of injustice, and I have suggested, following Medina, that the conclusion that Fricker has overlooked varieties of hermeneutical injustice that involve perpetrators is better motivated than the conclusion drawn by Dotson and Pohlhaus, that she has overlooked a distinct species of epistemic injustice. I have also laid out Dotson's order-of-change model of epistemic injustice and its sub-varieties; this has been very influential, but I remain sceptical that the key notion of what kind of change is needed to minimally address a given form of epistemic injustice is clear and determinate enough to allow us to distinguish different forms of epistemic injustice in the manner Dotson proposes.

I've closed this final chapter of Part 3 by returning to the starting point of this book, examining whether we need either or both of the notions of epistemic injustice (as understood according to Fricker's account) and epistemic oppression. I'm strongly inclined to think that philosophers engaged with the kinds of examples that animate this topic and this book should be open to employing both, and I've begun to explore what such a pluralist approach to our topic might look like, drawing on Dotson's discussion once more.

10.9 SUGGESTED FURTHER READINGS

Catala (2024) is a very helpful discussion of the differences between Fricker's epistemic injustice and Dotson's epistemic oppression; I drew on Catala's points in the chapter, but it's very worth reading the whole paper.

A number of philosophers have argued against Fricker's claim that hermeneutical injustice never has perpetrators, in addition to Medina. See, for instance, Maitra (2010), Dougherty (2023), Cull (2024), Luzzi (2024), and McGlynn (2025).

Despite being heavily influenced by Dotson's work, Berenstain (2020) rejects Dotson's ecumenical proposal discussed at the end of this chapter, and instead argues that Fricker's framework shouldbe replaced wholesale.

The point that there can be forms of hermeneutical injustice overlooked by Fricker that occur *after* fitting hermeneutical resources have been created has given rise to a small literature of its own. I lack space to give proper attention to the various contributions that have been made here, but see, for example, Jenkins (2017), Davis (2018), Bratu and Hänel (2021), George and Goguen (2021), Falbo (2022), Massami (2022: Chapter 11), Podosky (2023), Dular (2024), Edgoose (2024), Drury (2025), and Kok (2025).

Two important precursors to much of this literature, exploring the way that concepts can be robbed of their controversial political significance when they 'travel' into mainstream usage, are Lewis (2013) and Salem (2018). The example they focus on is the term 'intersectionality' and the associated concept, which I introduced in Chapter 1; this example is also discussed in Hawkins and Davis (2024), along with Du Bois's notion of double consciousness, introduced in Chapter 4. Another possible example is 'sexual harassment,' one of Fricker's principal examples of both hermeneutical justice and injustice, and the focus of Chapter 8 of this book: see Farley's (2017) piece 'I Coined the Term "Sexual Harassment".'

Corporations Stole It,' which I noted has a pessimistic tone when I quoted it in that earlier chapter.

For criticism of Medina's interpretation of the example of Tom Robinson as a hermeneutical injustice, see Curry (2017). I discussed Curry's more general worry about treating the example as involving an epistemic injustice in Chapter 5.

NOTES

1 Dotson has a related notion of an epistemological system that 'refers to our overall epistemic life ways,' and which 'includes operative, instituted social imaginaries, habits of cognition, attitudes about knowers and/or any relevant sensibilities that encourage or hinder the production of knowledge' (2014: 121).
2 Magnus Ferguson (forthcoming) observes that 'hermeneutical resources' and 'epistemic resources' are often treated as interchangeable in the literature, which is unfortunate given the point in the text. Ferguson advocates for a much more expansive conception of hermeneutical resources, so that in addition to concepts, expressions, and so on, we include comportments, habits and dispositions, and embodied skills, and he argues on this basis that we should accept that some hermeneutical resources are not epistemic resources. The point in the text, that hermeneutical resources of the sort Fricker discusses are epistemic resources, still stands even if we accept Ferguson's argument for broadening the former category beyond Fricker's conception of it. (See Crerar 2016 for an alternative suggestion concerning how we might expand what we count as hermeneutical resources.)
3 It's important to recognise that structural forms of injustice, even purely structural forms (if there are any), *do* involve the actions and behaviours of individuals agents. For example, I take hermeneutical marginalisation to be a structural phenomenon in the relevant sense (see Chapter 9), but the kind of pattern of exclusion from certain jobs, roles, and institutions that a group faces is of course made up of a lot of actions at the level of individuals: a Black woman receiving a rejection for a job or promotion she has applied for from a committee with a prejudiced member, for instance. The claim is that these individual agents don't count as perpetrators of the relevant injustice, not that they play no causal role in it. (As the example suggests, they may nonetheless count as perpetrators of the smaller injustices that contribute to the larger one.)

4 You may recall the related notions of 'situated knowledge' from Chapter 4 and 'reliable ignorance' from chapter 7.
5 Compare Catala (2024: 6).
6 See the suggested further readings at the end of this chapter for references to the literature on this point.
7 In one place, Dotson seems to acknowledge something like this point: see Dotson (2014: 127).
8 See relatedly Medina (2013: Chapter 2), though to pre-empt the discussion to follow a little, Medina puts the point in terms of hermeneutical injustice rather than suggesting we need to introduce a new category.
9 I have mostly focused on Dotson (2012) here, since it directly concerns the three varieties of epistemic injustice/oppression that we are considering. Dotson (2014) offers an appropriation of and elaboration on Plato's Allegory of the Cave in order to make some of the points discussed in the text, but also to argue that first- and second-order epistemic injustice are reducible to 'socially and historically contingent power relations' (2014: 116–117), while third-order epistemic injustice is an irreducible form of epistemic oppression which 'is difficult due to features of epistemological systems' themselves (2014: 116). See Veigl (2025) for a critical discussion of this aspect of Dotson's views.
10 See the suggested further readings at the end of this chapter for references to the wider literature on this.
11 Describing this as illustrating hermeneutical injustice needn't commit us to saying that there's no testimonial injustice in the example; rather, as Medina stresses, it seems like an illustration of how testimonial and hermeneutical injustice can work in unison. Compare the discussion of disability-positive testimony in the final section of Chapter 5.
12 There are some narrower characterisations of hermeneutical injustice in Fricker (2007: Chapter 7) that perhaps would exclude this example from counting: for instance, those that require there to be a lacuna—a gap—in the communal stock of hermeneutical resources, as there was on Fricker's interpretation of the injustice faced by Carmita Wood. However, these narrower definitions also exclude a number of other examples which seem like they should be included in a definition of hermeneutical injustice, including Fricker's own example of Edmund White's partly autobiographical novel *A Boy's Own Story* (White 1983), which tells the story of a gay teenager going through his adolescence and trying to make sense of his own sexual desires and experiences in the mid-20th century. In this example, there *is* a concept which should have been available as a resource to allow White to understand his experiences and his romantic and sexual desires, so in one sense,

there's no conceptual lacuna, but the concept available to him has been loaded with negative associations; homosexuality is unnatural, shameful, a sickness, associated with rape, dismissed as a passing phase, and so on (Fricker 2007: 163–165). See Falbo (2022) for further relevant discussion.
13 A very similar objection is made by Maitra (2010: 209–210).
14 Another concern along these lines is prompted by the observation made in Chapter 2, and reinforced in this chapter, that testimonial and hermeneutical injustice often seem to come entwinned, and that it may be hard in practice to separate them. That makes it different to see how 'minimally addressing' one form can be different, and less demanding, than doing so for the other.
15 These kinds of examples may be a variety of what Luvell Anderson calls 'hermeneutical impasses' (Anderson 2017).

REFERENCES

Anderson, Luvell. 2017. 'Hermeneutical Impasses.' *Philosophical Topics* 45 (2): 1–19. https://doi.org/10.5840/philtopics201745211

Bartunek, Jean and Michael Koch. 1987. 'First-Order, Second-Order, and Third-Order Change and Organization Development Interventions: A Cognitive Approach.' *The Journal of Applied Behavioral Science* 23 (4): 482–500. https://doi.org/10.1177/0021886387023004

Berenstain, Nora. 2020. 'White Feminist Gaslighting.' *Hypatia* 35 (4): 733–758. https://doi.org/10.1017/hyp.2020.31

Bratu, Christine and Hilkje Hänel. 2021. 'Varieties of Hermeneutical Injustice: A Blueprint.' *Moral Philosophy and Politics* 8 (2): 331–350. https://doi.org/10.1515/mopp-2020-0007

Catala, Amandine. 2024. 'Epistemic Injustice or Epistemic Oppression?' *KULA: Knowledge Creation, Dissemination, and Preservation Studies* 7 (1): 1–11. https://doi.org/10.18357/kula.294

Collins, Patricia Hills. 2000. *Black Feminist Thought: Knowledge, Consciousness, and the Politics of Empowerment* (Second Edition). New York and Oxon: Routledge.

Crerar, Charlie. 2016. 'Taboo, Hermeneutical Injustice, and Expressively Free Environments.' *Episteme* 13 (2): 195–207. https://doi.org/10.1017/epi.2015.35

Cull, Matthew. 2024. 'Trans Epistemology and Methodological Radicalism: Un Œuf, But Enough.' *Hypatia* 39 (1): 44–60. https://doi.org/10.1017/hyp.2023.102

Curry, Tommy J. 2017. 'This N*****'s Broken: Hyper-masculinity, the Buck, and the Role of Physical Disability in White Anxiety toward the Black Male Body.' *Journal of Social Philosophy* 48 (3): 321–343. https://doi.org/10.1111/josp.12193

Davis, Emmalon. 2018. 'On Epistemic Appropriation.' *Ethics* 128 (4): 702–727. https://doi.org/10.1086/697490

Dotson, Kristie. 2011. 'Tracking Epistemic Violence, Tracking Practices of Silencing.' *Hypatia* 26 (2): 236–257. https://doi.org/10.1111/j.1527-2001.2011.01177.x

Dotson, Kristie. 2012. 'A Cautionary Tale: On Limiting Epistemic Oppression.' *Frontiers: A Journal of Women Studies* 33 (1): 24–47. https://doi.org/10.1353/fro.2012.a472779

Dotson, Kristie. 2014. 'Conceptualizing Epistemic Oppression.' *Social Epistemology* 28 (2): 115–138. https://doi.org/10.1080/02691728.2013.782585

Dougherty, Emma C. 2023. 'Toward an Agential Conception of Hermeneutical Injustice: Isolation and Domestic Violence.' *Hypatia* 38 (4): 822–838. https://doi.org/10.1017/hyp.2023.75

Drury, Megan R. F. 2025. 'Concepts and Contexts: Towards a Theory of "Hermeneutical Bastardization".' *Hypatia* 40 (1): 206–227. https://doi.org/10.1017/hyp.2024.32

Dular, Nicole. 2023. 'One Too Many: Hermeneutical Excess as Hermeneutical Injustice.' *Hypatia* 38 (2): 423-438. https://doi.org/10.1017/hyp.2023.20

Edgoose, Han. 2024. 'Hermeneutical Sabotage.' *Australasian Journal of Philosophy* 102 (4): 879–895. https://doi.org/10.1080/00048402.2024.2351210

Falbo, Arianna. 2022. 'Hermeneutical Injustice: Distortion and Conceptual Aptness.' *Hypatia* 37 (2): 343–363. https://doi.org/10.1017/hyp.2022.4

Farley, Lin. 2017. 'I Coined the Term 'Sexual Harassment'. Corporations Stole It.' *The New York Times*, October 28, 2017. https://www.nytimes.com/2017/10/18/opinion/sexual-harassment-corporations-steal.html

Ferguson, Magnus. Forthcoming. 'What Are Hermeneutical Resources? Non-discursive Self-Interpretation and Gendered Embodiment.' *Hypatia*.

Fricker, Miranda. 2007. *Epistemic Injustice: Power and the Ethics of Knowing*. Oxford: Oxford University Press.

Fricker, Miranda. 2016. 'Epistemic Injustice and the Preservation of Ignorance.' In Rik Peels and Martijn Blaauw, eds. *The Epistemic Dimensions of Ignorance*: 160–177. Cambridge: Cambridge University Press.

George, B. R. and Stacey Goguen. 2021. 'Hermeneutical Backlash: Trans Youth Panics as Epistemic Injustice.' *Feminist Philosophy Quarterly* 7 (4): 1–34. https://doi.org/10.5206/fpq/2021.4.13518

Goetze, Trystan. 2018. 'Hermeneutical Dissent and the Species of Hermeneutical Injustice.' *Hypatia* 33 (1): 73–90. https://doi.org/10.1111/hypa.12384

Hawkins, Orlando and Emmalon Davis. 2024. 'The Future of Double Consciousness: Epistemic Virtue, Identity, and Structural Anti-Blackness.' *Ergo* 11 (3): 62–95. https://doi.org/10.3998/ergo.5708

Jenkins, Katharine. 2017. 'Rape Myths and Domestic Abuse Myths as Hermeneutical Injustices.' *Journal of Applied Philosophy* 34 (2): 191–205. https://doi.org/10.1111/japp.12174

Kok, Sara. 2025. 'The Epistemic Fata Morgana: Appropriation in the Institutional Context.' *Hypatia* 40 (4): 699–715. https://doi.org/10.1017/hyp.2024.91

Langton, Rae. 2010. '*Epistemic Injustice: Power and the Ethics of Knowing* by Miranda Fricker.' *Hypatia* 25 (2): 459–464. https://doi.org/10.1111/j.1527-2001.2010.01098.x

Lewis, Gail. 2013. 'Unsafe Travel: Experiencing Intersectionality and Feminist Displacements.' *Signs* 38 (4): 869–892. https://doi.org/10.1086/669609

Lugones, María. 1987. 'Playfulness, "World"-Travelling, and Loving Perception.' *Hypatia* 2 (2): 3–19. https://doi.org/10.1111/j.1527-2001.1987.tb01062.x

Luzzi, Federico. 2024. 'Deception-Based Hermeneutical Injustice.' *Episteme* 21 (1): 147–165. https://doi.org/10.1017/epi.2021.7

Maitra, Ishani. 2010. 'The Nature of Epistemic Injustice.' *Philosophical Books* 51 (4): 195–211. https://doi.org/10.1111/j.1468-0149.2010.00511.x

Massami, Michela. 2022. *Perspectival Realism*. New York: Oxford University Press.

McGlynn, Aidan. 2025. 'Epistemic Injustice: Phenomena and Theories.' In Jennifer Lackey and Aidan McGlynn, eds. *The Oxford Handbook of Social Epistemology*: 295–327. New York: Oxford University Press.

Medina, José. 2013. *The Epistemology of Resistance: Gender and Racial Oppression, Epistemic Injustice, and Resistant Imaginations*. Oxford: Oxford University Press.

Nikolaidis, A. C., Winston C. Thompson, and Miranda Fricker. 2023. 'Education, Epistemic Injustice, and Truthfulness: Miranda Fricker Interviewed by A. C. Nikolaidis and Winston C. Thompson.' *Journal of Philosophy of Education* 57 (4–5): 791–802. https://doi.org/10.1093/jopedu/qhad075

Ortega, Mariana. 2006. 'Being Lovingly, Knowingly Ignorant: White Feminism and Women of Color.' *Hypatia* 21 (3): 56–74. https://doi.org/10.1111/j.1527-2001.2006.tb01113.x

Podosky, Paul-Mikhail Catapang. 2023. 'Rethinking Epistemic Appropriation.' *Episteme* 20 (1): 142–162. https://doi.org/10.1017/epi.2021.8

Pohlhaus, Jr., Gaile. 2012. 'Relational Knowing and Epistemic Injustice: Towards a Theory of *Willful Hermeneutical Ignorance*.' *Hypatia* 27: 715–735. https://doi.org/10.1111/j.1527-2001.2011.01222.x

Pohlhaus Jr., Gaile. 2020. 'Epistemic Agency under Oppression.' *Philosophical Papers* 49 (2): 233–251. https://doi.org/10.1080/05568641.2020.1780149

Salem, Sara. 2018. 'Intersectionality and Its Discontents: Intersectionality as a Travelling Theory.' *European Journal of Women's Studies* 25 (4): 403–418. https://doi.org/10.1177/1350506816643999

Tremain, Shelley. 2017. 'Knowing Disability, Differently.' In Ian James Kidd, José Medina, and Gaile Pohlhaus Jr., eds. *The Routledge Handbook of Epistemic Injustice*: 175–184. Oxon: Routledge.

Veigl, Sophie Juliane. 2025. 'A Common Denominator? Epistemic Systems Bridge Epistemic Relativism and Epistemic Oppression.' *Hypatia* 40 (1): 125–143. https://doi.org/10.1017/hyp.2024.62

White, Edmund. 1983. *A Boy's Own Story*. London: Picador.

Part 4

PRIMARY HARMS OF EPISTEMIC INJUSTICE

11

IDENTIFYING PRIMARY HARMS OF TESTIMONIAL AND HERMENEUTICAL INJUSTICE

11.1 INTRODUCTION

We have looked in detail at Miranda Fricker's two species of epistemic injustice, testimonial and hermeneutical, in Parts 2 and 3 of this book. I want to start this chapter with what might initially seem like an odd question. Are testimonial and hermeneutical injustice really forms of epistemic injustice? It's tempting to reply 'Of course they are!'. This is just obvious. Moreover, Fricker picked these out as forms of epistemic injustice; isn't that proof enough by itself, given that she's the one who characterised epistemic injustice in the first place?

These are natural reactions, but I think they're misguided. Fricker has given us particular characterisations of testimonial injustice, hermeneutical injustice, and epistemic injustice, and the contention that testimonial and hermeneutical injustice are forms of epistemic injustice, understood as Fricker proposes, is a theoretical claim. It's neither obviously correct, nor the kind of thing that Fricker can simply stipulate in demarcating the phenomena she's interested in. Once we have her characterisations of these notions on the table, it seems to be a genuine question how they relate to one another. To miss this is to again render some of Fricker's central philosophical and

DOI: 10.4324/9781003281863-15

theoretical claims about epistemic injustice invisible, in a manner we should be familiar with by now.

If we take the notion of epistemic injustice broadly, as used in the title of this book, then testimonial and hermeneutical injustice do have claims to be obvious candidates. The former concerns testimony and credibility, while the latter also concerns testimony, along with interpretation, intelligibility, self-understanding, and self-knowledge, and so they both seem to clearly belong to the realm of the epistemic, generously construed. This point is irrelevant, though, when thinking about whether they are forms of epistemic injustice in Fricker's sense: whether they involve wrongs done to a person distinctively in their capacity as an epistemic agent. More needs to be said.

In fairness, Fricker doesn't leave these issues unaddressed or rest content with taking it for granted that testimonial and hermeneutical injustice are forms of epistemic injustice in the relevant sense, though her response is somewhat indirect. She starts by drawing a distinction between *primary* and *secondary* harms.[1] Primary harms are inherent in or essential to a particular kind of epistemic injustice, while secondary harms are contingent, and perhaps cumulative, side-effects. Fricker further divides secondary harms in turn into epistemic and practical harms. A secondary epistemic harm of testimonial justice might be that you lose confidence in what you are saying, and perhaps cease to believe it, thereby losing a piece of knowledge. Secondary practical harms are well illustrated by Fricker's *To Kill a Mockingbird* example, in which Tom Robinson is falsely convicted, imprisoned, and ultimately shot dead. As this example shows, there's no suggestion that labelling a harm as secondary indicates that it is not serious. So 'primary' and 'secondary' are not markers of severity, but rather relate only to whether a harm is an inherent aspect of a kind of epistemic injustice, or a contingent effect of it in a particular case or type of case.

Primary harms play a distinctive theoretical role in Fricker's framework, since the primary harm of a species of epistemic injustice is 'a form of the essential harm that is definitive of epistemic injustice in the broad' (2007: 44); that is, the primary harm identifies the way that a given species of epistemic injustice involves a harm done to someone in their capacity as an epistemic agent. Identifying the primary harms of testimonial and hermeneutical injustice, then, suffices to explain why we should think of these as species of epistemic injustice in Fricker's sense, and not just in some looser sense.

Fricker takes on the task of identifying primary harms in *Epistemic Injustice*, but her attempt can be frustrating in a number of respects. For one, her treatment of these issues is spread out across the book, and as we'll see, it's not always clear how to reconcile what she writes in one place with what she writes about the same topic in other places. Relatedly, we'll see that Fricker isn't always as clear as we might have hoped concerning which harms she takes to be primary and which she regards as secondary. Most notably, there's also surprisingly little by way of argument offered for this aspect of her views, as far as I've been able to tell. If you approach the topic of epistemic injustice sceptical that testimonial and hermeneutical injustice have any harms that are essential or inherent (perhaps on the grounds that there is a considerable amount of heterogeneity within each species, as we've seen in earlier chapters), it's not clear there's much in Fricker's discussion to convince you to change your mind.

The literature on this topic is also frustrating. A small cottage industry has developed offering criticisms of Fricker's account of the primary harm of testimonial injustice, and developing refinements or rivals that try to show how to improve on Fricker's account, but there has been virtually no discussion at all of the primary harm of hermeneutical injustice. This is odd—given the role of primary harms in Fricker's overall picture of epistemic injustice, expending so much energy on identifying a primary harm of testimonial injustice while ignoring hermeneutical injustice seems like heavily fortifying the front of a house while leaving the back door unguarded, unlocked, and wide open. Relatedly, the literature has rather uncritically inherited the problem of identifying a primary harm of testimonial injustice from Fricker, without any reflection on why this is a project we should be engaged in at all. I'm not just pointing fingers at others here; my own work on this topic (McGlynn 2020, 2021) is a perfect illustration of all of these problems.

This chapter will try to offer something of a corrective to these trends in the literature. I'll see how far we can push attempts to identify primary harms of testimonial *and* hermeneutical injustice, and my conclusions will be mostly negative. There are a number of relatively well-developed accounts of the primary harm of testimonial injustice in the literature, but it's not clear that any of them are entirely satisfactory. The real problem, though, is that the situation with respect to hermeneutical injustice is far worse; there are almost no proposals to consider, and those we have seem like non-starters. That's not to say that the discussion of these issues in the literature has been fruitless. Far from it; the debate has unearthed all kinds of rich theoretical resources for understanding many of the different ways in which different kinds of epistemic injustice can harm a subject. What it hasn't done, in my assessment, is vindicate the claim that there's a primary, essential harm shared by each instance of each kind of epistemic injustice, and it's this claim that Fricker's overall picture seems to presuppose.

I'll start by saying a little more about the distinction between primary and secondary harms (Section 11.2). I'll then survey attempts to find a primary harm of testimonial injustice, looking at Fricker's own proposals and the widespread criticisms they have attracted (Section 11.3), before examining whether any of the developments of or alternatives to her approach are more successful (Sections 11.4 and 11.5). I draw three morals about what the aims of identifying primary harms are meant to be (Section 11.6), before turning to hermeneutical injustice, where I argue that almost no progress has been made at all (Section 11.7). I also consider an interesting attempt to offer a unified treatment of both testimonial and hermeneutical injustice, and I'll contend that while it may deepen our understanding of some particularly significant secondary harms, it doesn't offer plausible candidates to be primary harms of epistemic injustice (Section 11.8).

11.2 PRIMARY AND SECONDARY HARMS

Let's start by elaborating a little on the distinction between primary and secondary harms. Testimonial injustice is associated with a wide range of secondary harms. Some of these are epistemic in nature. For example, a subject might react to being unfairly doubted by losing confidence in her own belief, perhaps thereby losing knowledge. If this happens persistently, she may lose her sense of epistemic self-trust more generally; this is a cumulative secondary harm, caused by persistent testimonial injustice. Some of these secondary harms are non-epistemic. Tom Robinson loses his freedom and ultimately his life as a result of the testimonial injustice he experiences at his trial. As I've pointed out already, this example shows that labelling these harms as secondary isn't meant to suggest that they aren't serious. Rather, secondary harms are ones that *may* arise as a downstream effect of testimonial injustice—but they may not. It's a contingent matter whether secondary harms arise in a given case, rather than being inherent in the nature of testimonial injustice itself. Instead of losing confidence after experiencing testimonial injustice, you might become all the more confident and determined to be heard. Though it wouldn't have suited Harper Lee's narrative, Robinson could have lived to win at a retrial, as Finch hoped. The crucial point for this chapter is that, even if *none* of these secondary harms arise, being subject to a testimonial injustice is to be subject to a harm: the primary harm. In line with the picture outlined at the start of this chapter, this primary harm is meant to reveal in what sense testimonial injustice is a form of epistemic injustice; it reveals how there's a distinctive harm done to one in one's capacity as an epistemic agent.

11.3 EPISTEMIC OBJECTIFICATION AND EPISTEMIC AGENCY

Fricker's own view, inspired by Edward Craig (1990), is that we should think of the primary harm of testimonial injustice as a kind of *epistemic objectification*. Craig drew a distinction between informants, who are 'epistemic agents who convey information,' and sources of information, which are 'states of affairs from which the inquirer may be in a position to glean information' (Fricker 2007: 132). Moreover, Craig suggested that sources of information are treated as 'objects from which services, in this case true belief, can be extracted' (Craig 1990: 36). What Fricker adds to this is the idea that testimonial injustice involves treating an informant as a mere source of information, thereby treating them as an object in the manner suggested by Craig, and so objectifying them. As Fricker sums up the proposal, testimonial injustice involves casting a testifier in 'the role of passive state of affairs from which knowledge might be gleaned,' treating them as having 'the same status as a felled tree whose age one might glean from the number of rings' (Fricker 2007: 132–133).

Fricker appeals to Martha Nussbaum's influential analysis of objectification to substantiate the claim that treating an informant as a mere source of information is a form of objectification. According to Nussbaum (1995: 257), there are many different ways to treat a person as a mere thing, and one of these is to treat a person as inert: that is, as lacking agency, in the sense we discussed in Chapter 1. The primary harm of testimonial injustice, on Fricker's account, is that one treats an informant as a mere source of information, thereby treating them as *epistemically inert*—as lacking epistemic agency. This makes vivid the sense in which testimonial injustice involves a person being wronged in their capacity as an epistemic agent: the speaker offering testimony is treated as lacking any such agency.

There's an obvious problem with this account, though. Primary harms are, by definition, those which are essential to an injustice, rather than merely contingently associated with it. However, there seem to be clear cases of testimonial injustice which don't involve the speaker being treated as lacking epistemic agency. I'll focus on just two here.[2] A point that I've stressed a number of times since Chapter 2 is that the prejudices involved in each of Fricker's central examples of testimonial injustice, Marge Sherwood from *The Talented Mr. Ripley* and Tom Robinson, target the speaker's credibility in somewhat different ways. Herbert Greenleaf's put-down represents Sherwood as epistemically incompetent; he clearly thinks that the way that she is reaching her conclusions cuts her off from the facts. The prejudices warping the jurors' perception of Tom Robinson are different, since they paint him as insincere rather than as incompetent. The jurors don't think Robinson is cut off from the facts about what happened between himself and Mayella Ewell; they think he knows fine well, but is unwilling, perhaps even incapable, of telling the truth about it. But thinking of someone as engaged in deception of this sort doesn't seem to be aptly thought of as denying that they are exercising epistemic agency; Fricker's comparison with the way that we treat a felled tree when we infer information from it seems totally out of place.[3]

The second problem for Fricker's account I'll discuss is based on Emmalon Davis's examples of prejudicial credibility excesses discussed already in Chapter 6. These involve speakers being treated like spokespersons for a homogeneous group, due to so-called positive stereotypes associated with that group. As we saw, Fricker claims that even if credibility excesses might have detrimental epistemic consequences for a speaker in the long-term—that's to say, even if they can be associated with cumulative secondary harms—they don't 'undermine, insult, or otherwise withhold proper respect for the speaker' (Fricker 2007: 20). However, Davis argues that her examples show that Fricker is wrong about this; some credibility excesses do involve insulting or withholding proper respect for a speaker in their role as an epistemic agent. Moreover, Davis points out that although giving someone a prejudicial credibility excess may be harmful, it doesn't seem plausible to say that this harm is that of treating the speaker as lacking epistemic agency:

> ...the targets of [credibility excesses] are not regarded simply as passive states of affairs or inert objects from which information might be gleaned nor are they excluded from epistemic participation.
>
> (2016: 489)

These two kinds of examples, and the others that have been produced in the literature, suggest that Fricker is wrong to diagnose the primary harm of testimonial injustice as that of treating a speaker as epistemically inert. There have been two broad reactions to this point in the literature. Most of the philosophers who have written about this issue have suggested that it motivates moving away from Fricker's account of the primary harm in terms of epistemic objectification, to an account that appeals to a notion of *epistemic othering*. The other reaction has been to argue that this shift is premature, since the epistemic objectification account, properly developed, has the resources to give a plausible account of the examples that have proved troublesome for Fricker.

11.4 OBJECTS OR OTHERS?

Gaile Pohlhaus Jr. (2014) has developed a version of the idea that testimonial injustice involves othering by appealing to Ann Cahill's notion of derivatisation, and several other philosophers have endorsed versions of Pohlhaus's proposal.[4] To derivatise, according to Cahill, is to 'portray, render, understand, or approach a being solely or primarily as the reflection, projection, or expression of another being's identity, desires, fears, etc.' (2011: 32). This is an attempt to give substance and precision to Simone de Beauvoir's notion of 'the Other' in *The Second Sex* (Beauvoir 1949/2009; Pohlhaus 2014: 104–105). Pohlhaus offers an account of epistemic othering that spells out what an epistemic version of derivatisation would look like:

> Epistemically speaking, we might say that the derivatizer treats the derivatized as though she has nothing unique to contribute to the intersubjective relations that maintain epistemic practices, even while he does recognize her as capable of some sorts of epistemic labor. In other words, she is treated as if her own lived experience from which she draws in order to add to the communal knowledge pool is simply a mirror (or perhaps shadow) of his own, but certainly not capable of contributing to our understanding of the world beyond (and in ways that might change the shape of) the scope of the derivatizer's experienced world.
>
> (2014: 106; see also 107)

To return to the kinds of examples that were problematic for Fricker, an audience might subject a speaker to a testimonial injustice without thereby treating them as lacking epistemic agency, but we can explain the harm done to that speaker in their capacity as an epistemic agent by observing that they are being epistemically derivatised by their audience in the manner described by Pohlhaus. They are treated as capable of 'epistemic labor,' and so not as epistemically inert, but they are not recognised as full epistemic agents in their own right.

However, Davis notes that Pohlhaus's account needs amendment if it's to accommodate Davis's own examples of credibility excesses (Davis 2016: 490). After all, in those examples, the speaker is given an excess of credibility precisely because the audience prejudicially expects them to offer testimony that is *not* a mere mirror or shadow of his own, but rather reflects the extraordinary abilities or experiences attributed to members of the stereotyped group; for instance, recall from Chapter 6 Davis's example of the Asian American student presumed to be unusually gifted at mathematics. Davis offers the following revised proposal:

> [W]e may characterize the primary, or intrinsic, harm of epistemic injustice as a form of epistemic othering, through which the capacities of a speaker are prejudicially assessed in such a way that bypasses or circumscribes the speaker's subjectivity.
>
> (2016: 490)

This preserves the core of Pohlhaus's proposal, as Davis sees it, namely, the idea that a speaker subject to a testimonial injustice is unable to simply testify in accordance with her own inclinations or lived experiences and be taken seriously. Her capacity to contribute something is always assessed with respect to the experiences of the dominant, so that she is liable to suffer a credibility deficit or excess if what she said conflicts with the dominant picture of the world or extends beyond it in an unexpected way.

This complicates Pohlhaus's account of the primary harm in terms of derivatisation. By itself, that's not much of a strike against it, but as observed in Chapter 6, Davis also suggests in passing an alternative treatment of her own examples which seems much simpler, and which points towards an alternative response to the examples that are problematic for Fricker's account. What Davis observes is that her examples feature speakers who are treated as *epistemically fungible*; rather than being treated as individuals with something unique to contribute with their testimony, their audience's prejudices mean that they are instead treated as an interchangeable representative of a homogeneous group, at least with respect to the topic at hand.

To see the significance of this point, recall Fricker's proposal; the primary harm of testimonial injustice is that the speaker is epistemically objectified, where objectification is to be understood along the lines suggested by Nussbaum's analysis. However, while Nussbaum identifies seven different ways that we can treat a person as a thing, Fricker's account of the primary harm only invokes one: treating them as lacking (epistemic) agency. Moreover, Nussbaum identifies treating someone as fungible as one of the other six ways of objectifying someone.[5] What this might suggest is that Fricker's mistake wasn't that she identified the primary harm as epistemic objectification, but that she construed objectification too narrowly, failing to avail herself of the concept's full richness by focusing too much on the denial of agency. Perhaps something in the spirit, if not the letter, of Fricker's account can accommodate the cases that proved problematic for her. This is the line of argument that I've defended in my earlier work on this issue (McGlynn 2020, 2021).

Of course, if this is to be a promising general defence of an account of the primary harm in terms of epistemic objectification, it will need to be extended to *all* of the problem examples, not just Davis's. It's not clear that this can be done. An account of epistemic objectification that appeals to the full breadth of Nussbaum's analysis has a much richer set of tools to work with, but that doesn't mean it has the right tools for the job. Take the testimonial injustice faced by Tom Robinson once again. We're no longer forced to say that Robinson is objectified by being treated as epistemically inert; in principle, we now have other options. That's progress, but we want details; what's the positive story about how he is objectified by the jurors' dismissal of his testimony as insincere? I've suggested that we might see the jurors as treating Robinson as an instrument for their own purposes when he testifies (McGlynn 2021: 172–173), instrumentality of this sort being one of the other forms of objectification recognised by Nussbaum. The idea is that Robinson offers his testimony with the aim of being treated as an informant—as informing them about what happened on the day in question and the nature of his wider relationship with Mayella Ewell—but instead his testimony is treated as fodder for all kinds of other inferences about what happened and about his intentions and actions, inferences that he does not intend and which it's not in his interests for them to make. There's a question mark over how informative or illuminating this account is.

More pressingly, you might also suspect the whole approach of being guilty of cheating. We're looking for an essential, inherent harm of testimonial injustice: a harm present in every instance of that injustice. Does the modification of Fricker's account I've proposed deliver this (assuming the point in the previous paragraph can be addressed)? In a sense, yes; in every case of testimonial injustice, the speaker is epistemically objectified. But it achieves this affirmative answer across a disparate range of cases precisely by exploiting the fact that on Nussbaum's analysis, there are a number of quite different ways of objectifying someone, and so we might well worry that this only delivers the superficial appearance of identifying a single harm in every case. I don't think that's a knockdown objection to the proposal, but it should give us pause.

11.5 STEADYING THE MIND

There's another thread in Fricker's discussion of the primary harm of testimonial injustice that is worth unpicking here, particularly since it has an analogue when we turn to hermeneutical injustice in later sections that will prove important. In Chapter 2 of *Epistemic Injustice*, Fricker appeals to Bernard Williams's (2002) idea that participation in 'mutually reliant, and so mutually trustful, dialogue with others' is an essential part of 'steadying the mind.' This, according to Williams, is the process by which 'wishes'—'contents that are entertained with no determinate attitude attached'—become either beliefs or desires (Fricker 2007: 51–52). Indeed, Fricker follows Williams in suggesting further that steadying the mind is an essential part of the process by which we develop an identity. So testimonial injustice 'marginalizes the subject in her participation in the very activity that steadies the mind and forges an essential aspect of identity—two processes of fundamental psychological importance for the individual' (Fricker 2007: 53–54).

The psychology on offer here might be debated. In particular, Williams's description of the process of sorting 'wishes' into beliefs and desires may not seem entirely psychologically realistic. However, his claims that beliefs are relatively steady states and that the process by which they are steadied is a social one, involving mutually trustful testimonial claims, seem to be separable from this and to enjoy considerable plausibility. Moreover, these may be sufficient for Fricker's purposes, namely to argue that systematic and persistent testimonial injustice can marginalise you in respects that can impede the formulation of your identity.

However, even if we accept Williams's claims, and accept that testimonial injustices can interfere with this process of steadying the mind, this shouldn't count as a *primary* harm of testimonial injustice, but rather as a particularly far-reaching secondary harm. The harm here, while serious, is both cumulative and contingent; these are not immediate and inherent harms of the sort which Fricker's picture of primary harms requires. As Fricker herself writes:

> It would be melodramatic to suggest that whenever someone suffers a testimonial injustice they are thereby inhibited, at least a tiny bit (whatever that would mean), in the formation of their identity.
>
> (2007: 54)

So the harm Fricker envisages here, the inhibition of the formation of your identity, is the result of a cumulative process, not a harm inherent in any instance of testimonial injustice. She goes on to argue that persistent and systematic injustices of this sort 'could' genuinely inhibit identity formation, and that someone subject to a testimonial injustice 'may not' have an alternative community in which to engage in the kind of trustful exchanges necessary for steadying one's mind (2007: 54), and she offers a plausible example to illustrate this possibility:

> Imagine a nineteenth-century middle-class woman who entertains a keen but frustrated interest in political affairs in a climate in which women lack the vote and are generally considered out of place in public life on the grounds that they are intellectually and temperamentally unsuited to political judgment. If when this woman expresses her beliefs and opinions around the dinner table she receives a blank wall of incredulity from her hoped-for conversational partners, is she not likely over time to be inhibited precisely in the development of an essential aspect of who she is?
>
> (2007: 54–55)

But as Fricker's language of 'could,' 'may not,' and 'likely over time' indicates, we seem to have the contingency and cumulativeness characteristic of secondary harms here. What she is describing is a particularly cutting kind of secondary epistemic harm, one that arises when someone without an alternative community in which to engage in trustful exchanges is subjected to persistent, systematic testimonial injustices. It's not a primary harm but rather, as Fricker puts it, an augmentation of the primary harm:

> Testimonial injustice may, depending on the context, exercise real social constructive power, and where such construction ensues, the primary harm of the injustice is grimly augmented [...] Putting the primary harm together with the extensive secondary harms it can cause, we now have a portrait of an injustice that shows it to be capable of running both deep and wide in a person's psychology and practical life.
>
> (2007: 58)

Taken as a thesis about how serious some of the secondary harms of testimonial injustice can be, I think this is, sadly, all too plausible. But whether you agree with this claim or not, this is a non-starter as a candidate to be the primary harm; Fricker's language here is again brimming with contingency and context-dependence, and this indicates that we're well inside the realm of the secondary here. I'll return to these issues in Section 11.7, and I'll also have something to say about why some of Fricker's readers seem to have been misled on this point.

11.6 THREE MORALS

Let's briefly draw some morals about what the point of identifying primary harms is meant to be from this survey of attempts to characterise the primary harm of testimonial injustice, which we can then carry into the second half of this chapter. First of all, any candidate for the primary harm of some species of epistemic injustice should identify a harm that is essential to it. This means that the harm should be present in every single case, not as a matter of contingency, and not only as a cumulative effect of persistent and systematic epistemic injustice of that sort; this is just what is *means* to say that a harm is primary, as I've already stressed. Second, the primary harm should also spell out the way that a species of epistemic injustice fits with Fricker's general characterisation: that is, it should explain in what sense that species involves a harm done to a person in their capacity as an epistemic agent.

Related to this there is also, I think, a third role played by the primary harm of a given species of epistemic injustice; it should illuminate its dual epistemic-ethical nature. Fricker contrasts the primary harm of testimonial injustice in this respect with its 'purely epistemic harm' (2007: 43), namely that knowledge fails to be passed to the prejudiced hearer. This purely epistemic harm completely ignores the ethical dimension of testimonial injustice, but the primary harm should show us how its epistemic and ethical dimensions are two sides of the same coin. We can see this role of the primary harm reflected in the kind of account Fricker offers of it, as well as in the alternatives presented in the literature. Both Fricker's epistemic objectification account and the rivals framed in terms of epistemic othering start with a notion that's of clear ethical significance, and characterise an epistemic version of it. This doesn't seem like the only strategy we could follow here, but it's a natural and potentially illuminating one.

Fricker's own account of the primary harm of testimonial injustice falls at the first hurdle, failing to identify a harm present in all cases. Indeed, if I'm right that Tom Robinson isn't treated as epistemically inert, she can't even claim to have offered an account that works for her own two central examples. The subsequent literature has produced refinements of Fricker's approach, as well as alternatives, and both mark genuine improvements in my view. Neither strategy seems entirely satisfactory, though, and deciding which kind of approach is best is a complicated matter. Still, when it comes to identifying the primary harm of testimonial injustice, we have options worth taking seriously and discussing further. As I signalled in the introduction to this chapter, the main problem lies instead with hermeneutical injustice. What we'll find is that when we take our three morals about what the point of identifying a primary harm is supposed to be and apply them to the few existing attempts to give an account of the primary harm of hermeneutical injustice, we emerge with nothing. Or so I'll argue.

11.7 SITUATED HERMENEUTICAL INEQUALITIES

A major shortcoming of the existing literature is that there has been almost no discussion of the primary harm of hermeneutical injustice. Fricker does address the issue, but her treatment of this is much less developed than her discussion of testimonial injustice, and it's puzzling in various respects. In the introduction to her book, she frames it in terms of there being a gap in the collective hermeneutical resources that prevents a subject from understanding their own experiences:

> The nature of the primary harm caused by hermeneutical injustice is analysed as a matter of someone suffering from a *situated hermeneutical inequality*: their social situation is such that a collective hermeneutical gap prevents them in particular from making sense of an experience which it is strongly in their interests to render intelligible.
>
> (2007: 7)

However, what Fricker in fact offers in her chapter on hermeneutical injustice is somewhat different, since it explains the notion of a situated hermeneutical inequality in terms of barriers to making yourself *communicatively intelligible* to others, rather than in terms of making your experiences intelligible to yourself:

> Let us say, then, that the primary harm of hermeneutical injustice consists in a *situated hermeneutical inequality*: the concrete situation is such that the subject is rendered unable to make communicatively intelligible something which it is particularly in his or her interests to be able to render intelligible.
>
> (2007: 162)

As we saw in Part 3, hermeneutical injustices sometimes involves a person struggling to make sense of their own experiences, and sometimes takes the form of a person encountering obstacles to making those experiences intelligible to others, particularly to others in dominantly situated social groups.[6] Each of Fricker's formulations of the 'situated hermeneutical inequality' that the primary harm supposedly consists in captures one of these forms of hermeneutical injustice, but ignores the other. Tristan Goetze spots this issue, and they suggest an amendment that encompasses both kinds of cases:

> I propose that the primary harm of hermeneutical injustice is that *the subject has some distinctive and important social experience that at some crucial moment lacks intelligibility.*
>
> (2018: 79)

However, this only make vivid the deeper problem with Fricker's suggestions. With testimonial injustice, Fricker offered us a characterisation of the phenomenon as a prejudicial credibility deficit, and then went on to identify the primary harm in richer, more ethically laden terms as a kind of epistemic objectification. She thereby tried to shed light on both the way in which testimonial injustice harms a person in their capacity as an epistemic agent and on this harm's dual ethical/epistemic character, in line with the morals we drew in Section 11.6. With hermeneutical injustice, in contrast, both Fricker and Goetze seem to be simply repeating the characterisation of *what hermeneutical injustice is* (minus an explicit specification that this moment of lack of intelligibility is due to hermeneutical marginalisation). This approach does well when it comes to the first requirement for an account of a primary harm that emerged above, at least in Goetze's unified formulation: it identifies a harm present in every case of hermeneutical injustice. But that's hardly surprising or much of an achievement if all that we've done is repeat part of the definition of hermeneutical injustice. It's no longer clear what the *point* of the notion of a primary harm is, if this counts as the identification of one.

Now, to be fair, Fricker does say more about the primary harm of hermeneutical injustice than the two brief remarks already quoted, and these additions offer a little more substance, and so might be thought to address part of the worry just raised. Her points both draw connections to aspects of her discussion of the primary harm of testimonial injustice. Let's take each in turn. First, in the continuation of the passage quoted above in which Fricker unpacks the primary harm as a matter of a subject being unable to make something communicatively intelligible, she connects this to the primary harm of testimonial injustice:

> Let us say, then, that the primary harm of hermeneutical injustice consists in a *situated hermeneutical inequality*: the concrete situation is such that the subject is rendered unable to make communicatively intelligible something which it is particularly in his or her interests to be able to render intelligible. This reveals another deep connection with the wrong of testimonial injustice. The primary harm of (the central case of) testimonial injustice concerns exclusion from the pooling of knowledge owing to identity prejudice on the part of the hearer; the primary harm of (the central case of) hermeneutical injustice concerns exclusion from the pooling of knowledge owing

to structural identity prejudice in the collective hermeneutical resource. The first prejudicial exclusion is made in relation to the speaker, the second in relation to what they are trying to say and/or how they are saying it. The wrongs involved in the two sorts of epistemic injustice, then, have a common epistemic significance running through them—prejudicial exclusion from participation in the spread of knowledge.

(2007: 162)

Fricker's characterisation of the primary harm of testimonial injustice in this passage is a bit thinner and less specific than the account she offers in terms of epistemic objectification and inertness. Still, the general idea is hopefully clear enough; in cases in which hermeneutical injustice takes the form of an obstacle to making yourself communicatively intelligible, the primary harm is similar to that of testimonial injustice. The problem is, of course, that any progress we've made here in offering a more substantive, illuminating account of the primary harm has come at the cost of proposing a candidate that covers all cases, since as Fricker acknowledges elsewhere, sometimes hermeneutical injustice is primarily a matter of having some of your significant social experiences left obscure to yourself due to a lack of fitting conceptual resources. Such a lack of self-understanding may also give rise to obstacles to contributing to the spread of knowledge, but this doesn't capture the essential harm done to someone who is unable to acquire such knowledge in the first place.

The other way Fricker supplements what she says about the primary harm of hermeneutical injustice is that she argues that hermeneutical injustice can impede a person being who they really are by constructing them as something they are not, noting that this is a power it shares with testimonial injustice on her account (as discussed in Section 11.5):

The primary harm of hermeneutical injustice, then, is to be understood not only in terms of the subject's being unfairly disadvantaged by some collective hermeneutical lacuna, but also in terms of the very construction (constitutive and/or causal) of selfhood. In certain social contexts, hermeneutical injustice can mean that someone is socially constituted as, and perhaps even caused to be, something they are not, and which it is not in their interests to be seen as. Thus, as we put the point previously in our discussion of the wrong of testimonial injustice, they may be prevented from becoming who they are. Testimonial and hermeneutical injustice have this identity-constructive power in common, then, as a possible feature of their primary harm.

(2007: 168)

I don't dispute that this is a genuine harm associated with some cases of hermeneutical injustice. However, it's not clear why Fricker bills this as a 'feature' of the primary harm of hermeneutical injustice, rather than as a particularly serious potential secondary harm. Again, primary harms are, by definition, inherent to the kind of injustice in question, while secondary harms are downstream, contingent, sometimes cumulative harms which may well be absent in many cases of the injustice in question; Fricker's talk of 'a possible feature' of the primary harm rather threatens to undermine our understanding of her own distinction. Moreover, as we saw above in Section 11.5, Fricker seems clearer that the analogous harm in the case of testimonial injustice is secondary rather than primary; it can 'grimly augment[...]' the primary harm, but it's not an inherent feature of testimonial injustice. I think her claims about hermeneutical injustice are best interpreted in the same spirit, but if so, her wording in the paragraph just quoted seems misleading.

11.8 RECOGNITION-FAILURE AS THE BASIS OF A UNIFIED ACCOUNT OF PRIMARY HARMS

The point just reiterated about the contingency of the 'identity-constructive' potential of both testimonial and hermeneutical injustice is important for assessing an alternative account of their primary harms. Like Pohlhaus's account of the primary harm of testimonial injustice, this account appeals to the idea of epistemic othering, but it is worth discussing separately since it promises a unified account of the primary harms of both testimonial and hermeneutical injustice.

This alternative approach to epistemic othering builds on Axel Honneth's development of some of Hegel's key ideas (e.g. Honneth 1995: Chapter 6). Honneth offers a rich theory of othering as various kinds of failure to *recognise* another person, and I'll only be able to offer a sketch of that theory here, so that we can see how it might be applied to the harms of epistemic injustice. On the picture Honneth develops, human flourishing requires self-realisation, and this in turn requires recognition from other people. Robinson Crusoe can't flourish on his island, since self-realisation requires struggling for and building relations of mutual recognition, and Crusoe can't even get started on this. A just society would be one in which, over and above there being a fair distribution of goods and opportunities, everyone stood in mutual relations of recognition sufficient for them to flourish. Injustice can involve various kinds of misrecognition or non-recognition, and Honneth usefully distinguishes three particularly significant ways in which this kind of (typically asymmetrical) failure of mutual recognition can prevent a person from flourishing: it can damage your 'basic self-confidence'—your sense of yourself as an individual with certain needs, who deserves to have those needs met (in part) by others; it can damage your sense of yourself as having standing as part of a community; and it can damage your sense of yourself and your accomplishments being valued by your community.

Philosophers working in this tradition, particularly Matthew Congdon (2017) and Paul Giladi (2017), have recently noted that it has largely untapped potential for illuminating the harms involved in testimonial injustice. Prejudicially failing to give someone the credibility that they deserve when testifying can involve a failure of recognition of a speaker in any and all of the ways distinguished by Honneth; it can call into question your sense of your epistemic achievements (your expertise in an area, for example) being acknowledged and valued by your community, your sense of having standing as a member of a community of inquirers, and even your self-confidence as a rational inquirer.[7] As discussed earlier in this chapter, Fricker worries that being subject to systematic testimonial injustice may 'inhibit the very formation of self' (2007: 55), and this Honneth-inspired account of the harms of testimonial injustice can explain this in terms of the consequences of facing repeated mis- or non-recognition: 'the experience of being disrespected carries with it the danger of an injury that can bring the identity of the person as a whole to the point of collapse' (Honneth 1995: 131–132).[8]

Unlike the other accounts of the harm of testimonial injustice in the literature, which we discussed in the first half of this chapter, this one has been explicitly extended to hermeneutical injustice too, with the proposal being that recognition theory offers a unified framework for thinking about primary harms of epistemic injustice in general. Giladi writes that:

> the principal harmfulness of hermeneutical injustice consists in depriving a victim of having access to the self-interpretational dimension of

rational agency: this represents a *specific* variety of alienation, because an indispensable feature of rational agency is one's ability to make sense of one's experiences. Due to individuals and/or groups being alienated from a crucial part of their rationality, asymmetrical cognitive resource distribution further entrenches the normative power of ideology. This seems to complement *and expand on* what Fricker writes here: 'The primary harm of hermeneutical injustice, then, is to be understood not only in terms of the subject's being unfairly disadvantaged by some collective hermeneutical lacuna, but also in terms of the very construction (constitutive and/or causal) of selfhood.'

(2017: 152–153)

Giladi understands ideology here as 'those social and cultural attitudes designed to further maintain domination over the oppressed by passively or actively encouraging those oppressed to accept/welcome their position of powerlessness' (2017: 152). The suggestion Giladi is making is that hermeneutical injustice involves an epistemic subject gaining social recognition, in Honneth's sense, only insofar as she conforms to the harmful controlling images or stereotypes built into the relevant ideology, and being subject to mis- or non-recognition otherwise. This leaves such subjects vulnerable to internalising the relevant harmful ideology.

I find the project of appealing to the rich recourses offered by Honneth's recognition theory in order to better understand and appreciate the harms of epistemic injustice promising and fascinating, and the specific proposals from Giladi, Congdon, and others deserve further consideration. However, it should already be clear from points made earlier in this chapter that we haven't yet been offered a plausible basis for an account of the primary harms of testimonial and hermeneutical injustice. What we have are potentially interesting and significant connections between the relevant notion of recognition on the one hand, and harms of epistemic injustice that are related to selfhood and identity on the other: but I've already argued that the latter harms are secondary, not primary. Given this, I'm not convinced this approach marks progress in identifying primary harms of epistemic injustice; the task of finding a plausible candidate to be the primary harm of hermeneutical injustice in particular looks as stubbornly difficult as when we started.

11.9 SUMMARY

This chapter has tried to clarify the role of primary harms in Fricker's account of epistemic injustice, and to look at the prospects of identifying such harms for each of her two varieties. With respect to testimonial injustice, the state of play isn't perhaps quite an embarrassment of riches, but there are a number of relatively well worked-out proposals, and there is already some literature engaging in the task of figuring out their strengths and weaknesses. I don't think it's obvious that any of these proposals, or some as-yet-unconsidered proposal, will triumph; equally, though, it's not obvious that all of these efforts will fail. The real cause for pessimism about this entire project, I have argued in this chapter, concerns the analogous effort to identify a primary harm of hermeneutical injustice. Here, I've contended that very little progress has been made, with the few proposals to be found in the literature failing to add anything to characterisations of what hermeneutical injustice is, or offering candidates which fail to apply to central cases, or which address themselves to harms which are, on reflection, contingent rather than essential. Given that it's not clear what the point of identifying a primary harm of testimonial injustice is, if this isn't an aspect of a more general and ambitious project, I think it's been a mistake for the literature to have adopted such a lopsided focus.

Where does all this leave us with respect to the question that opened this chapter, concerning whether testimonial and hermeneutical injustice should be counted as forms of epistemic injustice in Fricker's sense? Clearly, even if the pessimism of the previous paragraph is accepted, this does nothing to show that these *aren't* species of harms done to a person in their capacity as an epistemic agent. It may even be the case, compatible with everything I've argued here, that in each case of either testimonial or hermeneutical injustice, there's an immediate harm done to an epistemic agent that can be described in richer, more morally laden terms that helps illuminate its epistemic-ethical nature and articulates why it counts as an epistemic injustice; the troubles encountered in this chapter may be largely due to Fricker's assumption that there's a *single* distinctive harm that unifies all cases of a given species of epistemic injustice. I'm not sure this fallback position can be motivated or made to work, but I don't take it to be ruled out.[9] It also should go without saying that nothing argued here bears on whether testimonial and hermeneutical injustice count as epistemic injustices in a broader sense, one that relaxes Fricker's conception in various ways, as discussed in the introduction to this chapter.

Related to the points in the previous paragraph, even if all the harms associated with epistemic injustice prove to be contingent—none prove to be essential to any particular type of epistemic injustice—there is still all kinds of work to be done exploring these secondary harms, and I think Fricker is quite correct that some of these are especially interesting and serious. I also see no reason that the kinds of theoretical resources that have been thrown at the problem of identifying primary harms can't be repurposed for illuminating these secondary harms. I already made a version of this point in the previous section when discussing recognition theory and obstacles to authentically constructing one's self, but I intend the point generally to include the accounts of epistemic objectification and epistemic othering considered earlier in this chapter. So even if you are sceptical of the project of identifying primary harms of epistemic injustice, as I have increasingly become, it would be a mistake to conclude on this basis that this debate has all been a wrong turn; on the contrary, it remains significant and fertile ground for philosophers concerned with epistemic injustice and the harms it does inflicted.

11.10 SUGGESTED FURTHER READING

There are some further accounts of the primary harm of testimonial injustice, which I don't discuss in the chapter. One is offered in Pynn (2021): see Goldberg (2022) for some relevant discussion. A very recent alternative is offered in Pettigrew (2025), building on the account of the wrong of aesthetic injustice in Fraser (2024). Both Pynn and Pettigrew end up being very revisionary of the scope of testimonial injustice, excluding central examples (though see Pettigrew for helpful methodological discussion of this point).

The objection to Fricker's account of the primary harm of testimonial injustice as epistemic inertness covered in Section 11.2 is an instance of a more general worry with appeals to notions like objectification and dehumanisation (treating someone as subhuman or less than fully human) in explaining or analysing people's harmful treatment of others. The worry is that these harms often seem compatible with—indeed, to essentially involve—recognition of their victim's humanity (see e.g. Cahill 2011: Chapter 1 and Manne 2018: Chapter 5, and see Smith 2020 and McGlynn 2021, forthcoming for different replies).

McGlynn (2022 and forthcoming) attempts to defend a version of the familiar feminist critique that some pornography objectifies not only those women who perform in pornographic works, but women more generally, with appeal to the notion of epistemic fungibility discussed in this chapter.

The idea that recognition theory, in something like Honneth's sense, can illuminate the nature and harms of epistemic injustice goes back at least to McConkey (2004), but it has recently become a significant topic in the literature in its own right. My discussion in this chapter only scratches the surface, but Paul Giladi and Nicola McMillan have recently edited two collections of work on this issue: see Giladi and McMillan (2018, 2023).

See Dunne and Kotsonis (forthcoming) for a discussion of how harms relate to wrongs in the context of epistemic injustice—they use these terms very differently to how I have opted to in this book, however.

NOTES

1 Refering to primary *wrongs* might be more apt, given the way I suggested we understand the notions of harms and wrongs in Chapters 1 and 3. The literature is muddled on this, but it's mostly framed in terms of harms, and so I'll reluctantly follow suit for consistency.
2 For other criticisms of Fricker of this general sort, see Medina (2013: Chapter 3), Pohlhaus (2014), Congdon (2017), Hawley (2017), Carpan (2022), McGlynn (2024), and Pettigrew (2025).
3 See Congdon (2017) and McGlynn (2021) for versions of this objection.
4 E.g. Davis (2016), Cusick (2019), and Carpan (2022).
5 Nussbaum's seven ways of objectifying are: instrumentality, denial of autonomy, inertness, fungibility, violability, ownership, and denial of subjectivity (1995: 257).
6 For the latter, think in particular of the cases involving what Tristan Goetze (2018) calls hermeneutical dissent discussed in Chapter 10, where members of a marginalised group have developed their own hermeneutical resources but can't use them to communicate with people in their society from outside their own social group.
7 I have abstracted away somewhat from the details of their views, but see Giladi (2017: 146–148) and Congdon (2017: 248–250) for different developments of this kind of idea. While Congdon develops an account along these lines, his overall position seems to be the kind of pluralism I discuss in the summary of this chapter. See also Doan (2018).

8   See Congdon (2017: 248) and Giladi (2017: 155 n30). Honneth's claim here is slightly stronger than the analogue made by Fricker, since he is concerned not just with someone being inhibited in their self-formation, but also with the possibility of someone who already has a developed self-identity losing it.
9   Congdon (2017) and Carpan (2022) both make proposals of this sort, while Pynn describes this kind of pluralist position as 'tempting' without endorsing it (2021: 153).

REFERENCES

Beauvoir, Simone de. 1949/2009. *The Second Sex*. Translated by Constance Borde and Sheila Malovany-Chevallier. London: Random House, Inc.

Cahill, Anne. 2011. *Overcoming Objectification: A Carnal Ethics*. New York and Oxon: Routledge.

Carpan, Catalina. 2022. 'The Adultification of Black Girls as Identity-Prejudicial Credibility Excess.' *Ethical Theory and Moral Practice* 25: 793–807. https://doi.org/10.1007/s10677-022-10324-6

Congdon, Matthew. 2017. 'What's Wrong with Epistemic Injustice? Harm, Vice, Objectification, Misrecognition.' In Ian James Kidd, José Medina, and Gaile Pohlhaus Jr., eds. *The Routledge Handbook of Epistemic Injustice*: 243–253. Oxon: Routledge.

Craig, Edward. 1990. *Knowledge and the State of Nature: An Essay in Conceptual Synthesis*. Oxford: Oxford University Press.

Cusick, Carolyn. 2019. 'Testifying Bodies: Testimonial Injustice as Deritivization.' *Social Epistemology* 33 (2): 111–123. https://doi.org/10.1080/02691728.2019.1577919

Davis, Emmalon. 2016. 'Typecasts, Tokens, and Spokespersons: A Case for Credibility Excess as Testimonial Injustice.' *Hypatia* 31: 485–501. https://doi.org/10.1111/hypa.12251

Doan, Michael. 2018. 'Resisting Structural Epistemic Injustice.' *Feminist Philosophy Quarterly* 4 (4): 1–23. https://doi.org/10.5206/fpq/2018.4.6230

Dunne, Gerry and Alkis Kotsonis. Forthcoming. 'Carving at the Joints: Distinguishing Epistemic Wrongs from Epistemic Harms in Epistemic Injustice Contexts.' *Episteme*. https://doi.org/10.1017/epi.2023.62

Fraser, Rachel. 2024. 'Aesthetic Injustice.' *Ethics* 134 (4): 449–478. https://doi.org/10.1086/729708

Fricker, Miranda. 2007. *Epistemic Injustice: Power and the Ethics of Knowing*. Oxford: Oxford University Press.

Giladi, Paul. 2017. 'Epistemic Injustice: A Role for Recognition?' *Philosophy and Social Criticism* 44 (2): 141–158. https://doi.org/10.1177/0191453717707237

Giladi, Paul and Nicola McMillan (eds.). 2018. Special Issue on Epistemic Injustice and Recognition Theory. *Feminist Philosophy Quarterly* 4 (4).

Giladi, Paul and Nicola McMillan (eds.). 2023. *Epistemic Injustice and the Philosophy of Recognition*. Oxon: Routledge.

Goetze, Trystan. 2018. 'Hermeneutical Dissent and the Species of Hermeneutical Injustice.' *Hypatia* 33 (1): 73–90. https://doi.org/10.1111/hypa.12384

Goldberg, Sanford. 2022. 'What Is a Speaker Owed?' *Philosophy and Public Affairs* 50 (3): 375–407. https://doi.org/10.1111/papa.12219

Hawley, Katherine. 2017. 'Trust, Distrust, and Epistemic Injustice.' In Ian James Kidd, José Medina, and Gaile Pohlhaus Jr., eds. *The Routledge Handbook of Epistemic Injustice*: 69–78. Oxon: Routledge.

Honneth, Axel. 1995. *The Struggle for Recognition: The Moral Grammar of Social Conflicts*. Cambridge and Oxford: Polity Press.

Manne, Kate. 2018. *Down Girl: The Logic of Misogyny*. Oxford: Oxford University Press.

McConkey, Jane. 2004. 'Knowledge and Acknowledgement: 'Epistemic Injustice' as a Problem of Recognition.' *Politics* 24 (3): 198–205. https://doi.org/10.1111/j.1467-9256.2004.00220.x

McGlynn, Aidan. 2020. 'Objects or Others? Epistemic Agency and the Primary Harm of Testimonial Injustice.' *Ethical Theory and Moral Practice* 23: 831–845. https://doi.org/10.1007/s10677-020-10078-z

McGlynn, Aidan. 2021. 'Epistemic Objectification as the Primary Harm of Testimonial Injustice.' *Episteme* 18 (2): 160–176. https://doi.org/10.1017/epi.2019.9

McGlynn, Aidan. 2022. 'What Can Philosophy Contribute to 'Education to Address Pornography's Influence'?' *Journal of Philosophy of Education* 56 (5): 774–786. https://doi.org/10.1111/1467-9752.12695

McGlynn, Aidan. 2024. 'Making Life More Interesting: Trust, Trustworthiness, and Testimonial Injustice.' *Philosophical Psychology* 37 (1): 126–147. https://doi.org/10.1080/09515089.2022.2133695

McGlynn, Aidan. Forthcoming. 'Epistemic Objectification in Pornography.' *The Philosophical Quarterly*. https://doi.org/10.1093/pq/pqafo32

Medina, José. 2013. *The Epistemology of Resistance: Gender and Racial Oppression, Epistemic Injustice, and Resistant Imaginations*. Oxford: Oxford University Press.

Nussbaum, Martha. 1995. 'Objectification.' *Philosophy and Public Affairs* 24 (4): 249–291. https://doi.org/10.1111/j.1088-4963.1995.tb00032.x

Pettigrew, Richard. 2025. 'What Is the Characteristic Wrong of Testimonial Injustice?' *The Philosophical Quarterly* 75 (4): 1428–1451. https://doi.org/10.1093/pq/pqafo34

Pohlhaus Jr., Gaile. 2014. 'Discerning the Primary Epistemic Harm in Cases of Testimonial Injustice.' *Social Epistemology* 28 (2): 99–114. https://doi.org/10.1080/02691728.2013.782581

Pynn, Geoffrey. 2021. 'Testimonial Injustice and Epistemic Degradation.' In Jennifer Lackey, ed. *Applied Epistemology*: 151–170. New York: Oxford University Press.

Smith, David Livingstone. 2020. *On Inhumanity: Dehumanization and How to Resist It*. New York: Oxford University Press.

Williams, Bernard. 2002. *Truth and Truthfulness: An Essay in Genealogy*. Princeton, NJ: Princeton University Press.

Part 5

EPISTEMIC JUSTICE

12

TOWARDS EPISTEMIC JUSTICE

12.1 INTRODUCTION

Epistemologists (and perhaps philosophers more generally) are notoriously much better at coming up with problems and challenges than at solving them. This is true in more theoretical areas of the subject, but it's also proving true as epistemology increasingly takes the kind of applied turn illustrated by this book, and here the stakes are potentially higher. There can be value in helping to unearth and understand epistemic injustices, even if it remains unclear how to take concrete steps towards minimising, mitigating, or rectifying these injustices: towards *ameliorating* them, we'll say for short. Still, there's something undeniably disappointing about deep philosophical dives into problems that offer no solutions.

This chapter will only stem that disappointment to a limited degree, and this is for a few different reasons. For one, philosophers have simply had much more to say about the nature and scope of epistemic injustice—the kinds of issues that have preoccupied us up until this point—than about how to make progress towards epistemic justice. In that respect, my book is representative of where we are, sadly.

Perhaps the most important point is that there's a certain degree of generality demanded by the approach I've adopted in this book. While I've discussed both fictional and nonfictional examples throughout, my focus has been on broader questions and theoretical discussions about epistemic injustice rather than on the details of how these philosophical notions and debates might illuminate *particular* real-world applications in all of their messy details. I strongly suspect that some of the toughest examples of epistemic injustice require that kind of dedicated attention to detail, especially when it comes time to think about potential ameliorative responses. There may be some strategies that hold promise to be uniformly successful—but there may not, and I worry we'll only get so far with one-size-fits-all proposals. In my view, ameliorative strategies likely need to be tailored to particular kinds of epistemic injustice and particular domains in which epistemic injustice arises.[1]

Moreover, even focusing on a single kind of example, we have seen that epistemic injustices can be internally complex. One of the lessons of Part 3 of this book was that the kinds of injustices that broadly fall under what Fricker calls hermeneutical injustice take no one particular shape, but appear in a variety of different forms (only some of which we were able to explore in any detail). Even unjust dismissals of people's testimony, which seems like a relatively simple and unified phenomenon, emerged from Part 2 looking rather more heterogeneous than we might have expected. We shouldn't assume that there will be a single strategy for tackling any specific kind of epistemic injustice, given that they may each be rather fragmented in nature.[2]

Indeed, even focusing on a single example, we find complexity. Take Fricker's example of Tom Robinson in *To Kill a Mockingbird* one last time. In earlier chapters, we have seen that Gaile Pohlhaus Jr. and José Medina have made a strong case for recognising that Robinson isn't merely subject to testimonial injustice, but also faces obstacles to making his experiences intelligible to the jurors and others in the courtroom which contribute to the disastrous outcome of his trial. Whether we call this a form of hermeneutical injustice or something else, it shows that a single example can involve a complex interplay between different varieties of epistemic injustice, and this makes it harder to see how it might be possible to make meaningful progress towards epistemic justice.[3]

Given all of this, I think we should be a little sceptical of one-size-fits-all— or even two- or three-sizes-fit-all—approaches to ameliorating epistemic injustice. Again, I'm inclined to think different philosophers need to devote themselves to different varieties of epistemic injustice or different domains in which they arise, and be willing to get specific and practical. This will often involve drawing on the expertise of non-philosophers—academics and non-academics—to develop accurate and detailed accounts of particular examples or kinds of epistemic injustice, and what's needed to try to best mitigate or eliminate those injustices (Doan 2018).

That all said, the literature does contain a number of proposed general strategies for trying to take meaningful steps to ameliorate epistemic injustice, and I don't want to suggest there is no place for these, or that they should be dismissed out of hand. So in the remainder of this chapter, these will be my focus. I'll start by looking at Miranda Fricker's proposed virtues of epistemic justice, and some of the criticisms that have been made of them in the literature, before turning to a related but distinct set of proposals from José Medina. I'll close by taking stock of what this book has accomplished, and offering guidance on some further readings that offer interesting examples of different approaches to trying to secure a measure of epistemic justice in our deeply unjust world.

12.2 VIRTUES OF EPISTEMIC JUSTICE

Fricker's own proposed remedy involves cultivating certain virtues, one for each variety of epistemic injustice. The things we describe as virtues are disparate in kind, but in her helpful introduction and overview, Heather Battaly characterises them all as qualities that make one an excellent person (Battaly 2015: 5). It's common to make a separation between moral virtues, such as generosity or empathy, and epistemic or intellectual virtues: qualities which make one excellent as an epistemic agent, such as intellectual humility, open-mindedness, and curiosity.[4] Fricker argues that the virtues we must cultivate to avoid perpetrating epistemic injustices don't fit neatly into either category, moral or epistemic, but are rather 'hybrids'; the virtues of epistemic justice have the same kind of jointly epistemic-ethical profile that epistemic injustices themselves have (as discussed in the previous chapter). What do such virtues look like?

Acquiring the virtue of testimonial injustice, according to Fricker, involves cultivating a 'reflexive critical social awareness' (2007: 91): a capacity to recognise the ways that social identity is distorting your perceptions of credibility and to neutralise those distortions as much as possible. In particular, where it's possible to do so, this requires you to revise your initial degree of credibility upwards, closer to where it would have been, were it not for the prejudicial distortions (2007: 91–92). As discussed in Chapter 6, Fricker thinks of this in evidentialist terms; your credibility judgements ought to match the evidence you have that the speaker is telling the truth (Fricker 2007: 19), and so that's what you're aiming for. However, Fricker is clear that she doesn't think that this process of repairing your initial, low credibility judgement is an exact science; you just need to end up in the right ballpark (2007: 91–92). Repairing your distorted credibility judgements in light of your recognition that prejudice has played a role may initially involve some conscious effort, but it's the kind of thing that over time, you can—through something like the process Aristotle called *habituation*—come to do spontaneously (2007: 96–96); it can become second nature to you.[5]

What about hermeneutical injustice? Here too Fricker focuses on the virtues you can display as a hearer that has been presented with testimony. As we briefly discussed in Chapter 10, the virtue of hermeneutical justice is manifested by those who respond in the right kinds of ways to speakers trying to articulate and share their experiences, but who are struggling due to a lack of fitting shared hermeneutical resources. What the virtue of hermeneutical justice requires of you is context sensitive, in the sense that it demands more of you if you have time and resources to devote to attempting to find out what the speaker is saying than if you have less time and fewer resources. Fricker's proposal is that this virtue involves being attentive to the possibility that someone coming across as unintelligible may be struggling with a hermeneutical injustice, and trying to help them overcome the barriers to communicating their experiences, at least when investing that much time and care into an exchange is possible. When this kind of time and focus on what a speaker is saying isn't possible, but you are aware of the possibility that they are struggling due to facing a hermeneutical injustice, what virtue demands is simply keeping an open mind (Fricker 2007: 171–172).

12.3 A DROP IN THE OCEAN

Fricker's virtue theoretic approach to remedying epistemic injustice has been criticised on a number of interrelated grounds. Some of these criticisms relate to the fact that the prejudices that are operative in cases of epistemic injustice are meant to be below the level of consciousness, and are not typically seen as under our control. For example, Linda Alcoff writes:

> [I]f an identity prejudice operates via a collective imaginary, as [Fricker] suggests, through associated images and relatively unconscious connotations,

> can a successful antidote operate entirely as a conscious practice? Will volitional reflexivity, in other words, be sufficient to counteract a non-volitional prejudice?
>
> (Alcoff 2010: 132)

Alcoff's point in this passage is that it's not clear how 'non-volitional' and 'relatively unconscious' prejudices can be avoided, corrected, or managed by the conscious strategies by which we could cultivate or exercise the virtues of epistemic justice.[6] Krista Hyde has developed a version of this objection to Fricker in more detail, focusing on Fricker's virtue of testimonial justice. Hyde argues that the 'testimonial sensitivity' that Fricker thinks we need to develop (and which is maladjusted due to prejudice in cases of testimonial injustice) is best thought of as part of, or at least as involving, our suite of *mindreading capacities*: our capacities to attribute mental states to others on the basis of their verbal and nonverbal behaviour and other cues. Moreover, Hyde contends that once we think in these terms, there's little reason to think that the kinds of virtue that Fricker proposes will get any purchase on the kinds of failures of mindreading involved in testimonial injustice. Where there is empirical evidence bearing on this question, Hyde takes it to cut against Fricker's views.[7]

Hyde discusses several examples, but let's look at one by way of illustration. There is empirical evidence suggesting that infants who spend their first year of life in relatively racially segregated communities and spaces do worse at mindreading tasks that involve reading the facial expressions of people belonging to races other than the one they're used to being around. If such mindreading tasks are involved in credibility judgements—as seems plausible when we consider, for instance, the role that reading facial expressions often plays in our perception of a person as being sincere or not—then these prejudicial failures to accurately mindread will potentially generate testimonial injustices. However, Hyde observes that 'Fricker's virtue would not seem to address such missing capacities: the loss of facial recognition abilities does not appear reversible by conscious work' (2016: 865).

So far, we've been considering doubts about whether individuals really can develop virtues that would enable them to correct for epistemic injustices in the manner Fricker suggests. However, even if those objections can be met, a number of philosophers have raised concerns about how effective remedies that focus on the moral/epistemic development of individual epistemic agents are likely to be. Most influentially, Elizabeth Anderson has drawn parallels between Fricker's discussion of epistemic injustice, and other, more familiar cases of widespread and systematic injustice, where she thinks it's already clear that encouraging individuals to be virtuous achieves very little:

> [I]n the face of massive structural injustice, individual epistemic virtue plays a comparable role to the practice of individual charity in the context of massive structural poverty. Just as it would be better and more effective to redesign economic institutions so as to prevent mass poverty in the first place, it would be better to reconfigure epistemic institutions so as to prevent epistemic injustice from arising. Structural injustices call for structural remedies.
> (Anderson 2012: 171)

Anderson stresses that looking for remedies at the level of structural interventions need not rule out pursuing the kind of individualistic strategies Fricker advocates for. Indeed, structural, systematic changes can provide a background against which the kinds of individual virtues Fricker discusses can be more effective (Anderson 2012: 168). Here's an example Anderson offers to illustrate what she has in mind. People's judgements about who should be hired or who merits promotion within a large institution might be prejudiced in all kinds of ways. We might encourage people to try to detect and correct for any such prejudices in their own judgements, but this seems unlikely to be feasible or successful, for reasons we've already reviewed. Instead, the institution might identify explicit and objective criteria for hiring and promotion committees to use throughout the institution, to avoid any reliance on 'subjective assessment' which can be more likely to activate prejudices. This action at the level of the institution provides an environment in which individuals may be able to make judgements less distorted by prejudice, and so which are more virtuous by Fricker's lights.[8]

Now, it's worth stressing that Fricker doesn't deny the need for structural or systematic reforms; indeed, she highlights their importance at various junctures. For example, after laying out the form she thinks the virtue of hermeneutical justice should take, she writes:

> [H]ermeneutical marginalization is first and foremost the product of unequal relations of social power more generally, and as such is not the sort of thing that could itself be eradicated by what we do as virtuous hearers alone. Shifting the unequal relations of power that create the conditions of hermeneutical injustice (namely, hermeneutical marginalization) takes

more than virtuous individual conduct of any kind; it takes group political action for social change. The primary ethical role for the virtue of hermeneutical justice, then, remains one of mitigating the negative impact of hermeneutical injustice on the speaker. From the point of view of social change, this may be but a drop in the ocean; still, from the point of view of the individual hearer's virtue, not to mention the individual speaker's experience of their exchange, it is justice enough.

(2007: 174–175)

Given passages like these, it can be little unclear just how much disagreement there really is between Fricker and critics like Anderson. Fricker's recognition in the passage just quoted that what she is proposing is a mere 'drop in the ocean' seems very much of a piece with Anderson's insistence that 'in the face of massive structural injustice, individual epistemic virtue plays a role comparable to the practice of individual charity in the context of massive structural poverty' (2012: 171). We need to look more closely to determine why Anderson's point might be taken as an objection to Fricker's position, rather than a restatement of it.

Anderson worry isn't that Fricker has missed the need for wider political and institutional reforms, but that she doesn't pay them enough attention, and instead has overemphasised, as well as overestimated the effectiveness of, the cultivation of individual virtue; for example, Anderson contends that 'structural forms of testimonial injustice are *more pervasive than acknowledged in Fricker's work*, and that such structural injustices require structural remedies' (2012: 169, emphasis added). In this sense, the difference between Anderson and Fricker is best thought of as more one of degree than kind.[9] She is charging Fricker with focusing in the wrong place and thereby failing to give sufficient attention to the structural reforms that are needed. Still, it's hard to know how much significance to accord this point. For all the influence that Anderson's criticism of Fricker has enjoyed, it's not clear there's ultimately all that much distance between them concerning what they take epistemic justice to require, if this difference of emphasis and attention is all that separates them.[10]

12.4 EPISTEMIC VIRTUE AND EPISTEMIC FRICTION

Anderson concedes that a complete account of what would need to be accomplished for our institutions and social structures and practices to be epistemically just 'would require many books' (2012: 171), but she offers as a preliminary characterisation of what's required the notion of an *epistemic democracy*, which involves 'universal participation on terms of equality of all inquirers' (2012: 171–172). José Medina's has offered an approach to epistemic justice which, like Fricker's, involves the cultivation of epistemic virtues, though he explicitly conceives of this as a way of trying to realise Anderson's epistemic democracy.[11]

Medina also presents his approach as a development of some ideas that were central in Chapter 4, particularly Du Bois's notion of double consciousness.[12] Recall that Du Bois had in mind the way he was able to see not only what was happening on the other side of the 'veil' between his world and the world inhabited by white people, but also the way he could see how he and his world would look from the other side of the veil. Medina extends this by arguing that we have a responsibility to cultivate a 'kaleidoscopic consciousness' (2013: 44), involving awareness of how things seem from a multitude of different socially situated perspectives. Those who belong to oppressed social groups will tend to develop the epistemic virtue of open-mindedness, as they 'have no option but to acknowledge, respect, and (to some extent) inhabit alternative perspectives, in particular the perspectives of the dominant other(s)' (2013: 44). This puts such people a step ahead when it comes to achieving a kaleidoscopic consciousness, which Medina sees as stemming from open-mindedness. Medina intends these kinds of claims about how your social situation relates to epistemic virtue to capture the truth in standpoint epistemology, as characterised in Chapter 4. Standpoint epistemology holds that the standpoints associated with oppressed social groups have an epistemic advantage, and while Medina rejects such generalisations about entire social groups, he does think that members of oppressed groups will *tend* to form certain epistemic virtues.[13]

In contrast, members of dominant groups will tend to develop the epistemic vice of closed-mindedness, which will act as an obstacle to their coming to possess kaleidoscopic consciousness. However, that neither means that they *cannot* achieve this, nor does it absolve them of their responsibility to. How might you become more open-minded, in the relevant sense? Medina suggests we need to seek out other perspectives, and use them to generate 'beneficial epistemic friction': 'that is, a friction that enables us to acknowledge and engage alternative viewpoints and to reach epistemic equilibrium among alternative perspectives on a problem or phenomenon' (2013: 176). Medina is sensitive to the fact that there is little to be learned or gained from acknowledging and engaging with some viewpoints, such as irredeemably racist, homophobic, or transphobic perspectives on the world; in some cases, 'only a negative mode of engagement is possible or epistemically beneficial' (2013: 50).[14] Still, beneficial epistemic friction requires that even these views must be acknowledged, if only to be forcefully countered.

The aim of epistemic equilibrium involves 'searching for equilibrium in the interplay of cognitive forces, without some forces overpowering others, without some cognitive influences becoming unchecked and unbalanced'; Medina picks out aiming at equilibrium between your own perspective and the perspectives of others as of particular significance (2013: 50). Epistemic friction isn't always beneficial, but Medina holds that if we are guided by the two principles just sketched—the *principle of acknowledgement and engagement* and *the principle of epistemic equilibrium*—we will be able to engage with such friction productively.

As presented so far, this might all sound rather focused on the individual, and so like it might be subject to the same limitations as Fricker's proposal. However, we need to set these ideas about responsibility for making sure epistemic friction is beneficial, and for cultivating open-mindedness and kaleidoscopic consciousness, into the context of Medina's overall account of responsibility. To illustrate this account, Medina asks us to consider the true story of a Vanderbilt student who dropped a pig's head on the steps of the Ben Schulman Center for Jewish Life on campus, but who claimed to be ignorant both that the building had special significance and of the antisemitic symbolism of a pig's head (Medina 2013: 135). Medina is understandably sceptical that the student was as ignorant as he claimed to be, but he asks us to suspend disbelief for the sake of argument, and to suppose that the student was sincere when claiming this ignorance. On Medina's view, this ignorance isn't enough to get the student entirely off the hook; there were things he *should have known*, giving his place in campus life and the opportunities it afforded him to learn about the different people he interacts with. Neither, though, does the buck entirely stop with him; his community partly shares in the responsibility to make the campus a space in which epistemic friction will be beneficial, and some individuals will have a greater portion of that shared responsibility than others; epistemic responsibility is a socially situated matter.

That these are sites of shared responsibility may also help answer a concern you may have with Medina's proposed route to open-mindedness, namely that it may seem to involve a kind of circularity. You might have noticed that his principles for beneficial epistemic friction, particularly his principle of acknowledgement and engagement, are exactly the kind of thing that a closed-minded person would be inclined to disregard; what is it to be closed-minded, if not to fail to seek out other perspectives or to bring them into productive friction with your own take on the world? However, there's only a circularity here if each person has to be *self*-motivated to follow Medina's principles; if a community collectively works to keep each other in line with them, that may nudge individuals within that community in the direction of the virtue of open-mindedness even if that is not their natural inclination.

A community of people who possess kaleidoscopic consciousness is one that can consistently avail themselves of beneficial epistemic friction, and one of the benefits, on Medina's picture, is that this enables the collective repair or replacement of what's contained in the social imaginary, which he takes to be the 'repository of images and scripts' that 'constitutes the representational background against which people tend to share their thoughts and listen to each other in a culture' (2013: 67 fn4). Since prejudice and distortion in the social imaginary is responsible for both systematic testimonial injustice and hermeneutical injustice on Medina's view, this is one path to epistemic justice.[15]

12.5 WHATEVER WORKS

The cultivation of epistemic virtues as a response to epistemic injustice seems to do a bit better than it is often given credit for in the literature. Fricker's two virtues of epistemic justice don't look up to the task of adequately addressing structural aspects or varieties of epistemic injustice, but nobody, including Fricker, seems to have seriously suggested otherwise (with any disagreement concerning the degree to which such individual virtues are worth highlighting, given their limitations). Medina's picture broadens our focus, having us pay attention not just to individual epistemic agents, but to the socially and epistemically diverse communities they belong to, offering a complicated vision of how reform might be possible at a level bigger than the individual but smaller than an entire society.

I've focused on these proposals because they are prominent and perhaps promising examples of strategies for trying to address epistemic injustice in general, rather than specific forms or examples. However, to return to my starting point in this chapter, I think these general proposals need to be pursued in tandem with, rather than instead of, more focused and tailored strategies for particular examples, varieties, and domains.

Above all, my overall attitude to issues about how to ameliorate epistemic injustices and take meaningful steps towards epistemic justice is best captured by something Fricker says in passing. In her reply to Alcoff's concerns (which we discussed in Section 12.3 of this chapter), Fricker writes that when it comes to epistemic injustice, 'we should do whatever works' (2010a: 166). It's all very well to speculate from the armchair about what kinds of strategies and interventions at the level of individuals, groups, institutions, and societies might be most effective and beneficial, but what counts are actual results. Of course, what we should count as an approach *working* is itself an issue philosophers need to consider. This observation may provoke a few groans, but we may find there is room for creative and surprising answers.[16]

12.6 SUMMARY

In this final chapter, we have turned more squarely to issues about how epistemic injustice might be not just understood, but ameliorated. I started by noting that specific cases of epistemic injustice will often require tailored solutions, but I have left those aside here and instead focused on two general strategies, both of which find a crucial role for certain intellectual (and perhaps also moral) virtues. One theme throughout has been whether such strategies are overly focused on changes to individual epistemic agents when what's needed are interventions at a larger and more structural level.

If epistemic injustice can be as serious and as complex as the rest of this book has suggested, we shouldn't be too sanguine about what any of these strategies, or combinations of them, can achieve. By the same lights, though, we cannot afford to do nothing, and the strategies discussed in this chapter should offer some (perhaps small) hope that meaningful steps towards epistemic justice can be, and are being, taken.

12.7 CONCLUSION

Let's finish by returning to the questions I laid out in Chapter 1 to see what, if any, progress we have made.

- Are there, literally speaking, cases of epistemic injustice and/or epistemic oppression?

- What are they like? If they are not all alike, what different forms do they take?
- What is their significance?

I think the preceding chapters have made a pretty strong case that the first question can be answered affirmatively on both counts; there are, speaking perfectly literally rather than metaphorically or hyperbolically, cases of both epistemic injustice and epistemic oppression. Now, nothing I have written amounts to any kind of *proof* or *demonstration* of these claims. Though some people have offered empirical evidence in favour of not just the existence but also the prevalence of certain kinds of epistemic injustice (e.g. Carel and Kidd 2014; Yap 2017), there's an obvious limitation to proceeding this way. The forms of epistemic injustice and oppression we have examined tend to be quite insidious; they are difficult to spot even from the first-person perspective as either perpetrator or victim, let alone from a third-person, external perspective. I won't always know myself if my rejection of a person's testimony is due to prejudices or ignorance that I am carrying around with me; that's one reason that phenomena such as testimonial injustice are so difficult to address, as discussed in this final chapter. Suppose I present you with evidence suggesting that 73% of the members of a particular minority group have experienced testimonial injustice—I think the natural reply is 'how can they be sure?,' and this needn't be the expression of a doubt that testimonial injustice is a genuine and pervasive phenomenon, or a prejudice against the group in question. Add in the kinds of uncertainties that have been the focus of this book, concerning precisely how the different categories proposed by philosophers are to be defined and understood, and it increasingly seems that our (to be clear, fictitious) 73% statistic could at best be suggestive. That doesn't make such empirical work irrelevant, and I don't in the slightest mean to imply we should just ignore it where we have it. But it will inevitably involve a lot of interpretation, and at least some element of speculation (for example, about whether the relevant reactions were *really* the product of prejudice).[17]

In any case, this isn't how the literature on epistemic injustice has tended to proceed. Rather, we are given real-life or realistic fictional examples, typically in richer detail than the average philosophical thought-experiment; the examples I laid out in Chapter 2 are cases in point. We're also given a theoretical treatment of the relevant examples that picks out certain features as the key ones for abstracting from those particular instances to a more general phenomenon, and we're invited to recognise that pattern elsewhere (and in the case of the fictional examples, to thereby see that they represent a phenomenon with real instances). This is essentially the methodology I have adopted in this book too, though I have cautioned against a tendency to collapse the first two steps, and so mistake particular theoretical descriptions of the phenomena we're interested in with the phenomena themselves. Even with this note of caution in mind, it seems to me that the literature has done a good job of identifying plausible examples of various kinds of epistemic injustice and epistemic oppression. Again, there's no proof here, but we shouldn't expect one, nor does this put philosophical inquiry into these issues on a shakier foundation than most other philosophy.

In terms of what the examples are like, and the various ways they differ from each other, Parts 2 and 3 of this book have addressed these questions in considerable detail. We have spent longer than is usual working through many of the most familiar examples in the literature, sometimes with surprising upshots, and we've examined many of the different categories of epistemic injustice and epistemic oppression that philosophers have posited to taxonomise the various examples by capturing key points of similarity and contrast between them.

Finally, there is the question of the significance of these phenomena and of the different philosophical theories of them. One effect of making a clearer separation between phenomena and theories here is that it becomes clearer how there can be room for philosophical disagreement between people who all take the phenomena seriously. There's a philosophical complexity and richness to debates in the epistemic injustice literature that has sometimes been overlooked due to the tendencies I've pointed out in this book; as I have stressed throughout, Fricker has often been viewed as doing nothing more than exhibiting and naming the phenomena, and that leaves no room for real disagreement beyond denying that the examples are genuine and illustrate something significant, and no room for other theorists writing before or after Fricker to be doing anything beyond offering their own set of labels. In contrast to this flattened picture of the issues covered in this book, I've shown that we've been offered a variety of quite different theoretical approaches, each with their own strengths and weaknesses. I've also tried to convey what I think some of those strengths and weaknesses are, but those particular points are of much less importance than the general moral that a considerable amount of sophisticated theoretical work has been done on this topic by a number of philosophers and other thinkers, over a period stretching decades further back than the recent literature sparked by Fricker's work. This book also indicates that there remains a considerable amount more work of this kind ahead of us.

In terms of the significance of epistemic injustice and oppression beyond philosophy, I take that to have been more or less settled all the way back in Chapter 2, where I introduced a range of the examples that have preoccupied and motivated those working on these issues. As those examples show, epistemic forms of injustice and oppression are all too often aspects of larger systems of oppression, and can contribute to perpetuating those systems and to rendering them invisible, so that it becomes possible to think that the persistent disadvantages faced by some groups of people are either a matter of misfortune or of just deserts. Moreover, as Fricker often stresses, being dismissed, marginalised, or unrecognised when we attempt to participate in our society's collective epistemic practices isn't only bad because it can reinforce or hide *other* wrongs; these can be substantial wrongs in their own right. We are social creatures and we are inquiring creatures, and these are central aspects of what it is to be human, not to be suppressed or denied lightly. It's for all these reasons that understanding epistemic injustice and working towards epistemic justice rightly strike so many of us as urgent tasks.

12.8 SUGGESTED FURTHER READING

Sherman and Goguen (2019) is a collection of essays engaged in the kind of piecemeal work to address particular instances of epistemic injustice that I have suggested is necessary.

Battaly (2015) is a beautifully clear and accessible introduction to philosophical debates about virtues and vices, including epistemic virtues and vices. For further discussion of virtues and vices of epistemic injustice in particular, see Kotsonis (2023). One kind of objection I don't discuss in the chapter comes from what's often called the situationist challenge, which suggests that neither virtues nor vices exist, as usually understood: that how we act is too shaped by the particularities of the situations in which we act for us to meaningfully attribute, say, courage or cowardice to a person. This is a general challenge to virtue- and vice-theoretic approaches in both ethics and epistemology, though it's briefly discussed in the context of Fricker's virtues of epistemic justice in Sherman (2016). Subsequent work on the situationist challenge has found that the empirical results underwriting it have proved difficult to replicate, and so the challenge looks less pressing than it initially did; see Tanesini (2021) for relevant discussion.

There has been a lot of recent discussion about whether it's possible to educate people in a way that cultivates epistemic virtues. For a sample, see the essays in Baehr (2015), and for a recent discussion of the most effective approach, see Tanesini (2016), Tanesini (2021: Chapter 9), McGlynn (2024), and Hanel et al. (2023). Of course, educational contexts can also be sites and engines of epistemic injustice, as we noted in Chapter 4: see Kotzee (2017) and the papers collected in Dunne (2022) for recent discussion. Cassam (2019: Chapters 7 and 8) offer a useful examination of the difficulties involved in overcoming your own epistemic vices, but also of which strategies might be most effective. Madva (2020) offers an overview of different kinds of interventions with respect to implicit bias, which is of particular relevance for thinking about how to avoid testimonial injustice.

For further concerns that Fricker can't address structural forms of injustice, see Langton (2010) and Doan (2018).

An important development in Fricker's views which I don't discuss in the chapter is that in several places following her 2007 book, she has defended the claim that there can be genuinely *institutional* epistemic virtues, which are not reducible to the virtues of members of the relevant institutions, and which include virtues of epistemic justice: see for instance Fricker (2010b and 2013).

The chapter briefly discusses the notion of mindreading: our capacities for mental-state attribution. For recent introductions to the philosophical issues raised by mindreading, see Spaulding (2018) and Lavelle (2018), and see Spaulding (2018: Chapter 5) and Spaulding (2025) for further discussion of epistemic injustice and mindreading.

McKenna (2023: Chapter 7) offers a sympathetic reconstruction of Medina's account of responsibility and epistemic virtues and vices, which I found extremely helpful for constructing my own summary of Medina's complex views in this chapter. Hawkins and Davis (2024) offers criticisms of Medina's approach, particularly as it is presented as a development of Du Bois's metaphor of double consciousness.

A question that has come up at various points in the book is whether or not the concepts and theories developed in the literature on epistemic injustice, broadly construed, are helpful in the project of *decolonising* knowledge and epistemology or whether this literature—including, now, this book—should be a target of this project: whether it is just, as Mitova memorably puts it, 'white-people stuff' (Mitova forthcoming). Talk of decolonisation can mean several different things in this context, but one central idea is that former colonial powers still dictate to the rest of the world what counts as knowledge, evidence, rationality, objectivity, and so on, and to decolonise knowledge and epistemology is to work towards dismantling this kind of epistemic colonisation (e.g. Mitova 2020: 191). The literature on decolonising knowledge is vast, and even the segment of it focused on how it relates to epistemic injustice would require a larger survey than I can give it here. See Chapter 3 and the suggested readings for Chapter 7 for some relevant discussion and citations, and see also Mitova (2020), Pohlhaus (2020), Posholi (2020), Tobi (2020), Tobi (2022), Catala (2025), Landström (forthcoming), Masaka (forthcoming), and Mitova (forthcoming): see also the important exchange oriented around Dotson's notion of epistemic oppression in Berenstain, Dotson, Paredes, Ruíz, and Silva (2022).

Barnes (2016: Chapter 6) offers the fascinating suggestion that Pride movements can function to ameliorate epistemic injustice. In particular, Barnes proposes that Disability Pride can publicly contest the widespread misconceptions about disabled people that, or her view, both constitute a kind of hermeneutical injustice and lead to dismissals of their testimony, as discussed in Chapter 5 of this book. This proposal raises a version of the question I ended Section 12.5 with: what would it take for such a strategy to count as a meaningful step towards epistemic justice?

NOTES

1 A strand in my own work has involved trying to understand whether and how the notion of epistemic injustice might illuminate feminist critiques of mainstream sexist pornography, and the prospects for addressing these problems via certain forms of relationship and sex education (see, e.g. McGlynn 2019a, 2022, forthcoming-a). This kind of approach is tailored to the particular issues I identify; if it can be generalised or can offer a model for how other kinds of epistemic injustice might be addressed, that would be a welcome development, but the key thing for me is to identify the most effective ameliorative strategy for the particular problems I've focused on. Other philosophers are similarly engaged in their own more focused projects, which may

require quite different strategies; for example, see the 'phenomenological toolkit' developed by Havi Carel and advocated by Carel and Kidd as a way to ameliorate epistemic injustices in healthcare (see e.g. Carel and Kidd 2014: 536–538).

2   This is one way of putting some of the worries I raised with Kristie Dotson's attempt to rank different types of epistemic injustice within an orders-of-change model, as discussed in Chapter 10 (Dotson 2012, 2014). I take Dotson to offer an overly neat division between the different types, and to assume that we have a grasp of a minimal degree of change it would take to 'address' a specific type that I don't think we have.

3   Relatedly, following Jones (2002), Fricker acknowledges the 'grim possibility' that testimonial and hermeneutical injustice might feed off each other, with doubts about the speaker's credibility and doubts about whether they are saying anything intelligible compounding each other (Fricker 2007: 159); Fricker suggests that this kind of 'runaway credibility deflation' may have been Carmita Wood's situation, but Tom Robinson seems like a better example to me, in light of Pohlhaus and Medina's points.

4   These three epistemic virtues are accorded a particular significance in Medina's account (2013: Chapter 2), which we will discuss in the next section. It is standard to use 'intellectual' and 'epistemic' interchangeably in the literature on epistemic virtues and vices, and I'll follow that convention here.

5   Fricker (2007: 93–96) also considers whether, and under what conditions, a person can possess this virtue 'naïvely,' where a 'subject's credibility judgements are free from prejudice from the start, without her having done any self-monitoring (conscious or otherwise), let alone any correcting' (2007: 93).

6   See also Anderson (2012: 167–168) and Sherman (2016: 242–243). Fricker has replied to Alcoff by clarifying that she doesn't picture exercising the virtues of epistemic injustice as always volitional or conscious (Fricker 2010a: 166).

7   In particular, Hyde argues that the empirical studies appealed to in Fricker (2010a) as part of her reply to Alcoff's challenge have failed to replicate, and in some cases, further studies have provided some evidence that the kinds of strategies Fricker appeals to are ineffectual at reducing prejudice (Hyde 2016: 861–862). I'm not going to attempt to adjudicate this empirical issue here.

8   A related proposal is that where possible, we should anonymise processes used to evaluate testimony or to award jobs and other roles and responsibilities (by anonymising CVs, for instance). This kind of strategy is familiar from the literature on how to neutralise the influence of implicit biases more generally (e.g. Saul 2013: 52–53 and Zheng 2016: 73), and many of Fricker's critics also offer it as an illustration of how we might facilitate, or go beyond,

the cultivation of individual virtues (e.g. Anderson 2012: 168, Hyde 2016: 869–870 n11, and Pohlhaus 2020: 239). Fricker has in fact also endorsed such strategies both as a general approach to implicit bias (Fricker 2016: 47–50) and specifically when it comes to testimonial injustice (2010a: 165); however, given her general views about the role of stereotypes in our testimonial practices (as presented in Chapter 5), she will hold that there's no prospect of generalising a strategy of withholding information about social identity, since even if this was possible (which it's not), this would, on her picture, make our testimonial practices grind to a halt. We can think of these kinds of strategies as attempts to 'outsmart' our prejudices (Cassam 2019: 170, who gets this terminology from Banaji and Greenwald 2016).

9 In contrast, Pohlhaus charges Fricker with simply failing to recognise the 'structural aspects' of testimonial injustice (2014: 108): see McGlynn (2020: 839) for a response.
10 See McGlynn (forthcoming-b) for further relevant discussion.
11 See Medina (2013: Introduction).
12 Hawkins and Davis (2024) dispute the claim that Medina's views are really an extension of Du Bois's notion of double consciousness, properly interpreted.
13 See McGlynn (2019b) for a discussion of Medina's view and whether or not we should count it as a form of standpoint epistemology; Medina suggests that we should, and the literature has generally followed, but I remain unsure.
14 Medina's position on this is a little unclear, but I follow Ashton's interpretation here (2019: 332).
15 The details of this last aspect of Medina's picture are much more complex than I can do justice to here: see the later chapters of Medina (2013) for how he develops them.
16 An example of what I have in mind here is found in Nick Clanchy's work on how to address certain hermeneutical injustices (Clanchy 2024, forthcoming). Most strategies for tackling such injustices assume that the task is to enable members of marginalised groups to make more and more of their significant social experiences intelligible, to themselves or to others. Clanchy suggests that sometimes we should give that assumption up, and look for ways to meet the needs of members of marginalised groups which allow them to side-step requirements to make themselves more intelligible: for example, universal basic income would have allowed Carmita Wood to have money for herself and her family to live off even if she wasn't able to make her experiences of being harassed intelligible to the bureaucrats at the Department of Labor, and a policy of providing

gender-affirming healthcare to anyone who gives informed consent would enable trans people to access the healthcare they need without requiring them to make their experiences of being trans intelligible to certain (typically cis) healthcare professionals who get cast in a gatekeeping role within many current medical systems, such as the United Kingdom's National Health Service. For related ideas concerning testimonial injustice, see Doan (2018).

17 Fisher (forthcoming) makes similar points, and appeals to them in his defence of fictional examples, which he argues are often more psychologically transparent than cases involving real people.

REFERENCES

Alcoff, Linda Martín. 2010. 'Epistemic Identities.' *Episteme* 7 (2): 128–137. https://doi.org/10.3366/epi.2010.0003

Anderson, Elizabeth. 2012. 'Epistemic Justice as a Virtue of Social Institutions.' *Social Epistemology* 26 (2): 163–173. https://doi.org/10.1080/02691728.2011.652211

Ashton, Natalie. 2019. 'Relativising Epistemic Advantage.' Martin Kusch, ed. *The Routledge Handbook of Philosophy of Relativism*: 329–338. Oxon and New York: Routledge.

Baehr, Jason (ed.). 2015. *Intellectual Virtues and Education: Essays in Applied Virtue Epistemology*. London: Routledge.

Banaji, Mahzarin and Anthony Greenwald. 2016. *Blindspot: Hidden Biases of Good People*. New York: Bantam Books.

Barnes, Elizabeth. 2016. *The Minority Body: A Theory of Disability*. Oxford: Oxford University Press.

Battaly, Heather. 2015. *Virtue*. Cambridge: Polity Press.

Berenstain, Nora, Kristie Dotson, Julieta Paredes, Elena Ruíz, and Noenoe K. Silva. 2022. 'Epistemic Oppression, Resistance, and Resurgence.' *Contemporary Political Theory* 21: 283–314. https://doi.org/10.1057/s41296-021-00483-z

Carel, Havi and Ian James Kidd. 2014. 'Epistemic Injustice in Healthcare: A Philosophical Analysis.' *Medical Healthcare and Philosophy* 17: 529–540. https://doi.org/10.1007/s11019-014-9560-2

Cassam, Quassim. 2019. *Vices of the Mind: From the Intellectual to the Political*. Oxford: Oxford University Press.

Catala, Amandine. 2025. *The Dynamics of Epistemic Injustice: Situating Epistemic Power and Agency*. Oxford and New York: Oxford University Press.

Clanchy, Nick. 2024. 'Tackling Hermeneutical Injustices in Gender-Affirming Healthcare.' *Hypatia* 39 (4): 688–710. https://doi.org/10.1017/hyp.2024.15

Clanchy, Nick. Forthcoming. 'Infrapolitical Strategies for Preventing Hermeneutical Injustices Amidst the Global Trans Panic.' *Ergo*.

Doan, Michael. 2018. 'Resisting Structural Epistemic Injustice.' *Feminist Philosophy Quarterly* 4 (4): 1–23. https://doi.org/10.5206/fpq/2018.4.6230

Dotson, Kristie. 2012. 'A Cautionary Tale: On Limiting Epistemic Oppression.' *Frontiers: A Journal of Women Studies* 33 (1): 24–47. https://doi.org/10.1353/fro.2012.a472779

Dotson, Kristie. 2014. 'Conceptualizing Epistemic Oppression.' *Social Epistemology* 28 (2): 115–138. https://doi.org/10.1080/02691728.2013.782585

Dunne, Gerry (ed.). 2022. *Educational Philosophy and Theory: Special Issue on Epistemic Injustice and Education* 55 (3).

Fisher, Alex. Forthcoming. 'In Defence of Fictional Examples.' *The Philosophical Quarterly*. https://doi.org/10.1093/pq/pqaf036

Fricker, Miranda. 2007. *Epistemic Injustice: Power and the Ethics of Knowing*. Oxford: Oxford University Press.

Fricker, Miranda. 2010a. 'Replies to Alcoff, Goldberg, and Hookway on Epistemic Injustice.' *Episteme* 7 (2): 164–178. https://doi.org/10.3366/epi.2010.0006

Fricker, Miranda. 2010b. 'Can There Be Institutional Virtues?' *Oxford Studies in Epistemology* 3: 235–252.

Fricker, Miranda. 2013. 'Epistemic Justice as a Condition of Political Freedom?' *Synthese* 190: 1317–1332. https://doi.org/10.1007/s11229-012-0227-3

Fricker, Miranda. 2016. 'Fault and No-Fault Responsibility for Implicit Prejudice: A Space for Epistemic 'Agent-Regret'.' In Michael Brady and Miranda Fricker, eds. *The Epistemic Life of Groups: Essays in the Epistemology of Collectives*: 33–50. Oxford and New York: Oxford University Press.

Hanel, Paul, Deborah Roy, Samuel Taylor, Michael Franjieh, Chris Heffer, Alessandra Tanesini, and Gregory Maio. 2023. 'Using Self-Affirmation to Increase Intellectual Humility in Debate.' *The Royal Society* 10 (2): 1–13. https://doi.org/10.1098/rsos.220958

Hawkins, Orlando and Emmalon Davis. 2024. 'The Future of Double Consciousness: Epistemic Virtue, Identity, and Structural Anti-Blackness.' *Ergo* 11 (3): 62–95. https://doi.org/10.3998/ergo.5708

Hyde, Krista. 2016. 'Testimonial Injustice and Mindreading.' *Hypatia* 31 (4): 858–873. https://doi.org/10.1111/hypa.12273

Jones, Karen. 2002. 'The Politics of Credibility.' In Louise Anthony and Charlotte Witt, eds. *A Mind of One's Own: Feminist Essays on Reason and Objectivity* (Second Edition): 154–176. Boulder, CO: Westview Press.

Kotsonis, Alkis. 2023. 'On the Virtue of Epistemic Justice and the Vice of Epistemic Injustice.' *Episteme* 20 (3): 598–610. https://doi.org/10.1017/epi.2022.32

Kotzee, Ben. 2017. 'Education and Epistemic Injustice.' In Ian James Kidd, José Medina, & Gaile Pohlhaus Jr., eds. *The Routledge Handbook of Epistemic Injustice*: 324–335. Oxon: Routledge.

Landström, Karl. Forthcoming. 'On Epistemic Freedom and Epistemic Injustice.' *Inquiry*. https://doi.org/10.1080/0020174X.2024.2323561

Langton, Rae. 2010. '*Epistemic Injustice: Power and the Ethics of Knowing* by Miranda Fricker.' *Hypatia* 25 (2): 459–464. https://doi.org/10.1111/j.1527-2001.2010.01098.x

Lavelle, Jane Suilin. 2018. *The Social Mind: A Philosophical Introduction*. London and New York: Routledge.

Madva, Alex. 2020. 'Individual and Structural Interventions.' In Erin Beeghly and Alex Madva, eds. *An Introduction to Implicit Bias: Knowledge, Justice, and the Social Mind*: 233–270. Oxon and New York: Routledge.

Masaka, Dennis. Forthcoming. 'Overcoming Epistemic Injustice in Africa: A Global South Perspective.' *Inquiry*. https://doi.org/10.1080/0020174X.2025.2521663

McGlynn, Aidan. 2019a. 'Testimonial Injustice, Pornography, and Silencing.' *Analytic Philosophy* 60: 405–417. https://doi.org/10.1111/phib.12152

McGlynn, Aidan. 2019b. 'Redrawing the Map: Medina on Epistemic Vices and Skepticism.' *International Journal for the Study of Skepticism* 9 (3): 261–283. https://doi.org/10.1163/22105700-20191386

McGlynn, Aidan. 2020. 'Objects or Others? Epistemic Agency and the Primary Harm of Testimonial Injustice.' *Ethical Theory and Moral Practice* 23: 831–845. https://doi.org/10.1007/s10677-020-10078-z

McGlynn, Aidan. 2022. 'What Can Philosophy Contribute to 'Education to Address Pornography's Influence'?' *Journal of Philosophy of Education* 56 (5): 774–786. https://doi.org/10.1111/1467-9752.12695

McGlynn, Aidan. 2024. 'Educating for Intellectual Virtue in a Vicious World.' *Inquiry* 67 (2): 784–797. https://doi.org/10.1080/0020174X.2023.2174591

McGlynn, Aidan. Forthcoming-a. 'Epistemic Objectification in Pornography.' *The Philosophical Quarterly*. https://doi.org/10.1093/pq/pqaf032

McGlynn, Aidan. Forthcoming-b. 'Pessimism and Optimism in Non-Ideal Inquiry Epistemology.' *International Journal of Philosophical Studies*. https://doi.org/10.1080/09672559.2024.2444967

McKenna, Robin. 2023. *Non-Ideal Epistemology*. Oxford: Oxford University Press.

Medina, José. 2013. *The Epistemology of Resistance: Gender and Racial Oppression, Epistemic Injustice, and Resistant Imaginations*. Oxford: Oxford University Press.

Mitova, Veli. 2020. 'Decolonising Knowledge Here and Now.' *Philosophical Papers* 49 (2): 191–212. https://doi.org/10.1080/05568641.2020.1779606

Mitova, Veli. Forthcoming. 'Can Theorising Epistemic Injustice Help Us Decolonise?' *Inquiry*. https://doi.org/10.1080/0020174X.2024.2327489

Pohlhaus Jr., Gaile. 2014. 'Discerning the Primary Epistemic Harm in Cases of Testimonial Injustice.' *Social Epistemology* 28 (2): 99–114. https://doi.org/10.1080/02691728.2013.782581

Pohlhaus Jr., Gaile. 2020. 'Epistemic Agency under Oppression.' *Philosophical Papers* 49 (2): 233–251. https://doi.org/10.1080/05568641.2020.1780149

Posholi, Lerato. 2020. 'Epistemic Decolonization as Overcoming the Hermeneutical Injustice of Eurocentrism.' *Philosophical Papers* 49 (2): 279–304. https://doi.org/10.1080/05568641.2020.1779604

Saul, Jennifer. 2013. 'Implicit Bias, Stereotype Threat, and Women in Philosophy.' In Katrina Hutchison and Fiona Jenkins, eds. *Women in Philosophy: What Needs to Change?*: 39–60 Oxford and New York: Oxford University Press.

Sherman, Benjamin R. 2016. 'There's No (Testimonial) Justice: Why Pursuit of a Virtue Is Not the Solution to Epistemic Injustice.' *Social Epistemology* 30 (3): 229–250. https://doi.org/10.1080/02691728.2015.1031852

Sherman, Benjamin R. and Stacey Goguen (eds.). 2019. *Overcoming Epistemic Injustice: Social and Psychological Perspectives*. London and New York: Rowman and Littlefield International.

Spaulding, Shannon. 2018. *How We Understand Each Other: Philosophy and Social Cognition*. Oxon and New York: Routledge.

Spaulding, Shannon. 2025. 'How I Know What You Know.' In Jennifer Lackey and Aidan McGlynn, eds. *The Oxford Handbook of Social Epistemology*: 256–275. New York: Oxford University Press.

Tanesini, Alessandra. 2016. 'Teaching Virtue: Changing Attitudes.' *Logos & Episteme* 7 (4): 503–527. https://doi.org/10.5840/logos-episteme20167445

Tanesini, Alessandra. 2021. *The Mismeasure of the Self*. Oxford: Oxford University Press.

Tobi, Abraham. 2020. 'Towards a Plausible Account of Epistemic Decolonisation.' *Philosophical Papers* 49 (2): 253–278. https://doi.org/10.1080/05568641.2020.1779602

Tobi, Abraham. 2022. 'Epistemic Injustice and Colonisation.' *South African Journal of Philosophy* 41 (4): 337–346. https://doi.org/10.1080/02580136.2023.2199605

Yap, Audrey. 2017. 'Credibility Excess in the Social Imaginary in Cases of Sexual Assault.' *Feminist Philosophy Quarterly* 3: 1–24. https://doi.org/10.5206/fpq/2017.4.1

Zheng, Robin. 2016. 'Attributability, Accountability, and Implicit Bias.' In Michael Brownstein and Jennifer Saul, eds. *Implicit Bias and Philosophy Volume 2: Moral Responsibility, Structural Injustice, and Ethics*: 62–89. Oxford and New York: Oxford University Press.

Glossary of Key Terms

Agency the capacity to act rather than merely be acted upon. A thing or person lacking agency is inert.
Alien experiences experiences that contradict the dominant, widely accepted picture of social reality.
Analytic philosophy a tradition in 20th- and 21st-century philosophy, associated with figures such as Gottlob Frege, Bertrand Russell, G. E. Moore, and Ludwig Wittgenstein. It is often characterised as prizing clarity, analysis, and the use of formal tools such as logic, though its critics accuse it of retreating from answering big philosophical question, and instead focusing on narrow, abstract, and esoteric debates that make little progress.
Autonomy the capacity to act freely and to make your own choices about how to exercise your agency, without undue restrictions from others.
Concepts used in different ways across philosophy, but in this book they are mental representations used to classify and describe things in thought, as when someone classifies crayons according to our scheme of colour concepts.
Conceptual resources concepts that are available to allow people to make sense of and communicate things, particularly things about themselves (such as aspects of their identity, or significant experiences they have had).
Contributory injustice a form of epistemic oppression that involves members of a marginalised group who have engaged in hermeneutical dissent facing obstacles to making things intelligible to people belonging to more socially dominant social groups, where those obstacles are due to the situated ignorance of the latter groups.
Controlling images Patricia Hill Collins's term for the prejudicial stereotypes used to oppress and objectify minoritised groups, particularly Black women.

288 GLOSSARY OF KEY TERMS

Credibility   how likely a person comes across as willing and able to tell the truth. Sometimes used interchangeably with trustworthiness.

Credibility deficit   when a speaker receives less credibility that they deserve.

Credibility excess   when a speaker receives more credibility that they deserve.

Distributive injustice   when resources, goods, or opportunities are unfairly distributed, so that some have a bigger share than others without justification for this unequal arrangement.

Discriminatory injustice   injustice that is due to prejudice, either directly (as illustrated by testimonial injustice) or indirectly (as illustrated by hermeneutical injustice, where prejudice causes hermeneutical marginalisation).

Epistemic   relating to knowledge and other states and notions studied by epistemology, such as evidence, credibility, warrant, and so on.

Epistemic agency   in general, this is agency exercised with respect to our epistemic activities and practices, such as engaging in inquiry, making observations, swapping testimony, formulating and testing theories, trying to resolve disagreements, and so on. Kristie Dotson offers her own definition as (roughly) the capacity to use and revise the shared epistemic resources of a community in order to contribute to the production of knowledge.

Epistemic injustice   the general topic of this book, as when used in its title, or more specifically Miranda Fricker's central theoretical notion, which she defines as a harm or wrong done to one in one's capacity as a knower (or more generally, in one's capacity as an epistemic agent).

Epistemic luck   when a person or belief comes to have, or to lack, a particular epistemic status due to luck. Fricker often contrasts epistemic bad luck, when a subject is given a credibility deficit or struggles with a hermeneutical disadvantage due to luck rather than prejudice, with epistemic injustice.

Epistemic oppression   in general, when a person, group, or community faces persistent and unwarranted obstacles and constraints to exercising their epistemic agency (and perhaps also, to the extent that this is different, their autonomy). For Dotson, it involves persistent and unwarranted infringements on the epistemic agency of knowers that prevent them from contributing to the production of knowledge, where epistemic agency is understood according to her own particular definition.

Epistemic violence   an intentional or unintentional failure of an audience to appropriately reciprocate testimony offered to them, due to their pernicious ignorance.

Epistemology   the area of philosophy that studies the epistemic in all its forms, though traditionally it has had a particular focus on knowledge.

Evidence   often thought of as whatever justifies a person or group in believing some things rather than others, so that a person's body of evidence supports accepting certain claims and rejecting or suspending judgement on others. What kinds of things can be evidence is a contested matter; we often talk as if evidence consists of physical objects, which can be planted at the scene of a crime or stored in an 'evidence locker,' but a number of philosophers have contended that strictly speaking only propositions can be evidence.

Evidentialism   a view of epistemic justification, according to which what you are justified in believing is determined by the evidence you have, so that two people completely alike in their evidence are justified in believing the same things to the same degree. In discussions of epistemic injustice, it is sometimes used as a label

GLOSSARY OF KEY TERMS   289

for Miranda Fricker's view that a credibility deficit (or excess) occurs when you fail to match the credibility you give a speaker to the evidence you have that they are likely to be telling the truth.

Expressive resources   one kind of hermeneutical resources. These are the resources that are available for one to make things about oneself intelligible to others through communication. These will include words and longer linguistic expressions, as well as ways of expressing yourself (such as particular dialects).

Harm   to do something that results in a significant setback to a person's interests.

Hermeneutical disadvantage   when a person has trouble making things intelligible, to themselves or to other people, due to a lack of fitting hermeneutical resources. A hermeneutical disadvantage is a hermeneutical injustice if the lack of suitable resources is not mere misfortune but involves some elements of unfairness of discrimination; on Fricker's account, what's required is that the disadvantage be due to hermeneutical marginalisation. A mere hermeneutical disadvantage is one which is not an injustice.

Hermeneutical dissent   when hermeneutically marginalised groups create and utilise their own hermeneutical resources which may not be included in the shared stock of resources recognised and utilised by their wider society.

Hermeneutical injustice   a kind of epistemic injustice involving a person facing unjust obstacles to making their experiences (and perhaps other things) intelligible, either to themselves or to others, due to a lack of fitting hermeneutical resources in their society's shared stock. What makes a given case an injustice rather than a mere hermeneutical disadvantage, according to Fricker, is that it is due to hermeneutical marginalisation.

Hermeneutical marginalisation   when members of a social group are largely excluded from, and isolated within, the institutions, practices, and roles that have the most influence over which hermeneutical resources are created and become part of a society's shared stock of such resources that members of that society can rely on being available in almost any context.

Hermeneutical resources   resources that are available for rendering particular experiences and other things about yourself intelligible, to yourself or to others. Exactly what is included is disputed; Fricker mentions concepts and expressive resources such as expressions and ways of speaking about particular subject matters, but the recent literature suggests this may be too narrow a conception.

Identity   this is used in many different ways in different areas of philosophy (such as the longstanding debate in metaphysics on the nature of personal identity). In discussions of epistemic injustice, it typically refers to a person's social identity, where this is a matter of which social groups they belong to. The focus is on those social identities associated with oppressed social groups, such as people of particular races or genders, or who are disabled, fat, old, trans, gay or lesbian, bisexual, or who practice particular religions. However, the term is used more broadly; for example, being a philosopher or a dentist can be an aspect of a person's identity, in the relevant sense.

Identity prejudice   a prejudice concerning a person's identity: for example, a racist or transphobic prejudice, or a prejudice against philosophers of science.

Ignorance   a state of non-knowing. Some philosophers use this term more narrowly to pick out a state of non-knowing that isn't due to error; they use ignorance to pick out a person who lacks a true belief in some matter without having a false belief. This book understands the term in the more general way, not in this narrower sense.

Incidental epistemic injustice a non-systematic case of <u>epistemic injustice</u>, involving relatively local forms of <u>prejudice</u> and discrimination that are not aspects of a wider pattern of <u>oppression</u>.

Injustice when a person or group is harmed, where this harm is undeserved and due to an unfairness or inequality.

Intersectionality a way of understanding and studying systems of oppression, which emphasises the distinctive forms of oppression faced by people living in the overlap between such systems, rather than assuming that studying the effects of different systems of oppression individually suffices (as when someone might suggest it suffices to understand the ways that Black women are oppressed to examine the racialised oppression of Black men and the gendered oppression of white women).

Knowledge the central notion studied by epistemology, though it has proved notoriously difficult to characterise. On a standard conception, knowing that something is the case is a matter of truly believing that it's the case on the basis of <u>evidence</u> that justifies you in holding that belief and which rules out that it's just a matter of luck that your belief is true (see <u>epistemic luck</u>). More recently, epistemologists have become sceptical that any analysis of the nature of knowledge is possible, and some have proposed treating it as primitive. In addition to knowing that something is the case, you can also know how to do things, and you can know places and people.

Lived experience first-personal, direct experience of something.

Luck when something happens as a matter of accident or (mis)fortune.

Objectification to treat a person as a mere object, for instance by treating them as a mere instrument you can use for your own purposes.

Oppression when a group of people encounter unwarranted and persistent barriers to exercising their agency and/or autonomy. Marilyn Frye influentially pictured it as a cage, made out of wires which couldn't block a bird's flight in isolation but which are arranged so as to drastically restrict the bird's possible movements.

Pernicious ignorance a kind of <u>ignorance</u> that is both reliable (in the sense that it is a predictable part of ignorance of a whole domain) and that causes <u>harm</u>.

Prejudice a <u>stereotype</u> that associates a group with an attribute, typically negative, which is not only mistaken or unreliable, but is also resistant to correction by <u>evidence</u>.

Primary harms/wrongs a <u>harm</u> or <u>wrong</u> associated with a particular kind of <u>epistemic injustice</u> that is essential, inherent, and immediate.

Secondary harms/wrongs a <u>harm</u> or <u>wrong</u> associated with a particular kind of <u>epistemic injustice</u> that is contingent or cumulative rather than essential and immediate.

Silencing when a person (or sometimes a group) is unable to speak. This may mean they are literally unable to utter words, or have been coerced into not speaking, but it may be used more broadly to cover cases in which a person is able to utter the words they want to, but are systematically prevented from doing what they want to with their words.

Situated ignorance ignorance that follows from a person's social location (as when men in a patriarchal society are ignorant of domestic matters).

Standpoint epistemology/theory a family of views in epistemology and the philosophy of science that share a commitment to the claims that social identity shapes what a person or group are likely to know or to remain ignorant of, and that oppressed social groups are associated with certain forms of epistemic advantage. Standpoint epistemologies often accord more importance to lived experience and alien experiences than other kinds of epistemological theories do.

Stereotype as Miranda Fricker defines this, it's an association between a social group and a (positive or negative) attribute; stereotypes, so defined, are not inherently unreliable or problematic, but they can be if they are prejudicial. In ordinary talk, people often use 'stereotype' to mean something close to what Fricker means by 'prejudice.'

Structural injustice forms of injustice that result from the way social structures—for example, institutions, practices, and societies—are arranged and how they operate. A *purely* structural injustice would be a kind of injustice that arises just from these features of social structures, and so cannot be attributed to the actions and behaviour of particular agents (who we might call perpetrators or culprits of that injustice); whether there are any purely structural forms of epistemic injustice is a controversial issue.

Subjugated knowledge knowledge produced from a particular standpoint that is systematically not recognised as knowledge (particularly by the institutions and practices that a society relies on to validate certain claims or results as contributions to its collective knowledge, such as academia).

Systematic epistemic injustice forms of epistemic injustice that arise from prejudices or discrimination that 'track' a person through different spheres of social activity, rather than being local to particular kinds of activities; epistemic injustice due to localised prejudices or discrimination is incidental. Systematic forms of epistemic injustice tend to be aspects of larger patterns of oppression. Fricker describes systematic forms of different types of epistemic injustice as their 'central case.'

Testimonial Injustice a form of epistemic injustice, involving a speaker receiving a credibility deficit when offering testimony to an audience, due to prejudices held by that audience.

Testimonial knowledge knowledge acquired on the basis of someone's testimony.

Testimonial Smothering a form of silencing and epistemic violence, involving a speaker truncating the testimony they would give to an audience, due to the content of the testimony being risky and their audience failing to have demonstrated that they will understand it in the right way, where this is in turn due to that audience's (actual or suspected) pernicious ignorance.

Testimonial Quieting a form of silencing and epistemic violence, involving a speaker failing to be recognised as a knower when offering testimony due to prejudices, or more generally due to the pernicious ignorance of their audience.

Testimony telling another person that something is the case (either orally or in writing), usually with the intention that they will come to share your knowledge.

Trust when you rely on something, sometimes without evidence of its reliability. In the case of trusting people, it is often suggested that more is required, such as taking them to have undertaken a commitment to do the thing in question, or having made yourself vulnerable to betrayal; however, in the literature on testimony, it is sometimes used more loosely just to mean that you accepted what a person said.

Trustworthiness   the degree to which a person can be trusted. Fricker typically uses this to mean the same as credibility.

Vice   qualities that make a person fail to be excellent or to attain the good. Epistemic/intellectual vices are qualities that interfere with you acquiring and sharing knowledge and other epistemic goods; intellectual laziness and closed-mindedness are examples of qualities generally regarded as intellectual vices.

Virtue   qualities that make a person excellent, or attain the good. Epistemic/intellectual virtues are ways of being excellent in the context of our epistemic activities and practices; curiosity and open-mindedness are examples of qualities generally regarded as intellectual virtues.

Wilful hermeneutical ignorance   when members of a marginalised group who have engaged in hermeneutical dissent face obstacles to making their experiences intelligible to members of dominant groups due to the latter wilfully refusing to acknowledge and utilise the hermeneutical resources developed by that marginalised group. Possibly a species of contributory injustice or hermeneutical injustice (or both).

Wrong   in the relevant sense, a harm done to someone unjustly (as opposed to as a matter of desert or bad luck).

INDEX

Note: Page numbers followed by "n" denote endnotes.

adaptive preferences 104–108, 111n16
adultification 131
agency 9–10, 12–15, 17, 241, 258n5; *see also* epistemic agency
agential testimonial injustice 132, 137n14
Alcoff, Linda Martín 268–269, 281n7
ameliorating epistemic injustice *see* epistemic justice
analysis 23–25, 42–44, 46n8, 49, 124
analytic philosophy 4–5, 18n2, 36, 43, 45, 58
Anderson, Elizabeth 103, 269–272, 281n6, 282n8
applied turn in epistemology and philosophy 5, 42–44, 265
asylum seekers 32–33, 45
Austin, J. L. 155, 157n1
autonomy 9–10, 12–15, 17, 58, 68, 258n5; *see also* epistemic autonomy
avowals 110

Bain, Zara 157
Barnes, Elizabeth 31, 104–108, 110, 111n14, 111n16, 112n18, 112n19, 112n22, 280

Battaly, Heather 109, 267, 278
Beauvoir, Simone de 17, 86n15, 243
Berenstain, Nora 18n1, 37, 82, 84n5, 85n10, 156, 181n11, 181n15, 202n11, 228, 280
Black feminist thought *see* Patricia Hill Collins
Borgoni, Cristina 110
Brownmiller, Susan 169–170, 181n11, 181n14, 193

Cahill, Ann 17, 243, 257
Carel, Havi 45, 202n4, 281n1
Carpan, Catalina 131, 258n2, 258n4, 259n9
Catala, Amandine 62, 83, 85n14, 179, 224, 228, 280
Clanchy, Nick 168, 180n2, 197–199, 202n6, 202n7, 202n10, 202n11, 282–283n16
class 57
Coady, C. A. J. 94, 110n1
Coady, David 59, 61
Code, Lorraine 111n5

Collins, Patricia Hill 74–81, 84n6, 85n8, 85n9, 85n12, 120, 192; on subjugated knowledge 77, 80, 142, 205–206, 224; see also controlling images
concepts 39, 170–172, 181n7, 181n9, 205
confessions 33, 45, 131–132, 134–135
Congdon, Matthew 254–255, 258n2, 259n9
consciousness raising 70–71, 83n1, 169–170, 174–175, 178, 208
content-based epistemic injustice 18n3, 107
contributory injustice 202–203n12, 206, 209–211; compared to hermeneutical injustice 212
controlling images 74–78, 85n8–85n10, 112n17, 120, 130–131, 142–146
Craig, Edward 241
credibility 25–26, 96, 120, 122, 214
credibility deficits 118–126, 148–149, 151, 244
credibility excesses 118, 122–123, 126–133, 159n10, 242, 244
credibility judgements 96–97, 123, 136–137n5, 136n4, 221, 267–268
Crenshaw, Kimberlé 11, 73; see also intersectionality
Cull, Matthew 74, 202n4, 228
Curry, Tommy 38, 46n7, 109, 111n7, 201, 229

Dalit feminism 170
Davis, Emmalon 18n1, 18n3, 83–84n3, 84n5, 107, 129–130, 228, 242, 244–245, 279, 282n12
de Clérambault's Syndrome 188–189, 201–202n2
decolonising knowledge 53–54, 156, 222, 224, 279–280
dehumanisation 6, 111n8, 155–156, 160n16, 257
disability 31, 40, 62, 104–110, 111n14, 112n18, 112n22, 230n11, 280
discriminatory epistemic injustice 59, 62, 192, 226
discursive injustice 156
distributive epistemic injustice 58–59, 61–62, 226

distributive injustice 58, 127–128
Dotson, Kristie passim; see also contributory injustice; epistemic agency; epistemic oppression; epistemic violence
double-binds 12, 17, 75, 85n8
double consciousness 68, 82, 83–84n3, 272, 279, 282n12
Dougherty, Emma 190–191, 202n4, 228
Du Bois, W. E. B. 58, 67–69, 71–72, 78; see also double consciousness

education 57–60, 62, 62n5, 279, 280n1
epistemic agency 14–15, 53, 62, 79, 81, 132, 212, 241–244
epistemic autonomy 15, 81
epistemic bad luck see luck
epistemic friction 272–274
epistemic fungibility 130, 244–245, 258
epistemic inertness see epistemic agency
epistemic injustice: Fricker's definition of 51–55, 60; meaning of 9, 15–16, 25, 49–50
epistemic justice 44, 173, 176–179, 220–223, 265–275, 278–280, 281n2, 282–283n16
epistemic objectification see objectification
epistemic oppression 5–7, 13–15, 79–82, 181n8, 205–206, 211–212, 230n9; compared to epistemic injustice 81–82, 144, 149, 223–224
epistemic othering see othering
epistemic resources 80, 205, 212, 220, 229n2
epistemic system 205, 220, 223–224, 229n1
epistemic violence 5–7, 146, 152–153, 159–160n12; compared to testimonial injustice 148–150
erotomania see de Clérambault's Syndrome
evidentialism about credibility deficits 120–124, 127–128, 135, 136n1, 136n2, 137n5, 267–268
expressions 171–172, 181n9, 205

INDEX

Falbo, Arianna 202n6, 228, 231n12
Farley, Lin 172–179, 182n17, 228–229
fiction 36–37, 45, 283n17
Fisher, Alex 36, 45, 283n17
formal testimony 94
Fraser, Rachel 18n4, 179–180, 180n6, 202n6, 257
Freire, Paulo 58, 61
Fricker, Miranda passim
Friedan, Betty 39, 46n5, 85n11, 192
Frye, Marilyn 9–13, 17, 37, 45, 75, 81; see also double binds; oppression

Giladi, Paul 254–255, 258, 259n8
Goetze, Tristan 208, 250–251
Govier, Trudy 119–122
Greenleaf, Herbert 28, 35–36, 38, 52–53, 55, 99, 101–103, 107, 126, 151, 219, 242
Grice, H. P. 42

Hänel, Hilkje 17, 228
harm 7–13, 17, 51–52, 144, 146, 150, 153, 258, 258n1
harm principle 9, 17
Hawley, Katharine 62, 109, 123, 258n2
healthcare 31–32, 44–45, 157, 281n1, 282–283n16
hermeneutical disadvantage 195–197, 207
hermeneutical dissent 208–209, 211, 213, 216, 219–220, 223; see also contributory injustice; willful hermeneutical ignorance
hermeneutical gap see hermeneutical lacuna
hermeneutical injustice 102–104, 107–108, 112n22; definition 55–56, 168, 180n1; as purely structural injustice 104, 207, 213–220; without hermeneutical marginalisation 190–191, 216
hermeneutical lacuna 178, 193, 230–231n12, 249–250
hermeneutical marginalisation 39–40, 75–76, 168–169, 171–172, 185–203, 207, 217–218; Fricker's definition 193–194, 207–208
hermeneutical resources 39–40, 56, 71, 77, 80, 169, 172, 175, 178, 192, 199, 205–206, 208–212, 220, 222–224, 229n2, 250
hermeneutics 55, 167
Hill, Anita 73, 120
Honneth, Axel 253–254, 258, 259n8
hooks, bell 11, 130
Hornsby, Jennifer 143, 155, 157n1
Hyde, Krista 269, 281n7, 282n8

identity 246–248, 252–255, 259n8; see also social identity
identity prejudice 98, 112n19, 131–132, 137n15
ideology 255
ignorance 157, 159n9, 210; and responsibility 273; see also pernicious ignorance
illness example 196–197, 207, 209–210, 213, 222–223
implicit bias 97, 109, 268–269, 279, 281–282n8
incidental epistemic injustice 34, 98, 185–203
injustice 7–9, 12, 18n5
Intemann, Kristen 83
interrogations 29–30; see also confessions
intersectionality 11–12, 80, 228

Jenkins, Katharine 18n4, 202n6, 228
Johnson, Harriet McBryde 31, 37, 40, 104

Kidd, Ian James 45, 202n4, 281n1
knowledge how 4, 62
Kukla, Quill 156

Lackey, Jennifer 18n1, 45, 110n1, 118–119, 123–124, 128, 131–133, 135, 136n2, 137n6, 137n14
Langton, Rae 214, 221–223, 279

lived experience 80–81, 86n15, 205, 243–244
Lorde, Audre 73–74, 82
luck 105, 133–135, 150, 196–197, 199–201, 207, 209–211, 213, 225
Lugones, Maria 215
Luzzi, Federico 125, 136, 137n8, 149, 160n13, 202n4, 203n12, 228

MacKinnon, Catharine 155, 172
Maitra, Ishani 46n4, 133–135, 136n2, 137n15, 177, 182n16, 210–211, 219, 228, 231n13
Manne, Kate 36, 38, 44, 101–102, 129, 181n12, 257
Marxism 69, 83
Mason, Elinor 17, 155
Mason, Rebecca 178, 181n15, 202n6
McKenna, Robin 109, 279
McMillan Cottom, Tressie 31–32, 38, 44, 56, 141, 144
Medina, José 18n1, 40–41, 46n7, 84n3, 128–129, 136n2, 158n3, 158n4, 159n8, 160n15, 160n17, 197, 216–220, 229, 230n8, 230n11, 258n2, 266, 272–274, 279, 281n4, 282n12–282n15
metaphor 5–6, 13, 70, 83–84n3, 179–180
Mill, J. S. 9, 17, 84n4
Mills, Charles 11, 71–72, 79, 82, 157, 158n3
mindreading 269, 279
Mitova, Veli 280
Morrison, Toni 73

naming 45, 74, 174, 176, 178
Nussbaum, Martha 17, 241, 245–246, 258n5

objectification 17, 76–77, 241, 245–246, 257–258, 258n5
oppression 9–15, 17, 18n5, 226
order-of-change 214–215, 220–224, 281n2
Ortega, Mariana 215
othering 76–77; as deritivisation 243–244; as recognition failure 253–255, 258

pain reports 31–32, 44–45, 56, 144, 157
pernicious ignorance 144–146, 149–150, 157–158n2, 158n3–158n6, 159n12
Pettigrew, Richard 17, 257, 258n2
Piovarchy, Adam 18n1, 109, 125
pluralism about epistemic injustice 154, 207, 225–227
Pohlhaus Jr., Gaile 216–220, 243, 258n2, 266, 280, 282n8; see also primary harms; willful hermeneutical ignorance
pornography 155–156, 258, 280n1
postpartum depression see Wendy Sanford
pre-emptive testimonial injustice 102–103, 148, 155
prejudice 61, 97, 103–106, 112n19, 119, 121, 123–124, 133–136, 136–137n5, 137n8, 137n14, 137n15, 144–145, 149, 157, 159n9, 210, 267, 270, 274, 276
primary harms 137n8, 238–255; contrast with secondary harms 238, 240–241, 247–248, 253
Pynn, Geoffrey 257, 259n9

rape see sexual violence
reciprocity 143–144, 155
responsibility 74–75, 109, 272–274, 279
Riggs, Wayne 109
Robinson, Tom 28–29, 35–38, 40–41, 51, 56, 59, 98–104, 108, 112n20, 125, 129, 213, 216–217, 229, 238, 240–242, 245, 249, 266, 281n3
Romdenh-Romluc, Komarine 180n2, 195–196, 202n6, 202n8, 202n9
Rose, Joe 30, 37, 56, 187–189, 191–192, 194–201, 201–202n2, 201n1, 202–203n12, 202n3, 202n7, 208
Russell, Bertrand 4, 43

Sanford, Wendy 170–173, 178, 190, 193, 195, 213
Sauvigné, Karen 170, 176–177, 181n14
selfhood see identity
sexual harassment 13, 120; see also Carmita Wood
sexuality 190, 197, 230–231n12

sexual violence 13, 29–30, 35–38, 188, 200–201, 210
Sherwood, Marge 28, 35–36, 38, 52–53, 55, 98–99, 101–102, 104, 126, 151, 219, 242
silencing 78, 143–144, 146, 155–156, 157n1
Simion, Mona 61, 190–191, 202n5, 202n6
social identity 98
speak-outs *see* consciousness raising
speech acts *see* silencing
Spivak, Gayatri 18n1, 146, 156
stalking 188, 197, 200, 202n3
standpoint epistemology 69–72, 76, 79, 83, 282n13; achievement thesis 69–70; and deferential epistemology 84n4; epistemic advantage thesis 69, 79, 272; situated knowledge thesis 69, 72; strong epistemic disadvantage thesis 72
standpoint theory *see* standpoint epistemology
stereotypes 74, 96–97, 121, 123, 130, 133–135, 210–211, 282n8
structural injustice 103–104, 111n12, 189, 229n3, 270–271, 279

Táíwò, Olúfémi 84n4, 101
Tanesini, Alessandra 17, 279
testimonial injustice: central case of 98; definition of 55–56, 97; *see also* testimonial quieting
testimonial quieting 143–146; compared to testimonial injustice 148–151, 212
testimonial smothering 146–148, 151–152, 159n7, 160n14–160n16, 212
testimony 55; anti-reductionism and reductionism about 95–96, 110n3; definition of 94–95

Tilton, Emily 38, 72
Tobi, Abraham 111n9, 280
Toole, Briana 18n5, 70–71, 84n4
tracking prejudices 98–99, 186
Traister, Rebecca 177, 182n16
trans identities 180n2, 190; and healthcare 282–283n16
Tremain, Shelley 109, 196, 208–209, 216
trust 109, 222, 246
trustworthiness *see* credibility

vices 109, 218–219, 278–279, 281n4
virtue 109, 267–274, 278–279, 281n4–281n6; of hermeneutical injustice 218, 221–222, 268; of testimonial injustice 221, 267–268

White, Edmund 230–231n12
Wiggleton-Little, Jada 44–45, 157
willful hermeneutical ignorance 213–214
Williams, Bernard 246–247
Williams, Patricia 28, 36–37, 55, 98, 111n6, 141, 145–146
Wood, Carmita 29, 36, 38–40, 46n3, 51, 56, 79, 169–179, 180n5, 190, 193, 195, 208, 212–213, 216, 221, 281n3, 282n16
'world'-travelling 215, 222; *see also* decolonising knowledge
wrongs 8–9, 17, 51–52, 133–135, 149–150, 258, 258n1

Yap, Audrey 38, 129, 276